THE DHAMMAPADA

BIBLIOTHECA INDO-BUDDHICA No.—73

THE DHAMMAPADA

Verses & Stories

TRANSLATED
BY
DAW MYA TIN, M. A.,

Edited By
THE EDITORIAL COMMITTEE

SRI SATGURU PUBLICATIONS
A Division of
INDIAN BOOKS CENTRE
DELHI—INDIA

Published by :
SRI SATGURU PUBLICATIONS
Indological and Oriental Publishers
A Division of
INDIAN BOOKS CENTRE
40/5. Shakti Nagar
Delhi-110007
(INDIA)

ISBN.-81-7030-221-8

Published with the Arrangements of
'Burma Pitaka Association, Rangoon, Burma.

First Reprint Edition—Delhi 1990

Published in India.

Printed at :
Mohindra Offset Press, Delhi.

Namo tassa bhagavato arahato sammāsambuddhassa

Veneration to the Exalted One, the
Homage-Worthy, the Perfectly
Self-Enlightened

The Buddha is an Arahat and he is worthy of the highest veneration. All beings including devas and Brahmās venerate the Buddha because the Buddha is the Supreme One, who has extinguished all defilements, who has become perfectly self-enlightened through realization of the Four Noble Truths, and who is endowed with the six great qualities of glory, namely, *Issariya* (supremacy), *Dhamma* (Knowledge of the Path to Nibbāna), *Yasa* (fame and following), *Sirī* (noble splendour of appearance), *Kāma* (power of accomplishment) and *Payatta* (diligent mindfulness).

Publisher's Note

To save the Cost of Production of the Book, the list of the Donors is not included in the present Edition.

Publishers are, however, grateful to Association for giving Permission to Reprint it.

PREFACE

Dhammapada is one of the best known books of the Piṭaka. It is a collection of the teachings of the Buddha expressed in clear, pithy verses. These verses were culled from various discourses given by the Buddha in the course of forty-five years of his teaching, as he travelled in the valley of the Ganges (Gaṅgā) and the sub-mountain tract of the Himalayas. These verses are often terse, witty and convincing. Whenever similes are used, they are those that are easily understood even by a child, e.g., the cart's wheel, a man's shadow, a deep pool, flowers. Through these verses, the Buddha exhorts one to achieve that greatest of all conquests, the conquest of self; to escape from the evils of passion, hatred and ignorance; and to strive hard to attain freedom from craving and freedom from the round of rebirths. Each verse contains a truth (dhamma), an exhortation, a piece of advice.

Dhammapada verses are often quoted by many in many countries of the world and the book has been translated into many languages. One of the earliest translations into English was made by Max Muller in 1870. Other translations that followed are those by F.L. Woodward in 1921, by Wagismara and Saunders in 1920, and by A.L. Edmunds (Hymns of the Faith) in 1902. Of the recent translations, that by Nārada Mahāthera is the most widely known. Dr. Walpola Rahula also has translated some selected verses from the Dhammapada and has given them at the end of his book "What the Buddha Taught," revised edition. The Chinese translated the Dhammapada from Sanskrit. The Chinese version of the Dhammapada was translated into English by Samuel Beal (Texts from the Buddhist Canon known as Dhammapada) in 1878.

In Burma, translations have been made into Burmese, mostly in prose, some with paraphrases, explanations and abridgements of stories relating to the verses. In recent years, some books on Dhammapada with both Burmese and English translations, together with Pāḷi verses, have also been published.

The Dhammapada is the second book of the Khuddaka Nikāya of the Suttanta Piṭaka, consisting of four hundred and twenty-three verses in twenty-six chapters arranged under various heads. In the Dhammapada are enshrined the basic tenets of the Buddha's Teaching.

Verse (21) which begins with "Appamādo amatapadaṁ" meaning "Mindfulness is the way to Nibbāna, the Deathless," is a very important and significant verse. Mindfulness is the most important element in Tranquillity and Insight Meditation. The last exhortation of the Buddha just before he passed away was also to be mindful and to endeavour diligently (to complete the task of attaining freedom from the round of rebirths through Magga and Phala). It is generally accepted that it was on account of this verse on mindfulness that the Emperor Asoka of India and King Anawrahta of Burma became converts to Buddhism. Both kings had helped greatly in the propagation of Buddhism in their respective countries.

In verse (29) the Buddha has coupled his call for mindfulness with a sense of urgency. The verse runs: "Mindful amongst the negligent, highly vigilant amongst the drowsy, the wise man advances like a race-horse, leaving the jade behind."

Verses (1) and (2) illustrate the immutable law of Kamma, under which every deed, good or bad, comes back to the doer. Here, the Buddha emphasizes the importance of mind in all our actions and speaks of the inevitable consequences of our deeds, words and thoughts.

Verses (153) and (154) are expressions of sublime and intense joy uttered by the Buddha at the very moment of his Enlightenment. These two verses give us a graphic account of the culmination of the Buddha's search for Truth. They tell us about the Buddha finding the 'house-builder,' Craving, the cause of repeated births in Saṁsāra. Having rid of Craving, for him no more houses (khandhas) shall be built by Craving, and there will be no more rebirths.

Verses (277), (278) and (279) are also important as they tell us about the impermanent, unsatisfactory and the non-self nature of all conditioned things. It is very important that one should perceive the true nature of all conditioned things and become weary of the khandhas, for this is the Path to Purity.

Then the Buddha shows us the Path leading to the liberation from round of rebirths, i.e., the Path with eight constituents (Aṭṭhaṅgiko Maggo) in Verse (273). Further, the Buddha exhorts us to make our own effort in Verse (276) saying, "You yourselves should make the effort, the Tathāgatas only show the way." Verse (183) gives us the teaching of the Buddhas. It says, "Do no evil, cultivate merit, purify one's mind; this is the teaching of the Buddhas."

In Verse (24) the Buddha shows us the way to success in life, thus: "If a person is energetic, mindful, pure in thought, word and deed, if he does everything with care and consideration, restrains his senses, earns his living according to the Dhamma and is not unheedful, then, the fame and fortune of that mindful person increase."

These are some of the examples of the gems to be found in the Dhammapada. Dhammapada is, indeed, a philosopher, guide and friend to all.

This translation of verses is from Pāḷi into English. The Pāḷi text used is the Dhammapada Pāḷi approved by the Sixth International Buddhist Synod. We have tried to make the translation as close to the text as possible, but sometimes it is very difficult, if not impossible, to find an English word that would exactly correspond to a Pāḷi word. For example, we cannot yet find a single English word that can convey the real meaning of the word "dukkha" used in the exposition of the Four Noble Truths. In this translation, wherever the term "dukkha" carries the same meaning as it does in the Four Noble Truths, it is left untranslated, but only explained.

When there is any doubt in the interpretation of the dhamma concept of the verses or when the literal meaning is vague or unintelligible, we have referred to the Commentary (in Pāḷi) and the Burmese translation of the Commentary by the Nyaunglebin Sayadaw, a very learned thera. On many occasions we have also consulted the teachers of the Dhamma (dhammācariyas) for elucidation of perplexing words and sentences.

In addition we have also consulted Burmese translations of the Dhammapada, especially the translation by the Union Buddha Sāsana Council, the translation by the Saṅgajā Sayadaw (1805-1876), a leading mahā thera in the time of King Mindon and King Thibaw, and also the translation by Sayadaw U Thittila, an Ovādācariya mahā thera of the Burma Piṭaka Association. The book by the Saṅgajā Sayadaw also includes paraphrases and abridgements of the Dhammapada stories.

Dhammapada Stories

Summaries of the Dhammapada stories are given in the second part of the book as it is generally believed that the Dhammapada Commentary written by Buddhaghosa (5th. century A.D.) is a great help towards a better understanding of the Dhammapada. Three hundred and five stories are included in the Commentary. Most of the incidents mentioned in the stories took place during the life-time of the Buddha. In some stories, some facts about some past existences were also retold.

In writing summaries of stories we have not tried to translate the Commentary. We have simply culled the facts of the stories and have rewritten them briefly. A translation of the verses is given at the end of each story.

It only remains for me now to express my deep and sincere gratitude to the members of the Editorial Committee, Burma Piṭaka Association, for having meticulously gone through the script; to Sayagyi Dhammācariya U Aung Moe and to U Thein Maung, editor, Burma Piṭaka Association, for helping in the translation of the verses.

May the reader find the Path to Purity.

20th April, 1984. Daw Mya Tin

CONTENTS

Part I - Verses

Page

Part II ... Stories

Page

Contents

Contents

Page

KHUDDAKA NIKĀYA

The Dhammapada

(Path of the Buddha's Teaching)

Namo Tassa Bhagavato Arahato Sammāsambuddhassa.

Chapter I

The Pairs (Yamakavagga)

I. (1) Cakkhupālatthera Vatthu

Verse 1

1. Manopubbaṅgamā dhammā[1]
manoseṭṭhā manomayā
manasā ce paduṭṭhena[2]
bhāsati vā karoti vā
tato naṁ dukkhamanveti
cakkaṁva vahato padaṁ.

1. All mental phenomena have mind as their fore-runner; they have mind as their chief; they are mind-made. If one speaks or acts with an evil mind, 'dukkha'[3] follows him just as the wheel follows the hoof-print of the ox that draws the cart.

---

1. **manopubbaṅgamā dhammā**: All mental phenomena have Mind as their forerunner in the sense that Mind is the most dominant, and it is the cause of the other three mental phenomena, namely, Feeling (vedanā), Perception (saññā) and Mental Formations or Mental Concomitants (saṅkhāra). These three have Mind or Consciousness (viññāṇa) as their forerunner, because although they arise simultaneously with Mind they cannot arise if Mind does not arise. (The Commentary)

2. **manasā ce paduṭṭhena** (Verse 1) and **manasā ce pasannena** (Verse 2): Manasā here means intention or volition (cetanā); volition leads one to the performance of volitional actions, both good and evil. This volition and the resultant actions constitute kamma; and kamma always follows one to produce results. Cakkhupāla's blindness (Verse 1) was the consequence of his having acted with an evil intention in a previous existence and Maṭṭhakuṇḍali's happy existence in Tāvatiṁsa celestial world (Verse 2) was the result of his mental devotion (manopasāda) to the Buddha.

3. **dukkha**: In this context, *dukkha* means suffering, or physical or mental pain, misfortune, unsatisfactoriness, evil consequences, etc., and rebirth in the lower planes of existence or in the lower strata of human society if born in the human world.

I. (2) Maṭṭhakuṇḍalī Vatthu

Verse 2

2. Manopubbaṅgamā dhammā
manoseṭṭhā manomayā
manasā ce pasannena
bhāsati vā karoti vā
tato naṁ sukha[1]manveti
chāyāva anapāyinī.

2. All mental phenomena have mind as their forerunner; they have mind as their chief; they are mind-made. If one speaks or acts with a pure mind, happiness (sukha) follows him like a shadow that never leaves him.

I. (3) Tissatthera Vatthu

Verses 3 and 4

3. Akkocchi maṁ avadhi maṁ
ajini maṁ ahāsi me
ye ca taṁ upanayhanti
veraṁ tesaṁ na sammati.

4. Akkocchi maṁ avadhi maṁ
ajini maṁ ahāsi me
ye ca taṁ nupanayhanti
veraṁ tesūpasammati.

3. "He abused me, he ill-treated me, he got the better of me, he stole my belongings;"... the enmity of those harbouring such thoughts cannot be appeased.

4. "He abused me, he ill-treated me, he got the better of me, he stole my belongings;"... the enmity of those not harbouring such thoughts can be appeased.

---

1. sukhaṁ/sukha: in this context, happiness, satisfactoriness, fortune, etc., and rebirth in the three upper planes of happy existence.

I. (4) Kāḷayakkhinī Vatthu

Verse 5

5. Na hi verena verāni
sammantīdha kudācanaṁ
averena ca sammanti
esa dhammo sanantano[1].

5. Hatred is, indeed, never appeased by hatred in this world. It is appeased only by loving-kindness. This is an Ancient Law.

I. (5) Kosambaka Vatthu

Verse 6

6. Pare ca na vijānanti[2]
mayamettha yamāmase[3]
ye ca tattha vijānanti[4]
tato sammanti medhagā.

6. People, other than the wise, do not realize, "We in this world must all die," (and not realizing it continue their quarrels). The wise realize it and thereby their quarrels cease.

---

1. **esa dhammo sanantano:** This is the same as "porāṇako dhammo," the doctrine followed by the Buddha and his disciples. The exhortation is not to return hatred for hatred but to conquer it by loving-kindness (absence of hatred).

2. **pare ca na vijānanti:** 'Pare' means 'others'; in this context, people other than the wise. These people do not realize that they must die, and behave as if they were never going to die and keep on quarrelling. Therefore, they are sometimes referred to as the ignorant or the foolish, or those who are not worthy of love and respect.

3. **mayamettha yamāmase:** lit., "We here must die," meaning we, of this world, must die; or all men are mortal.

4. **ye ca tattha vijānanti:** in the case of those who understand, meaning the wise. The wise understand (or realize) that all men are mortal.

I. (6) Mahākāḷatthera Vatthu

Verses 7 and 8

7. Subhānupassiṁ viharantaṁ
indriyesu asaṁvutaṁ
bhojanamhi cāmattaññuṁ
kusītaṁ hīnavīriyaṁ
taṁ ve pasahati Māro[1]
vāto rukkhaṁva dubbalaṁ.

8. Asubhānupassiṁ viharantaṁ
indriyesu susaṁvutaṁ
bhojanamhi ca mattaññuṁ
saddhaṁ[2] āraddhavīriyaṁ
taṁ ve nappasahati Māro
vāto selaṁva pabbataṁ.

7. He who keeps his mind on pleasant objects, who is uncontrolled in his senses, immoderate in his food, and is lazy and lacking in energy, will certainly be overwhelmed by Māra[1], just as stormy winds uproot a weak tree.

8. He who keeps his mind on the impurities (of the body), who is well-controlled in his senses, and is full of faith and energy, will certainly be not overwhelmed by Māra, just as stormy winds cannot shake a mountain of rock.

---

1. **Māro/Māra**: in this context kilesamāra, the defilements hindering the realization of Nibbāna.

2. **saddhaṁ/saddhā** : According to the Commentary,

   (a) unwavering (unshakable) faith in the Buddha, the Dhamma (the Doctrine) and the Saṁgha (the Buddhist Religious Order) and

   (b) faith or belief in kamma (action) and its results

I. (7) Devadatta Vatthu

Verses 9 and 10

9. Anikkasāvo kāsāvaṁ[1]
yo vatthaṁ paridahissati
apeto damasaccena
na so kāsāvamarahati.

10. Yo ca vantakasāv'assa[2]
sīlesu susamāhito
upeto damasaccena
sa ve kāsāvamarahati.

9. He who is not free from taints of moral defilements (kilesas) and yet dons the yellow robe, who lacks restraint and (speaks not the) truth, is unworthy of the yellow robe.

10. He who has discarded all moral defilements (kilesas), who is established in moral precepts, is endowed with restraint and (speaks the) truth, is indeed worthy of the yellow robe.

I. (8) Sāriputtatthera Vatthu

Verses 11 and 12

11. Asāre[3] sāramatino
sāre[4] cāsāradassino
te sāraṁ[5] nādhigacchanti
micchāsaṅkappagocarā.

---

1. **kāsāvaṁ** or **kāsāvaṁ vatthaṁ:** the yellow or reddish yellow robe donned by members of the Buddhist Religious Order. There is a play on words in the above stanzas; 'anikkasāvo' meaning, not free from faults of moral defilements and therefore, stained; and kāsāvaṁ, the yellow robe, dyed sombre in some astringent juice and is therefore stained.
2. **vantakasāv'assa:** lit., has vomited all moral defilements; it means, has discarded all moral defilements through the four Path Knowledge (Magga ñāṇa).
3. **asāre:** lit., essenceless; according to the Commentary, wrong view, i. e., untruth.
4. **sāre:** lit., essence; according to the Commentary, right view, i.e., truth.
5. **sāraṁ:** Truth—According to the Commentary, essence of the Dhamma. The essence of the Dhamma comprises sīla (moral precepts or morality), samādhi (concentration), paññā (knowledge), vimutti (liberation), vimutti-ñāṇadassana (Knowledge of and Insight into liberation) haramattha (ultimate truth) and Nibbāna.

12. Sārañca sārato ñatvā
asārañca asārato
te sāraṁ adhigacchanti
sammāsaṅkappagocarā.

11. They take untruth for truth; they take truth for untruth; such persons can never arrive at the truth, for they hold wrong views.

12. They take truth for truth; they take untruth for untruth; such persons arrive at the truth, for they hold right views.

I. (9) Nandatthera Vatthu

Verses 13 and 14

13. Yathā agāraṁ ducchannaṁ
vuṭṭhi samativijjhati
evaṁ abhāvitaṁ cittaṁ
rāgo samativijjhati.

14. Yathā agāraṁ suchannaṁ
vuṭṭhī na samativijjhati
evaṁ subhāvitaṁ cittaṁ
rāgo na samativijjhati.

13. Just as rain penetrates a badly-roofed house, so also, passion (rāga) penetrates a mind not cultivated in Tranquillity and Insight Development (Samatha and Vipassanā).

14. Just as rain cannot penetrate a well-roofed house, so also, passion (rāga) cannot penetrate a mind well-cultivated in Tranquillity and Insight Development (Samatha and Vipassanā).

I. (10) Cundasūkarika Vatthu

Verse 15

15. Idha socati pecca socati
pāpakārī ubhayattha socati
so socati so vihaññati
disvā kammakiliṭṭhamattano.

15. Here he grieves, hereafter he grieves; the evil-doer grieves in both existences. He grieves and he suffers nguish when he sees the depravity of his own deeds

I. (11) Dhammika-upāsaka Vatthu

Verse 16

16. Idha modati pecca modati
katapuñño ubhayattha modati
so modati so pamodati
disvā kammavisuddhimattano.

16. Here he rejoices, hereafter he rejoices; one who performs meritorious deeds rejoices in both existences. He rejoices and greatly rejoices when he sees the purity of his own deeds.

I. (12) Devadatta Vatthu

Verse 17

17. Idha tappati pecca tappati
pāpakārī ubhayattha tappati
pāpaṁ me katanti tappati
bhiyyo tappati duggatiṁ[1] gato.

17. Here he is tormented, hereafter he is tormented; the evil-doer is tormented in both existences. He is tormented, and he laments: "Evil have I done." He is even more tormented when he is reborn in one of the lower worlds (apāya).

I. (13) Sumanādevī Vatthu

Verse 18

18. Idha nandati pecca nandati
katapuñño ubhayattha nandati
puññaṁ me katanti nandati
bhiyyo nandati suggatiṁ[2] gato.

18. Here he is happy, hereafter he is happy; one who performs meritorious deeds is happy in both existences. Happily he exclaims: "I have done meritorious deeds." He is happier still when he is reborn in a higher world (suggati).

---

1. **duggatiṁ/duggati:** unhappy destinations, the four lower worlds (apāya). In the case of Devadatta, avīci niraya, the lowest niraya, (place of torment).

2. **suggatiṁ/suggati:** happy existence.

I. (14) Dvesahāyakabhikkhu Vatthu

Verses 19 and 20

19. Bahumpi ce saṁhita bhāsamāno
na takkaro hoti naro pamatto
gopova gāvo gaṇayaṁ paresaṁ
na bhāgavā sāmaññassa hoti.

20. Appampi ce saṁhita bhāsamāno
dhammassa hoti anudhammacārī
rāgañca dosañca pahāya mohaṁ
sammappajāno suvimuttacitto [1]
anupādiyāno idha vā huraṁ vā
sa bhāgavā sāmaññassa hoti.[2]

19. Though he recites much the Sacred Texts (Tipiṭaka), but is negligent and does not practise according to the Dhamma, like a cowherd who counts the cattle of others, he has no share in the benefits of the life of a bhikkhu (i.e., Magga-phala).

20. Though he recites only a little of the Sacred Texts (Tipiṭaka), but practises according to the Dhamma, eradicating passion, ill will and ignorance, clearly comprehending the Dhamma, his mind freed from moral defilements and no longer clinging to this world or to the next, he shares the benefits of the life of a bhikkhu (i.e., Magga-phala).

End of Chapter One: the Pairs.

---

1. **suvimuttacitto:** Mind freed from moral defilements; this has been achieved through perfect practice and clear comprehension of the Dhamma.

2. **sa bhāgavā sāmaññassa hoti:** lit., shares the benefits of the life of a samaṇa (a bhikkhu). According to the Commentary, in this context, it means "Shares the benefits of Magga-phala."

Chapter II

Mindfulness (Appamādavagga)

II. (1) Sāmāvatī Vatthu

Verses 21, 22 and 23

21. Appamādo [1] amatapadaṁ [2]
pamādo maccuno padaṁ [3]
appamattā na mīyanti [4]
ye pamattā yathā matā. [5]

22. Evaṁ visesato ñatvā
appamādamhi paṇḍitā
appamāde pamodanti
ariyānaṁ gocare ratā. [6]

23. Te jhāyino [7] sātatikā
niccaṁ daḷhaparakkamā
phusanti dhīrā nibbānaṁ [8]
yogakkhemaṁ [9] anuttaraṁ.

21. Mindfulness is the way to the Deathless (Nibbāna), unmindfulness is the way to Death. Those who are mindful do not die; those who are not mindful are as if already dead.

22. Fully comprehending this, the wise, who are mindful, rejoice in being mindful and find delight in the domain of the Noble Ones (ariyas).

23. The wise, constantly cultivating Tranquillity and Insight Development Practice, being ever mindful and steadfastly striving, realize Nibbāna: Nibbāna, which is free from the bonds of yoga; Nibbāna, the Incomparable!

---

1. **appamāda**: According to the Commentary, it embraces all the meanings of the words of the Buddha in the Tipiṭaka, and therefore appamāda is to be interpreted as being ever mindful

in doing meritorious deeds; to be in line with the Buddha's Teaching in Mahāsatipaṭṭhāna Sutta, "appamādo amatapadaṁ," in particular, is to be interpreted as "Cultivation of Insight Development Practice is the way to Nibbāna."

2. **amata:** lit., no death / deathless; it does not mean eternal life or immortality. The Commentary says: "Amata means Nibbāna. It is true that Nibbāna is called "Amata" as there is no ageing (old age) and death because there is no birth."

3. **pamādo maccuno padaṁ :** lit., unmindfulness is the way to Death. According to the Commentary. one who is unmindful cannot be liberated from rebirth; when reborn, one must grow old and die; so unmindfulness is the cause of Death.

4. **appamattā na mīyanti:** Those who are mindful do not die. It does not mean that they do not grow old or die. According to the Commentary, the mindful develop mindful signs (i.e.,cultivate Insight Development Practice); they soon realize Magga-Phala (i.e., Nibbāna) and are no longer subject to rebirths. Therefore, whether they are, in fact, alive or dead, they are considered not to die.

5. **ye pamattā yathā matā:** as if dead. According to the Commentary, those who are not mindful are like the dead; because they never think of giving in charity, or keeping the moral precepts, etc., and in the case of bhikkhus, because they do not fulfil their duties to their teachers and preceptors, nor do they cultivate Tranquillity and Insight Development Practice.

6. **ariyānaṁ gocare ratā:** lit., "finds delight in the domain of the ariyas." According to the Commentary the domain of the ariyas consists of the Thirty-seven Factors of Enlightenment (Bodhipakkhiya) and the nine Transcendentals, viz., the four Maggas, the four Phalas, and Nibbāna.

7. **jhāyino:** those cultivating Tranquillity and Insight Development Practice.

8. **phusanti dhīrā nibbānaṁ:** the wise realize Nibbāna. Lit., *phusati* means, to touch, to reach. According to the Commentary, the realization takes place through contact or experience, which may be either through Insight (Magga-Ñāṇa) or through Fruition (Phala). In this context, contact by way of Fruition is meant.

9. **yogakkhemaṁ:** an attribute of Nibbāna. Lit., it means free or secure from the four bonds which bind people to the round of rebirths. The four bonds of yoga are: sense pleasures (kāma), existence (bhava), wrong belief (diṭṭhi), and ignorance of the Four Noble Truths (avijjā).

II. (2) Kumbhaghosakaseṭṭhi Vatthu

Verse 24

24. Uṭṭhānavato satīmato
sucikammassa nisammakārino
saññatassa dhammajīvino
appamattassa yaso bhivaḍḍhati.

24. If a person is energetic, mindful, pure in his thought, word and deed, and if he does everything with care and consideration, restrains his senses, earns his living according to the Law (Dhamma), and, is not unheedful, then, the fame and fortune of that mindful person steadily increase.

II. (3) Cūḷapanthaka Vatthu

Verse 25

25. Uṭṭhānena' ppamādena
saṁyamena damena ca
dīpaṁ kayirātha medhāvī [1]
yaṁ ogho [2] nābhikīrati.

25. Through diligence, mindfulness, discipline (with regard to moral precepts) and control of his senses, let the man of wisdom make (of himself) an island which no flood can overwhelm.

II. (4) Bālanakkhattasaṅghuṭṭha Vatthu

Verses 26 and 27

26. Pamādamanuyuñjanti
bālā dummedhino janā [3]
appamādañca medhāvī
dhanaṁ seṭṭhaṁva rakkhati.

---

1. **dīpaṁ kayirātha medhāvī**=island + make + the wise, meaning let the man of wisdom make an island. The 'island', in this context, stands for arahatship. Arahatship is here linkened to an island because it enables one to escape from the stormy waters of Saṁsāra (round of rebirths).

2. **ogho** : flood or torrent. It is used metaphorically of evils or passions which overwhelm humanity.

3. **bālā dummedhino janā**: the foolish and the ignorant. The foolish mentioned in the story were the hooligans who were given up to wild revelry and disorder during the Bālanakkhatta festival. They were not mindful of others or of the consequence for themselves in this world and the next.

27. Mā pamādamanuyuñjetha
mā kāmaratisanthavaṁ
appamatto hi jhāyanto
pappoti vipulaṁ sukhaṁ.

26. The foolish and the ignorant give themselves over to negligence; whereas the wise treasure mindfulness as a precious jewel.

27. Therefore, one should not be negligent, nor be addicted to sensual pleasures; for he who is established in mindfulness, through cultivation of Tranquillity and Insight Development Practice, experiences supreme happiness (i.e., realizes Nibbāna).

II. (5) Mahākassapatthera Vatthu

Verse 28

28. Pamādaṁ appamādena
yadā nudati paṇḍito
paññāpāsādamāruyha
asoko sokiniṁ pajaṁ
pabbataṭṭhova bhūmaṭṭhe
dhīro[1] bāle[2] avekkhati.

28. The wise one dispels negligence by means of mindfulness; he ascends the tower of wisdom and being free from sorrow looks at the sorrowing beings. Just as one on the mountain top looks at those on the plain below, so also, the wise one (the arahat) looks at the foolish and the ignorant (worldlings).

II. (6) Dvesahāyakabhikkhu Vatthu

Verse 29

29. Appamatto pamattesu
suttesu bahujāgaro
abalassaṁva sīghasso
hitvā yāti sumedhaso[3].

29. Mindful amongst the negligent, highly vigilant amongst the drowsy, the man of wisdom advances like a race-horse, leaving the jade behind.

---

1. **dhīro**: the wise one; in this context, the arahat.
2. **bāle**: the foolish; in this context, the worldings.
3. **sumedhaso**: the wise one: the wise one advances steadily until he realizes Magga, Phala and Nibbāna, leaving the negligent ones behind in the round of relirths (saṁsāra).

II. (7) Magha Vatthu

Verse 30

30. Appamādena[1] maghavā
devānaṁ seṭṭhataṁ gato
appamādaṁ pasaṁsanti
pamādo garahito sadā.

30. Through mindfulness (in doing meritorious deeds) Magha became king of the devas. Mindfulness is always praised, but negligence is always blamed.

II. (8) Aññatarabhikkhu Vatthu

Verse 31

31. Appamādarato bhikkhu[2]
pamāde bhayadassi[3] vā
saṁyojanaṁ aṇuṁ thūlaṁ
ḍahaṁ aggīva gacchati.

31. A bhikkhu who takes delight in mindfulness and sees danger in negligence advances like fire, burning up all fetters, great and small.

II. (9) Nigamavāsitissatthera Vatthu

Verse 32

32. Appamādarato bhikkhu
pamāde bhayadassi vā
abhabbo parihānāya[4]
nibbānasseva santike.

32. A bhikkhu who takes delight in mindfulness and sees danger in negligence cannot fall away; he is, indeed, very close to Nibbāna.

End of Chapter Two: Mindfulness.

---

1. **appamādena**: through mindfulness ; i. e., mindfulness in doing meritorious deeds. In the above story, Magha, the young man from Macala village, by cleaning and clearing land and making roads was reborn as Indra or Sakka, king of the devas. (The devas are celestial beings.)
2. **appamādarato bhikkhu**: a bhikkhu who takes delight in mindfulness, i. e., in the practice of Tranquillity and Insight Development.
3. **pamāde bhayadassi**: seeing danger in negligence, i. e., negligence which would lead to continued existenc in the round of rebirths (saṁsāra).
4. **abhabbo parihānāya**: Unable to fall away; here it means, unable to fall away from the practice of Tranquillity and Insight Development and the benefits thereof i. e., Magga and Phala. (The Commentary)

Chapter III

The Mind (Cittavagga)

III. (1). Meghiyatthera Vatthu

Verses 33 and 34

33. Phandanaṁ capalaṁ cittaṁ
dūrakkhaṁ[1] dunnivārayaṁ[2]
ujuṁ karoti[3] medhāvī
usukārova tejanaṁ.

34. Vārijova thale khitto
okamokata ubbhato
pariphandatidaṁ cittaṁ
māradheyyaṁ pahātave.

33. The mind is excitable and unsteady; it is difficult to control and to restrain. The wise one trains his mind to be upright as a fletcher straightens an arrow.

34. As a fish quivers when taken out of its watery home and thrown on to dry ground, so does the mind quiver when it is taken out of the sensual world to escape from the realm of Māra (i. e., kilesa vaṭṭa, round of moral defilements).

III. (2) Aññatarabhikkhu Vatthu

Verse 35

35. Dunniggahassa lahuno
yatthakāmanipātino[4]
cittassa damatho sādhu
cittaṁ dantaṁ sukhāvahaṁ[5].

35. The mind is difficult to control; swiftly and lightly, it moves and lands wherever it pleases. It is good to tame the mind, for a well-tamed mind brings happiness.

---

1. **dūrakkhaṁ :** difficult to keep the mind fixed on a single object when meditating.
2. **dunnivārayaṁ :** difficult to restrain the mind from drifting towards sensual pleasures.
3. **ujuṁ karoti :** straightens:
 (a) the fletcher straightens the arrow.
 (b) the wise man trains his sensuous, unruly mind by means of Tranquillity and Insight Development Practice (Samatha and Vipassanā). (The Commentary)
4. **yatthakāmanipātino:** moving about wherever it pleases, landing on any sense object without any control.
5. **sukhāvahaṁ:** brings happiness, fortune, satisfaction etc., and also, Maggas, Phalas and Nibbāna. (The Commentary)

III. (3) Ukkaṇṭhitabhikkhu Vatthu

Verse 36

36. Sududdasaṁ sunipuṇaṁ
yatthakāmanipātinaṁ
cittaṁ rakkeտha medhāvī
cittaṁ guttaṁ sukhāvahaṁ.

36. The mind is very difficult to see, very delicat and subtle; it moves and lands wherever it pleases The wise one should guard his mind, for a guarded mind brings happiness.

III. (4) Saṁgharakkhitatthera Vatthu

Verse 37

37. Dūraṅgamaṁ ekacaraṁ[1]
asarīraṁ guhāsayaṁ[2]
ye cittaṁ saṁyamissanti
mokkhanti mārabandhanā.

37. The mind wanders far and moves about alone; it is non-material; it lies in the cave (chamber of the heart). Those who control their mind will be free from the bonds of Māra.

III. (5) Cittahatthatthera Vatthu

Verses 38 and 39

38. Anavaṭṭhitacittassa
saddhammaṁ avijānato
pariplavapasādassa
paññā na paripūrati.

---

1. **ekacaraṁ:** walking alone, moves about alone. It means conceiving one thought at a time, i.e., one thought arises only when another ceases.

2. **guhāsayaṁ:** lit., lying or sleeping in a cave; mind lies and arises continually in the cave / chamber of the heart (hadayavatthu), the seat of consciousness.

39. Anavassutacittassa
ananvāhatacetaso
puññapāpapahīnassa [1]
natthi jāgarato [2] bhayaṁ.

38. If a man's mind is unsteady, if he is ignorant of the true Dhamma, and if his faith is wavering, then his knowledge will never be perfect.

39. If a man's mind is free from passion, if he is free from ill will, if he has abandoned both good and evil, and if he is vigilant, for such a man there is no danger.

III. (6) Pañcasatabhikkhu Vatthu

Verse 40

40. Kumbhūpamaṁ kāyamimaṁ viditvā
nagarūpamaṁ cittamidaṁ ṭhapetvā
yodhetha māraṁ paññāvudhena
jitañca rakkhe anivesano siyā [3].

40. Knowing that this body is (fragile) like an earthen jar, making one's mind secure like a fortified town, one should fight Māra with the weapon of knowledge. (After defeating Māra) one should still continue to guard one's mind, and feel no attachment to that which has been gained (i.e., jhāna ecstasy and serenity gained through meditation).

---

1. **puññapāpapahīnassa:** one who has abandoned both good and evil: i.e., an arahat. An arahat does not commit any morally good or morally bad volitional action; all his actions are non-kamma-producing.

2. **jāgarato:** one who is awake or vigilant, i.e., an arahat. Whether awake or asleep, an arahat is regarded as vigilant as the moral qualities, viz., faith, diligence, mindfulness, concentration and wisdom, are ever present in him.

3. **anivesano siyā:** not to be attached; in this context not to be attached to jhāna ecstasy and serenity gained through meditation, but to proceed further with Insight meditation practices until the attainment of arahatship. (The Commentary)

III. (7) Pūtigattatissatthera Vatthu

Verse 41

41. Aciraṁ vata' yaṁ kāyo
pathaviṁ adhisessati
chuddho apetaviññāṇo
niratthaṁva kaliṅgaraṁ.

41. Before long, alas! this body, deprived of consciousness, will lie on the earth, discarded like a useless log.

III. (8) Nandagopālaka Vatthu

Verse 42

42. Diso[1] disaṁ yaṁ taṁ kayirā
verī vā pana verinaṁ
micchāpaṇihitaṁ cittaṁ
pāpiyo naṁ tato kare.

42. A thief may harm a thief; an enemy may harm an enemy; but a wrongly directed mind can do oneself far greater harm.[2]

III. (9) Soreyya Vatthu

Verse 43

43. Na taṁ mātā pitā kayirā
aññe vāpi ca ñātakā
sammāpaṇihitaṁ cittaṁ
seyyaso[3] naṁ tato kare.

43. Not a mother, nor a father, nor any other relative can do more for the well-being of one than a rightly-directed mind can.

End of Chapter Three : The Mind

---

1. **diso** : lit., an enemy; a thief in this context. (The Commentary)
2. According to the Commentary, the mind, wrongly set on the ten-fold evil path, will cause ruin and destruction not only in this life, but also, even in a hundred thousand future existences in Apāya.
3. **seyyaso** : still better; here it means much better service; because it (the rightly-directed mind) can lead one to the well-being of a man and of a deva and even to the realization of Nibbāna.

Chapter IV

Flowers (Pupphavagga)

IV. (1) Pañcasatabhikkhu Vatthu

Verses 44 and 45

44. Ko imaṁ pathaviṁ vicessati
yamalokañca imaṁ sadevakaṁ
ko dhammapadaṁ sudesitaṁ[1]
kusalo pupphamiva pacessati.

45. Sekho pathaviṁ vicessati
yamalokañca imaṁ sadevakaṁ
sekho dhammapadaṁ sudesitaṁ
kusalo pupphamiva pacessati.

44. Who shall examine this earth (i. e., this body), the world of Yama (i. e., the four apayas) and the wold of man together with the world of devas? Who shall examine the well-taught Path of Virtue (Dhammapada) as an expert florist picks and chooses flowers?

45. The Ariya Sekha shall examine this earth (i.e., the body), the world of Yama (i. e., the four apāyas) and the world of man together with the world of devas. The Ariya Sekha shall examine the well-taught Path of Virtue (Dhammapada) as an expert florist picks and chooses flowers.

---

1. **dhammapadaṁ sudesitaṁ**: the well-taught Path of Virtue; here it means the thirty-seven Factors of Enlightenment (Bodhipakkhiya Dhamma).

2. **sekho/sekhapuggala**: one who is practising the Dhamma, and has entered the Path, but has not yet become an arahat. The term is applied to the first seven ariyapuggalas, the eighth or arahat being asekho.

IV. (2) Maricikammaṭṭhānika bhikkhu Vatthu

Verse 46

46. Pheṇūpamaṁ[1] kāyamimaṁ viditvā
marīcidhammaṁ[2] abhisambudhāno
chetvāna mārassa papupphakāni[3]
adassanaṁ maccurājassa gacche[4].

46. One who knows that this body is impermanent like froth, and comprehends that it is insubstantial as a mirage, will cut the flowers of Māra (i. e., the three kinds of vaṭṭa or rounds), and pass out of sight of the King of Death.

IV. (3) Viṭaṭūbha Vatthu

Verse 47

47. Pupphāni heva pacinantaṁ
byāsattamanasaṁ naraṁ
suttaṁ gāmaṁ mahoghova
maccu ādāya gacchati.

47. Like one who picks and chooses flowers, a man who has his mind attached to sensual pleasures is carried away by Death, just as a great flood sweeps away a sleeping village.

---

1. **pheṇūpamaṁ:** like froth; it means that this body is perishable and impermanent like froth.

2. **marīcidhammaṁ:** lit., mirage + nature; nature of a mirage i. e., insubstantial like a mirage.

3. **mārassa papupphakāni:** flowers or flower-tipped arrows of Māra. These flowers or arrows of Māra represent the tivaṭṭaṁ or the three kinds of vaṭṭaṁ (rounds), viz., kilesavaṭṭaṁ (the round of moral defilements), kammavattaṁ (the round of volitional action) and vipākavaṭṭaṁ (the round of resultant effects). According to the Commentary, this chain or round is broken when cut by the sword of ariya magga ñāṇa.

4. **adassanaṁ maccurājassa gacche:** In this context, out of sight of the King of Death means the realization of Nibbāna.

IV. (4) Patipūjikakumāri Vatthu

Verse 48

48 Pupphāni heva pacinantaṁ
byāsattamanasaṁ naraṁ
atittaññeva kāmesu
antako kurute vasaṁ.

48. Like one who picks and chooses flowers, a man who has his mind attached to sensual pleasures and is insatiate in them is overpowered by Death.

IV. (5) Macchariyakosiyaseṭṭhi Vatthu

Verse 49

49. Yathāpi bhamaro pupphaṁ
vaṇṇagandhamaheṭhayaṁ
paleti rasamādāya
evaṁ gāme munī care.

49. As the bee collects nectar and flies away without damaging the flower or its colour or its scent, so also, let the bhikkhu dwell and act in the village (without affecting the faith and generosity or the wealth of the villagers).

IV. (6) Pāveyya ājīvaka Vatthu

Verse 50

50. Na paresaṁ vilomāni
na paresaṁ katākataṁ
attanova avekkheyya
katāni akatāni ca.

50. One should not consider the faults of others, nor their doing or not doing good or bad deeds. One should only consider whether one has done or not done good or bad deeds.

IV. (7) Chattapāṇi upāsaka Vatthu

Verses 51 and 52

51. Yathāpi ruciraṁ pupphaṁ
vaṇṇavantaṁ agandhakaṁ
evaṁ subhāsitā vācā
aphalā hoti akubbato.

52. Yathāpi ruciraṁ pupphaṁ
vaṇṇavantaṁ sagandhakaṁ
evaṁ subhāsitā vācā
saphalā hoti kubbato.

51. Just as a beautiful flower, lacking in scent, cannot give the wearer the benefit of its scent, so also, the well-preached words of the Buddha cannot benefit one who does not practise the Dhamma.

52. Just as a flower, beautiful as well as fragrant, will give the wearer the benefit of its scent, so also, the well-preached words of the Buddha will benefit one who practises the Dhamma.

IV. (8) Visākhā Vatthu

Verse 53

53. Yathāpi puppharāsimhā
kayirā mālāguṇe bahū
evaṁ jātena maccena
kattabbaṁ kusalaṁ bahuṁ[1].

53. As from a collection of flowers many a garland can be made by an expert florist, so also, much good can be done (with wealth, out of faith and generosity,) by one subject to birth and death.

IV. (9) Ānandattherapañhā Vatthu

Verses 54 and 55

54. Na pupphagandho paṭivātameti
na candanaṁ tagara mallikā vā
satañca gandho paṭivātameti
sabbā disā sappuriso[2] pavāyati.

55. Cadanaṁ tagaraṁ vāpi
uppalaṁ atha vassikī
etesaṁ gandhajātānaṁ
sīlagandho anuttaro.

54. The scent of flowers cannot go against the wind; nor the scent of sandalwood, nor of rhododendron

---

1. **kattabbaṁ kusalaṁ bahuṁ:** much good may be done. According to the Commentary, it means many deeds of merit should be done with wealth, out of faith and generosity.

2. **sappuriso/sappurisa:** good and pious people; virtuous persons. The virtuous are the Noble Ones (the ariyas) and the virtuous worldlings (kalyāṇa puthujjana).

(tagara), nor of jasmin (mallikā[1]); only the reputation of good people can go against the wind. The reputation of the virtuous ones (sappurisa) is wafted abroad in all directions.

55 There are the scents of sandalwood, rhododendron, lotus and jasmin (vassikā[2]); but the scent of virtue surpasses all scents.

IV. (10) Mahākassapatthera Vatthu

Verse 56

56. Appamatto ayaṁ gandho
yāyaṁ tagaracandanī
yo ca sīlavataṁ gandho
vāti devesu uttamo.

56. The scents of rhododendron and of sandalwood are very faint; but the scent (reputation) of the virtuous is the strongest; it spreads even to the abodes of the devas.

IV. (11) Godhikattheraparinibbāna Vatthu

Verse 57

Tesaṁ sampannasīlānaṁ
appamādavihārinaṁ
sammadaññā vimuttānaṁ
Māro maggaṁ na vindati.

57. Māra cannot find the path taken by those who are endowed with virtue, who live mindfully, and have been freed from moral defilements by Right Knowledge.[3]

IV. (12) Garahadinna Vatthu

Verses 58 and 59

58. Yathā saṅkāradhānasmiṁ
ujjhitasmiṁ mahāpathe
padumaṁ tattha jāyetha
sucigandhaṁ manoramaṁ.

---

1. **mallikā**: Arabian jasmin.
2. **vassikā**: Spanish jasmin.

3. Arahats having eradicated moral defilements are no longer subject to rebirths; so Māra, for all his power, cannot find out where such arahats go after death. (The Commentary)

59. Evaṁ saṅkārabhūtesu[1]
andhabhūte puthujjane[2]
atirocati paññāya
sammāsambuddhasāvako.

58, 59. As a sweet smelling and beautiful lotus flower may grow upon a heap of rubbish thrown on the highway, so also, out of the rubbish heap of beings may appear a disciple of the Buddha, who with his wisdom shines forth far above the blind (ignorant) worldlings.

End of Chapter Four : Flowers.

---

1. **saṅkārabhūtesu:** rubbish heap of beings.
2. **andhabhūte puthujjane:** blind worldlings. The worldlings are like the blind because they are lacking in knowledge.

Chapter V

The Fool (Bālavagga)[1]

V. (1) Aññatarapurisa Vatthu

Verse 60

60. Dīghā jāgarato ratti
dīghaṁ santassa yojanaṁ[2]
dīgho bālāna saṁsāro
saddhammaṁ avijānataṁ.

60. Long is the night to one who is wakeful; long is (the journey of) one yojana to the traveller who is tired; long is saṁsāra (round of rebirths) to the fool who is ignorant of the true Dhamma (the Teaching of the Buddha).

V. (2) Mahākassapa saddhivihārika Vatthu

Verse 61

61. Carañce nādhigaccheyya
seyyaṁ sadisamattano
ekacariyaṁ daḷhaṁ kayirā
natthi bāle sahāyatā.

61. If a person seeking a companion cannot find one who is better than or equal to him, let him resolutely go on alone; there can be no companionship with a fool.

V. (3) Ānandaseṭṭhi Vatthu

Verse 62

62. Puttā[3] ma'tthi dhanaṁ ma' tthi
iti bālo vihaññati
attā hi attano natthi
kuto puttā kuto dhanaṁ.

62. "I have sons, I have wealth"; with this (feeling of attachment) the fool is afflicted. Indeed, he himself is not his own, how can sons and wealth be his?

---

1. **Bālavagga:** Chapter on the Fool.
Bāla is the opposite of paṇḍita; it means those who are ignorant, stupid and mentally dull. They cannot think or act right.
2. **yojanaṁ/yojana:** a measure of length, about twelve miles.
3. **puttā;** sons, also means both son and daughter.

V. (4) Gaṇṭhibhedakacora Vatthu

Verse 63

63. Yo bālo maññati bālyaṁ
paṇḍitovāpi tena so
bālo ca paṇḍitamānī
sa ve bāloti vuccati.

63. The fool who knows that he is a fool can for that reason be a wise man; but the fool who thinks that he is wise is, indeed, called a fool.

V. (5) Udāyitthera Vatthu

Verse 64

64. Yāvajīvampi ce bālo
paṇḍitaṁ payirupāsati
na so dhammaṁ vijānāti
dabbī sūparasaṁ yathā.

64. A fool, even though he is associated with a wise man all his life, does not understand the Dhamma, just as a ladle does not know the taste of soup.

V. (6) Tiṁsapāveyyakabhikkhu Vatthu

Verse 65

65. Muhuttamapi ce viññū
paṇḍitaṁ payirupāsati
khippaṁ dhammaṁ vijānāti
jivhā sūparasaṁ yathā.

65. An intelligent man, even though he is associated with a wise man only for a moment, quickly understands the Dhamma, just as the tongue knows the taste of soup.

V. (7) Suppabuddhakuṭṭhi Vatthu

Verse 66

66. Caranti bālā dummedhā
amitteneva attanā
karontā pāpakaṁ kammaṁ
yaṁ hoti kaṭukapphalaṁ.

66. With themselves as their own enemies, fools lacking in intelligence move about doing evil deeds, which bear bitter fruits.

V. (8) Kassaka Vatthu

Verse 67

67. Na taṁ kammaṁ kataṁ sādhu
yaṁ katvā anutappati
yassa assumukho rodaṁ
vipākaṁ paṭisevati.

67. That deed is not well done if one has to repent for having done it, and if, with a tearful face, one has to weep as a result of that deed.

V. (9) Sumanamālākāra Vatthu

Verse 68

68. Tañca kammaṁ kataṁ sādhu
yaṁ katvā nānutappati
yassa patīto sumano
vipākaṁ paṭisevati.

68. That deed is well done if one has not to repent for having done it, and if one is delighted and happy with the result of that deed.

V. (10) Uppalavaṇṇattherī Vatthu

Verse 69

69. Madhuṁvā maññati bālo
yāva pāpaṁ na paccati
yadā ca paccati pāpaṁ
atha dukkhaṁ nigacchati.

69. As long as the evil deed does not bear fruit, the fool thinks it is sweet like honey; but when his evil deed does bear fruit, the fool suffers for it.

V. (11) Jambukatthera Vatthu

Verse 70

70. Māse māse kusaggena
bālo bhuñjeyya bhojanaṁ
na so saṅkhātadhammānaṁ
kalaṁ agghati soḷasiṁ.

70. Even though, month after month, the fool (living in austerity) takes his food sparingly with the tip of a grass blade, he is not worth even one-sixteenth part of those who have comprehended the Truth (i.e., ariyas)

V. (12) Ahipeta Vatthu

Verse 71

71. Na hi pāpaṁ kataṁ kammaṁ
sajju khīraṁva muccati
ḍahantaṁ bālamanveti
bhasmacchannova pāvako.

71. An evil deed does not immediately bear fruit, just as the newly-drawn milk does not curdle at once; but it follows the fool, burning him like live coal covered with ashes.

V. (13) Saṭṭhikūṭapeta Vatthu

Verse 72

72. Yāvadeva anatthāya
ñattaṁ bālassa jāyati
hanti bālassa sukkaṁsaṁ[1]
muddhamassa[2] vipātayaṁ.

72. The skill of a fool can only harm him; it destroys his merit and his wisdom (lit., it severs his head).

V. (14) Cittagahapati Vatthu

Verses 73 and 74

73. Asantaṁ bhāvanamiccheyya
purekkhārañca bhikkhusu
āvāsesu ca issariyaṁ
pūjaṁ parakulesu[3] ca.

74. Mameva kata maññantu
gihī[4] pabbajitā ubho
mamevātivasā assu
kiccākiccesu kismici
iti bālassa saṅkappo
icchā māno ca vaḍḍhati.

73. The foolish bhikkhu desires praise for qualities he does not have, precedence among bhikkhus, authority

---

1. **sukkaṁsa:** sukka+aṁsa: sukka means white, bright, pure or good; aṁsa means portion. According to the Commentary, sukkaṁsa means merit.
2. **muddha:** head, top, summit. According to the Commentary, it means knowledge.
3. **parakulesu:** those outside the family; (para = outside or others).
4. **gihī:** short form for gahapati, householder.

in the monasteries, and veneration from those unrelated to him.

74. "Let both laymen and bhikkhus think that things are done because of me; let them obey me in all matters, great and small." Such being the thoughts of the fool, his greed and his pride grow.

V. (15) Vanavāsitissasāmaṇera Vatthu

Verse 75

75. Aññā hi lābhūpanisā
aññā nibbānagāminī
evametaṁ abhiññāya
bhikkhu Buddhassa sāvako
sakkāraṁ nābhinandeyya
vivekamanubrūhaye[1].

75. Indeed, the path that leads to worldly gain is one, and the Path that leads to Nibbāna is another. Fully comprehending this, the bhikkhu, the disciple of the Buddha, should not take delight in worldly gain and honour, but devote himself to solitude, detachment and the realization of Nibbāna.

End of Chapter Five: The Fool.

---

1. **vivekamanubrūhaye** = (vivekaṁ + anubrūhaye).
viveka: solitary seclusion. According to the Commentary, the three kinds of vivekas are kāyaviveka (seclusion of the body or solitude); cittaviveka (detachment of the mind from human passions) and upadhiviveka (Nibbāna).

Chapter VI

The Wise (Paṇḍitavagga)

VI. (1) Rādhatthera Vatthu

Verse 76

76. Nidhīnaṁva pavattāraṁ
yaṁ passe vajjadassinaṁ
niggayhavādiṁ medhāviṁ
tādiṣaṁ paṇḍitaṁ bhaje
tādisaṁ bhajamānassa
seyyo hoti na pāpiyo.

76. One should follow a man of wisdom who rebukes one for one's faults, as one would follow a guide to some buried treasure. To one who follows such a wise man, it will be an advantage and not a disadvantage.

VI. (2) Assajipunabbasuka Vatthu

Verse 77

77. Ovadeyyā'nusāseyya[1]
asabbhā ca nivāraye
sataṁ hi so piyo hoti
asataṁ hoti appiyo.

77. The man of wisdom should admonish othars; he should give advice and should prevent others from doing wrong; such a man is held dear by the good; he is disliked only by the bad.

VI. (3) Channatthera Vatthu

Verse 78

78. Na bhaje pāpake mitte
na bhaje purisādhame
bhajetha mitte kalyāṇe
bhajetha purisuttame.

78. One should not associate with bad friends, nor with the vile. One should associate with good friends, and with those who are noble.

---

1. **anusāseyya:** to give advice in advance; also to give advice repeatedly.

Verse 79

VI. (4) Mahākappinatthera Vatthu

79. Dhammapīti sukhaṁ seti
vippasannena cetasā
ariyappavedite dhamme
sadā ramati paṇḍito.

79. He who drinks in the Dhamma lives happily with a serene mind; the wise man always takes delight in the Dhamma (Bodhipakkhiya Dhamma) expounded by the Noble Ones (ariyas).

Verse 80

VI. (5) Paṇḍitasāmaṇera Vatthu

80. Udakaṁ hi nayanti nettikā
usukārā namayanti[1] tejanaṁ
dāruṁ namayanti tacchakā
attānaṁ damayanti paṇḍitā.

80. Farmers (lit., makers of irrigation canals) channel the water; fletchers straighten the arrows; carpenters work the timber; the wise tame themselves.

Verse 81

VI. (6) Lakuṇḍakabhaddiyatthera Vatthu

81. Selo yathā ekaghano
vātena na samīrati
evaṁ nindāpasaṁsāsu
na samiñjanti paṇḍitā.

81. As a mountain of rock is unshaken by wind, so also, the wise are unperturbed by blame or by praise.

Verse 82

VI. (7) Kāṇamātā Vatthu

82. Yathāpi rahado gambhīro
vippasanno anāvilo
evaṁ dhammāni sutvāna
vippasīdanti paṇḍitā.

82. Like a lake which is deep, clear and calm, the wise after listening to the Teaching (Dhamma) become serene.

---

1. **namayanti**: to bend, to incline a person's heart or will. In the case of fletchers, to make the arrows straight; in the case of carpenters, to make the timber into things that people want, by cutting, sawing and planing.

VI. (8) Pañcasatabhikkhu Vatthu

Verse 83

83. Sabbattha ve sappurisā cajanti
na kāmakāmā lapayanti santo
sukhena phuṭṭhā atha vā dukhena
na uccāvacaṁ paṇḍitā dassayanti.

83. Indeed, the virtuous give up all (i.e., attachment to the five khandhas, etc.); the virtuous (lit., the tranquil) do not talk with sensual desire; when faced with joy or sorrow, the wise do not show elation or depression.

VI. (9) Dhammikatthera Vatthu

Verse 84

84. Na attahetu na parassa hetu
na puttamicche na dhanaṁ na raṭṭhaṁ
na iccheyya adhammena samiddhimattano
sa sīlavā paññavā dhammiko siyā.

84. For his own sake or for the sake of others he does no evil; nor does he wish for sons and daughters or for wealth or for a kingdom by doing evil; nor does he wish for success by unfair means: such a one is indeed virtuous, wise and just.

VI. (10) Dhammassavana Vatthu

Verses 85 and 86

85. Appakā te manussesu
ye janā pāragāmino
athāyaṁ itarā pajā
tīramevānudhāvati[1].

86. Ye ca kho sammadakkhāte
dhamme dhammānuvattino
te janā pāramessanti[2]
maccudheyyaṁ[3] suduttaraṁ.

---

1. **tīramevānudhāvati : tīraṁ + eva + anudhāvati:** shore + only this + run up and down: according to the Commentary 'only this shore' in this context means sakkāyadiṭṭhi (ego belief).

2. **pāramessanti:** pāraṁ + essanti: the other shore + will reach. The other or opposite shore is metaphorically used for Nibbāna.

3. **maccudheyyaṁ :** the realm of Death (or saṁsāra, round of rebirths.)

85. Few among men reach the other shore (Nibbâna); all the others only run up and down on this shore.

86. But those who practise according to the well--expounded Dhamma will reach the other shore(Nibbāna), having passed the realm of Death (i. e., saṁsāra), very difficult as it is to cross.

VI. (11) Pañcasaṭa Āgantukabhikkhu Vatthu

Verses 87, 88 and 89

87. Kaṇhaṁ dhammaṁ vippahāya
sukkaṁ bhāvetha paṇḍito
okā anokamāgamma[1]
viveke[2] yattha dūramaṁ.

88. Tatrābhiratimiccheyya
hitvā kāme akiñcano[3]
pariyodapeyya attānaṁ
cittaklesehi[4] paṇḍito.

89. Yesaṁ sambodhiyaṅgesu[5]
sammā cittaṁ subhāvitaṁ
ādānapaṭinissagge
anupādāya ye ratā
khīṇāsavā[6] jutimanto[7]
te loke parinibbutā.[8]

87, 88. The man of wisdom, leaving the home of craving and having Nibbāna as his goal, should give up dark, evil ways and cultivate pure, good ones. He should seek great delight in solitude, detachment and Nibbāna, which an ordinary man finds so difficult to enjoy. He should also give up sensual pleasures, and clinging to nothing, should cleanse himself of all impurities of the mind.

89. Those, with mind well-developed in the Seven Factors of Enlightenment (bojjhaṅgā), and who have rid themselves of all craving, rejoice in their abandonment of attachment. Such men, with all moral intoxicants eradicated, and powerful with the light of Arahatta Maggañāṇa have realized Nibbāna in this world (i. e., with khandha aggregates remaining).

---

1. **okā anokamāgamma** : lit., having gone from home to the homeless. In this context interpreted as leaving the seat of carving and having Nibbāna as a goal.

2. **viveke: viveka:** solitude, detachment, Nibbāna.

3. **akiñcano:** lit., having nothing; clinging to nothing. (The term kiñcana may include any of the kilesas or defilements such as passion, ill will, ignorance, etc; it also means clinging or attachment to the world.)

4. **cittaklesehi: citta kilesa:** impurities of the mind.

5. **sambodhiyaṅgesu: sambojjhaṅga:** the Factors of Enlightenment or requisites for attaining Magga Insight.

6. **khīṇāsava:** one in whom human passions are extinguished; an arahat.

7. **jutimanta:** one endowed with the power of Arahatta Maggañāṇa.

8. **te loke parinibbutā:** the realization of Nibbāna in the realm of the five aggregates (khandhas), or in other words, in this world. But according to the Commentary, in this context, both Sa-upādisesa and Anupādisesa Nibbāna are meant. Sa-upādisesa or Kilesā Nibbāna is Nibbāna with groups of existence or khandhas remaining; it is realized by an arahat on the attainment of arahatship. Anupādisesa or Khandha Nibbāna is Nibbāna without groups of existence or khandhas remaining. It takes place on the death of an arahat.

End of Chapter Six: The Wise.

Chapter VII

The Arahat (Arahantavagga)

VII. (1) Jīvakapañha Vatthu

Verse 90

90. Gataddhino [1] visokassa
vippamuttassa sabbadhi
sabbaganthappahīnassa[2]
pariḷāho na vijjati.

90. For him (an arahat) whose journey is ended, who is free from sorrow and from all (e.g., khandha aggregates), who has destroyed all fetters, there is no more distress.

VII. (2) Mahākassapatthera Vatthu

Verse 91

91. Uyyuñjanti satīmanto
na nikete ramanti te
haṁsāva pallalaṁ hitvā
okamokaṁ jahanti te.

91. The mindful strive diligently (in the Tranquillity and Insight Development Practice); they take no delight in the home (i.e., in the life of sensual pleasures); like swans (haṁsa) that forsake the muddy pool, they abandon all homelife (i.e., all craving).

---

1. **gataddhino:** the journey is ended. Here 'the journey' means round of rebirths (saṁsāra).
2. **sabbaganthappahīnassa:** one who has destroyed all fetters. Here 'fetters' means greed, ill will, and wrong view.

VII. (3) Belaṭṭhasisatthera Vatthu

Verse 92

92. Yesaṁ sannicayo[1] natthi
ye pariññātabhojanā[2]
suññato[3] animitto[4] ca
vimokkho[5] yesaṁ gocaro
ākāseva sakuntānaṁ
gati tesaṁ durannayā[6].

92. Arahats do not hoard (anything); when taking food they reflect well over it (i.e., in accordance with the three pariññās). They have as their object liberation from existence, i.e., Nibbāna which is Void and Signless. Their destination, like the course of birds in the air, cannot be traced.

VII. (4) Anuruddhatthera Vatthu

Verse 93

93. Yassāsavā parikkhīṇā
āhāre ca anissito
suññato animitto ca
vimokkho yassa gocaro
ākāseva sakuntānaṁ
padaṁ tassa durannayaṁ.

93. The arahat is free from moral intoxicants (āsavas); he is not attached to food. He has as his object liberation from existence, i.e., Nibbāna which is Void and Signless. His path, like that of birds in the air, cannot be traced.

---

1. **sannicayo:** hoarding. According to the Commentary, it means accumulating either kamma and its effects or any of the four requisites.
2. **pariññātabhojanā:** to take food according to the three pariññās. According to the Commentary, there are three pariññās that the bhikkhu should have concerning food, viz., (a) ñātapariññā, knowing the exact nature of the food being taken, (b) tīraṇapariññā, being convinced of the vileness of material food, and (c) pahānapariññā, rejection of all pleasure in eating.
3. **suññata:** the Void. According to the Commentary, it means void of craving. It is an epithet of Nibbāna.
4. **animittaṁ:** the Signless. According to the Commentary, it means no sign of craving, ill will and ignorance. It is also an epithet of Nibbāna.
5. **vimokkho:** liberation from existence; Nibbāna.
6. **gati tesaṁ durannayā:** their destination cannot be traced because arahats have eradicated craving and are no more subject to rebirths.

VII. (5) Mahākaccāyanatthera Vatthu

Verse 94

94. Yassindriyāni samathaṅgatāni
assā yathā sārathinā sudantā
pahīnamānassa anāsavassa
devāpi tassa pihayanti tādino[1].

94. The arahat whose sense-faculties are calm like horses well-tamed by the charioteer, who is free from pride and moral intoxicants — such an arahat is held dear even by the devas.

VII. (6) Sāriputtatthera Vatthu

Verse 95

95. Pathavisamo no virujjhati
indakhilupamo tādi subbato
rahadova apetakaddamo[2]
saṁsārā na bhavanti tādino.

95. Like the earth, the arahat is patient and is not provoked to respond in anger; like the door-post he is firm; he is unperturbed by the ups and downs of life; he is serene and pure like a lake free from mud. For such an arahat there will be no more rebirth.

VII. (7) Kosambivāsitissattherasāmaṇera Vatthu

Verse 96

96. Santaṁ tassa manaṁ hoti
santā vācā ca kamma ca
sammadaññā vimuttassa
upasantassa tādino.

96. An arahat is calm in his mind, calm in his speech, and also in his deed; truly knowing the Dhamma, such an arahat is free from moral defilements and is unperturbed by the ups and downs of life.

1. **tādino:** one who is calm and tranquil or unperturbed by the ups and downs of life (Lokadhamma).

2. **apetakaddamo:** free from mud. The lake water being free from mud is unpolluted; the arahat being free from defilements is also serene and pure.

VII. (8) Sāriputtatthera Vatthu

Verse 97

97. Assaddho akataññū ca
sandhicchedo ca yo naro
hatāvakāso vantāso[1]
sa ve uttamaporiso.

97. He who is not credulous, who has realized the Unconditioned (Nibbāna), who has cut off the links of the round of rebirths, who has destroyed all consequences of good and bad deeds, who has discarded all craving, is indeed the noblest of all men (i.e., an arahat).

VII. (9) Khadiravaniyarevatatthera Vatthu

Verse 98

98. Gāme vā yadi vāraññe
ninne vā yadi vā thale
yattha arahanto viharanti
taṁ bhūmirāmaṇeyyakaṁ.

98. In a village or in a forest, in a valley or on a hill, wherever the arahats dwell, that place is delightful.

VII. (10) Aññatara itthi Vatthu

Verse 99

99. Ramaṇīyāni araññāni
yattha na ramatī jano
vītarāgā ramissanti
na te kāmagavesino.

99. Forests are delightful, but the worldlings find no delight in them; only those who are free from passion will find delight in them, for they do not seek sensual pleasures.

End of Chapter Seven: The Arahat.

---

1. **vantāso:** one who has discarded all craving (lit., one who has vomited all craving).

Chapter VIII

The Thousands (Sahassavagga)

VIII. (1) Tambadāṭhika Coraghātaka Vatthu

Verse 100

100 Sahassamapi ce vācā
anatthapadasaṁhitā
ekaṁ atthapadaṁ seyyo
yaṁ sutvā upasammati.

100. Better than a thousand words that are senseless and unconnected with the realization of Nibbāna, is a single word of sense, if on hearing it one is calmed.

VIII. (2) Bāhiyadāruciriya Vatthu

Verse 101

101. Sahassamapi ce gāthā
anatthapadasaṁhitā
ekaṁ gāthāpadaṁ seyyo
yaṁ sutvā upasammati.

101. Better than a thousand verses that are senseless and unconnected with the realization of Nibbāna, is a single verse, if on hearing it one is calmed.

VIII. (3) Kuṇḍalakesitherī Vatthu

Verses 102 and 103

102. Yo ca gāthā sataṁ bhāse
anatthapadasaṁhitā
ekaṁ Dhammapadaṁ seyyo
yaṁ sutvā upasammati.

103. Yo sahassaṁ sahassena
saṅgāme mānuse jine
ekañca jeyyamattānaṁ
sa ve saṅgāmajuttamo.

102. Better than the recitation of a hundred verses that are senseless and unconnected with the realization of Nibbāna, is the recitation of a single word of the Teaching (Dhamma), if on hearing it one is calmed.

103. A man may conquer a million men in battle but one who conquers himself is, indeed, the greatest of conquerors.

VIII. (4) Anatthapucchakabrāhmaṇa Vatthu

Verses 104 and 105

104. Attā have jitaṁ seyyo
yā cāyaṁ itarā pajā
attadantassa posassa
niccaṁ saññatacārino.

105. Neva devo na gandhabbo
na Māro saha Brahmunā
jitaṁ apajitaṁ kayirā
tathārūpassa jantuno.

104, 105. It is better indeed, to conquer oneself than to conquer others. Neither a deva, nor a gandhabba, nor Māra together with Brahmā can turn into defeat the victory of the man who controls himself.

VIII. (5) Sāriputtattherassa Mātula Brāhmaṇa Vatthu

Verse 106

106. Māse māse sahassena [1]
yo vajetha sataṁ samaṁ
ekañca bhāvitattānaṁ
muhuttamapi pūjaye
sā yeva pūjanā seyyo
yañce vassasataṁ hutaṁ.

106. Month after month for a hundred years, one may make offerings (to ordinary people) to the value of a thousand kahāpaṇas; yet if, only for a moment, one pays homage to a bhikkhu who has practised Insight Development, this homage is, indeed, better than a hundred years of making offerings (to ordinary people).

VIII. (6) Sāriputtattherassa bhāgineyya Vatthu

Verse 107

107. Yo ca vassasataṁ jantu
aggiṁ paricare vane
ekañca bhāvitattānaṁ
muhuttamapi pūjaye
sā yeva pūjanā seyyo
yañce vassasataṁ hutaṁ.

---

1. **sahassa:** one thousand; in this context, one thousand kahāpaṇas. A kahāpaṇa coin can be in copper, silver or gold,

107. For a hundred years, a man may tend the sacred fire in the forest; yet if, only for a moment, one pays homage to a bhikkhu who has practised Insight Development, this homage is, indeed, better than a hundred years of making sacrifices (in fire-worship).

VIII. (7) Sāriputtattherassa sahāyaka brāhmaṇa Vatthu

Verse 108

108. Yaṁkiñci yiṭṭhaṁ va hutaṁ va loke
saṁvaccharaṁ yajetha puññapekkho
sabbampi taṁ na catubhāgameti
abhivādanā ujjugatesu seyyo.

108. In this world, one may make sacrificial offerings, great and small, all the year round, in order to gain merit; all these offerings are not worth a quarter of the merit gained by worshipping the Noble Ones (ariyas) who walk the right path.

VIII (8) Āyuvaḍḍhanakumāra Vatthu

Verse 109

109. Abhivādanasīlissa
niccaṁ vuḍḍhāpacāyino
cattāro dhammā vaḍḍhanti
āyu vaṇṇo sukhaṁ balaṁ.

109. For one who always respects and honours those who are older and more virtuous, four benefits, viz., longevity, beauty, happiness and strength, will increase.

VIII. (9) Saṁkiccasāmaṇera Vatthu

Verse 110

110. Yo ca vassasataṁ jīve
dussīlo asamāhito
ekāhaṁ jīvitaṁ seyyo
sīlavantassa jhāyino.

110. Better than a hundred years in the life of an immoral person who has no control over his senses, is a day in the life of a virtuous person who cultivates Tranquillity and Insight Development Practice.

VIII. (10) Khāṇu Koṇḍaññatthera Vatthu

Verse 111

111. Yo ca vassasataṁ jīve
duppañño asamāhito
ekāhaṁ jīvitaṁ seyyo
paññavantassa jhāyino.

111. Better than a hundred years in the life of an ignorant person, who has no control over his senses, is a day in the life of a wise man who cultivates Tranquillity and Insight Development Practice.

VIII. (11) Sappadāsatthera Vatthu

Verse 112

112. Yo ca vassasataṁ jīve
kusīto [1] hīnavīriyo
ekāhaṁ jīvitaṁ seyyo
vīriyamārabhato daḷhaṁ.

112. Better than a hundred years in the life of a person who is idle and inactive, is a day in the life of one who makes a zealous and strenuous effort (in Tranquillity and Insight Development Practice).

VIII. (12) Paṭācārātherī Vatthu

Verse 113

113. Yo ca vassasataṁ jīve
apassaṁ udayabbayaṁ [2]
ekāhaṁ jīvitaṁ seyyo
passato udayabbayaṁ.

113. Better than a hundred years in the life of a person who does not perceive the arising and the dissolving of the five aggregates (khandhas), is a day in the life of one who perceives the arising and the dissolving of the five aggregates.

---

1. **kusīto:** an idle person; according to the Commentary, an idle person is one who passes his time only in evil thoughts.

2. **udayabbayaṁ:** the arising and the dissolving of the five aggregates (khandhas). Udayabbayañāṇa is the knowledge acquired through Insight Development Practice, indicating the impermanent characteristics of the five aggregates.

VIII. (13) Kisāgotamī Vatthu

Verse 114

114. Yo ca vassasataṁ jīve
apassaṁ amataṁ padaṁ
ekāhaṁ jīvitaṁ seyyo
passato amataṁ padaṁ.

114. Better than a hundred years in the life of a person who does not perceive the Deathless (Nibbāna), is a day in the life of one who perceives the Deathless (Nibbāna).

VIII. (14) Bahuputtikattherī Vatthu

Verse 115

115. Yo ca vassasataṁ jīve
apassaṁ dhammamuttamaṁ[1]
ekāhaṁ jīvitaṁ seyyo
passato dhammamuttamaṁ.

115. Better than a hundred years in the life of a person who does not comprehend the Noble Dhamma (Dhammamuttamaṁ), is a day in the life of one who comprehends the Noble Dhamma.

End of Chapter Eight: The Thousands.

---

1. **dhammamuttamaṁ**: the Noble Dhamma or the Highest Dhamma (the Nine Transcendentals).

The Nine Transcendentals are: four Maggas, four Phalas and Nibbāna.

Chapter IX

Evil (Pāpavagga)

IX. (1) Cūḷekasāṭaka Vatthu

Verse 116

116. Abhittharetha kalyāṇe
pāpā cittaṁ nivāraye
dandhaṁ hi karoto puññaṁ
pāpasmiṁ ramatī mano.

116. One should make haste in doing good deeds; one should restrain one's mind from evil; for the mind of one who is slow in doing good tends to take delight in doing evil.

IX. (2) Seyyasakatthera Vatthu

Verse 117

117. Pāpañce puriso kayirā
na naṁ kayirā punappunaṁ
na tamhi chandaṁ kayirātha
dukkho pāpassa uccayo.

117. If a man does evil, he should not do it again and again; he should not take delight in it; the accumulation of evil leads to dukkha.

IX. (3) Lājadevadhītā Vatthu

Verse 118

118. Puññañce puriso kayirā
kayirā naṁ punappunaṁ
tamhi chandaṁ kayirātha
sukho puññassa uccayo.

118. If a man does what is good, he should do it again and again; he should take delight in it; the accumulation of merit leads to happiness.

IX. (4) Anāthapiṇḍikaseṭṭhi Vatthu

Verses 119 and 120

119. Pāpopi passati bhadraṁ
yāva pāpaṁ na paccati
yadā ca paccati pāpaṁ
atha pāpo pāpāni passati.

119. Even an evil person may still find happiness so long as his evil deed does not bear fruit; but when his evil deed does bear fruit he will meet with evil consequences.

120. Bhadropi passati pāpaṁ
yāva bhadraṁ na paccati
yadā ca paccati bhadraṁ
atha bhadro bhadrāni passati.

120. Even a good person may still meet with suffering so long as his good deed does not bear fruit; but when it does bear fruit he will enjoy the benefits of his good deed.

IX. (5) Asaññataparikkhāra Vatthu

Verse 121

121. Māvamaññetha pāpassa
na mandaṁ āgamissati
udabindunipātena
udakumbhopi pūrati
bālo pūrati pāpassa
thokaṁ thokampi ācinaṁ.

121. One should not think lightly of doing evil, imagining "A little will not affect me"; just as a water-jar is filled up by falling drops of rain, so also, the fool is filled up with evil, by accumulating it little by little.

IX (6) Biḷālapādakaseṭṭhi Vatthu

Verse 122

122. Māvamaññetha puññassa
na mandaṁ āgamissati
udabindunipātena
udakumbhopi pūrati
dhīro pūrati puññassa
thokaṁ thokampi ācinaṁ.

122. One should not think lightly of doing good, imagining "A little will not affect me"; just as a water-jar is filled up by falling drops of rain, so also, the wise one is filled up with merit, by accumulating it little by little.

IX. (7) Mahādhanavāṇija Vatthu

Verse 123

123. Vāṇijova bhayaṁ maggaṁ
appasattho mahaddhano
visaṁ jīvitukāmova
pāpāni parivajjaye.

123. Just as a wealthy merchant with few attendants avoids a dangerous road, just as one who desires to go on living avoids poison, so also, one should avoid evil.

IX. (8) Kukkuṭamittanesāda Vatthu

Verse 124

124. Pāṇimhi ce vaṇo nāssa
hareyya pāṇinā visaṁ
nābbaṇaṁ visamanveti
natthi pāpaṁ akubbato.

124. If there is no wound on the hand, one may handle poison; poison does not affect one who has no wound; there can be no evil for one who has no evil intention.

IX. (9) Kokasunakhaluddaka Vatthu

Verse 125

125. Yo appaduṭṭhassa narassa [1] dussati
suddhassa posassa [1] anaṅgaṇassa
tameva bālaṁ pacceti pāpaṁ
sukhumo rajo paṭivātaṁva khitto.

125. If one wrongs a person who should not be wronged, one who is pure and is free from moral defilements viz., an arahat, the evil falls back upon that fool, like fine dust thrown against the wind.

---

1. narassa/posassa: an arahat.

IX. (10) Maṇikārakulūpaka Tissatthera Vatthu

Verse 126

126. Gabbhameke uppajjanti [1]
nirayaṁ pāpakammino
saggaṁ sugatino yanti
parinibbanti anāsavā. [2]

126. Some are reborn as human beings, the wicked are reborn in a place of continuous torment (niraya), the righteous go to the deva world, and those who are free from moral intoxicants (viz., the arahats) realize Nibbāna.

IX. (11) Tayojana Vatthu

Verse 127

127. Na antalikkhe na samuddamajjhe
na pabbatānaṁ vivaraṁ pavissa
na vijjatī so jagatippadeso
yatthaṭṭhito mucceyya pāpakammā.

127. Not in the sky, nor in the middle of the ocean, nor in the cave of a mountain, nor anywhere else, is there a place, where one may escape from the consequences of an evil deed.

IX. (12) Suppabuddhasakya Vatthu

Verse 128

128. Na antalikkhe na samuddamajjhe
na pabbatānaṁ vivaraṁ pavissa
na vijjatī so jagatippadeso
yatthaṭṭhitaṁ nappasaheyya maccu.

128. Not in the sky, nor in the middle of the ocean, nor in the cave of a mountain, nor anywhere else, is there a place where one cannot be oppressed by Death.

End of Chapter Nine: Evil.

---

1. **Gabbhameke uppajjanti**: lit., some enter the womb; in this context, "some are reborn as human beings."

2. **anāsavā**: free from moral intoxicants or passions (āvas) i.e., they have become kāiṇāsava or anāsava or arahatssa

Chapter X

Punishment (Daṇḍavagga)

X. (1) and (2) Chabbaggiya Bhikkhu Vatthu

Verses 129 and 130

129. Sabbe tasanti daṇḍassa
sabbe bhāyanti maccuno
attānaṁ upamaṁ katvā
na haneyya na ghātaye.

130. Sabbe tasanti daṇḍassa
sabbesaṁ jīvitaṁ piyaṁ
attānaṁ upamaṁ katvā
na haneyya na ghātaye.

129. All are afraid of the stick, all fear death. Putting oneself in another's place, one should not beat or kill others.

130. All are afraid of the stick, all hold their lives dear. Putting oneself in another's place, one should not beat or kill others.

X. (3) Sambahula Kumāraka Vatthu

Verses 131 and 132

131. Sukhakāmāni bhūtāni
yo daṇḍena vihiṁsati
attano sukhamesāno
pecca so na labhate sukhaṁ.

132. Sukhakāmāni bhūtāni
yo daṇḍena na hiṁsati
attano sukhamesāno
pecca so labhate sukhaṁ.

131. He who seeks his own happiness by oppressing others who also desire to have happiness will not find happiness in his next existence.

132. He who seeks his own happiness by not oppressing others who also desire to have happiness will find happiness in his next existence.

X. (4) Koṇḍadhānatthera Vatthu

Verses 133 and 134

133. Māvoca pharusaṁ kañci
vuttā paṭivadeyyu taṁ
dukkhā hi sārambhakathā[1]
paṭidaṇḍā phuseyyu taṁ.

134. Sace neresi attānaṁ
kaṁso upahato yathā
esa pattosi nibbānaṁ
sārambho te na vijjati.

133. Do not speak harshly to anyone; those who are thus spoken to will retort. Malicious talk is indeed the cause of trouble (dukkha) and retribution will come to you.

134. If you can keep yourself calm and quiet, like a broken gong which is no longer resonant, you are sure to realize Nibbāna; there will be no harshness in you.

X. (5) Uposathika Itthīnaṁ Vatthu

Verse 135

135. Yathā daṇḍena gopālo
gāvo pājeti gocaraṁ
evaṁ jarā ca maccu ca
āyuṁ pājenti pāṇinaṁ.

135. As with a stick the cowherd drives his cattle to the pasture, so also, Aging and Death drive the life of beings.

X. (6) Ajagarapeta Vatthu

Verse 136

136. Atha pāpāni kammāni
karaṁ bālo na bujjhati
sehi kammehi dummedho
aggiḍaḍḍhova tappati.

136. A fool while doing evil deeds does not know them as being evil; but that fool suffers for his evil deeds like one who is burnt by fire.

---

1. **sārambhakathā** : malicious talk. According to the Commentary it means talk belittling others.

X. (7) Mahā Moggallānatthera Vatthu

Verses 137,138,139 and 140

137. Yo daṇḍena adaṇḍesu
appaduṭṭhesu dussati
dasannamaññataraṁ ṭhānaṁ
khippameva nigacchati.

138. Vedanaṁ pharusaṁ jāniṁ
sarīrassa va bhedanaṁ
garukaṁ vāpi ābādhaṁ
cittakkhepaṁ va pāpuṇe.

139. Rājato vā upasaggaṁ
abbhakkhānaṁ va dāruṇaṁ
parikkhayaṁ va ñātīnaṁ
bhogānaṁ va pabhaṅguraṁ.

140. Atha vāssa agārāni
aggi ḍahati pāvako
kāyassa bhedā duppañño
nirayaṁ so papajjati.

137. He who does harm with weapons to those who are harmless and should not be harmed will soon come to any of these ten evil consequences:

138 to 140. He will be subject to severe pain, or impoverishment, or injury to the body (e.g., loss of limbs), or serious illness (e.g., leprosy), or lunacy, or misfortunes following the wrath of the king, or wrongful and serious accusations, or loss of relatives, or destruction of wealth, or the burning down of his houses by fire or by lightning. After the dissolution of his body, the fool will be reborn in the plane of continuous suffering (niraya).

X. (8) Bahubhaṇḍika Bhikkhu Vatthu

Verse 141

141. Na naggacariyā na jaṭā na paṅkā
nānāsakā thaṇḍilasāyikā vā
rajojallaṁ ukkuṭikappadhānaṁ
sodhenti maccaṁ avitiṇṇakaṅkhaṁ.

141. Not going naked, nor having matted hair, nor smearing oneself with mud, nor fasting, nor sleeping on

bare ground, nor covering oneself with dust, nor striving by squatting can purify a being, who has not yet overcome doubt.

X. (9) Santati Mahāmatta Vatthu

Verse 142

142. Alaṅkato cepi samaṁ careyya
santo danto niyato brahmacārī
sabbesu bhūtesu nidhāya daṇḍaṁ
so brāhmaṇo so samaṇo sa bhikkhu.[1]

142. Though he is gaily decked, if he is calm, free from moral defilements, and has his senses controlled, if he is established in Magga Insight, if he is pure and has laid aside enmity (lit., weapons) towards all beings, he indeed is a brāhmaṇa, a samaṇa, and a bhikkhu.

X. (10) Pilotikatissatthera Vatthu

Verses 143 and 144

143. Hirīnisedho puriso
koci lokasmi vijjati
yo niddaṁ apabodheti
asso bhadro kasāmiva.

144. Asso yathā bhadro kasāniviṭṭho
ātāpino saṁvegino bhavātha
saddhāya sīlena ca vīriyena ca
samādhinā dhammavinicchayena[2] ca
sampannavijjācaraṇā patissatā
jahissatha dukkhamidaṁ anappakaṁ.

143. Rare in this world is the kind of person who out of a sense of shame restrains from doing evil and keeps himself awake like a good horse that gives no cause to be whipped.

---

1. According to the Commentary, in this context, brāhmaṇa, samaṇa, and bhikkhu are all arahats.

2. **dhammavinicchayena**: (dhamma + vinicchaya) — discernment of the Dhamma or Law. It is explained by the Commentary as karaṇākaraṇā jānanaṁ, i.e., knowing right and wrong causes of things.

144. Like a good horse stirred at a touch of the whip, be diligent and get alarmed by endless round of rebirths (i.e., saṁsāra). By faith, morality, effort, concentration, and discernment of the Dhamma, be endowed with knowledge and practice of morality and with mindfulness, leave this immeasurable dukkha (of saṁsāra) behind.

X. (11) Sukhasāmaṇera Vatthu

Verse 145

145. Udakaṁ hi nayanti nettikā
usukārā namayanti tejanaṁ
dāruṁ namayanti tacchakā
attānaṁ damayanti subbatā.

145. Farmers (lit., makers of irrigation canals) channel the water; fletchers straighten the arrows; carpenters work the timber; the wise tame themselves.

End of Chapter Ten: Punishment.

Chapter XI

Aging (Jarāvagga)

XI. (1) Visākhāya Sahāyikānaṁ Vatthu

Verse 146

146. Ko nu hāso kimānando
niccaṁ pajjalite[1] sati
andhakārena[2] onaddhā
padīpaṁ[3] na gavesatha.

146. Why is there laughter? Why is there joy although (the world) is always burning? Shrouded in darkness why not seek the light?

XI. (2) Sirimā Vatthu

Verse 147

147. Passa cittakataṁ bimbaṁ
arukāyaṁ samussitaṁ
āturaṁ bahusaṅkappaṁ[4]
yassa natthi dhuvaṁ ṭhiti.

147. Look at this dressed up body, a mass of sores, supported (by bones), sickly, a subject of many thoughts (of sensual desire). Indeed, that body is neither permanent nor enduring.

XI. (3) Uttarātherī Vatthu

Verse 148

148. Parijiṇṇamidaṁ rūpaṁ
roganiḷaṁ pabhaṅguraṁ
bhijjati pūtisandeho
maraṇantaṁ hi jīvitaṁ.

148. This body is worn out with age, it is the seat of sickness, it is subject to decay. This putrid body disintegrates; life, indeed, ends in death.

---

1. **pajjalite:** burning; in this context, it means burning with fires of passion, etc. (The Commentary)
2. **andhakārena:** darkness; in this context, ignorance of the Four Noble Truths. (The Commentary)
3. **padīpaṁ:** light; in this context, wisdom. (The Commentary)
4. **bahusaṅkappaṁ:** the body, which is the subject of many thoughts of sensual desire and admiration.

XI. (4) Sambahula Adhimānikabhikkhu Vatthu

Verse 149

149. Yānimāni apatthāni
alābūneva sārade
kāpotakāni aṭṭhīni
tāni disvāna kā rati.

149. Like gourds thrown away in autumn are these dove-grey bones; what pleasure is there in seeing them?

XI. (5) Janapadakalyāṇī Rūpanandātherī Vatthu

Verse 150

150. Aṭṭhīnaṁ nagaraṁ kataṁ
maṁsalohitalepanaṁ
yattha jarā ca maccu ca
māno makkho ca ohito.

150. This body (lit., the city) is built up with bones which are covered with flesh and blood; within this dwell (lit., are deposited) decay and death, pride and detraction (of others' virtues and reputation).

XI. (6) Mallikādevī Vatthu

Verse 151

151. Jīranti ve rājarathā sucittā
atho sarīrampi jaraṁ upeti
satañca dhammo[1] na jaraṁ upeti
santo have sabbhi pavedayanti.

151. The much ornamented royal carriages do wear out, the body also grows old, but the Dhamma[1] of the Virtuous does not decay. Thus, indeed, say the Virtuous among themselves.

XI. (7) Lāḷudāyī Thera Vatthu

Verse 152

152. Appassutāyaṁ puriso
balībaddova jīrati
maṁsāni tassa vaḍḍhanti
paññā tassa na vaḍḍhati.

152. This man of little learning grows old like an ox ; only his flesh grows but not his wisdom.

---

1. **dhammo/dhamma**: The nine Transcendentals, viz., the four Maggas, the four Phalas and Nibbāna. (The Commentary)

XI. (8) Udāna Vatthu

Verses 153 and 154 [1]

153. Anekajātisaṁsāraṁ
sandhāvissaṁ anibbisaṁ
gahakāraṁ gavesanto[2]
dukkhā jāti punappunaṁ[3]

154. Gahakāraka diṭṭhosi[4]
puna gehaṁ na kāhasi[5]
sabbā te phāsukā bhaggā[6]
gahakūṭaṁ visaṅkhataṁ[7]
visaṅkhāragataṁ cittaṁ[8]
taṇhānaṁ khayamajjhagā.[9]

153. I, who have been seeking the builder of this house (body), failing to attain Enlightenment (Bodhi ñāṇa or Sabbaññuta ñāṇa) which would enable me to find him, have wandered through innumerable births in saṁsāra. To be born again and again is, indeed, dukkha!

154. Oh housebuilder! You are seen, you shall build no house (for me) again. All your rafters are broken, your roof-tree is destroyed. My mind has reached the Unconditioned (i.e., Nibbāna); the end of craving (Arahatta Phala) has been attained.

XI. (9) Mahādhanaseṭṭhiputta Vatthu

Verses 155 and 156.

155. Acaritvā brahmacariyaṁ
aladdhā yobbane dhanaṁ
jiṇṇakoñcāva jhāyanti
khīṇamaccheva pallale.

156. Acaritvā brahmacariyaṁ
aladdhā yobbane dhanaṁ
senti cāpātikhīṇāva
purāṇāni anutthunaṁ.

155. They, who in youth have neither led the Life of Purity, nor have acquired wealth, waste away in dejection like decrepit herons on a drying pond deplete of fish.

156. They, who in youth have neither led the Life of Purity, nor have acquired wealth, lie helplessly like arrows that have lost momentum, moaning and sighing after the past.

---

1. **Footnotes to Verses 153 and 154:** These two verses are expressions of intense and sublime joy the Buddha felt at the

very moment of his attainment of Enlightenment; as such, they are replete with a wealth of sublime meaning and deep feeling.

2. **gahakāraṁ gavesanto:** lit., "I who have tried to find the builder of the house". The house is the body, the builder is Craving (Taṇhā). The meaning of Verse (153) as given in the Commentary is as follows:

   I who have been seeking the builder of this house, knowing that he could be seen only with a certain wisdom, have been trying to attain such wisdom (Bodhi ñāṇa) ever since Dīpaṅkara Buddha prophesied that I would, one day, become a Buddha like him. But failing to attain Bodhi ñāṇa, I have wandered through this course of hundreds of thousands of existences in the endless round of rebirths.

3. **dukkhā jāti punappunaṁ:** To be born again and again is dukkha. This is the reason for trying to find the builder of this house, the Carpenter Craving.

   Birth which comes together with aging, disease and death is dukkha; that is why I have been incessantly looking for the Housebuilder Craving.

4. **diṭṭhosi:** You are seen: I have seen you now that I have attained Enlightenment or Bodhi ñāṇa, the all comprehending wisdom, with my own Insight.

5. **puna gehaṁ na kāhasi:** No house shall be built again: You shall not build another house (for me) in this round of rebirths.

6. **sabbā te phāsukā bhaggā:** All your rafters are broken: I have destroyed all the remaining defilements.

7. **gahakūṭaṁ visaṅkhataṁ:** The roof-tree has been destroyed: I have dispelled ignorance.

8. **visaṅkhāragataṁ cittaṁ:** lit., my mind has reached the Unconditioned; having Nibbāna as its object, my mind has realized Nibbāna.

9. **taṇhānaṁ khayamajjhagā:** The end of craving has been attained: I have attained Arahatta Fruition.

End of Chapter Eleven: Aging.

Chapter XII
Self (Attavagga)

XII. (1) Bodhirājakumrāra Vatthu
Verse 157

157. Attānañce piyaṁ jaññā
rakkheyya naṁ surakkhitaṁ
tiṇṇaṁ aññataraṁ yāmaṁ [1]
paṭijaggeyya paṇḍito.

157. If one knows that one is dear to oneself, one should protect oneself well. During any of the three watches (of life) the wise man should be on guard (against evil).

XII. (2) Upanandasakyaputtatthera Vatthu
Verse 158

158. Attānameva paṭhamaṁ
patirūpe nivesaye
athaññamanusāseyya
na kilisseyya paṇḍito.

158. One should first establish oneself in what is proper; then only one should teach others. A wise man should not incur reproach.

XII. (3) Padhānikatissatthera Vatthu
Verse 159

159. Attānañce tathā kayirā
yathāññamanusāsati
sudanto vata dametha
attā hi kira duddamo.

159. One should act as one teaches others; only with oneself thoroughly tamed should one tame others. To tame oneself is, indeed, difficult.

---

1. yāmaṁ: A night is divided into three watches. According to the Commentary, the watches in this context are the three stages in Man's life, viz., childhood, youth and old age.

XII. (4) Kumārakassapamātuttherī Vatthu

Verse 160

160. Attā hi attano nātho
ko hi nātho paro siyā
attanā hi sudantena
nāthaṁ labhati dullabhaṁ.

160. One indeed is one's own refuge; how can others be a refuge to one? With oneself thoroughly tamed, one can attain a refuge (i.e., Arahatta Phala), which is so difficult to attain.

XII. (5) Mahākāla Upāsaka Vatthu

Verse 161

161. Attanā hi kataṁ pāpaṁ
attajaṁ attasambhavaṁ
abhimatthati dummedhaṁ
vajiraṁva'smamayaṁ maṇiṁ.

161. The evil done by oneself, arising in oneself, and caused by oneself, destroys the foolish one, just as a diamond grinds the rock from which it is formed.

XII. (6) Devadatta Vatthu

Verse 162

162. Yassa accantadussilyaṁ
māluvā sālamivotthataṁ
karoti so tatha'ttānaṁ
yathā naṁ icchatī diso.

162. As the creeper (māluvā) strangles the sal tree, so also, a really immoral person (overwhelmed by Craving) does to himself just what his enemy wishes him to do.

XII. (7) Saṁghabhedaparisakkana Vatthu

Verse 163

163. Sukarāni asadhūni
attano ahitāni ca
yaṁ ve hitañca sādhuñca
taṁ ve paramadukkaraṁ.

163. It is easy to do things that are bad and unbeneficial to onself, but it is, indeed, most difficult to do things that are beneficial and good.

XII. (8) Kālatthera Vatthu

Veres 164

164. Yo sāsanaṁ arahataṁ
ariyānaṁ dhammajīvinaṁ
paṭikkosati dummedho
diṭṭhiṁ nissāya pāpikaṁ
phalāni kaṭṭhakasseva
attaghātāya phallati.

164. The foolish man who, on account of his wrong views, scorns the teaching of the homage-worthy Noble Ones (Ariyas) who live according to the Dhamma, is like the bamboo which bears fruit for its own destruction.

XII. (9) Cūḷakāla Upāsaka Vatthu

Verse 165

165. Attanā hi kataṁ pāpaṁ
attanā saṁkilissati
attanā akataṁ pāpaṁ
attanāva visujjhati
suddhī asuddhi paccattaṁ
nāñño aññaṁ visodhaye.

165. By oneself indeed is evil done and by oneself is one defiled; by oneself is evil not done and by oneself is one purified. Purity and impurity depend entirely on oneself; no one can purify another.

XII. (10) Attadatthatthera Vatthu

Verse 166

166. Attadatthaṁ[1] paratthena
bahunāpi na hāpaye
attadatthamabhiññāya
sadatthapasuto siyā.

166. For the sake of another's benefit, however great it may be, do not neglect one's own (moral) benefit. Clearly perceiving one's own benefit one should make every effort to attain it.

End of Chapter Twelve: Self.

---

1. **Attadatthaṁ:** one's own benefit. According to the Commentary, in this context, one's own benefit means Magga, Phala and Nibbāna. (N.B. The above was uttered by the Buddha in connection with Insight Meditation.)

Chapter XIII
The World (Lokavagga)

XIII. (1) Daharabhikkhu Vatthu

Verse 167

167. Hīnaṁ dhammaṁ na seveyya
pamādena na saṁvase
micchādiṭṭhiṁ na seveyya
na siyā lokavaḍḍhano.

167. Do not follow ignoble ways, do not live in negligence, do not embrace wrong views, do not be the one to prolong saṁsāra (lit., the world[1]).

XIII. (2) Suddhodana Vatthu

Verses 168 and 169

168. Uttiṭṭhe nappamajjeyya
dhammaṁ sucaritaṁ[2] care
dhammacārī sukhaṁ seti
asmiṁ loke paramhi ca.

169. Dhammaṁ care sucaritaṁ
na naṁ duccaritaṁ[3] care
dhammacārī sukhaṁ seti
asmiṁ loke paramhi ca.

168. Do not neglect the duty of going on alms-round; observe proper practice (in going on alms-round). One who observes proper practice lives happily both in this world and in the next.

169. Observe proper practice (in going on alms-round); do not observe improper practice. One who observes proper practice lives happily both in this world and in the next.

---

1. **the world:** Loka: it means the five khandhas, the continuity of which in the round of existences (saṁsāra) is prolonged by the above three factors.

2. **dhammaṁ sucaritaṁ:** proper practice. The Commentary says that here proper practice means stopping for alms-food at one house after another in the course of the alms-round except where it is not proper to go (such as a courtesan's house).

3. **na naṁ duccaritaṁ:** improper practice. Here it means not observing the above rules.

XIII. (3) Pañcasatavipassakabhikkhu Vatthu

Verse 170

170. Yathā pubbuḷakaṁ passe
yathā passe marīcikaṁ
evaṁ lokaṁ avekkhantaṁ[1]
maccurājā na passati.

170. If a man looks at the world (i.e., the five khandhas), in the same way as one looks at a bubble or a mirage, step the King of Death will not find him.

XIII. (4) Abhayarājakumāra Vatthu

Verse 171

171. Etha passathimaṁ lokaṁ
cittaṁ rājarathūpamaṁ
yattha bālā visīdanti
natthi saṅgo vijānataṁ.

171. Come, look at this world (i.e., the five khandhas), which is like an ornamented royal carriage. Fools flounder in this world of the khandhas, but the wise are not attached to it.

XIII. (5) Sammajjanatthera Vatthu

Verse 172

172. Yo ca pubbe pamajjitvā
pacchā so nappamajjati
so'maṁ lokaṁ pabhāseti
abbhā muttova candimā.

172. He who has been formerly unmindful, but is mindful later on, lights up the world (with the light of Magga Insight) as does the moon freed from clouds.

---

1. **evaṁ lokaṁ avekkhantaṁ**: one who looks at the world in the same way, i.e., looks at the world as being impermanent as a bubble and as non-material as a mirage.

XIII. (6) Aṅgulimālatthera Vatthu

Verse 173

173. Yassa pāpaṁ kataṁ kammaṁ
kusalena[1] pidhīyati
so'maṁ lokaṁ pabhāseti
abbhā muttova candimā.

173. He who overwhelms with good the evil that he has done lights up this world (with the light of Magga Insight), as does the moon freed from clouds.

XIII. (7) Pesakāradhitā Vatthu

Verse 174

174. Andhabhūto ayaṁ loko
tanuke'ttha vipassati
sakuṇo jālamuttova
appo saggāya gacchati.

174. Blind are the people of this world; only a few in this world see clearly (with Insight). Just as only a few birds escape from the net, so also, only a few get to the world of the devas, (and Nibbāna).

XIII. (8) Tiṁsabhikkhu Vatthu

Verse 175

175. Haṁsā' diccapathe yanti
ākāse yanti iddhiyā
nīyanti dhīrā lokamhā
jetvā māraṁ savāhiniṁ.

175. Swans travel in the sky; those with supernormal powers travel through space; the wise, having conquered Māra together with his army, go out of this world (i.e., realize Nibbāna).

---

1. **kusalena:** with good deed; the good in this context means Arahatta Magga, the fourth and final Path knowledge. (The Commentary)

XIII. (9) Ciñcamāṇavikā Vatthu

Verse 176

176. Ekaṁ dhammaṁ atītassa
musāvādissa jantuno
vitiṇṇaparalokassa
natthi pāpaṁ akāriyaṁ.

176. For one who transgresses the Truth, and is given to lying, and who is unconcerned with the life hereafter, there is no evil that he dare not do.

XIII. (10) Asadisadāna Vatthu

Verse 177

177. Na ve kadariyā devalokaṁ vajanti
bālā have nappasaṁsanti dānaṁ
dhīro ca dānaṁ anumodamāno
teneva so hoti sukhī parattha.

177. Indeed, misers do not go to the abode of the devas; fools do not praise charity; but the wise rejoice in charity and so gain happiness in the life hereafter.

XIII. (11) Anāthapiṇḍikaputtakāla Vatthu

Verse 178

178. Pathabyā ekarajjena
saggassa gamanena vā
sabbalokādhipaccena
sotāpattiphalaṁ varaṁ.

178. Far better than sovereignty over the earth, or far better than going to the abodes of the devas, or far better than ruling supreme over the entire universe, is (the attainment of) Sotāpatti Fruition.

End of Chapter Thirteen: The World.

Chapter XIV

The Buddha (Buddhavagga)

XIV. (1) Māradhītara Vatthu

Verses 179 and 180

179. Yassa jitaṁ nāvajīyati[1],
jitaṁ yassa no'yāti koci loke[2]
taṁ buddhamanantagocaraṁ[3]
apadaṁ[4] kena padena nessatha.

180. Yassa jālinī visattikā
taṇhā natthi kuhiñci netave
taṁ buddhamanantagocaraṁ
apadaṁ kena padena nessatha[5].

179. The Buddha, whose conquest (of moral defilements) is complete, in whom there cannot arise any further defilements in this world,– that Buddha of infinite range of wisdom, who is trackless, by what track will you lead him?

180. The Buddha, in whom there is no craving, which like a net would bring him back to any existence (in saṁsāra),— that Buddha of infinite range of wisdom, who is trackless, by what track will you lead him?

---

1. **jitaṁ nāvajīyati:** 'the conquest is complete' means there is no need for further conquests as there are no more moral defilements to be conquered.

2. **jitaṁ yassa** no'yāti koci **loke:** lit., whose conquered defilements cannot be followed by any further defilements in this world.

3. **anantagocaraṁ:** The range of wisdom of the Buddha is infinite by reason of his omniscience, Sabbaññuta ñāṇa. (The Commentary)

4. **apadaṁ:** lit., 'trackless'. The Buddha, being free from conditions of rebirth, such as craving, clinging, passion, etc., his track or passage through saṁsāra has come to an end. (The Com.)
[The same idea is conveyed in verses 92 and 93 which express the idea that the arahat passes away, leaving no more trace of existence than a bird leaves its passage through the air.]

5. **kena padena nessatha:** lit., by what track will you lead him? It means he cannot be lured by any temptation whatsoever.

XIV. (2) Devorohaṇa Vatthu

Verse 181

181. Ye jhānapasutā dhīrā
nekkhammūpasame ratā
devāpi tesaṁ pihayanti
sambuddhānaṁ satīmataṁ.

181. The wise who practise jhāna concentration and Insight Meditation take delight in the peace of liberation from sensual pleasures and moral defilements. Such wise and mindful ones, who truly comprehend the Four Noble Truths (i.e., arahats and Buddhas), are held dear also by the devas.

XIV. (3) Erakapattanāgarāja Vatthu

Verse 182

182. Kiccho manussapaṭilābho
kicchaṁ maccāna jīvitaṁ
kicchaṁ saddhammassavanaṁ
kiccho buddhānamuppādo.

182. Hard to gain is birth as man; hard is the life of mortals; hard to get is the opportunity of hearing the Ariya Dhamma (Teaching of the Buddhas); hard it is for a Buddha to appear.

XIV. (4) Ānandattherapañha Vatthu

Verses 183,184 and 185

183. Sabbapāpassa akaraṇaṁ
kusalassa upasampadā
sacittapariyodapanaṁ
etaṁ buddhāna sāsanaṁ.

184. Khantī paramaṁ tapo titikkhā
nibbānaṁ paramaṁ vadanti buddhā
na hi pabbajito parūpaghātī
na samaṇo hoti paraṁ viheṭhayanto.

185. Anūpavādo anūpaghāto
pātimokkhe ca saṁvaro
mattaññutā ca bhattasmiṁ
pantañca sayanāsanaṁ
adhicitte ca āyogo
etaṁ buddhāna sāsanaṁ

183. Not to do evil, to cultivate merit, to purify one's mind — this is the Teaching of the Buddhas.

184. The best moral practice is patience and forbearance; "Nibbāna is Supreme", said the Buddhas. A bhikkhu does not harm others; one who harms others is not a bhikkhu.

185. Not to revile, not to do any harm, to practise restraint according to the Fundamental Instructions for the bhikkhus, to be moderate in taking food, to dwell in a secluded place, to devote oneself to higher concentration — this is the Teaching of the Buddhas.

XIV. (5) Anabhiratabhikkhu Vatthu

Verses 186 and 187

186. Na kahāpaṇavassena
titti kāmesu vijjati
appassādā dukhā kāmā
iti viññāya paṇḍito.

187. Api dibbesu kāmesu
ratiṁ so nādhigacchati
taṇhakkhayarato hoti
sammāsambuddhasāvako

186, 187. Not by a shower of coins can sensual desires be satiated; sensual desires give little pleasure and are fraught with evil consequences (dukkha). Knowing this, the wise man, who is the disciple of the Buddha, does not find delight even in the pleasures of the devas, but rejoices in the cessation of craving (Nibbāna).

XIV. (6) Aggidattabrāhmaṇa Vatthu

Verses 188, 189, 190, 191 and 192

188. Bahuṁ ve saraṇaṁ yanti
pabbatāni vanāni ca
ārāmarukkhacetyāni
manussā bhayatajjitā.

189. Netaṁ kho saraṇaṁ khemaṁ
netaṁ saraṇamuttamaṁ
netaṁ saraṇamāgamma
sabbadukkhā pamuccati.

190. Yo ca buddhañca dhammañca
saṁghañca saraṇaṁ gato
cattāri ariyasaccāni
sammappaññāya passati.

191. Dukkhaṁ dukkhasamuppādaṁ
dukkhassa ca atikkamaṁ
ariyaṁ caṭṭhaṅgikaṁ maggaṁ
dukkhūpasamagāminaṁ.

192. Etaṁ kho saraṇaṁ khemaṁ
etaṁ saraṇamuttamaṁ
etaṁ saraṇamāgamma
sabbadukkhā pamuccati.

188. When threatened with danger, men go to many a refuge,— to mountains and forests, to parks and gardens, and to sacred trees.

189. But such a refuge is not a safe refuge, not the best refuge. One is not liberated from all evil consequences of existence (dukkha) for having come to such a refuge.

190, 191. One who takes refuge in the Buddha, the Dhamma and the Saṁgha, sees with Magga Insight the Four Noble Truths, viz., Dukkha, the Cause of Dukkha, the Cessation of Dukkha, and the Noble Path of Eight Constituents which leads to the Cessation of Dukkha.

192. This,[1] indeed, is the safe refuge; this is the best refuge. Having come to this refuge, one is liberated from all dukkha.

XIV. (7) Ānandattherapañha Vatthu

Verse 193

193. Dullabho purisājañño [2]
na so sabbattha jāyati
yattha so jāyati dhīro
taṁ kulaṁ sukhamedhati.[3]

193. It is hard to find the noblest of men; he is not born everywhere nor in every clan. To whatever clan such a wise man is born, that clan prospers.

---

1. This: Here refers to the refuge in the Three Gems (Buddha, Dhamma and Saṁgha)
2. **purisājañño:** According to the Commentary, a Buddha is intended.
3. **sukhamedhati:** lit., attains happiness or thrives in happiness.

XIV. (8) Sambahulabhikkhu Vatthu

Verse 194

194. Sukho buddhānamuppādo
sukhā saddhammadesanā
sukhā saṁghassa sāmaggī
samaggānaṁ tapo sukho.

194. Happy is the arising of a Buddha; happy is the exposition of the Ariya Dhamma; happy is the harmony amongst the Saṁgha; happy is the practice of those in harmony.

XIV. (9) Kassapadasabalassa Suvaṇṇacetiya Vatthu

Verses 195 and 196

195. pūjārahe pūjayato
buddhe yadi va sāvake
papañcasamatikkante[1]
tiṇṇasokapariddave.

196. Te tādise pūjayato
nibbute akutobhaye
na sakkā puññaṁ saṅkhātuṁ
imettamapi kenaci.

195 He pays homage to those who are worthy of veneration, whether they are the Buddhas or their disciples who have overcome obstacles (to Insight Development) and have rid themselves of sorrow and lamentation.

196. The merit gained by such a person who pays homage to those who have been freed from moral defilements and have nothing to fear, cannot be measured by anyone, as this much or that much.

End of Chapter Fourteen: The Buddha.

---

1. papañcasamatikkante: lit., who have got rid of craving, pride and wrong view, factors lengthening saṁsāra.

Chapter XV

Happiness (Sukhavagga)

XV. (1) Ñātikalahavūpasamana Vatthu

Verses 197,198 and 199

197. Susukhaṁ vata jīvāma
verinesu averino
verinesu manussesu
viharāma averino.

198. Susukhaṁ vata jīvāma
āturesu [1] anāturā
āturesu manussesu
viharāma anāturā.

199. Susukhaṁ vata jīvāma
ussukesu anussukā
ussukesu manussesu
viharāma anussukā.

197. Indeed we live very happily, not hating anyone among those who hate; among men who hate we live without hating anyone.

198. Indeed we live very happily, in good health among the ailing; among men who are ailing we live in good health.

199. Indeed we live very happily, not striving (for sensual pleasures) among those who strive (for them); among those who strive (for them) we live without striving.

XV. (2) Māra Vatthu

Verse 200

200. Susukhaṁ vata jīvāma
yesaṁ no natthi kiñcanaṁ[2]
pītibhakkhā bhavissāma
devā ābhassarā[3] yathā.

---

1. **āturesu/ātura:** ailing or ailment; moral ailment is meant here.

2. **natthi kiñcanaṁ:** without any anxiety; here it means without greed, ill will and ignorance (rāga, dosa and moha).

3. **devā ābhassarā:** Ābhassara brahmās are the radiant brahmās of the abode of the second Rūpāvacara Jhāna Brahmāloka.

200. Indeed we live very happily, without any anxiety (i.e., without greed, ill will and ignorance); like the Ābhassara brahmās we shall live on delightful satisfaction (pīti) as our food.

XV. (3) Kosalaraññо Parājaya Vatthu

Verse 201

201. Jayaṁ veraṁ pasavati
dukkhaṁ seti parājito
upasanto[1] sukhaṁ seti
hitvā jayaparājayaṁ.

201. Conquest begets enmity; the conquered live in misery; the peaceful live happily having renounced conquest and defeat.

XV. (4) Aññatarakuladārikā Vatthu

Verse 202

202. Natthi rāgasamo aggi
natthi dosasamo kali
natthi khandhasamā dukkhā
natthi santiparaṁ sukhaṁ.

202. There is no fire like passion; there is no evil like hatred; there is no ill like (the burden of) khandhas; there is no bliss that surpasses the Perfect Peace (i.e., Nibbāna).

XV. (5) Eka Upāsaka Vatthu

Verse 203

203. Jighacchāparamā rogā
saṅkhāraparamā dukhā
etaṁ ñatvā yathābhūtaṁ
nibbānaṁ paramaṁ sukhaṁ.

203. Hunger is the greatest ailment, khandhas[2] are the greatest ill. The wise, knowing them as they really are, realize Nibbāna, the greatest bliss.

---

1. **upasanto**: the peaceful: one who has extinguished the fire of moral defilements.

2. Both **saṅkhāra** and **khandhas** are used to denote the five aggregates.

XV. (6) Pasenadikosala Vatthu

Verse 204

204. Ārogyaparamā lābhā
santuṭṭhiparamaṁ dhanaṁ
vissāsaparamā[1] ñāti
nibbānaṁ paramaṁ sukhaṁ.

204. Health is the greatest gift, contentment is the greatest wealth, a trusted friend is the best relative, Nibbāna is the greatest bliss.

XV. (7) Tissatthera Vatthu

Verse 205

205. Pavivekarasaṁ pitvā
rasaṁ upasamassa ca
niddaro hoti nippāpo
dhammapītirasaṁ pivaṁ.

205. Having had the taste of solitude and the taste of Perfect Peace of Nibbāna, one who drinks in the joy of the essence of the Dhamma is free from fear and evil.

XV. (8) Sakka Vatthu

Verses 206, 207 and 208

206. Sāhu dassanamariyānaṁ
sannivāso sadā sukho
adassanena bālānaṁ
niccameva sukhī siyā.

207. Bālasaṅgatacārī hi
dīghamaddhāna socati
dukkho bālehi saṁvāso
amitteneva sabbadā
dhīro ca sukhasaṁvāso
ñātīnaṁva samāgamo.

208. Tasmā hi
dhīrañca paññañca bahussutañca
dhorayhasīlaṁ vatavantamariyaṁ
taṁ tādisaṁ sappurisaṁ sumedhaṁ
bhajetha nakkhattapathaṁva candimā.

---

1. **vissāsaparamā**: vissāsa + paramā: vissāsa here means trust; also interpreted as intimacy.

206. It is good to see the Noble Ones (ariyas); to live with them is always a pleasure; not seeing fools is also always a pleasure.

207. He who walks in the company of fools has to grieve for a long time. Association with fools is ever painful, as living with an enemy; association with the wise is a pleasure, as living with relatives.

208. Therefore, one should follow a resolute, intelligent, learned, persevering and dutiful ariya; follow such a virtuous and wise man, as the moon follows the path of the stars.

End of Chapter Fifteen: Happiness.

Chapter XVI
Affection (Piyavagga)

XVI. (1) TayojanapabbajitaVatthu

Verses 209,210 and 211

209. Ayoge yuñja'mattānaṁ
yogasmiñca ayojayaṁ
atthaṁ hitvā piyaggāhī
piheta'ttānuyoginaṁ.

210. Mā piyehi samāgañchi
appiyehi kudācanaṁ
piyānaṁ adassanaṁ dukkhaṁ
appiyānañca dassanaṁ.

211. Tasmā piyaṁ na kayirātha
piyāpāyo hi pāpako
ganthā tesaṁ na vijjanti
yesaṁ natthi piyāppiyaṁ.

209. He who does what should not be done and fails to do what should be done, who forsakes the noble aim of life (i.e., Morality, Concentration and Insight) and grasps at sensual pleasure, covets the benefits gained by those who exert themselves (in meditation).

210. Do not associate with those who are dear, and never with those who are not dear to you; not seeing the dear ones is painful, and seeing those who are not dear to you is also painful.

211. Therefore, one should hold nothing dear; separation from the loved ones is painful; there are no fetters for those who do not love or hate.

XVI. (2) Aññatarakuṭumbika Vatthu

Verse 212

212. Piyato jāyatī soko
piyato jāyatī bhayaṁ
piyato vippamuttassa
natthi soko kuto bhayaṁ.

212. Affection begets sorrow, affection begets fear. For him who is free from affection there is no sorrow; how can there be fear for him?

XVI. (3) Visākhā Vatthu

Verse 213

213. Pemato jāyatī soko
pemato jāyatī bhayaṁ
pemato vippamuttassa
natthi soko kuto bhayaṁ.

213. Endearment begets sorrow, endearment begets fear. For him who is free from endearment there is no sorrow; how can there be fear for him?

XVI. (4) Licchavī Vatthu

Verse 214

214. Ratiyā jāyatī soko
ratiyā jāyatī bhayaṁ
ratiyā vippamuttassa
natthi soko kuto bhayaṁ.

214. Attachment (to sensual pleasures) begets sorrow, attachment begets fear. For him who is free from attachment there is no sorrow; how can there be fear for him?

XVI. (5) Anitthigandhakumāra Vatthu

Verse 215

215. Kāmato jāyatī soko
kāmato jāyatī bhayaṁ
kāmato vippamuttassa
natthi soko kuto bhayaṁ.

215. Lust begets sorrow, lust begets fear. For him who is free from lust there is no sorrow; how can there be fear for him?

XVI. (6) Aññatarabrāhmaṇa Vatthu

Verse 216

216. Taṇhāya jāpatī soko
taṇhāya jāyatī bhayaṁ
taṇhāya vippamuttassa
natthi soko kuto bhayaṁ.

216. Craving begets sorrow, craving begets fear. For him who is free from craving there is no sorrow; how can there be fear for him?

XVI. (7) Pañcasatadāraka Vatthu

Verse 217

217. Sīladassanasampannaṁ
dhammaṭṭhaṁ saccavedinaṁ
attano kamma kubbānaṁ
taṁ jano kurute piyaṁ.

217. He who is endowed with Virtue and Insight, who is established in the Dhamma, who has realized the Truth and performs his own duties, is loved by all men.

XVI. (8) Eka Anāgāmitthera Vatthu

Verse 218

218. Chandajāto anakkhāte
manasā ca phuṭo siyā
kāmesu ca appaṭibaddhacitto
"uddhaṁsoto"[1] ti vuccati.

218. He who has developed a desire for the Ineffable (i.e., Nibbāna), whose mind reaches the same and is no longer attached to the sensual world (kāmaloka), is called one who is bound upstream (uddhaṁsoto).

XVI. (9) Nandiya Vatthu

Verses 219 and 220

219. Cirappavāsiṁ purisaṁ
dūrato sotthimāgataṁ
ñātimittā suhajjā ca
abhinandanti āgataṁ.
220. Tatheva katapuññampi
asmā lokā paraṁ gataṁ
puññāni paṭigaṇhanti
piyaṁ ñātīva āgataṁ.

219. A man who has long been absent and has returned home safely from a distance is welcomed with joy by relatives, friends and well-wishers on his return.

220. In the same way, his good deeds will receive him who has done good when he goes from this world to the other, as relatives receive a dear one on his return.

End of Chapter Sixteen: Affection.

---

1. **uddhaṁsoto:** one who is going upstream, i.e., one who is bound for the "Pure Abodes", (Suddhāvāsa Brahmaloka). The reference is to the anāgāmī or non-returner, who is born in the Avihā Suddhāvāsa and from there passes upwards till he reaches the Akaniṭṭha Suddhāvāsa, the highest of the five Pure Abodes. (The Commentary)

Chapter XVII

Anger (Kodhavagga)

XVII. (1) Rohinīkhattiyakaññā Vatthu

Verse 221

221. Kodhaṁ jahe vippajaheyya mānaṁ
saṁyojanaṁ[1] sabbamatikkameyya
taṁ nāmarūpasmimasajjamānaṁ
akiñcanaṁ[2] nānupatanti dukkhā.

221. Give up anger, abandon conceit, overcome all fetters. Ills of life (dukkha) do not befall one who does not cling to mind and body and is free from moral defilements.

XVII. (2) Aññatarabhikkhu Vatthu

Verse 222

222. Yo ve uppatitaṁ kodhaṁ
rathaṁ bhantaṁva vāraye
tamahaṁ sārathiṁ brūmi
rasmiggāho itaro jano.

222. He who restrains his rising anger as a skilful charioteer checks a speeding chariot,—him I call a true charioteer; other charioteers only hold the reins.

XVII. (3) Uttarā Upāsika Vatthu

Verse 223

223. Akkodhena jine kodhaṁ
asādhuṁ sādhunā jine
jine kadariyaṁ dānena
saccenā' likavādinaṁ.

223. Conquer the angry one by not getting angry (i.e., by loving-kindness); conquer the wicked by goodness; conquer the stingy by generosity, and the liar by speaking the truth.

---

1. **saṁyojanaṁ:** a fetter. There are ten fetters of human passion which bind man to the round of rebirths; these are cast off at different stages of Magga Insight.

2. **akiñcanaṁ:** free from kiñcanā: the three kiñcanā are passion, ill will and ignorance.

XVII. (4) Mahāmoggallānapañha Vatthu

Verse 224

224. Saccaṁ bhaṇe na kujjheyya
dajjā appampi yācito
etehi tīhi ṭhānehi
gacche devāna santike.

224. One should speak the truth, one should not yield to anger, one should give when asked even if it is only a little. By means of these three, one may go to the world of the devas.

XVII. (5) Buddhapitubrāhmaṇa Vatthu

Verse 225

225. Ahiṁsakā ye munayo
niccaṁ kāyena saṁvutā
te yanti accutaṁ[1] ṭhānaṁ
yattha gantvā na socare.

225. The arahats, who do not harm others and are always restrained in their actions, go to the deathless Nibbāna, where there is no sorrow.

XVII. (6) Puṇṇadāsī Vatthu

Verse 226

226. Sadā jāgaramānānaṁ
ahorattānusikkhinaṁ
nibbānaṁ adhimuttānaṁ
atthaṁ gacchanti āsavā.

226. In those who are ever vigilant, who by day and by night train themselves in the three sikkhas (i.e., sīla, samādhi and paññā), and who have their mind directed towards Nibbāna, moral intoxicants become extinct.

---

1. **accutaṁ:** changeless; deathless. It does not mean immortality.

XVII. (7) Atula Upāsaka Vatthu

Verses 227, 228, 229 and 230

227. Porāṇametaṁ Atula
netaṁ ajjatanāmiva
nindanti tuṇhimāsīnaṁ
nindanti bahubhāṇinaṁ
mitabhāṇimpi nindanti
natthi loke anindito.

228. Na cāhu na ca bhavissati
na cetarahi vijjati
ekantaṁ nindito poso
ekantaṁ vā pasaṁsito.

229. Yaṁ ce viññū pasaṁsanti
anuvicca suve suve
acchiddavuttiṁ medhāviṁ
paññāsīlasamāhitaṁ.

230. Nikkhaṁ jambonadasseva[1]
ko taṁ ninditumarahati
devāpi naṁ pasaṁsanti
brahmunāpi pasaṁsito.

227. It is not new, O Atula! It has always been done from ancient times. They blame one who is silent, they blame one who speaks much, and they blame one who speaks little. There is no one in this world who is not blamed.

228. There never has been, there never will be, nor is there now, anyone who is always blamed or always praised.

229, 230. If the wise praise him day after day, knowing him to be truly faultless, wise and endowed with knowledge and virtue, who would blame him, who is like a nikkha of pure gold? The devas praise him; he is praised even by the great Brahmā.

---

1. **nikkaṁ jambonadasseva**: like a nikkha of jambonada gold. Jambonada gold which comes from Jambu river is the finest gold. A **nikkha** can be a weight-unit of gold, an ornament or a coin.

XVIII. (8) Chabbaggiya Vatthu

Verses 231,232,233 and 234

231. Kāyappakopaṁ rakkheyya
kāyena saṁvuto siyā
kāyaduccaritaṁ hitvā
kāyena sucaritaṁ care.

232. Vacīpakopaṁ rakkheyya
vācāya saṁvuto siyā
vacīduccaritaṁ hitvā
vācāya sucaritaṁ care.

233. Manopakopaṁ rakkheyya
manasā saṁvuto siyā
manoduccaritaṁ hitvā
manasā sucaritaṁ care.

234. Kāyena saṁvutā dhīrā
atho vācāya saṁvutā
manasā saṁvutā dhīrā
te ve suparisaṁvutā.

231. Guard against evil deeds, control your body Giving up evil deeds, cultivate good deeds.

232. Guard against evil speech, control your speech. Giving up evil speech, cultivate good speech.

233. Guard against evil thoughts, control your mind. Giving up evil thoughts, cultivate good thoughts.

234. The wise are controlled in deed, they are controlled in speech, they are controlled in thought. Indeed, they are perfectly self-controlled.

End of Chapter Seventeen: Anger

Chapter XVIII

Impurities (Malavagga)

XVIII. (1) Goghātakaputta Vatthu

Verses 235,236,237 and 238

235. Paṇḍupalāsova dānisi
yamapurisāpi ca te upaṭṭhitā
uyyogamukhe[1] ca tiṭṭhasi
pātheyyampi ca te na vijjati.

236. So karohi dīpamattano
khippaṁ vāyama paṇḍito bhava
niddhantamalo anaṅgaṇo
dibbaṁ ariyabhūmiṁ[2] upehisi.

237. Upanītavayo ca dānisi
sampayātosi yamassa santikaṁ
vāso te natthi antarā
pātheyyampi ca te na vijjati.

238. So karohi dīpamattano
khippaṁ vāyama paṇḍito bhava
niddhantamalo anaṅgaṇo
na punaṁ jātijaraṁ upehisi.

235. You are now like a withered leaf; the messengers of death are near you; you are about to set out on a long journey; (yet) you have no provisions (for the journey).

236. Make a firm support for yourself; hasten to strive hard; and be wise. Having removed impurities and being free from moral defilements, you shall enter the abodes of the ariyas (i.e., Suddhāvāsa brahmā realm).

237. Now you are of advanced age, you are going to the presence of the King of Death and you cannot stop on the way; (yet) you have no provisions (for the journey).

238. Make a firm support for yourself; hasten to strive hard and be wise. Having removed impurities and being free from moral defilements, you will no longer be subject to rebirth and decay.

---

1. **uyyogamukhe:** lit., about to set out on a long journey, i.e., the journey of saṁsāra.
2. **dibbaṁ ariyabhūmiṁ:** the celestial plane of the ariyas. The reference is to the Suddhāvāsa brahmā realm or the Pure Abodes which are exclusively inhabited by the anāgāmīs (the Never-Returners).

XVIII. (2) Aññatara brāhmaṇa Vatthu

Verse 239

239. Anupubbena medhāvī
thokaṁ thokaṁ khaṇe khaṇe
kammāro rajatasseva
niddhame malamattano.

239. By degrees, little by little, from moment to moment, a wise man removes his own impurities (moral defilements), as a smith removes the dross of silver or gold.

XVIII. (3) Tissatthera Vatthu

Verse 240

240. Ayasāva malaṁ samuṭṭhitaṁ
tatuṭṭhāya tameva khādati
evaṁ atidhonacārinaṁ[1]
sāni kammāni nayanti duggatiṁ.

240. Just as rust is formed from iron, and corrodes the iron from which it is formed, so also, his own deeds lead the transgressor to a lower plane of existence (duggati).

XVIII. (4) Lāḷudāyī Vatthu

Verse 241

241. Asajjhāyamalā mantā
anuṭṭhānamalā gharā
malaṁ vaṇṇassa kosajjaṁ
pamādo rakkhato malaṁ.

241. Non-recitation is the taint of learning; non--maintenance is the taint of houses; indolence is the taint of beauty; unmindfulness is the taint of one who keeps watch.

XVIII (5) Aññatarakuḷaputta Vatthu

Verses 242 and 243

242. Malitthiyā duccaritaṁ
maccheraṁ dadato malaṁ
malā ve pāpakā dhammā
asmiṁ loke paramhi ca.

---

1. atidhonacārinaṁ: transgressor: i.e., one who transgresses or indulges too much in the use of 'dhona', the four requisites of a bhikkhu.

243. Tato malā malataraṁ
avijjā paramaṁ malaṁ
etaṁ malaṁ pahantvāna
nimmalā hotha bhikkhavo.

242. Sexual misconduct is the taint of a woman; stinginess is the taint of a giver; evil ways are indeed taints in this world as well as in the next.

243. A taint worse than these is ignorance (of the Truth), which is the greatest of taints. O Bhikkhus, abandon this taint and be taintless.

XVIII. (6) Cūḷasāribhikkhu Vatthu

Verses 244 and 245

244. Sujīvaṁ ahirikena
kākasūrena dhaṁsinā
pakkhandinā pagabbhena
saṁkiliṭṭhena jīvitaṁ.

245. Hirīmatā ca dujjīvaṁ
niccaṁ sucigavesinā
alīnenā' ppagabbhena
suddhājīvena passatā.

244. Life is easy for one who is shameless and bold as a crow, who slanders others and is pretentious, aggressive and corrupt.

245. Life is hard for one with a sense of shame, who always seeks purity, who is free from attachment, who is modest and who sees clearly what is proper livelihood.

XVIII. (7) Pañca Upāsaka Vatthu

Verses 246, 247 and 248

246. Yo pāṇamatipāteti
musāvādañca bhāsati
loke adinnamādiyati
paradārañca gacchati.

247. Surāmerayapānañca
yo naro anuyuñjati
idheva meso lokasmiṁ
mūlaṁ khaṇati attano.

248. Evaṁ bho purisa jānāhi
pāpadhammā asaññatā
mā taṁ lobho adhammo ca
ciraṁ dukkhāya randhayuṁ.

246, 247. He who destroys life, tells lies, takes what is not given him, commits adultery, and takes intoxicating drinks, digs up his own roots even in this very life.

248. Know this, O man! Not restraining oneself is evil; do not let greed and ill will subject you to prolonged misery.

XVIII. (8) Tissadahara Vatthu

Verses 249 and 250

249. Dadāti ve yathāsaddhaṁ
yathāpasādanaṁ jano
tattha yo ca maṅku bhavati
paresaṁ pānabhojane
na so divā vā rattiṁ vā
samādhimadhigacchati.

250. Yassa cetaṁ samucchinnaṁ
mūlaghaccaṁ samūhataṁ
sa ve divā vā rattiṁ vā
samādhimadhigacchati.

249. People give according to their faith and their devotion; one who is displeased with others receiving food and drink cannot attain concentration (samādhi) by day or by night.

250. He, who has this feeling of displeasure cut off, sprooted and removed, will surely attain concentration uamādhi) by day or by night.

XVIII. (9) Pañca Upāsaka Vatthu

Verse 251

251. Natthi rāgasamo aggi
natthi dosasamo gaho
natthi mohasamaṁ jālaṁ
natthi taṇhāsamā nadī.[1]

---

1. **natthi taṇhāsamā nadī:** There is no river like craving. This is because although a river can be full at times, craving can never be full, i.e., satiated.

251. There is no fire like passion, there is no grip like ill will, there is no net like ignorance, there is no river like craving.

XVIII. (10) Meṇḍakaseṭṭhi Vatthu

Verse 252

252. Sudassaṁ vajjamaññesaṁ
attano pana duddasaṁ
paresaṁ hi so vajjāni
opunāti yathā bhusaṁ
attano pana chādeti
kaliṁva kitavā saṭho [1].

252. It is easy for one to see the faults of others, but difficult to see one's own. That man broadcasts the faults of others like winnowing chaff in the wind, but hides his own faults as a crafty fowler covers himself.

XVIII. (11) Ujjhānasaññitthera Vatthu

Verse 253

253. Paravajjānupassissa
niccaṁ ujjhānasaññino
āsavā tassa vaḍḍhanti
ārā so āsavakkhayā.

253. In one who constantly sees the faults of others and is always disparaging them, moral intoxicants (āsavas) increase; he is far from extinction of moral intoxicants (i. e., he is far from attainment of arahatship).

XVIII. (12) Subhaddaparibbājaka Vatthu

Verses 254 and 255

254. Ākāseva padaṁ natthi
samaṇo natthi bāhire
papañcābhiratā pajā
nippapañcā tathāgatā.

255. Ākāseva padaṁ natthi
samaṇo natthi bāhire
saṅkhārā sassatā natthi
natthi buddhānamiñjitaṁ.

---

1. **saṭho**: a cheat, a gambler. According to the Commentary, it means a crafty fowler.

254. In the sky there is no track; outside the Buddha's Teaching there is no ariya bhikkhu (samaṇa). All beings take delight in fetters (i. e., craving, pride and wrong view) that prolong saṁsāra; all the Buddhas are free from these fetters.

255. In the sky there is no track; outside the Buddha's Teaching there is no ariya bhikkhu (samaṇa). There is no conditioned thing that is permanent; all the Buddhas are unperturbed (by craving, pride and wrong view).

End of Chapter Eighteen: Impurities.

Chapter XIX

The Just or the Righteous (Dhammaṭṭhavagga)

XIX. (1) Vinicchayamahāmatta Vatthu

Verses 256 and 257

256. Na tena hoti dhammaṭṭho
yenatthaṁ sāhasā naye
yo ca atthaṁ anatthañca
ubho niccheyya paṇḍito.

257. Asāhasena dhammena
samena nayatī pare
dhammassa gutto medhāvī
"dhammaṭṭho" ti pavuccati.

256. He is not just if he decides a case arbitrarily; the wise man should decide after considering both what is right and what is wrong.

257. The wise man who decides not arbitrarily, but in accordance with the law is one who safeguards the law; he is called 'one who abides by the law' (dhammaṭṭho).

XIX. (2) Chabbaggiya Vatthu

Verse 258

258. Na tena paṇḍito hoti
yāvatā bahu bhāsati
khemī averī abhayo
"paṇḍito" ti pavuccati.

258. He is not a wise man just because he talks much; only he who is peaceful, free from enmity, and does no harm to others, is called 'a wise man'.

XIX. (3) Ekudānakhīṇāsava Vatthu

Verse 259

259. Na tāvatā dhammadharo
yāvatā bahu bhāsati
yo ca appampi sutvāna
dhammaṁ kāyena passati
sa ve dhammadharo hoti
yo dhammaṁ nappamajjati.

259. He is not "one versed in the Dhamma" (Dhammadhara) just because he talks much. He who hears only a little but comprehends the Dhamma, and is not unmindful is, indeed, "one versed in the Dhamma".

XIX. (4) Lakuṇḍakabhaddiyatthera Vatthu

Verses 260 and 261

260. Na tena thero so hoti
yenassa palitaṁ siro
paripakko vayo tassa
"moghajiṇṇo" ti vuccati.

261. Yamhi saccañca dhammo ca
ahiṁsā saṁyamo damo
sa ve vantamalo[1] dhīro
"thero"[2] iti pavuccati.

260. He is not a thera just because his head is grey; he who is ripe only in years is called "one grown old in vain."

261. Only a wise man who comprehends the Four Noble Truths and the Dhamma, who is harmless and virtuous, who restrains his senses and has rid himself of moral defilements is indeed called a thera.

XIX (5) Sambahulabhikkhu Vatthu

Verses 262 and 263

262. Na vākkaraṇamattena
vaṇṇapokkharatāya vā
sādhurūpo naro hoti
issukī maccharī saṭho.

263. Yassa cetaṁ samucchinnaṁ
mūlaghaccaṁ samūnataṁ
sa vantadoso medhāvī
"sādhurūpo" ti vuccati.

262. Not by fine talk, nor by good looks could one be a good-hearted man, if he were envious, miserly and crafty.

263. A wise man who has cut off, uprooted and removed these and has rid himself of moral defilements is, indeed, called a good-hearted man.

---

1. **vantamalo**: lit., has vomited impurities.
2. **thero**: an Elder, i. e. a senior member of the Buddhist Order; but often applied to bhikkhus in general.

XIX. (6) Hatthaka Vatthu

Verses 264 and 265

264. Na muṇḍakena samaṇo
abbato alikaṁ bhaṇaṁ
icchālobhasamāpanno
samaṇo kiṁ bhavissati.

265. Yo ca sameti pāpāni
aṇuṁthūlāni sabbaso
samitattā hi pāpānaṁ
"samaṇo" ti pavuccati.

264. Not by a shaven head does a man become a samaṇa, if he lacks morality and austere practices, and tells lies. How could he who is full of covetousness and greed be a samaṇa?

265. He who has totally subdued all evil, great and small, is called a samaṇa because he has overcome all evil.

XIX. (7) Aññatarabrāhmana Vatthu

Vers s 266 and 267

266. Na tena bhikkhu so hoti
yāvatā bhikkhate[1] pare
vissaṁ dhammaṁ samādāya
bhikkhu hoti na tāvatā.

267. Yo'dha puññañca pāpañca
bāhetvā brahmacariyavā
saṅkhāya loke carati
sa ve "bhikkhū" ti vuccati.

266. He does not become a bhikkhu merely because he stands at the door for alms. He cannot become a bhikkhu because he acts according to a faith which is not in conformity with the Dhamma.

267. In this world, he who lays aside both good and evil, who leads the life of purity, and lives meditating on the khandha aggregates is, indeed, called a bhikkhu.

---

1. **bhikkhate**: lit., begs.

XIX. (8) Titthiya Vatthu

Verses 268 and 269

268. Na monena munī hoti
mūḷharūpo aviddasu
yo ca tulaṁva paggayha
varamā[1]dāya paṇḍito.

269. Pāpāni parivajjeti
sa munī tena so muni
yo munāti ubho loke[2]
"muni" tena pavuccati.

268, 269. Not by silence does one become a muni, if one is dull and ignorant. Like one holding a pair of scales, the wise takes what is good and rejects what is evil. For this reason he is a muni. He who understands both internal and external aggregates is also, for that reason, called a muni.

XIX. (9) Bālisika Vatthu

Verse 270

270. Na tena ariyo hoti
yena pāṇāni hiṁsati
ahiṁsā sabbapāṇānaṁ
"ariyo" ti pavuccati.

270. He who harms living beings is, for that reason, not an ariya (a Noble One); he who does not harm any living being is called an ariya[3].

XIX. (10) Sambahulasīlādisampannabhikkhu Vatthu

Verses 271 and 272

271. Na sīlabbatamattena
bāhusaccena vā pana
atha vā samādhilābhena
vivittasayanena vā.

---

1. **varaṁ**: the best, the good, the noble. In this context, it means morality (sīla), concentration (samādhi) and knowledge (paññā), etc. (The Commentary)

2. **ubho loke**: lit., both worlds, meaning internal and external aggregates, or one's own aggregates as well as those of others.

3. **ariya**: one who has realized one of the four maggas.

272. Phusāmi nekkhammasukhaṁ [1]
aputhujjanasevitaṁ
bhikkhu vissāsamāpādi
appatto āsavakkhayaṁ.

271, 272. Not by mere moral practice, nor by much learning, nor by acquiring concentration, nor by dwelling in seclusion, nor by assuring oneself "I enjoy the bliss of Anāgāmi Fruition that is not enjoyed by common worldlings (puthujjanas)" should the bhikkhu rest content without attaining the extinction of moral intoxicants (āsavas) [i.e., without attaining arahatship].

End of Chapter Nineteen: The Just or the Righteous.

---

1. **nekkhammasukhaṁ:** In this context, Anāgāmisukhaṁ, i.e., Anāgāmi Fruition, the fruition that follows the attainment of Anāgāmi Magga.

Chapter XX

The Path (Maggavagga)

XX. (1) Pañcasatabhikkhu Vatthu

Verses 273, 274 and 275

273. Maggānaṭṭhaṅgiko[1] seṭṭho
saccānaṁ caturo padā[2]
virāgo seṭṭho dhammānaṁ[3]
dvipādānañca cakkhumā.

274. Eseva maggo natthañño
dassanassa visuddhiyā
etañhi tumhe paṭipajjatha
mārassetaṁ pamohanaṁ.

275. Etañhi tumhe paṭipannā
dukkhassantaṁ karissatha
akkhāto vo mayā maggo
aññāya sallakantanaṁ.

276. Tumhehi kiccamātappaṁ
akkhātāro tathāgatā
paṭipannā pamokkhanti
jhāyino mārabandhanā.

273. Of paths, the Path of Eight Constituents is the noblest; of truths, the Four Noble Truths are the noblest; of the dhammas, the absence of craving (i.e., Nibbāna) is the noblest; of the two-legged beings, the All-Seeing Buddha is the noblest.

274. This is the only Path, and there is none other for the purity of vision. Follow this Path; it will bewilder Māra.

---

1. **aṭṭhaṅgiko:** Ariya Aṭṭhaṅgika Magga, or the Noble Path of Eight Constituents. This is the Path pointed out by the Buddha for liberation from the round of existences. The Eight Constituents are: right view, right thinking, right speech, right action, right living, right effort, right mindfulness and right concentration.

2. **caturo padā:** Cattāri Ariyasaccāni, or the Four Noble Truths. These are the four Truths upon which the whole doctrine of the Buddha is based. They are: (a) the Noble Truth of Dukkha; (b) the Noble Truth of the Cause of Dukkha, i.e., craving; (c) the Noble Truth of the Cessation of Dukkha; and (d) the Noble Truth of the Path leading to the Cessation of Dukkha. (N.B. Dukkha, in this context, means the five aggregates of attachment or Pañcupādānakkhandha).

3. **dhammā:** both conditioned and unconditioned things.

275. Following this Path, you will make an end of dukkha. Having myself known the Path which can lead to the removal of the thorns of moral defilements, I have shown you the Path.

276. You yourselves should make the effort; the Tathāgatas (Buddhas) can only show the way. Those who practise the Tranquillity and Insight Meditation are freed from the bond of Māra.

XX. (2), (3) and (4) Aniccalakkhaṇa, Dukkhalakkhaṇa and Anattalakkhaṇa Vatthu

Verses 277, 278 and 279

277. "Sabbe saṅkhārā aniccā" ti
yadā paññāya[1] passati
atha nibbindati dukkhe
esa maggo visuddhiyā.

278. "Sabbe saṅkārā dukkhā" ti
yadā paññāya passati
atha nibbindati dukkhe
esa maggo visuddhiyā.

279. "Sabbe dhammā anattā" ti
yadā paññāya passati
atha nibbindati dukkhe
esa maggo visuddhiyā.

277. "All conditioned phenomena are impermanent"; when one sees this with Insight-wisdom, one becomes weary of dukkha (i.e., the khandhas). This is the Path to Purity.

278. "All conditioned phenomena are dukkha"; when one sees this with Insight-wisdom, one becomes weary of dukkha (i.e., the khandhas). This is the Path to Purity.

279. "All phenomena (dhammas) are without Self"; when one sees this with Insight-wisdom, one becomes weary of dukkha (i.e., the khandhas). This is the Path to Purity.

---

1. **paññā**: Insight-wisdom (Vipassanā paññā).

XX. (5) Padhānakammikatissatthera Vatthu

Verse 280

280. Uṭṭhānakālamhi anuṭṭhahāno
yuvā balī ālasiyaṁ upeto
saṁsanna saṅkappamano kusīto
paññāya maggaṁ alaso na vindati.

280. The idler who does not strive when he should be striving, who though young and strong is given to idleness, whose thoughts are weak and wandering, will not attain Magga Insight which can only be perceived by wisdom.

XX. (6) Sūkarapeta Vatthu

Verse 281

281. Vācānurakkhī manasā susaṁvuto
kāyena ca nākusalaṁ kayirā
ete tayo kammapathe visodhaye
ārādhaye magga' misippaveditaṁ.

281. One should be careful in speech, be well-restrained in mind, and physically, too, one should do no evil. One should purify these three courses of action and accomplish the practice of the Path of Eight Constituents made known by the Buddhas.

XX. (7) Poṭṭhilatthera Vatthu

Verse 282

282. Yogā ve jāyatī bhūri
ayogā bhūrisaṅkhayo
etaṁ dvedhāpathaṁ ñatvā
bhavāya vibhavāya ca
tathā'ttānaṁ niveseyya
yathā bhūri pavaḍḍhati.

282. Indeed, wisdom is born of meditation; without meditation wisdom is lost. Knowing this twofold path of gain and loss of wisdom, one should conduct oneself so that wisdom may increase.

XX. (8) Pañcamahallakabhikkhu Vatthu

Verses 283 and 284

283. Vanaṁ chindatha mā rukkhaṁ
vanato jāyate bhayaṁ
chetvā vanañca vanathañca
nibbanā hotha bhikkhavo.

284. Yāva hi vanatho na chijjati
aṇumattopi narassa nārisu
paṭibaddhamanova tāva so
vaccho khīrapakova mātari.

283. O Bhikkhus, cut down the forest of craving, not the real tree; the forest of craving breeds danger (of rebirth). Cut down the forest of craving as well as its undergrowth and be free from craving.

284. So long as craving of man for woman is not cut down and the slightest trace of it remains, so long is his mind in bondage as the calf is bound to its mother.

XX. (9) Suvaṇṇakāratthera Vatthu

Verse 285

285. Ucchinda sinehamattano
kumudaṁ sāradikaṁva pāṇinā
santimaggameva[1] brūhaya
Nibbānaṁ sugatena desitaṁ.

285. Cut off your craving as one plucks an autumn lily with the hand. Nibbāna has been expounded on by the Buddha; cultivate that Path which leads to it.

XX. (10) Mahādhanavāṇija Vatthu

Verse 286

286. Idha vassaṁ vasissāmi
idha hemantagimhisu
iti bālo vicinteti
antarāyaṁ na bujjhati.

286. "Here will I live in the rainy season; here will I live in the cold season and the hot season," so imagines the fool, not realizing the danger (of approaching death).

1. santimaggaṁ: the Path that leads to Nibbāna, i.e., the Path with Eight Constituents.

XX. (11) Kisāgotamī Vatthu

Verse 287

287. Taṁ puttapasusammattaṁ
byāsattamanasaṁ naraṁ
suttaṁ gāmaṁ mahoghova
maccu ādāya gacchati.

287. The man who dotes on his children and his herds of cattle, whose mind longs for and is attached to sensual pleasures, is carried away by Death even as a sleeping village is swept away by a great flood.

XX. (12) Paṭācārā Vatthu

Verses 288 and 289

288. Na santi puttā tāṇāya
na pitā nāpi bandhavā
antakenā' dhipannassa
natthi ñātisu tāṇatā.

289. Etamatthavasaṁ ñatvā
paṇḍito sīlasaṁvuto
nibbānagamanaṁ maggaṁ
khippameva visodhaye.

288. Not sons, nor parents, nor close relatives can protect one assailed by Death; indeed, neither kith nor kin can give protection.

289. Knowing this, the wise man restrained by morality should quickly clear (the obstacles to) the Path leading to Nibbāna.

End of Chapter Twenty : The Path.

Chapter XXI
Miscellaneous (Pakiṇṇakavagga)

XXI.(1) Attanopubbakamma Vatthu

Verse 290

290. Mattā sukhapariccagā
passe ce vipulaṁ sukhaṁ
caje mattāsukhaṁ dhīro
sampassaṁ vipulaṁ sukhaṁ.

290. If by giving up small pleasures, great happiness is to be found, the wise should give up small pleasures seeing (the prospect of) great happiness.

XXI. (2) Kukkuṭaṇḍakhādikā Vatthu

Verse 291

291. Paradukkhūpadhānena
attano sukhamicchati
verasaṁsaggasaṁsaṭṭho
verā so na parimuccati.

291. He who seeks his own happiness by inflicting pain on others, being entangled by bonds of enmity, cannot be free from enmity.

XXI. (3) Bhaddiyānaṁ bhikkhūnaṁ Vatthu

Verses 292 and 293

292. Yaṁ hi kiccaṁ apaviddhaṁ
akiccaṁ pana kariyati
unnaḷānaṁ pamattānaṁ
tesaṁ vaḍḍhanti āsavā.

293. Yesañca susamāraddhā
niccaṁ kāyagatā sati
akiccaṁ te na sevanti
kicce sātaccakārino
satānaṁ sampajānānaṁ
atthaṁ gacchanti āsavā.

292. In those who leave undone what should indeed be done but do what should not be done, who are conceited and unmindful, moral intoxicants increase.

---

1. **vipulaṁ sukhaṁ**: According to the Commentary, it means the bliss of Nibbāna.

293. In those who always make a good effort in meditating on the body, who do not do what should not be done but always do what should be done, who are also mindful and endowed with clear comprehension, moral intoxicants come to an end.

XXI. (4) Lakuṇḍaka Bhaddiya Vatthu

Verses 294 and 295

294. Mātaraṁ pitaraṁ hantvā
rājāno dve ca khattiye
raṭṭhaṁ sānucaraṁ hantvā
anīgho yāti[1] brāhmaṇo.

295. Mātaraṁ pitaraṁ hantvā
rājāno dve ca sotthiye
veyagghapañcamaṁ[2] hantvā
anīgho yāti[1] brāhmaṇo.

294. Having killed mother (i . e., Craving), father (i. e., Conceit), and the two kings (i. e., Eternity-belief and Annihilation-belief), and having destroyed the kingdom (i. e., the sense bases and sense objects) together with its revenue officer (i.e,, attachment), the brāhmaṇa (i. e., the arahat) goes free from dukkha.

295. Having killed mother, father, the two brahmin kings and having destroyed the hindrances of which the fifth (i.e., doubt) is like a tiger-infested journey, the brāhmaṇa (i.e., the arahat) goes free from dukkha.

XXI. (5) Dārusākaṭikaputta Vatthu

Verses 296, 297, 298, 299, 300 and 301

296. Suppabuddhaṁ pabujjhanti
sadā gotamasāvakā
yesaṁ divā ca ratto ca
niccaṁ buddhagatā sati.

297. Suppabuddhaṁ pabujjhanti
sadā gotamasāvakā
yesaṁ divā ca ratto ca
niccaṁ dhammagatā sati.

---

1. **anīgho yāti;** goes unharmed, i.e., liberated from the round of rebirths (saṁsāra).

2. **veyagghapañcamaṁ;** veyaggha + pañcamaṁ, i.e., like a tiger + the fifth. There are five hindrances, nīvaraṇas. The reference here is to the fifth hindrance, viz., doubt (vicikicchā).

298. Suppabuddhaṁ pabujjhanti
sadā gotamasāvakā
yesaṁ divā ca ratto ca
niccaṁ saṁghagatā sati.

299. Suppabuddhaṁ pabujjhanti
sadā gotamasāvakā
yesaṁ divā ca ratto ca
niccaṁ kāyagatā sati.

300. Suppabuddhaṁ pabujjhanti
sadā gotamasāvakā
yesaṁ divā ca ratto ca
ahiṁsāya rato mano.

301. Suppabuddhaṁ pabujjhanti
sadā gotamasāvakā
yesaṁ divā ca ratto ca
bhāvanāya rato mano.

296. Fully alert and ever vigilant are Gotama Buddha's disciples, who by day and by night are always mindful of the qualities of the Buddha.

297. Fully alert and ever vigilant are Gotama Buddha's disciples, who by day and by night are always mindful of the qualities of the Dhamma.

298. Fully alert and ever vigilant are Gotama Buddha's disciples, who by day and by night are always mindful of the qualities of the Saṁgha.

299. Fully alert and ever vigilant are Gotama Buddha's disciples, who by day and by night are always mindful of the component parts of the body.

300. Fully alert and ever vigilant are Gotama Buddha's disciples, whose mind by day and by night always takes delight in being compassionate(lit.,harmless).

301. Fully alert and ever vigilant are Gotama Buddha's disciples, whose mind by day and by night always takes delight in the cultivation (of good-will towards all).

XXI. (6) Vajjiputtakabhikkhu Vatthu

Verse 302

302. Duppabbajjaṁ durabhiramaṁ
durāvāsā gharā dukhā
dukkho' samānasaṁvāso
dukkhānupatitaddhagū
tasmā na caddhagū siyā
na ca dukkhānupatito siyā.

302. It is hard to become a bhikkhu; it is hard to be happy in the practice of a bhikkhu. The hard life of a householder is painful; to live with those of a different temperament is painful. A traveller in saṁsāra is continually subject to dukkha; therefore, do not be a traveller in saṁsāra; do not be the one to be subject to dukkha again and again.

XXI. (7) Cittagahapati Vatthu

Verse 303

303. Saddho sīlena sampanno
yasobhogasamappito
yaṁ yaṁ padesaṁ bhajati
tattha tattheva pūjito.

303. He, who is full of faith and virtue, who also possesses fame and fortune, is held in reverence wherever he goes.

XXI. (8) Cūḷasubhaddā Vatthu

Verse 304

304. Dūre santo pakāsenti
himavantova pabbato
asantettha na dissanti
rattiṁ khittā yathā sarā.

304. Like the Himalayas, the good are visible even from afar; like arrows shot in the night, the wicked are not seen even though they may be near.

XXI. (9) Ekavihāritthera Vatthu

Verse 305

305. Ekāsanaṁ ekaseyyaṁ
eko caramatandito
eko damayamattānaṁ
vanante ramito siyā.

305. He who sits alone, lies down alone, walks[1] alone in diligent practice, and alone tames himself should find delight in living in the forest.

End of Chapter Twenty-One : Miscellaneous.

---

1. All these postures are connected with the cultivation of Insight Development. (The Commentary)

Chapter XXII

The Chapter on Niraya (Nirayavagga)

XXII. (1) Sundarīparibbājikā Vatthu

Verse 306

306. Abhūtavādī nirayaṁ upeti
yo vāpi katvā na karomi' cāha
ubhopi te pecca samā bhavanti
nihīnakammā manujā parattha.

306. One who tells lies (about others) goes to niraya; one who has done evil and says, "I did not do it," also goes to niraya. Both of them being evil-doers, suffer alike (in niraya) in their next existence.

XXII. (2) Duccaritaphalapīḷita Vatthu

Verse 307

307. Kāsāvakaṇṭhā bahavo
pāpadhammā asaññatā
pāpā pāpehi kammehi
nirayaṁ te upapajjare.

307. Many men wearing the yellow robe up to their necks who have an evil disposition and are unrestrained in thought, word and deed are reborn in niraya on account of their evil deeds.

XXII. (3) Vaggumudātīriya Bhikkhu Vatthu

Verse 308

308. Seyyo ayoguḷo bhutto
tatto aggisikhūpamo
yañce bhuñjeyya dussīlo
raṭṭhapiṇḍamasaññato.

308. It is better for one to eat a red-hot lump of iron burning like a flame than to eat alms-food offered by the people, if one is without morality (sīla) and unrestrained in thought, word and deed.

XXII. (4) Khemakaseṭṭhiputta Vatthu

Verses 309 and 310

309. Cattāri ṭhānāni naro pamatto
āpajjati paradārūpasevī
apuññalābhaṁ na nikāmaseyyaṁ
nindaṁ tatīyaṁ nirayaṁ catutthaṁ.

310. Apuññalābho ca gatī ca pāpikā
bhītassa bhītāya ratī ca thokikā
rājā ca daṇḍaṁ garukaṁ paṇeti
tasmā naro paradāraṁ na seve.

309. Four misfortunes befall a man who is unmindful of right conduct and commits sexual misconduct with another man's wife: acquisition of demerit, disturbed sleep, reproach, and suffering in niraya.

310. Thus, there is the acquisition of demerit, and there is rebirth in the evil apāya realms. The enjoyment of a scared man with a scared woman is short-lived, and the king also metes out severe punishment. Therefore, a man should not commit sexual misconduct with another man's wife.

XXII. (5) Dubbacabhikkhu Vatthu

Verses 311, 312 and 313

311. Kuso yathā duggahito
hatthamevā' nukantati
sāmaññaṁ dupparāmaṭṭhaṁ
nirayāyu' pakaḍḍhati

312. Yaṁ kiñci sithilaṁ kammaṁ
saṁkiliṭṭhañca yaṁ vataṁ
saṅkassaraṁ brahmacariyaṁ
na taṁ hoti mahapphalaṁ.

313. Kayirā ce kayirāthenaṁ
daḷhamenaṁ parakkame
sithilo hi paribbājo
bhiyyo ākirate rajaṁ.

311. Just as kusa grass if badly held cuts that very hand, so also, the ill-led life of a bhikkhu drags that bhikkhu down to niraya.

312. An act perfunctorily performed, or a practice that is depraved, or a questionable conduct of a bhikkhu is not of much benefit.

313. If there is anything to be done, do it well; do it firmly and energetically: for the slack life of a bhikkhu scatters much dust (of moral defilements).

XXII. (6) Issāpakata Itthi Vatthu

Verse 314

314. Akataṁ dukkaṭaṁ seyyo
pacchā tappati dukkaṭaṁ
katañca sukataṁ seyyo
yaṁ katvā nānutappati.

314. It is better not to do an evil deed; an evil deed torments one later on. It is better to do a good deed as one does not have to repent for having done it.

XXII (7) Sambahulabhikkhu Vatthu

Verse 315

315. Nagaraṁ yathā paccantaṁ
guttaṁ santarabāhiraṁ
evaṁ gopetha attānaṁ[1]
khaṇo vo mā upaccagā
khaṇātītā hi socanti
nirayamhi samappitā.

315. As a border town is guarded both inside and outside, so guard yourself. Let not the right moment go by; for those who miss this moment come to grief when they fall into niraya.

---

1. **evaṁ gopetha attānaṁ**: so guard yourself; i.e., to guard the internal as well as the external senses. The six internal senses (sense bases) are eye, ear, nose, tongue, body and mind; the six external senses (sense objects) are visible object, sound, odour, taste, touch and idea.

XXII. (8) Nigaṇṭha Vatthu

Verses 316 and 317

316. Alajjitāye lajjanti
lajjitāye na lajjare
micchādiṭṭhisamādānā
sattā gacchanti duggatiṁ.

317. Abhaye bhayadassino
bhaye cābhayadassino
micchādiṭṭhisamādānā
sattā gacchanti duggatiṁ.

316. Those beings who are ashamed of what should not be ashamed of, who are not ashamed of what should be ashamed of, and who hold wrong views go to a lower plane of existence (duggati).

317. Those beings who see danger in what is not dangerous, who do not see danger in what is dangerous, and who hold wrong views go to a lower plane of existence (duggati).

XXII. (9) Titthiyasāvaka Vatthu

Verses 318 and 319

318. Avajje vajjamatino
vajje cāvajjadassino
micchādiṭṭhisamādānā
sattā gacchanti duggatiṁ.

319. Vajjañca vajjato ñatvā
avajjañca avajjato
sammādiṭṭhisamādānā
sattā gacchanti suggatiṁ.

318. Beings who imagine wrong in what is not wrong, who do not see wrong in what is wrong, and who hold wrong views go to a lower plane of existence (duggati).

319. Beings who know what is wrong as wrong, who know what is right as right, and who hold right views go to a happy plane of existence (suggati).

End of Chapter Twenty-two: Niraya.

Chapter XXIII
The Elephant (Nāgavagga)

XXIII. (1) Attadanta Vatthu
Verses 320, 321 and 322

320. Ahaṁ nāgova saṅgāme
cāpato patitaṁ saraṁ
ativākyaṁ titikkhissaṁ
dussīlo hi bahujjano.

321. Dantaṁ nayanti samitiṁ
dantaṁ rājā' bhirūhati
danto seṭṭho manussesu
yo' tivākyaṁ titikkhati.

322. Varamassatarā dantā
ājānīyā ca sindhavā
kuñjarā ca mahānāgā
attadanto tato varaṁ.

320. As an elephant in battlefield withstands the arrow shot from a bow, so shall I endure abuse. Indeed, many people are without morality.

321. Only the trained (horses and elephants) are led to gatherings of people; the king mounts only the trained (horses and elephants). Noblest among men are the tamed, who endure abuse.

322. Mules, thoroughbred horses, horses from Sindh, and great elephants are noble only when they are trained; but one who has tamed himself (through Magga Insight) is far nobler.

XXIII. (2) Hatthācariyapubbaka Bhikkhu Vatthu
Verse 323

323. Na hi etehi yānehi
gaccheyya agataṁ disaṁ
yathā' ttanā sudantena
danto dantena gacchati.

323. Indeed, not by any means of transport (such as elephants and horses) can one go to the place one has never been before (i.e., Nibbāna); but by thoroughly taming oneself, the tamed one[1] can get to that place (i.e., Nibbāna).

---

1. **The tamed one:** One, who having first controlled the senses, has later developed Magga Insight. (The Commentary)

XXIII. (3) Parijiṇṇa Brāhmaṇaputta Vatthu

Verse 324

324. Dhanapālo nāma kuñjaro
kaṭukabhedano dunnivārayo
baddho kabaḷaṁ na bhuñjati
sumarati nāgavanassa kuñjaro.

324. The elephant called Dhanapāla, in severe must and uncontrollable, being in captivity, eats not a morsel, yearning for his native forest (i.e., longing to look after his parents).

XXIII. (4) Pasenadikosala Vatthu

Verse 325

325. Middhī yadā hoti mahagghaso ca
niddāyitā samparivattasāyī
mahāvarāhova nivāpaputṭho
punappunaṁ gabbhamupeti mando.

325. The stupid one, who is lazy, gluttonous, and drowsy, who just wallows like a well-fed pig, is subject to repeated rebirths.

XXIII. (5) Sānusāmaṇera Vatthu

Verse 326

326. Idaṁ pure cittamacāri cārikaṁ
yenicchakaṁ yatthakāmaṁ yathāsukhaṁ
tadajjahaṁ niggahessāmi yoniso
hatthippabhinnaṁ viya aṅkusaggaho.

326. In the past, this mind has wandered as it liked, wherever it liked, at its own pleasure. Now I will control my mind wisely, as a mahout with his goad controls an elephant in must.

XXIII. (6) Pāveyyakahatthi Vatthu

Verse 327

327. Appamādaratā hotha
sacittamanurakkhatha
duggā uddharath' attānaṁ
paṅke sannova kuñjaro.

327. Take delight in mindfulness, guard your mind well. As an elephant stuck in mire pulls itself out, so also, pull yourself out of the mire of moral defilements.

XXIII. (7) Sambahulabhikkhu Vatthu

Verses 328, 329 and 330

328. Sace labhetha nipakaṁ sahāyaṁ
saddhiṁ caraṁ sādhuvihāri dhīraṁ
abhibhuyya sabbāni parissayāni
careyya tena' ttamano satīmā.

329. No ce labhetha nipakaṁ sahāyaṁ
saddhiṁ caraṁ sādhuvihāri dhīraṁ
rājāva raṭṭhaṁ vijitaṁ pahāya
eko care mātaṅga' raññeva nāgo.

330. Ekassa caritaṁ seyyo
natthi bāle sahāyatā
eko care na ca pāpāni kayirā
appossukko mātaṅga' raññeva nāgo.

328. If one finds a sagacious friend, who is a virtuous and steadfast companion, one should live with him joyfully and mindfully, overcoming all dangers.

329. If one cannot find a sagacious friend, who is a virtuous and steadfast companion, one should live alone like the king who gave up and left the country he had won, and like the elephant Mātaṅga roaming alone in the forest.

330. It is better to live alone; there is no fellowship with a fool. So one should live alone, do no evil, and be carefree like the elephant Mātaṅga roaming alone in the forest.

XXIII. (8) Māra Vatthu

Verses 331, 332 and 333

331. Atthamhi jātamhi sukhā sahāyā
tuṭṭhī sukhā yā itarītarena
puññaṁ sukhaṁ jīvitasaṅkhayamhi
sabbassa dukkhassa sukhaṁ pahānaṁ.

332. Sukhā matteyyatā loke
atho petteyyatā sukhā
sukhā sāmaññatā loke
atho brahmaññatā sukhā.

333. Sukhaṁ yāva jarā sīlaṁ
sukhā saddhā patiṭṭhitā
sukho paññāya paṭilābho
pāpānaṁ akaraṇaṁ sukhaṁ.

331. It is good to have friends when the need arises; it is good to be content with anything that is available; it is good to have merit when life is about to end: it is good to be rid of all dukkha.

332. In this world it is good to be dutiful to one's mother; also it is good to be dutiful to one's father. In this world also it is good to minister unto samaṇas[1]; also, it is good to minister unto brāhmaṇas[2].

333. It is good to have virtue till old age, it is good to have unshakeable faith, it is good to gain wisdom, it is good to do no evil.

End of Chapter Twenty-three: The Elephant.

---

1. samaṇas: recluses.
2. brāhmaṇas: here means Buddhas, paccekabuddhas or arahats. (The Commentary)

Chapter XXIV
Craving (Taṇhāvagga)

XXIV, (1) Kapilamaccha Vatthu

Verses 334, 335, 336 and 337

334. Manujassa pamattacārino
taṇhā vaḍḍhati māluvā viya
so plavatī hurā huraṁ
phalamicchaṁva vanasmi vānaro.

335. Yaṁ esā sahate jammī
taṇhā loke visattikā
sokā tassa pavaḍḍhanti
abhivaṭṭhaṁva bīraṇaṁ.

336. Yo cetaṁ sahate jammiṁ
taṇhaṁ loke duraccayaṁ
sokā tamhā papatanti
udabinduva pokkharā.

337. Taṁ vo vadāmi bhaddaṁ vo
yāvante' ttha samāgatā
taṇhāya mūlaṁ khaṇatha
usīratthova bīraṇaṁ
mā vo naḷaṁva sotova
māro bhañji punappunaṁ.

334. In a man who is unmindful craving grows like a creeper. He runs from birth to birth, like a monkey seeking fruits in the forest.

335. In this world, sorrow grows in one who is overwhelmed by this vile craving that clings to the senses, just as (well-watered) bīraṇa grass grows luxuriantly.

336. In this world, sorrow falls away from one who overcomes this vile craving that is difficult to get rid of, just as water-drops fall away from a lotus leaf.

337. Therefore, I will deliver this worthy discourse to all of you who have assembled here. Dig up the root of craving just as one who wishes to have the fragrant root digs up the bīraṇa grass. Do not let Māra destroy you again and again, as the flood destroys the reed.

XXIV. (2) Sūkarapotikā Vatthu

Verses 338,339,340,341,342 and 343

338. Yathāpi mūle anupaddave daḷhe
chinnopi rukkho punareva rūhati
evampi taṇhānusaye anūhate
nibbattatī dukkhamidaṁ punappunaṁ.

339. Yassa chattiṁsati sotā
manāpasavanā bhusā
mahā vahanti duddiṭṭhiṁ
saṅkappā rāganissitā.

340. Savanti sabbadhi sotā
latā uppajja tiṭṭhati
tañca disvā lataṁ jātaṁ
mulaṁ paññāya chindatha.

341. Saritāni sinehitāni ca
somanassāni bhavanti jantuno
te sātasitā sukhesino
te ve jātijarūpagā narā.

342. Tasiṇāya purakkhatā pajā
parisappanti sasova bandhito
saṁyojanasaṅgasattakā
dukkhamupenti punappunaṁ cirāya.

343. Tasiṇāya purakkhatā pajā
parisappanti sasova bandhito
tasmā tasiṇaṁ vinodaye
ākaṅkhanta virāgamattano.

338. Just as a tree with roots undamaged and firm grows again even though cut down, so also, if latent craving is not rooted out, this dukkha (of birth, ageing and death) arises again and again.

339. That man of wrong views, in whom the thirty-six streams (of craving) that flow towards pleasurable objects are strong, is carried away by his many thoughts connected with passion.

340. The stream of craving flows towards all sense objects; the creeper of craving arises (at the six sense-doors) and fixes itself (on the six sense objects). Seeing that creeper of craving growing, cut off its roots with Magga Insight.

341. In beings, there flows happiness that is smeared with craving; those beings attached to pleasure and seeking pleasure are, indeed, subject to birth and ageing.

342. People beset with craving are terrified like a hare caught in a snare; held fast by fetters and bonds they undergo dukkha (round of rebirths) again and again, for a long time.

343. People beset with craving are terrified like a hare caught in a snare. Therefore, one who wishes to free himself from craving should eradicate craving.

XXIV. (3) Vibbhantabhikkhu Vatthu

Verse 344

344. Yo nibbanatho vanādhimutto
vanamutto vanameva ḍhāvati
taṁ puggalametha passatha
mutto bandhanameva ḍhāvati.

344. Having left the forest of desire (i.e., the life of a householder), he takes to the forest of the practice (i.e., the life of a bhikkhu); but when he is free from the forest of desire he rushes back to that very forest. Come, look at that man who having become free rushes back into that very bondage.

XXIV. (4) Bandhanāgāra Vatthu

Verses 345 and 346

345. Na taṁ daḷhaṁ bandhanamāhu ḍhīrā
yadāyasaṁ dārujapabbajañca
sārattarattā maṇikuṇḍalesu
puttesu dāresu ca yā apekkhā.

346. Etaṁ daḷhaṁ bandhanamāhu ḍhīrā
ohārinaṁ sithilaṁ ḍuppamuñcaṁ
etampi chetvāna paribbajanti
anapekkhino kāmasukhaṁ pahāya.

345, 346. The wise do not say that bonds made of iron, of wood, and of hemp are strong bonds; they say that only passionate attachment to and care for gems and jewellery, children and wives are strong bonds. These drag one down (to lower planes of existence) and although they seem yielding are difficult to unfasten. The wise, cutting off this bond (of craving) and resolutely giving up sensual pleasures, renounce the world.

XXIV. (5) Khemātherī Vatthu

Verse 347

347. Ye rāgarattā'nupatanti sotaṁ
sayaṁkataṁ makkaṭakova jālaṁ
etampi chetvāna vajanti dhīrā
anapekkhino sabbadukkhaṁ pahāya.

347. Beings who are infatuated with lust fall back into the Stream of Craving they have generated, just as a spider does in the web it has spun. The wise, cutting off the bond of craving, walk on resolutely, leaving all ills (dukkha) behind.

XXIV. (6) Uggasena Vatthu

Varse 348

348. Muñca pure[1] muñca pacchato[2]
majjhe[3] muñca bhavassa pāragū[4]
sabbattha vimuttamānaso
na punaṁ jātijaraṁ upehisi.

348. Give up the past, give up the future, give up the present. Having reached the end of existences, with a mind freed from all (conditioned things), you will not again undergo birth and decay.

XXIV. (7) Cūḷadhanuggaha Paṇḍita Vatthu

Verses 349 and 350

349. Vitakkamathitassa jantuno
tibbarāgassa subhānupassino
bhiyyo taṇhā pavaḍḍhati
esa kho daḷhaṁ karoti bandhanaṁ.

1,2,3. **pure, pacchato, majjhe**: The reference is to attachment to the past, future and present khandha aggregates.

4. **bhavassa pāragū**: one who has gone to the other shore or end of existences (i. e., Nibbāna); an arahat.

350. Vitakkūpasame ca yo rato
asubhaṁ bhāvayate sadā sato
esa kho byanti kāhiti
esa checchati mārabandhanaṁ.

349. In a man who is disturbed by (sensual) thoughts, whose passions are strong, and who keeps seeing objects as being pleasant, craving grows more and more. Indeed, he makes his bondage strong.

350. A man who takes delight in calming (sensual) thoughts, who is ever mindful, and meditates on the impurity (of the body, etc.) will certainly get rid (of craving); this man will cut the bond of Māra.

XXIV. (8) Māra Vatthu

Verses 351 and 352

351. Niṭṭhaṅgato asantāsī
vītataṇho anaṅgaṇo
acchindi bhavasallāni
antimoyaṁ samussayo.

352. Vītataṇho anādāno
niruttipadakovido[1]
akkharānaṁ sannipātaṁ
jaññā pubbāparāni ca
sa ve "antimasārīro
mahāpañño mahāpuriso" ti vuccati.

351. He who has attained arahatship is free from fear, free from craving, and free from moral defilements. He has cut off the thorns of existence (such as lust). This is the last existence[2] (for him).

352. He who is free from craving and from attachment, who is skilled in the knowledge of the significance of terms, who knows the grouping of letters and their sequence is indeed called "one who has lived his last, a man of great wisdom, a great man".

---

1. **niruttipadakovido** : skilled in niruttipaṭisambhidā i.e., skilled in the knowledge of words.

2. lit,, body.

XXIV. (9) Upakājīvaka Vatthu

Verse 353

353. Sabbābhibhū sabbavidūhamasmi
sabbesu dhammesu anūpalitto
sabbañjaho taṇhakkhaye vimutto
sayaṁ abhiññāya kamuddiseyyaṁ.

353. I have overcome all, I know all, I am detached from all, I have given up all; I am liberated from moral defilements having eradicated Craving (i.e., I have attained arahatship). Having comprehended the Four Noble Truths by myself, whom should I point out as my teacher?

XXIV. (10) Sakkapañha Vatthu

Verse 354

354. Sabbadānaṁ dhammadānaṁ jināti
sabbarasaṁ dhammaraso jināti
sabbaratiṁ dhammarati jināti
taṇhakkhayo sabbadukkhaṁ jināti.

354. The gift of the Dhamma excels all gifts; the taste of the Dhamma excels all tastes; delight in the Dhamma excels all delights. The eradication of Craving (i.e., attainment of arahatship) overcomes all ills (saṁsāra dukkha)[1].

XXIV. (11) Aputtakaseṭṭhi Vatthu

Verse 355

355. Hananti bhogā dummedhaṁ
no ca pāragavesino
bhogataṇhāya dummedho
hanti aññeva attanaṁ.

355. Wealth destroys the foolish; but it cannot destroy those who seek the other shore (i.e., Nibbāna). By his craving for wealth the fool destroys himself, as he would destroy others.

---

1. The eradication of Craving leads to cessation of khandha aggregates, which means the end of rebirths.

XXIV. (12) Aṅkura Vatthu

Verses 356, 357, 358 and 359

356. Tiṇadosāni khettāni
rāgadosā ayaṁ pajā
tasmā hi vītarāgesu
dinnaṁ hoti mahapphalaṁ.

357. Tiṇadosāni khettāni
dosadosā ayaṁ pajā
tasmā hi vītadosesu
dinnaṁ hoti mahapphalaṁ.

358. Tiṇadosāni khettāni
mohadosā ayaṁ pajā
tasmā hi vītamohesu
dinnaṁ hoti mahapphalaṁ.

359. Tiṇadosāni khettāni
icchādosā ayaṁ pajā
tasmā hi vigaticchesu
dinnaṁ hoti mahapphalaṁ.

356. Weeds damage fields; lust spoils all beings. Therefore, giving to those free from lust yields great benefit.

357. Weeds damage fields; ill will spoils all beings. Therefore, giving to those free from ill will yields great benefit.

358. Weeds damage fields; ignorance spoils all beings. Therefore, giving to those free from ignorance yields great benefit.

359. Weeds damage fields; covetousness spoils all beings. Therefore, giving to those free from covetousness yields great benefit.

End of Chapter Twenty-four: Craving.

Chapter XXV
The Bhikkhu (Bhikkhuvagga)

XXV. (1) Pañcabhikkhu Vatthu

Verses 360 and 361

360. Cakkhunā saṁvaro sādhu
sādhu sotena saṁvaro
ghānena saṁvaro sādhu
sādhu jivhāya saṁvaro.

361. Kāyena saṁvaro sādhu
sādhu vācāya saṁvaro
manasā saṁvaro sādhu
sādhu sabbattha saṁvaro
sabbattha saṁvuto bhikkhu
sabbadukkhā pamuccati.

360. Restraint in the eye is good, good is restraint in the ear; restraint in the nose is good, good is restraint in the tongue.

361. Restraint in body is good, good is restraint in speech; restraint in mind is good, good is restraint in all the senses. A bhikkhu restrained in all the senses is freed from all ills (saṁsāra dukkha).

XXV. (2) Haṁsaghātakabhikkhu Vatthu

Verse 362

362. Hatthasaṁyato pādasaṁyato
vācāsaṁyato saṁyatuttamo
ajjhattarato samāhito
eko santusito tamāhu bhikkhuṁ.

362. He who controls his hand, controls his foot, controls his speech, and has complete control of himself; who finds delight in Insight Development Practice and is calm; who stays alone and is contented;—him they call a bhikkhu.

XXV. (3) Kokālika Vatthu

Verse 363

363. Yo mukhasaṁyato bhikkhu
mantabhāṇī anuddhato
atthaṁ dhammañca dīpeti
madhuraṁ tassa bhāsitaṁ.

363. The bhikkhu who controls his mouth (speech), who speaks wisely with his mind composed, who explains the meaning and the text of the Dhamma;– sweet are the words of that bhikkhu.

XXV. (4) Dhammārāmatthera Vatthu

Verse 364

364. Dhammārāmo dhammarato
dhammaṁ anuvicintayaṁ
dhammaṁ anussaraṁ bhikkhu
saddhammā[1]na parihāyati.

364. The bhikkhu, who abides in the Dhamma, who delights in the Dhamma, who meditates on the Dhamma, and is ever mindful of the Dhamma, does not fall away from the Dhamma of the virtuous[1].

XXV. (5) Vipakkhasevaka Bhikkhu Vatthu

Verses 365 and 366

365. Salābhaṁ nātimaññeyya
nā' ññesaṁ pihayaṁ care
aññesaṁ pihayaṁ bhikkhu
samādhiṁ nādhigacchati.

366. Appalābhopi ce bhikkhu
salābhaṁ nātimaññati
taṁ ve devā pasaṁsanti
suddhājiviṁ atanditaṁ.

365. One should not despise what one has received (by proper means), nor should one envy others their gains. The bhikkhu who envies others cannot attain concentration (samādhi).

366. Though he receives only a little, if a bhikkhu does not despise what he has received (by proper means), the devas will surely praise him who leads a pure life and is not slothful.

---

1. **saddhammā**: the Dhammā of the virtuous; i.e., the thirty-seven Factors of Enlightenment (Bodhipakkhiya Dhamma) and the nine Transcendentals (Lokuttara Dhamma).

XXV. (6) Pañcaggadāyaka Brāhmaṇa Vatthu

Verse 367

367. Sabbaso nāmarūpasmiṁ
yassa natthi mamāyitaṁ
asatā ca na socati
sa ve "bhikkhū" ti vuccati

367. He who does not take the mind-and-body aggregate (nāma-rūpa) as "I and mine", and who does not grieve over the dissolution (of mind-and-body) is, indeed, called a bhikkhu.

XXV. (7) Sambahulabhikkhu Vatthu

Verses 368 to 376

368. Mettāvihārī yo bhikkhu
pasanno buddhasāsane
adhigacche padaṁ santaṁ
saṅkhārūpasamaṁ sukhaṁ.

369. Siñca bhikkhu imaṁ nāvaṁ
sittā te lahumessati
chetvā rāgañca dosañca
tato nibbānamehisi.

370. Pañca[1] chinde pañca[2] jahe
pañca [3] cuttari bhāvaye
pañcasaṅgātigo[4] bhikkhu
"oghatiṇṇo" ti vuccati.

---

1. **The lower five fetters (Orambhāgiya saṁyojanā)** are: ego belief (sakkāyadiṭṭhi); doubt (vicikkicchā); wrong views of morality and practices (sīlabbataparāmāsa); sensual desire (kāmarāga) and ill will (byāpāda). These can be got rid of by the first, second and third Maggas.

2 **The upper five fetters (Uddhambhāgiya saṁyojanā)** are: craving for fine material existences (rūpa rāga); craving for non-material existences (arūpa rāga); pride (māna); restlessness (uddhacca) and ignorance (avijjā). These five can be got rid of by arahatship.

3 **The five controlling faculties (Pañcindriyā)** are: faith (saddhā); diligence (viriya); mindfulness (sati); concentration (samādhi) and wisdom (paññā).

4, **The five saṅgas** are: passion ill will, ignorance, pride and wrong views.

371. Jhāya bhikkhu mā pamādo
mā te kāmaguṇe ramessu cittaṁ
mā lohaguḷaṁ gilī pamatto
mā kandi "dukkhamidan" ti ḍayhamāno.

372. Natthi jhānaṁ apaññassa
paññā natthi ajhāyato
yamhi jhānañca paññā ca
sa ve nibbānasantike.

373. Suññāgāraṁ paviṭṭhassa
santacittassa bhikkhuno
amānusī rati hoti
sammā dhammaṁ vipassato.

374. Yato yato sammasati
khandhānaṁ udayabbayaṁ
labhatī pītipāmojjaṁ
amataṁ taṁ vijānataṁ.

375. Tatrāyamādi bhavati
idha paññassa bhikkhuno
indriyagutti santuṭṭhi
pātimokkhe ca saṁvaro.

376. Mitte bhajassu kalyāṇe
suddhājīve atandite
paṭisanthāravutyassa
ācārakusalo siyā
tato pāmojjabahulo [1]
dukkhassantaṁ karissati.

368. The bhikkhu, who lives exercising loving-kindness and is devoted to the Teaching of the Buddha, will realize Nibbāna— the Tranquil, the Unconditioned, the Blissful.

369. O Bhikkhu, bale out the water (of wrong thoughts) from this boat (your body); when empty it will sail swiftly; having cut off passion and ill will you will realize Nibbāna.

370. Cut off the five (the lower five fetters); give up the five (the upper five fetters); and develop the five (controlling faculties). The bhikkhu who has freed himself of the five bonds (passion, ill will, ignorance, pride and wrong view) is called "One who has crossed the flood (of saṁsāra)".

1. **pāmojjabahulo**: lit., much joy; according to the Commentary, in this context, frequently feeling joy.

371. O Bhikkhu, meditate, and do not be unmindful; do not let your mind rejoice in sensual pleasures. Do not be unmindful and swallow the (hot) lump of iron; as you burn (in niraya), do not cry, "This, indeed, is suffering".

372. There can be no concentration in one who lacks wisdom; there can be no wisdom in one who lacks concentration. He who has concentration as well as wisdom is, indeed, close to Nibbāna.

373. The bhikkhu who goes into seclusion (to meditate), whose mind is tranquil, who clearly perceives the Dhamma, experiences the joy which transcends that of (ordinary) men.

374. Every time he clearly comprehends the arising and the perishing of the khandhas, he finds joy and rapture. That, to the wise, is the way to Nibbāna (the Deathless).

375. For a wise bhikkhu in this Teaching, this is the beginning (of the practice leading to Nibbāna): control of the senses, contentment, and restraint according to the Fundamental Precepts.

376. Associate with good friends, who are energetic and whose livelihood is pure; let him be amiable and be correct in his conduct. Then, (frequently) feeling much joy he will make an end of dukkha (of the round of rebirths).

XXV. (8) Pañcasatabhikkhu Vatthu

Verses 377

377. Vassikā viya pupphāni
maddavāni pamuñcati
evaṁ rāgañca dosañca
vippamuñcetha bhikkhavo.

377. O Bhikkhus! As the jasmin (vassikā) plant sheds its withered flowers, so also, should you shed passion and ill will.

XXV. (9) Santakāyatthera Vatthu

Verse 378

378. Santakāyo santavāco
santavā susamāhito
vantalokāmiso bhikkhu
"upasanto" ti vuccati.

378. The bhikkhu who is calm in body, calm in speech, calm in mind, who is well-composed and has given up (lit., vomited) worldly pleasures, is called a "Tranquil One."

XXV. (10) Naṅgalakulatthera Vatthu

Verses 379 and 380

379. Attanā codayattānaṁ
paṭimaṁsetha attanā
so attagutto satimā
sukhaṁ bhikkhu vihāhisi.

380. Attā hi attano nātho
(ko hi nātho paro siyā)[1]
attā hi attano gati
tasmā saṁyamamattānaṁ
assaṁ bhadraṁva vāṇijo.

379. O Bhikkhu, by yourself exhort yourself, and examine yourself; thus guarding yourself and being mindful, you will live in peace.

380. One indeed is one's own refuge, (how could anyone else be one's refuge?)[1] One indeed is one's own haven; therefore, look after yourself as a horse dealer looks after a thoroughbred.

XXV. (11) Vakkalitthera Vatthu

Verse 381

381. Pāmojjabahulo bhikkhu
pasanno buddhasāsane
adhigacche padaṁ santaṁ
saṅkhārūpasamaṁ sukhaṁ.

381. The bhikkhu who frequently feels joy and is devoted to the Teaching of the Buddha will realize Nibbāna --- the Tranquil, the Unconditioned, the Blissful.

---

1. Not found in some foreign versions.

XXV. (12) Sumanasāmaṇera Vatthu

Verse 382

382. Yo have daharo bhikkhu
yuñjati buddhasāsane
so' maṁ lokaṁ pabhāseti
abbhā muttova candimā.

382. A bhikkhu who, though young, devotes himself to the Teaching of the Buddha lights up the world, as does the moon freed from a cloud.

End of Chapter Twenty-five : The Bhikkhu.

Chapter XXVI

Brāhmaṇa or Arahat (Brāhmaṇavagga)

XXVI. (1) Pasādabahulabrāhmaṇa Vatthu

Verse 383

383. Chinda sotaṁ parakkamma
kāme panuda brāhmaṇa
saṅkhārānaṁ khayaṁ ñatvā
akataññūsi brāhmaṇa.

283. O Brāhmaṇa, cut off the stream f craving with diligence, and abandon sense desires. O Brāhmaṇa perceiving the cessation of the Conditioned, be an arahat who realizes Nibbāna, the Unconditioned.

XXVI. (2) Sambahulabhikkhu Vatthu

Verse 384

384. Yadā dvayesu dhammesu
pāragū hoti brāhmaṇo
athassa sabbe saṁyogā
atthaṁ gacchanti jānato.

384. When the brāhmaṇa is well-established in the two dhammas (i.e., the practice of Tranquillity and Insight Meditation), then, in that knowing one, all fetters are destroyed.

XXVI. (3) Māra Vatthu

Verse 385

385. Yassa pāraṁ apāraṁ vā
pārāpāraṁ na vijjati
vītaddaraṁ visaṁyuttaṁ
tamahaṁ brūmi brāhmaṇaṁ.

385. Him I call a brāhmaṇa, who has for him neither this shore (i. e., the sense bases) nor the other shore (i. e., the sense objects), and who is undistressed and free from moral defilements.[1]

---

1. "This shore" and 'the other shore' are used in the sense of the internal and the external āyatanas. The internal āyatanas are the sense bases, viz., the eye, the ear, the nose, the tongue, the body and the mind; the external āyatanas are the sense objects, viz., visible object, sound, odour. taste, touch and mind-object.

For a true brahmaṇa (i. e., arahat) there is neither 'this shore' nor 'the other shore'; which means that the senses of the arahat are calmed, and his passions extinguished.

XXVI. (4) Aññatarabrāhmaṇa Vatthu

Verse 386

386. Jhāyiṁ viraja' māsīnaṁ
katakicca' manāsavaṁ
uttamattha' manuppattaṁ
tamahaṁ brūmi brāhmaṇaṁ.

386. Him I call a brāhmaṇa who dwells in seclusion practising Tranquillity and Insight Meditation and is free from taints (of moral defilements), who has performed his duties and is free from moral intoxicants (āsavas) and has reached the highest goal (arahatship).

XXVI. (5) Ānandatthera Vatthu

Verse 387

387. Divā tapati ādicco
ratti' mābhāti candimā
sannaddho khattiyo tapati
jhāyī tapati brāhmaṇo
atha sabbamahorattiṁ
buddho tapati tejasā.

387. By day shines the sun; by night shines the moon; in regalia shines the king; in meditation shines the arahat; but the Buddha in his glory shines at all times, by day and by night.

XXVI. (6) Aññatarabrāhmaṇa Pabbajita Vatthu

Verse 388

388. Bāhitapāpoti brāhmaṇo
samacariyā [1] "samaṇo" ti vuccati
pabbājayamattano malaṁ
tasmā "pabbajito [2]" ti vuccati.

388. Because he has discarded evil he is called a 'brāhmaṇa'; because he lives calmly he is called a 'samaṇa'; and because he gets rid of his impurities he is called a 'pabbajita.'

---

1. **samacariyā:** lit., living calmly, i.e., practising for eradication of moral defilements.

2. **pabbajita:** one who leaves the household life for the homeless life of a recluse; in Buddhism it means one who has given up the impurities of the household life to become a bhikkhu.

XXVI. (7) Sāriputtatthera Vatthu

Verses 389 and 390

389. Na brāhmaṇassa pahareyya
nāssa muñcetha brāhmaṇo
dhī brāhmaṇassa hantāraṁ
tato dhī yassa muñcati.

390. Na brāhmaṇasse' tadakiñci seyyo
yadā nisedho manaso piyehi
yato yato hiṁsamano nivattati
tato tato sammatimeva dukkhaṁ.

389. One should not strike a brāhmaṇa ; a brāhmaṇa should not get angry with his assailant; it is shameful to strike a brāhmaṇa; it is more shameful to get angry with one's assailant.

390. For a brāhmaṇa there is no benefit at all, if he does not restrain from anger to which his mind is prone. Inasmuch as the intention to harm is desisted, to that extent dukkha ceases.

XXVI. (8) Mahāpajāpatigotamī Vatthu

Verse 391

391. Yassa kāyena vācāya
manasā natthi dukkaṭaṁ
saṁvutaṁ tīhi ṭhānehi
tamahaṁ brūmi brāhmaṇaṁ.

391. Him I call a brāhmaṇa who does no evil in deed or word or thought, who is restrained in these three respects.

XXVI. (9) Sāriputtatthera Vatthu

Verse 392

392. Yamhā dhammaṁ vijāneyya
sammāsambuddhadesitaṁ
sakkaccaṁ taṁ namasseyya
aggihuttaṁva brāhmaṇo.

392. If from somebody one should learn the Teaching of the Buddha, he should respectfully pay homage to that teacher, as a brahmin worships the sacrificial fire.

XXVI. (10) Jaṭilabrāhmaṇa Vatthu

Verse 393

393. Na jaṭāhi na gottena
na jaccā hoti brāhmaṇo
yamhi saccañca[1] dhammo[2] ca
so sucī so ca brāhmaṇo.

393. Not by wearing matted hair, nor by lineage, nor by caste, does one become a brāhmaṇa; only he who realizes the Truth and the Dhamma is pure; he is a brāhmaṇa.

XXVI. (11) Kuhakabrāhmaṇa Vatthu

Verse 394

394. Kiṁ te jaṭāhi dummedha
kiṁ te ajinasāṭiyā
abbhantaraṁ te gahanaṁ
bāhiraṁ parimajjasi.

394. O foolish one! What is the use of your wearing matted hair? What is the use of your wearing a garment made of antelope skin? In you, there is a forest (of moral defilements); you clean yourself only externally.

XXVI. (12) Kisāgotamī Vatthu

Verse 395

395. Paṁsukūladharaṁ jantuṁ
kisaṁ dhamanisanthataṁ
ekaṁ vanasmiṁ jhāyantaṁ
tamahaṁ brūmi brāhamaṇaṁ.

395. Him I call a brāhmaṇa, who wears robes made from rags (picked up from a dust heap), who is lean with veins standing out, who meditates alone in the forest.

---

1. **sacca**: the Four Noble Truths.
2. **dhamma** : the nine Transcendentals, viz., the four Maggas, the four Phalas and Nibbāna.

XXVI. (13) Eka brāhmaṇa Vatthu

Verse 396

396. Na cāhaṁ brāhmaṇaṁ brūmi
yonijaṁ mattisambhavaṁ
bhovādi[1] nāma so hoti
sace hoti sakiñcano
akiñcanaṁ anādānaṁ
tamahaṁ brūmi brāhmaṇaṁ.

396. I do not call him a brāhmaṇa just because he is born from the womb of a brāhmaṇa mother. He is just a bhovādi brahmin if he is not free from moral defilements. Him I call a brāhmaṇa, who is free from moral defilements and attachment.

XXVI. (14) Uggasenaseṭṭhiputta Vatthu

Verse 397

397. Sabbasaṁyojanaṁ chetvā
yo ve na paritassati
saṅgātigaṁ visaṁyuttaṁ
tamahaṁ brūmi brāhamaṇaṁ.

397. Him I call a brāhmaṇa, who has cut off all fetters and is fearless, who is beyond attachment and is free from moral defilements.

XXVI. (15) Dve brāhmaṇa Vatthu

Verse 398

398. Chetvā naddhiṁ varattañca
sandānaṁ sahanukkamaṁ
ukkhittapalighaṁ buddhaṁ
tamahaṁ brūmi brāhamaṇaṁ.

398. Him I call a brāhmaṇa, who has cut the strap (of ill will), the thong (of craving) and the cord (of wrong views together with latent defilements), who has lifted the bar that fastens the door (of ignorance), and who knows the Truth.

---

1. **bhovādi:** 'Bho' is a familiar term of address used to inferiors and equals. The epithet 'bhovādi', therefore, implies arrogance. Brahmins usually addressed the Buddha as 'Bho Gotama!' The term 'bhovādi' is applied reproachfully by the Buddhists to the brahmins.

XXVI. (16) Akkosakabhāradvāja Vatthu

Verse 399

399. Akkosaṁ vadhabandhañca
aduṭṭho yo titikkhati
khantībalaṁ balānīkaṁ
tamahaṁ brūmi brāhmaṇaṁ.

399. Him I call a brāhmaṇa, who, without anger, endures abuse, beating and being bound, to whom the strength of patience is like the strength of an army.

XXVI. (17) Sāriputtatthera Vatthu

Verse 400

400. Akkodhanaṁ vatavantaṁ
sīlavantaṁ anussadaṁ
dantaṁ antimasārīraṁ[1]
tamahaṁ brūmi brāhmaṇaṁ.

400. Him I call a brāhmaṇa, who is free from anger, who practises austerity, who is virtuous and free from craving, who is controlled in his senses and for whom this body (i. e., existence) is the very last.

XXVI. (18) Uppalavaṇṇā Therī Vatthu

Verse 401

401. Vāri pokkharapatteva
āraggeriva sāsapo
yo na limpati kāmesu
tamahaṁ brūmi brāhmaṇaṁ.

401. Him I call a brāhmaṇa, who does not cling to sensual pleasures, just as water does not cling to a lotus leaf, or the mustard seed to the tip of an awl.

---

1. **antimasārīraṁ:** lit., one who has the last body. This is his last body because he will not be reborn; he is an arahat.

XXVI. (19) Aññatarabrāhmaṇa Vatthu

Verse 402

402. Yo dukkhassa pajānāti
idheva khayamattano
pannabhāraṁ visaṁyuttaṁ
tamahaṁ brūmi brahmaṇaṁ.

402. Him I call a brāhmaṇa, who even in this existence realizes the end of dukkha (i.e., Nibbāna), who has laid down the burden (of the khandhas), and who is free from moral defilements.

XXVI. (20) Khemābhikkhunī Vatthu

Verse 403

403. Gambhīrapaññaṁ medhāviṁ
maggāmaggassa kovidaṁ[1]
uttamattha' manuppattaṁ
tamahaṁ brūmi brāhmaṇaṁ.

403. Him I call a brāhmaṇa, who is wise and is profound in his knowledge, who knows the right way from the wrong way, and who has attained the highest goal (i.e., arahatship).

XXVI. (21) Pabbhāravāsitissatthera Vatthu

Verse 404

404. Asaṁsaṭṭhaṁ gahaṭṭhehi
anāgārehi cūbhayaṁ
anokasāri' mappicchaṁ
tamahaṁ brūmi brāhmaṇaṁ.

404. Him I call a brāhmaṇa, who associates not with the householder or with the homeless one, or with both, who is free from sensual desire, and has few wants.

---

1. **maggâmaggassa kovidaṁ**: skilful in differentiating the right way from the wrong way, i.e., knowledge of what does and what does not lead to the realization of Nibbāna.

XXVI. (22) Aññatarabhikkhu Vatthu

Verse 405

405. Nidhāya daṇḍaṁ bhūtesu[1]
tasesu thāvaresu[2] ca
yo na hanti na ghāteti
tamahaṁ brūmi brāhmaṇaṁ.

405. Him I call a brāhmaṇa, who has laid aside the use of force towards all beings, the perturbed as well as the unperturbed (i.e., the arahats), and who does not kill or cause others to kill.

XXVI. (23) Sāmaṇerānaṁ Vatthu

Verse 406

406. Aviruddhaṁ viruddhesu
attadaṇḍesu nibbutaṁ
sādānesu anādānaṁ
tamahaṁ brūmi brāhmaṇaṁ.

406. Him I call a brāhmaṇa, who is not hostile to those who are hostile, who is peaceful (i.e., has laid aside the use of force) to those with weapons, and who is without attachment to objects of attachment.

XXVI. (24) Mahāpanthakatthera Vatthu

Verse 407

407. Yassa rāgo ca doso ca
māno makkho ca pātito
sāsaporiva āraggā
tamahaṁ brūmi brāhmaṇaṁ.

407. Him I call a brāhmaṇa, from whom passion, ill will, pride and detraction have fallen off, like a mustard seed from the tip of an awl.

---

1. **nidhāya daṇḍaṁ bhūtesu:** has laid aside the use of the stick towards all beings.

2. **tasesu thāvaresu:** the perturbed and the unperturbed. The perturbed are those who still have craving and are therefore easily shaken. The unpertarbed are those who have given up craving and are therefore firm and tranquil; they are the arahats.

XXVI. (25) **Pilindavacchatthera Vatthu**

Verse 408

408. Akakkasaṁ viññāpaniṁ
giraṁ sacca' mudīraye
yāya nābhisaje kañci
tamahaṁ brūmi brāhmaṇaṁ.

408. Him I call a brāhmaṇa, who speaks gentle, instructive and true words, and who does not offend anyone by speech.

XXVI. (26) **Aññataratthera Vatthu**

Verse 409

409. Yo'dha dīghaṁ va rassaṁ vā
aṇuṁ thūlaṁ subhāsubhaṁ
loke adinnaṁ nādiyati
tamahaṁ brūmi brāhmaṇaṁ.

409. Him I call a brāhmaṇa, who, in this world, takes nothing that is not given him, be it long or short, big or small, good or bad.

XXVI. (27) **Sāriputtatthera Vatthu**

Verse 410

410. Āsā yassa na vijjanti
asmiṁ loke paramhi ca
nirāsāsaṁ visaṁyuttaṁ
tamahaṁ brūmi brāhmaṇaṁ.

410. Him I call a brāhmaṇa, who has no desire either for this world or for the next, who is free from rcaving and from moral defilements.

XXVI. (28) **Mahāmoggallānatthera Vatthu**

Verse 411

411. Yassālayā na vijjanti
aññāya akathaṁkathī
amatogadha' manuppattaṁ
tamahaṁ brūmi brāhmaṇaṁ.

411. Him I call a brāhmaṇa, who has no craving, who through knowledge of the Four Noble Truths is free from doubt, and has realized Nibbāna the Deathless.

XXVI. (29) Revatatthera Vatthu

Verse 412

412. Yo'dha puññañca pāpañca
ubho saṅga'mupaccagā
asokaṁ virajaṁ suddhaṁ
tamahaṁ brūmi brāhmaṇaṁ.

412. Him I call a brāhmaṇa, who, in this world, has transcended both ties good and evil; who is sorrowless and, being free from the taints of moral defilements, is pure

XXVI. (30) Candābhatthera Vatthu

Verse 413

413. Candaṁva vimalaṁ suddhaṁ
vippasannamanāvilaṁ
nandībhavaparikkhīṇaṁ[1]
tamahaṁ brūmi brāhmaṇaṁ.

413. Him I call a brāhmaṇa, who, like the moon (in a cloudless sky), is pure, clear and serene, and in whom craving for existence is extinct.

XXVI. (31) Sivalitthera Vatthu

Verse 414

414. Yo'maṁ palipathaṁ duggaṁ
saṁsāraṁ mohamaccagā
tiṇṇo pāraṅgato jhāyī
anejo akathaṁkathī
anupādāya nibbuto
tamahaṁ brūmi brāhmaṇaṁ.

414. Him I call a brāhmaṇa, who, having traversed this dangerous swamp (of passion), this difficult road (of moral defilements), the ocean of life (saṁsāra), and the darkness of ignorance (moha), and having crossed the fourfold Flood has reached the other shore (Nibbāna), who practises Tranquillity and Insight Meditation, who is free from craving and from doubt, who clings to nothing and remains in perfect peace.

---

1. **nandībhavaparikkhīṇaṁ:** one in whom craving for continued existence, either in the current sensual existence or in a better and higher plane of existence in the rūpa (fine material) or arūpa (non-material) brahmā realms, is extinct.

XXVI. (32) Sundarasamuddatthera Vatthu

Verse 415

415. Yo'dha kāme pahantvāna
anāgāro paribbaje
kāmabhavaparikkhīṇaṁ
tamahaṁ brūmi brāhmaṇaṁ.

415. Him I call a brāhmaṇa, who, in this world, has given up sensual pleasures, and leaving the home--life has become a bhikkhu; who has eradicated sensual desires and has come to the end of existence.

XXVI. (33) Jaṭilatthera Vatthu

XXVI. (34) Jotikatthera Vatthu

Verse 416

416. Yo'dha taṇhaṁ pahantvāna
anāgāro paribbaje
taṇhābhavaparikkhīṇaṁ
tamahaṁ brūmi brāhmaṇaṁ.

416. Him I call a brāhmaṇa, who, in this world, has given up craving, and leaving the home-life has become a bhikkhu ; who has eradicated craving and has come to the end of existence.

XXVI. (35) Naṭaputtakatthera Vatthu

Verse 417

417. Hitvā mānusakaṁ yogaṁ
dibbaṁ yogaṁ upaccagā
sabbayogavisaṁyuttaṁ
tamahaṁ brūmi brāhmaṇaṁ.

417. Him I call a brāhmaṇa, who has given up attachment to (sensual pleasures of) human life, has transcended attachment to (sensual pleasures of) deva life and is completely free from all attachment.

XXVI. (36) Naṭaputtakatthera Vatthu

Verse 418

418. Hitvā ratiṁ ca aratiṁ ca
sītibhūtaṁ nirūpadhiṁ[1]
sabbalokābhibhuṁ[2] vīraṁ
tamahaṁ brūmi brāhmaṇaṁ.

418. Him I call a brāhmaṇa, who has given up taking delight (in sensual pleasures) and not taking delight (in solitude); who has attained perfect peace and is free from moral defilements; who has overcome all the five khandhas (lit., the world) and is diligent.

XXVI. (37) Vaṅgīsatthera Vatthu

Verses 419 and 420

419. Cutiṁ yo vedi sattānaṁ
upapattiñca sabbaso
asattaṁ sugataṁ buddhaṁ
tamahaṁ brūmi brāhmaṇaṁ.

420. Yassa gatiṁ na jānanti
devā gandhabbamānusā
khīṇāsavaṁ arahantaṁ
tamahaṁ brūmi brāhmaṇaṁ.

419. Him I call a brāhmaṇa, who knows the death and rebirth of beings in every detail, who is detached, who follows the good practice and knows the Four Noble Truths.

420. Him I call a brāhmaṇa, whose destination the devas or gandhabbas or men do not know, who has eradicated moral intoxicants and is an arahat.

XXVI. (38) Dhammadinnā Therī Vatthu

Verse 421

421. Yassa pure ca pacchā ca
majjhe ca natthi kiñcanaṁ
akiñcanaṁ anādānaṁ
tamahaṁ brūmi brāhmaṇaṁ.

---

1. **nirūpadhiṁ:** according to the Commentary, "nirūpadhiṁ ti nirūpakkilesaṁ", i.e., free from substratum or free from moral defilements (kilesā).
2. **sabbalokābhibhuṁ:** lit., one who has conquered all the world, i.e., one who has put an end to rebirths, or the arising of the khandhas.

421. Him I call a brāhmaṇa, who does not cling to the past, future and present khandha aggregates and who is free from moral defilements and attachment.

XXVI. (39) Aṅgulimālatthera Vatthu

Verse 422

422. Usabhaṁ pavaraṁ vīraṁ
mahesiṁ vijitāvinaṁ
anejaṁ nhātakaṁ[1] buddhaṁ
tamahaṁ brūmi brāhmaṇaṁ.

422. Him I call a brāhmaṇa, who is fearless like a bull, who is noble and diligent, who is a seeker of high moral virtues and a conqueror (of three Māras)[2], who is free from craving, who has been cleansed of moral defilements and knows the Four Noble Truths.

XXVI. (40) Devahitabrāhmaṇa Vatthu

Verse 423

423. Pubbenivāsaṁ yo vedi
saggāpāyañca passati
atho jātikkhayaṁ patto
abhiññāvosito muni
sabbavositavosānaṁ
tamahaṁ brūmi brāhmaṇaṁ.

423. Him I call a brāhmaṇa, who knows past existences, who sees the celestial as well as the lower worlds, who has reached the end of rebirths, who, with Magga Insight, has become an arahat and has accomplished all that is to be accomplished for the eradication of moral defilements.

End of Chapter Twenty-six: The Brāhmaṇa.
The end of the Dhammapada Verses.

---

1. **nhātakaṁ:** made clean (of moral defilements) ; an allusion to the ceremonial bathing of the brahmin after finishing his course of studies.

2. **three Māras:** moral defilements (kilesamāra), death (maraṇamāra), the evil one (devaputtamāra).

Chapter I

The Pairs (Yamakavagga)

Verse 1

I (1) The Story of Thera Cakkhupāla

While residing at the Jetavana monastery in Sāvatthi, the Buddha uttered Verse (1) of this book, with reference to Cakkhupāla, a blind thera[1].

On one occasion, Thera Cakkhupāla came to pay homage to the Buddha at the Jetavana monastery. One night, while pacing up and down in meditation, the thera accidentally stepped on some insects. In the morning, some bhikkhus visiting the thera found the dead insects. They thought ill of the thera and reported the matter to the Buddha. The Buddha asked them whether they had seen the thera killing the insects. When they answered in the negative, the Buddha said, "Just as you had not seen him killing, so also he had not seen those living insects. Besides, as the thera had already attained arahatship he could have no intention of killing and so was quite innocent." On being asked why Cakkhupāla was blind although he was an arahat[2], the Buddha told the following story:

Cakkhupāla was a physician in one of his past existences. Once, he had deliberately made a woman patient blind. That woman had promised him to become his slave, together with her children, if her eyes were completely cured. Fearing that she and her children would have to become slaves, she lied to the physician. She told him that her eyes were getting worse when, in fact, they were perfectly cured. The physician knew she was deceiving him, so in revenge, he gave her another ointment, which made her totally blind. As a result of this evil deed the physician lost his eyesight many times in his later existences.

---

1. **thera**: an Elder, i.e., a senior member of the Buddhist Order; but often applied to bhikkhus in general.

2. **arahat**: one who has attained the fourth and final Magga,

Then the Buddha spoke in verse as follows:

Verse 1. All mental phenomena have mind as their forerunner; they have mind as their chief; they are mind-made. If one speaks or acts with an evil mind, 'dukkha' follows him just as the wheel follows the hoofprint of the ox that draws the cart.

At the end of the discourse, thirty thousand bhikkhus attained arahatship together with Analytical Insight (Paṭisambhidā).

Verse 2

I (2) The Story of Maṭṭhakuṇḍalī

While residing at the Jetavana monastery in Sāvatthi, the Buddha uttered Verse (2) of this book, with reference to Maṭṭhakuṇḍalī, a young brahmin.

Maṭṭhakuṇḍalī was a young brahmin, whose father, Adinnapubbaka, was very stingy and never gave anything in charity. Even the gold ornaments for his only son were made by himself to save payment for workmanship. When his son fell ill, no physician was consulted, until it was too late. When he realized that his son was dying, he had the youth carried outside on to the verandah, so that people coming to his house would not see his possessions.

On that morning, the Buddha arising early from his deep meditation of compassion saw, in his Net of Knowledge, Maṭṭhakuṇḍalī lying on the verandah. So when entering Sāvatthi for alms-food with his disciples, the Buddha stood near the door of the brahmin Adinnapubbaka. The Buddha sent forth a ray of light to attract the attention of the youth, who was facing the interior of the house. The youth saw the Buddha; and as he was very weak he could only profess his faith mentally. But that was enough. When he passed away with his heart in devotion to the Buddha he was reborn in the Tāvatiṁsa celestial world.

From his celestial abode the young Maṭṭhakuṇḍalī, seeing his father mourning over him at the cemetery, appeared to the old man in the likeness of his old self. He told his father about his rebirth in the Tāvatiṁsa world and also urged him to approach and invite the Buddha to a meal. At the house of Adinnapubbaka the question of whether one could or could not be reborn in a celestial world simply by mentally professing profound faith in the Buddha, without giving in charity or observing the moral precepts, was brought up. So the Buddha willed that Maṭṭhakuṇḍalī should appear in person; Maṭṭhakuṇḍalī soon appeared fully decked with celestial ornaments and told them about his rebirth in the Tāvatiṁsa world. Then only, the audience became convinced that the son of the brahmin Adinnapubbaka by simply devoting his mind to the Buddha had attained much glory.

Then the Buddha spoke in verse as follows:

Verse 2. All mental phenomena have mind as their forerunner; they have mind as their chief; they are mind-made. If one speaks or acts with a pure mind, happiness (sukha) follows him like a shadow that never leaves him.

At the end of the discourse Maṭṭhakuṇḍalī and his father Adinnapubbaka attained Sotāpatti Magga and Phala.[1] Adinnapubbaka also donated almost all his wealth to the cause of the Buddha's Teaching.

Verses (3) and (4)

I (3) The Story of Thera Tissa

While residing at the Jetavana monastery in Sāvatthi, the Buddha uttered Verses (3) and (4) of this book, with reference to Thera Tissa.

Tissa, son of the Buddha's maternal aunt, was at one time staying with the Buddha. He had become a bhikkhu only in his old age, but he posed as a senior bhikkhu and was very pleased when visiting bhikkhus asked his permission to do some service for him. On the other hand, he failed to perform the duties expected of junior bhikkhus; besides, he often quarrelled with the younger bhikkhus. Should anyone rebuke him on account of his behaviour he would go complaining to the Buddha, weeping, very much dissatisfied and very upset. The others also followed him to the presence

---

1. **Sotāpatti Magga and Phala:** Sotāpatti Magga is the first Magga, attained by one who has entered the current of emancipation. This is followed immediately by Sotāpatti Phala, 'the fruit' or 'fruition' of stream-entering.

of the Buddha. The Buddha told them not to harbour thoughts of enmity, for enmity could only be appeased by not harbouring enmity.

Then the Buddha spoke in verse as follows:

Verse 3. "He abused me, he ill-treated me, he got the better of me, he stole my belongings;"... the enmity of those harbouring such thoughts cannot be appeased.

Verse 4. "He abused me, he ill-treated me, he got the better of me, he stole my belongings;" ... the enmity of those not harbouring such thoughts can be appeased.

At the end of the discourse, one hundred thousand bhikkhus attained Sotāpatti Fruition.

Verse 5

I. (4) The Story of Kāḷayākkhinī

While residing at the Jetavana monastery in Sāvatthi, the Buddha uttered Verse (5) of this book, with reference to a certain woman who was barren and her rival.

Once there lived a householder, whose wife was barren; later he took another wife. The feud started when the elder wife caused abortion of the other one, who eventually died in childbirth. In later existences the two were reborn as a hen and a cat; a doe and a leopardess; and finally as the daughter of a nobleman in Sāvatthi and an ogress named Kāli. The ogress (Kālayakkhinī) was in hot pursuit of the lady with the baby, when the latter learned that the Buddha was nearby, giving a religious discourse at the Jetavana monastery. She fled to him and placed her son at his feet for protection. The ogress was stopped at the door by the guardian spirit of the monastery and was refused admission. She was later called in, and both the lady and the ogress were reprimanded by the Buddha. The Buddha told them about their past feuds as rival wives of a common husband, as a cat and a hen, and as a doe and a leopardess. They were made to see that hatred could only cause more hatred, and that it could only cease through friendship, understanding and goodwill.

Then the Buddha spoke in verse as follows:

Verse 5. Hatred is, indeed, never appeased by hatred in this world. It is appeased only by loving-kindness. This is an ancient law.

At the end of the discourse, the ogress was established in Sotāpatti Fruition and the long-standing feud came to an end.

Verse 6

I (5) The Story of Kosambī Bhikkhus

While residing at the Jetavana monastery in Sāvatthi, the Buddha uttered Verse (6) of this book, with reference to the bhikkhus[1] of Kosambī.

The bhikkhus of Kosambī had formed into two groups. One group followed the master of Vinaya[2] and the other followed the teacher of the Dhamma[3] and they were often quarrelling among themselves. Even the Buddha could not stop them from quarrelling; so he left them and spent the vassa, residence period of the rains, all alone in Rakkhita Grove near Pālileyyaka forest. There, the elephant Pālileyya waited upon the Buddha.

The lay disciples of Kosambī, on learning the reason for the departure of the Buddha, refused to make offerings to the remaining bhikkhus. This made them realize their mistake and reconciliation took place among themselves. Still, the lay disciples would not treat them as respectfully as before, until they owned up their fault to the Buddha. But the Buddha was away and it was in the middle of the vassa; so the bhikkhus of Kosambī spent the vassa in misery and hardship.

At the end of the vassa, the Venerable Ānanda and five hundred bhikkhus approached the Buddha and gave the message from Anāthapiṇḍika and other lay disciples imploring him to return. In due course the Buddha returned to the Jetavana monastery in Sāvatthi. The bhikkhus followed him there, fell down at his feet, and owned up their fault. The Buddha rebuked them for

---

1. **bhikkhu:** a member of the Buddhist Order.
2. **Vinaya:** the Disciplinary Rules of the Order (the Saṁgha).
3. **Dhamma:** the Doctrines of the Buddha.

disobeying him. He told them to remember that they must all die some day and therefore, they must stop their quarrels and must not act as if they would never die.

Then the Buddha spoke in verse as follows:

Verse 6. People, other than the wise, do not realize, "We in this world must all die," (and not realizing it continue their quarrels). The wise realize it and thereby their quarrels cease. At the end of the discourse, all the assembled bhikkhus were established in Sotāpatti Fruition.

Verses 7 and 8

I (6) The Story of Thera Māhākāḷa

While residing in the neighbourhood of the town of Setabya, the Buddha uttered Verses (7) and (8) of this book, with reference to Mahākāḷa and his brother Cūḷakāḷa. Mahākāḷa and Cūḷakāḷa were two merchant brothers from the town of Setabya. While travelling about with their merchandise on one occasion, they had a chance to listen to a religious discourse given by the Buddha. After hearing the discourse Mahākāḷa asked the Buddha for admission to the Order of the bhikkhus. Cūḷakāḷa also joined the Order but with the intention of coming out of the Order and to bring out his brother along with him.

Mahākāḷa was serious in his ascetic practice at the cemetery (Sosānika dhutiṅga) and diligently meditated on decay and impermanence. He finally gained Insight and attained arahatship.

Later, the Buddha and his disciples, including the brothers, happened to be staying in the forest of Simsapa, near Setabya. While staying there, the former wives of Cūḷakāḷa invited the Buddha and his disciples to their house. Cūḷakaḷa himself went ahead to prepare seating arrangements for the Buddha and his disciples. Once there, the former wives of Cūḷakāḷa made him change into lay clothes.

The next day, the wives of Mahākāḷa invited the Buddha and his disciples to their house hoping to do the same with Mahākāḷa as the wives of Cūḷakāḷa had done to Cūḷakāḷa. After the meal they requested the

Buddha to let Mahākāḷa remain to "express appreciation" (anumodanā). So the Buddha and the other disciples left.

Arriving at the village gate the bhikkhus expressed their dissatisfaction and apprehension. They were dissatisfied because Mahākāḷa was permitted to stay behind and they were afraid that, like Cūḷakāḷa, his brother, Mahākāḷa, too, would be made to leave the Order by his former wives. To this, the Buddha replied that the two brothers were not alike. Cūḷakāḷa indulged in sensual pleasures and was lazy and weak; he was just like a weak tree. Mahākāḷa, on the other hand, was diligent, steadfast and strong in his faith of the Buddha, the Dhamma and the Saṁgha; he was like a mountain of rock.

Then the Buddha spoke in verse as follows:

Verse 7. He who keeps his mind on pleasant objects, who is uncontrolled in his senses, immoderate in his food, and is lazy and lacking in energy, will certainly be overwhelmed by Māra, just as stormy winds uproot a weak tree.

Verse 8. He who keeps his mind on the impurities (of the body), who is well-controlled in his senses, and is full of faith and energy, will certainly be not overwhelmed by Māra, just as stormy winds cannot shake a mountain of rock.

Meanwhile, the former wives of Mahākāḷa surrounded him and tried to remove his yellow robes. The thera, sensing their attitude, stood up and rising up into the air by his supernormal powers passed through the roof of the house into the sky. He landed at the feet of the Buddha at the very moment the master was coming to the end of his utterance of the above two stanzas. At the same time, all the bhikkhus assembled there were established in Sotāpatti Fruition.

Verses 9 and 10

1 (7) The Story of Devadatta

While residing at the Jetavana monastery in Sāvatthi, the Buddha uttered Verses (9) and (10) of this book, with reference to Devadatta.

Once the two Chief Disciples, the Venerable Sāriputta and the Venerable Mahā Moggallāna, went from Sāvatthi to Rājagaha. There, the people of Rājagaha invited them, with their one thousand followers, to a morning meal. On that occasion someone handed over a piece of cloth, worth one hundred thousand, to the organizers of the alms giving ceremony. He instructed them to dispose of it and use the proceeds for the ceremony should there be any shortage of funds, or if there were no such shortage, to offer it to anyone of the bhikkhus they thought fit. It so happened that there was no shortage of anything and the cloth was to be offered to one of the theras. Since the two Chief Disciples visited Rājagaha only occasionally, the cloth was offered to Devadatta, who was a permanent resident of Rājagaha.

Devadatta promptly made the cloth into robes and moved about pompously, wearing them. Then, a certain bhikkhu from Rājagaha came to Sāvatthi to pay homage to the Buddha, and told him about Devadatta and the robe, made out of cloth worth one hundred thousand. The Buddha then said that it was not the first time that Devadatta was wearing robes that he did not deserve. The Buddha then related the following story.

Devadatta was an elephant hunter in one of his previous existences. At that time, in a certain forest, there lived a large number of elephants. One day, the hunter noticed that these elephants knelt down to the paccekabuddhas[1] on seeing them. Having observed that, the hunter stole an upper part of a yellow robe and covered his body and hand with it. Then, holding a spear in his hand, he waited for the elephants on their usual route. The elephants came, and taking him for a paccekabuddha fell down on their knees to pay obeisance. They easily fell a prey to the hunter. Thus, one by one, he killed the last elephant in the row each day for many days.

The Bodhisatta (the Buddha-to-be) was then the leader of the herd. Noticing the dwindling number of his followers he decided to investigate and followed his

---

1. **paccekabuddha :** one who, like the Buddha, is Self-Enlightened in the Four Noble Truths and has uprooted all the moral defilements (kilesas). However, he cannot teach others. Paccekabuddhas appear during the absence of the Buddha Sāsanā (Teaching).

herd at the end of the line. He was alert, and was therefore able to evade the spear. He caught hold of the hunter in his trunk and was about to dash him against the ground, when he saw the yellow robe. Seeing the yellow robe, he desisted and spared the life of the hunter.

The hunter was rebuked for trying to kill under cover of the yellow robe and for committing such an act of depravity. The hunter clearly did not deserve to put on the yellow robe.

Then the Buddha spoke in verse as follows:

Verse 9. He who is not free from taints of moral defilements (kilesas) and yet dons the yellow robe, who lacks restraint in his senses and (speaks not the) truth is unworthy of the yellow robe.

Verse 10. He who has discarded all moral defilements (kilesas), who is established in moral precepts, is endowed with restraint and (speaks the) truth is, indeed, worthy of the yellow robe.

At the end of the discourse, many bhikkhus were established in Sotāpatti Fruition.

Verses 11 and 12

I (8) The Story of Thera Sāriputta

While residing at Veḷuvana, the Bamboo Grove monastery in Rājagaha, the Buddha uttered Verses (11) and (12) of this book, with reference to Sañjaya, a former teacher of the Chief Disciples, the Venerable Sāriputta and the Venerable Moggallāna (formerly Upatissa and Kolita).

Upatissa and Kolita were two youths from Upatissa and Kolita, two villages near Rājagaha. While looking at a show they realized the insubstantiality of things and they decided to seach for the way to liberation. First, they approached Sañjaya, the wandering ascetic at Rājagaha, but they were not satisfied with his teachings. So they went all over Jambudīpa and came back to their native place, after searching for, but not finding the true dhamma. At this point they came to an understanding that one who found the true dhamma should inform the other.

One day, Upatissa came across Thera Assaji and learned from him the substance of the dhamma. The thera uttered the verse beginning with "Ye dhammā hetuppabhavā", meaning, "those phenomena which proceed from a cause". Listening to the verse, Upatissa became established in the Sotāpatti Magga and Phala. Then, as promised, he went to his friend Kolita, explained to him that he, Upatissa, had attained the state of Deathlessness and repeated the verse to his friend. Kolita also become established in Sotāpatti Fruition at the end of the verse. They both remembered their former teacher and so went to Sañjaya and said to him, "We have found one who could point out the Path to Deathlesseness; the Buddha has appeared in the world; the Dhamma has appeared; the Saṁgha has appeared... Come, let us go to the Teacher." They had hoped that their former teacher would go along with them to the Buddha and by listening to the discourses he, too, would come to realize Magga and Phala. But Sañjaya refused.

So Upatissa and Kolita, with two hundred and fifty followers, went to the Buddha, at Veḷuvana. There, they were initiated and admitted into the Order as bhikkhus. Upatissa as son of Rūpasārī became known as Thera Sāriputta; Kolita as son of Moggalī became known as Thera Mahā Moggallāna. On the seventh day after the initiation Mahā Moggallāna attained Arahatship. Thera Sāriputta achieved the same a fortnight after initiation. On that day, the Buddha made them his two Chief Disciples (Agga-Sāvaka).

The two Chief Disciples then related to the Buddha how they went to the Giragga festival, the meeting with Thera Assaji and their attainment of Sotāpatti Fruition. They also told the Buddha about their former teacher Sañjaya, who refused to accompany them. Sañjaya had said, "Having been a teacher to so many pupils, for me to become his pupil would be like a jar turning into a drinking cup. Besides, only few people are wise and the majority are foolish; let the wise go to the wise Gotama, the foolish would still come to me. Go your way, my pupils."

Thus, as the Buddha pointed out, Sañjaya's false pride was preventing him from seeing truth as truth; he was seeing untruth as truth and would never arrive at the real truth.

Then the Buddha spoke in verse as follows:

Verse 11. They take untruth for truth; they take truth for untruth; such persons can never arrive at the truth, for they hold wrong views.

Verse 12. They take truth for truth; they take untruth for untruth; such persons arrive at the truth, for they hold right views.

At the end of the discourse, many people came to be established in Sotāpatti Fruition.

Verses 13 and 14

I (9) The Story of Thera Nanda

While residing at the Jetavana monastery in Sāvatthi, the Buddha uttered Verses (13) and (14) of this book, with reference to Thera Nanda, a cousin of the Buddha.

Once the Buddha was residing at the Veḷuvana monastery in Rājagaha when his father King Suddhodana repeatedly sent messengers to the Buddha requesting him to visit the city of Kapilavatthu. Accordingly, the Buddha made the journey in the company of twenty thousand arahats. On arrival at Kapilavatthu he related the Vessantara Jātaka to the assembly of his relatives. On the second day, he entered the city, where by reciting the verse beginning with "Uttiṭṭhe Nappamajjeyya..." (i. e., One should arise and should not be unmindful...) he caused his father to be established in Sotāpatti Fruition. On arrival at the palace, the Buddha recited another verse beginning with "Dhammaṁ care sucaritaṁ..." (i. e., One should practise the Dhamma...) and established the king in Sakadāgāmi Fruition.[1] After the meal he narrated the Candakinnarī Jātaka, with reference to the virtues of Rāhula's mother.

On the third day, there was the marriage ceremony of Prince Nanda, a cousin of the Buddha. The Buddha went there for alms and handed over the alms bowl to Prince Nanda. The Buddha then departed without taking back the bowl. So the prince, holding the bowl, had to follow the Buddha. The bride, Princess

---

1. **Sakadāgāmi Fruition:** Sakadāgāmi Phala, 'fruit' or 'fruition'. This immediately follows Sakadāgāmi Magga which is the second Magga or the second stage of Enlightenment attained by one who has practised Insight Meditation.

Janapadakalyāṇī, seeing the prince following the Buddha rushed forth and cried out to the prince to come back soon. At the monastery, the prince was admitted into the Order as a bhikkhu.

Later, the Buddha moved into the monastery built by Anāthapiṇḍika, at Jeta Park in Sāvatthi. While residing there Nanda was discontented and half-hearted and found little pleasure in the life of a bhikkhu. He wanted to return to the life of a householder because he kept on remembering the words of Princess Janapadakalyāṇī, imploring him to return soon.

Knowing this, the Buddha, by supernormal power, showed Nanda, the beautiful female devas of the Tāvatiṁsa world who were far prettier than Princess Janapadakalyāṇī. He promised to get them for Nanda, if the latter strove hard in the practice of the Dhamma. Other bhikkhus ridiculed Nanda by saying that he was like a hireling who practised the Dhamma for the sake of beautiful women, etc. Nanda felt very much tormented and ashamed. So, in seclusion, he tried very hard in the practice of the Dhamma and eventually attained arahatship. As an arahat his mind was totally released from all attachments, and the Buddha was also released from his promise to Nanda. All this had been foreseen by the Buddha right from the very beginning.

Other bhikkhus, having known that Nanda was not happy in the life of a bhikkhu, again asked him how he was faring. When he answered that he had no more attachments to the life of a householder, they thought Nanda was not speaking the truth. So they informed the Buddha about the matter, at the same time expressing their doubts. The Buddha then explained to them that, previously, the nature of Nanda was like that of an ill-roofed house, but now, it had grown to be like a well-roofed one.

Then the Buddha spoke in verse as follows:

Verse 13. Just as rain penetrates a badly-roofed house, so also, passion (rāga) penetrates a mind not cultivated in Tranquillity and Insight Development (Samatha and Vipassanā).

Verse 14. Just as rain cannot penetrate a well-roofed house, so also, passion (rāga) cannot penetrate a mind well-cultivated in Tranquillity and Insight Development (Samatha and Vipassanā).

Verse 15

I (10) The Story of Cundasūkarika

While residing at the Veḷuvana monastery in Rājagaha, the Buddha uttered Verse (15) of this book, with reference to Cunda, the pork-butcher.

Once, in a village not far away from the Veḷuvana monastery, there lived a very cruel and hard-hearted pork-butcher, by the name of Cunda. Cunda was a pork-butcher for over fifty-five years; all this time he had not done a single meritorious deed. Before he died, he was in such great pain and agony that he was grunting and squealing and kept on moving about on his hands and knees like a pig for seven whole days. In fact, even before he died, he was suffering as if he were in Niraya. On the seventh day, the pork-butcher died and was reborn in Avīci Niraya. Thus, the evil-doer must always suffer for the evil deeds done by him; he suffers in this world as well as in the next.

In this connection, the Buddha spoke in verse as follows:

Verse 15. Here he grieves, hereafter he grieves; the evil-doer grieves in both existences. He grieves and he suffers anguish when he sees the depravity of his own deeds.

Verse 16

I (11) The Story of Dhammika Upāsaka

While residing at the Jetavana monastery in Sāvatthi, the Buddha uttered Verse (16) of this book, with reference to Dhammika, a lay disciple.

Once there lived in Sāvatthi, a lay disciple by the name of Dhammika, who was virtuous and very fond of giving in charity. He generously offered food and other requisites to the bhikkhus regularly and also on special occasions. He was, in fact, the leader of five hundred virtuous lay disciples of the Buddha who lived in Sāvatthi. Dhammika had seven sons and seven

---

1. **Niraya or Naraka:** a place of continuous torment sometimes compared with hell; but it is different from hell because suffering in Niraya is not everlasting like suffering in hell. Avīci Niraya is the most fearful of all Nirayas.

daughters and all of them, like their father, were virtuous and devoted to charity. When Dhammika was very ill and was on his death-bed he made a request to the Saṁgha to come to him and recite the sacred texts by his bedside. While the bhikkhus were reciting the Mahāsatipaṭṭhāna Sutta, six decorated chariots from six celestial worlds arrived to invite him to their respective worlds. Dhammika told them to wait for a while for fear of interrupting the recitation of the Sutta. The bhikkhus, thinking that they were being asked to stop, stopped and left the place.

A little while later, Dhammika told his children about the six decorated chariots waiting for him. Then and there he decided to choose the chariot from the Tusita world and asked one of his children to throw a garland on to it. Then he passed away and was reborn in the Tusita world. Thus, the virtuous man rejoices in this world as well as in the next.

Then the Buddha spoke in verse as follows:

Verse 16. Here he rejoices, hereafter he rejoices; one who performed meritorious deeds rejoices in both existences. He rejoices and greatly rejoices when he sees the purity of his own deeds.

Verse 17

I (12) The Story of Devadatta

While residing at the Jetavana monastery in Sāvatthi, the Buddha uttered Verse (17) of this book, with reference to Devadatta.

Devadatta was at one time residing with the Buddha in Kosambī. While staying there he realized that the Buddha was receiving much respect and honour as well as offerings. He envied the Buddha and aspired to head the Order of the bhikkhus. One day, while the Buddha was preaching at the Veḷuvana monastery in Rājagaha, he approached the Buddha and on the ground that the Buddha was getting old, he suggested that the Order be entrusted to his care. The Buddha rejected his offer and rebuked him, saying that he was a swallower of other people's spittle. The Buddha next asked the Saṁgha to carry out an act of proclamation (Pakāsanīya kamma[1]) regarding Devadatta.

Devadatta felt aggrieved and vowed vengeance against the Buddha. Three times, he attempted to kill the Buddha: first, by employing some archers; secondly, by climbing up the Gijjhakūṭa hill and rolling down a big piece of rock on to the Buddha; and thirdly, by causing the elephant Nāḷāgiri to attack the Buddha. The hired assassins returned after being established in Sotāpatti Fruition, without harming the Buddha. The big piece of rock rolled down by Devadatta hurt the big toe of the Buddha just a little, and when the Nāḷāgīri elephant rushed at the Buddha, it was made docile by the Buddha. Thus Devadatta failed to kill the Buddha, and he tried another tactic. He tried to break up the Order of the bhikkhus by taking away some newly admitted bhikkhus with him to Gayāsīsa; however, most of them were brought back by Thera Sāriputta and Thera Mahā Moggallāna.

Later, Devadatta fell ill. He had been ill for nine months when he asked his pupils to take him to the Buddha, and subsequently made the trip to the Jetavana monastery. Hearing that Devadatta was coming, the Budddha told his disciples that Devadatta would never get the opportunity to see him.

When Devadatta and his party reached the pond in the Jetavana monastery compound the carriers put down the couch on the bank of the pond and went to take a bath. Devadatta also rose from his couch and placed both his feet on the ground. Immediately, his feet sank into the earth and he was gradually swallowed up. Devadatta did not have the opportunity to see the Buddha because of the wicked deeds he had done to the Buddha. After his death, he was reborn in Avīci Niraya, a place of intense and continuous torment.

---

1. **Pakāsanīya kamma:** An act of Proclamation carried out by the Order of the Saṁgha regarding a member declaring that as his conduct was of one kind before and is of another kind now, henceforth all his physical and verbal actions are only his and have nothing to do with the Buddha, the Dhamma and the Saṁgha.

Then the Buddha spoke in verse as follows:

Verse 17. Here he is tormented, hereafter he is tormented; the evil-doer is tormented in both existences. He is tormented, and he laments: "Evil have I done." He is even more tormented when he is reborn in one of the lower worlds (Apāya).

Verse 18

I (13) The Story of Sumanadevī

While residing at the Jetavana monastery in Sāvatthi, the Buddha uttered Verse (18) of this book, with reference to Sumanadevī, the youngest daughter of Anāthapiṇḍika.

In Sāvatthi, at the house of Anāthapiṇḍika and the house of Visākhā, two thousand bhikkhus were served with food daily. At the house of Visākhā, the offering of alms-food was supervised by her granddaughter. At the house of Anāthapiṇḍika, the supervision was done, first by the eldest daughter, next by the second daughter and finally by Sumanadevī, the youngest daughter. The two elder sisters attained Sotāpatti Fruition by listening to the Dhamma, while serving food to the bhikkhus. Sumanadevī did even better and she attained Sakadāgāmi Fruition.

Later, Sumanadevī fell ill and on her death-bed she asked for her father. Her father came, and she addressed her father as "younger brother" (Kaniṭṭha bhātika) and passed away soon after. Her form of address kept her father wondering and made him uneasy and depressed, thinking that his daughter was delirious and not in her right senses at the time of her death. So, he approached the Buddha and reported to him about his daughter, Sumanadevī. Then the Buddha told the noble rich man that his daughter was in her right senses and fully self--possessed at the time of her passing away. The Buddha also explained that Sumanadevī had addressed her father as "younger brother" because her attainment of Magga and Phala was higher than that of her father's. She was a Sakadāgāmī whereas her father was only a Sotāpanna. Anāthapiṇḍika was also told that Sumanadevī was reborn in the Tusita deva world.

Then the Buddha spoke in verse as follows:

Verse 18. Here he is happy, hereafter he is happy; one who performs meritorious deeds is happy in both existences. Happily he exclaims: "I have done meritorious deeds." He is happier still when he is reborn in a higher world (suggati).

Verses 19 and 20

I (14) The Story of Two Friends

While residing at the Jetavana monastery, the Buddha uttered Verses (19) and (20) of this book, with reference to two bhikkhus who were friends.

Once there were two friends of noble family, two bhikkhus from Sāvatthi. One of them learned the Tipiṭaka and was very proficient in reciting and preaching the sacred texts. He taught five hundred bhikkhus and became the instructor of eighteen groups of bhikkhus. The other bhikkhu striving diligently and ardently in the course of Insight Meditation attained arahatship together with Analytical Insight.

On one occasion, when the second bhikkhu came to pay homage to the Buddha, at the Jetavana monastery, the two bhikkhus met. The master of the Tipiṭaka did not realize that the other had already become an arahat. He looked down on the other, thinking that this old bhikkhu knew very little of the sacred texts, not even one out of the five Nikāyas or one out of the three Piṭakas. So he thought of putting questions to the other, and thus embarass him. The Buddha knew about his unkind intention and he also knew that as a result of giving trouble to such a noble disciple of his, the learned bhikkhu would be reborn in a lower world.

So, out of compassion, the Buddha visited the two bhikkhus to prevent the scholar from questioning the other bhikkhu. The Buddha himself did the questioning. He put questions on jhānas and maggas to the master of the Tipiṭaka; but he could not answer them because he had not practised what he had taught. The other bhikkhu, having practised the Dhamma and having attained arahatship, could answer all the questions. The Buddha praised the one who practised the Dhamma (i.e., a vipassaka), but not a single word of praise was spoken for the learned scholar(i.e., a ganthika).

The resident disciples could not understand why the Buddha had words of praise for the old bhikkhu and not for their learned teacher. So, the Buddha explained the matter to them. The scholar who knows a great deal but does not practise in accordance with the Dhamma is like a cowherd, who looks after the cows for wages, while the one who practises in accordance with the Dhamma is like the owner who enjoys the five kinds of produce of the cows[1]. Thus, the scholar enjoys only the services rendered to him by his pupils but not the benefits of Magga-phala. The other bhikkhu, though he knows little and recites only a little of the sacred texts, having clearly comprehended the essence of the Dhamma and having practised diligently and strenuously, is an 'anudhammacārī[2]', who has eradicated passion, ill will and ignorance. His mind being totally freed from moral defilements and from all attachments to this world as well as to the next he truly shares the benefits of Magga-phala.

Then the Buddha spoke in verse as follows:

Verse 19. Though he recites much the Sacred Texts (Tipiṭika), but is negligent and does not practise according to the Dhamma, like a cowherd who counts the cattle of others, he has no share in the benefits of the life of a bhikkhu (i.e., Magga-phala).

Verse 20. Though he recites only a little of the Sacred Texts (Tipiṭika), but practises according to the Dhamma, eradicating passion, ill will and ignorance, clearly comprehending the Dhamma, with his mind freed from moral defilements and no longer clinging to this world or to the next, he shares the benefits of the life of a bhikkhu (i.e.,Magga-phala).

End of Chapter One: The Pairs.

---

1. Milk, cream, butter, butter-milk and ghee.
2. **anudhammacārī:** one who practises in conformity with the Dhamma.

Chapter II

Mindfulness (Appamādavagga)

Verses 21, 22 and 23

II. (1) The Story of Sāmāvatī

While residing at the Ghosita monastery near Kosambī, the Buddha uttered Verses (21), (22) and (23) of this book, with reference to Sāmāvatī, one of the chief queens of Udena, king of Kosambī.

Sāmāvatī had five hundred maids-of-honour staying with her at the palace; she also had a maid servant called Khujjuttarā. The maid had to buy flowers for Sāmāvatī from the florist Sumana everyday. On one occasion, Khujjuttarā had the opportunity to listen to a religious discourse delivered by the Buddha, at the home of Sumana and she attained Sotāpatti Fruition. She repeated the discourse of the Buddha to Sāmāvatī and the five hundred maids-of-honour, and they also attained Sotāpatti Fruition. From that day, Khujjuttarā did not have to do any menial work, but took the place of mother and teacher to Sāmāvatī. She listened to the discourses of the Buddha and repeated them to Sāmāvatī and her maids. In course of time, Khujjuttarā mastered the Tipiṭaka.

Sāmāvatī and her maids wished very much to see the Buddha and pay obeisance to him; but they were afraid the king might be displeased with them. So, making holes in the walls of their palace, they looked through them and paid obeisance to the Buddha everyday as he was going to the houses of the three rich men, namely, Ghosaka, Kukkuṭa and Pāvāriya.

At that time, King Udena had also another chief queen by the name of Māgandiyā. She was the daughter of Māgandiya, a brahmin. The brahmin seeing the Buddha one day thought the Buddha was the only person who was worthy of his very beautiful daughter. So, he hurriedly went off to fetch his wife and daughter and offered to give his daughter in marriage to the Buddha. Turning down his offer, the Buddha said, "Even after seeing Taṇhā, Arati and Ragā, the daughters of Māra, I felt no desire in me for sensual pleasures; after all, what is this which is full of urine and filth and which I don't like to touch even with my foot."

On hearing those words of the Buddha, both the brahmin and his wife attained Anāgāmi Magga and Phala. They entrusted their daughter to the care of her uncle and themselves joined the Order. Eventually, they attained arahatship. The Buddha knew from the beginning that the brahmin and his wife were destined to attain Anāgāmi Fruition that very day, hence his reply to the brahmin in the above manner. However, the daughter Māgandiyā became very bitter and sore and she vowed to take revenge if and when an opportunity arose.

Later, her uncle presented Māgandiyā to King Udena and she became one of his chief queens. Māgandiyā came to learn about the arrival of the Buddha in Kosambī and about how Sāmāvatī and her maids paid obeisance to him through holes in the walls of their living quarters. So, she planned to take her revenge on the Buddha and to harm Sāmāvatī and her maids who were ardent devotees of the Buddha. Māgandiyā told the king that Sāmāvatī and her maids had made holes in the walls of their living quarters and that they had outside contacts and were disloyal to the king. King Udena saw the holes in the walls, but when the truth was told he did not get angry.

But Māgandiyā kept on trying to make the king believe Sāmāvatī was not loyal to him and was trying to kill him. On one occasion, knowing that the king would be visiting Sāmāvatī within the next few days and that he would be taking along his lute with him, Māgandiyā inserted a snake into the lute and closed the hole with a bunch of flowers. Māgandiyā followed King Udena to Sāmāvatī's quarters after trying to stop him on the pretext that she had some presentiment and felt worried about his safety. At Sāmāvatī's place Māgandiyā removed the bunch of flowers from the hole of the lute. The snake came out hissing and coiled itself on the bed. When the king saw the snake he believed Māgandiyā's words that Sāmāvatī was trying to kill him. The king was furious. He commanded Sāmāvatī to stand and all her ladies to line up behind her. Then he fitted his bow with an arrow dipped in poison and shot the arrow. But Sāmāvatī and her ladies bore no ill will towards the king and through the power of goodwill (mettā), the arrow turned back, although an arrow shot by the king usually went even through a rock. Then, the king realized the innocence of Sāmāvatī and he gave her permission to invite the Buddha and his disciples to the palace for alms-food and for delivering discourses.

Māgandiyā, realizing that none of her plans had materialized, made a final, infallible plan. She sent a message to her uncle with full instructions to go to Sāmāvatī's place and burn down the building with all the women inside. As the house was burning, Sāmāvatī and her maids-of-honour, numbering five hundred, kept on meditating. Thus, some of them attained Sakadāgāmi Fruition, and the rest attained Anāgāmi Fruition.

As the news of the fire spread, the king rushed to the scene, but it was too late. He suspected that it was done at the instigation of Māgandiyā; but he did not show that he was suspicious. Instead, he said, "While Sāmāvatī was alive I had been fearful and alert thinking I might be harmed by her; only now, my mind is at peace. Who could have done this? It must have been done only by someone who loves me very dearly." Hearing this, Māgandiyā promptly admitted that it was she who had instructed her uncle to do it. Whereupon, the king pretended to be very pleased with her and said that he would do her a great favour, and honour all her relatives. So, the relatives were sent for and they came gladly. On arrival at the palace, all of them, including Māgandiyā, were seized and burnt in the palace courtyard, by the order of the king.

When the Buddha was told about these two incidents, he said that those who are mindful do not die; but those who are negligent are as good as dead even while living.

Then the Buddha spoke in verse as follows:

Verse 21. Mindfulness is the way to the Deathless (Nibbāna); unmindfulness is the way to Death. Those who are mindful do not die; those who are not mindful are as if already dead.

Verse 22. Fully comprehending this, the wise, who are mindful, rejoice in being mindful and find delight in the domain of the Noble Ones (Ariyas).

Verse 23. The wise, constantly cultivating Tranquillity and Insight Development Practice, being ever mindful and steadfastly striving, realize Nibbāna: Nibbāna, which is free from the bonds of yoga[1]; Nibbāna, the Incomparable!

Verse 24

II (2) The Story of Kumbhaghosaka, the Banker

While residing at the Veḷuvana monastery, the Buddha uttered Verse (24) of this book, with reference to Kumbhaghosaka, the banker.

At one time, a plague epidemic broke out in the city of Rājagaha. In the house of the city banker, the servants died on account of this disease; the banker and his wife were also attacked by the same. When they were both down with the disease they told their young son Kumbhaghosaka to leave them and flee from the house and to return only after a long time. They also told him that at such and such a place they had buried a treasure worth forty crores. The son left the city and stayed in a forest for twelve years and then came back to the city.

By that time, he was quite a grown up youth and nobody in the city recognized him. He went to the place where the treasure was hidden and found it was quite intact. But he reasoned and realized that there was no one who could identify him and that if he were to unearth the buried treasure and make use of it people might think a young poor man had accidentally come upon buried treasure and they might report it to the king. In that case, his property would be confiscated and he himself might be manhandled or put in captivity. So he concluded it was not yet time to unearth the treasure and that meanwhile he must find work for his living. Dressed in old clothes Kumbhaghosaka looked for work. He was given the work of waking up and rousing the people to get up early in the morning and of going round announcing that it was time to prepare food, time to fetch carts and yoke the bullocks, etc.

---

1. The bonds of yoga are four in number, viz., sense-pleasures (kāma), existence (bhava), wrong belief (diṭṭhi) and ignorance of the Four Noble Truths (i.e., avijjā).

One morning, King Bimbisāra heard him. The king who was a keen judge of voices commented, "This is the voice of a man of great wealth." A maid, hearing the king's remark, sent someone to investigate. He reported that the youth was only a hireling of the labourers. In spite of this report the king repeated the same remark on two subsequent days. Again, enquiries were made but with the same result. The maid thought that this was very strange, so she asked the king to give her permission to go and personally investigate.

Disguised as rustics, the maid and her daughter set out to the place of the labourers. Saying that they were travellers, they asked for shelter and was given accommodation in the house of Kumbhaghosaka just for one night. However, they managed to prolong their stay there During that period, twice the king proclaimed that a certain ceremony must be performed in the locality of the labourers, and that every household must make contributions. Kumbhaghosaka had no ready cash for such an occasion. So he was forced to get some coins (Kahāpaṇas) from his treasure. As these coins were handed over to the maid, she substituted them with her money and sent the coins to the king. After some time, she sent a message to the king asking him to send some men and summon Kumbhaghosaka to the court. Kumbhaghosaka, very reluctantly, went along with the men. The maid and her daughter also went to the palace, ahead of them.

At the palace, the king told Kumbhaghosaka to speak out the truth and gave him assurance that he would not be harmed on this account. Kumbhaghosaka then admitted that those Kahāpaṇas were his and also that he was the son of the city banker of Rājagaha, who died in the plague epidemic twelve years ago. He further revealed the place where the treasure was hidden. Subsequently, all the buried treasure was brought to the palace; the king made him a banker and gave his daughter in marriage to him.

Afterwards, taking Kumbhaghosaka along with him, the king went to the Buddha at the Veḷuvana monastery and told him how the youth, though rich, was earning his living as a hireling of the labourers, and how he had appointed the youth a banker.

Then the Buddha spoke in verse as follows:

Verse 24. If a person is energetic, mindful, pure in his thought, word and deed, and if he does everything with care and consideration, restrains his senses, earns his living according to the Law (Dhamma) and is not unheedful, then, the fame and fortune of that mindful person steadily increase.

At the end of the discourse, Kumbhaghosaka attained Sotāpatti Fruition.

Verse 25

II (3) The Story of Cūḷapanthaka

While residing at the Veḷuvana monastery, the Buddha uttered Verse (25) of this book, with reference to Cūḷapanthaka, a grandson of a banker of Rājagaha.

The banker had two grandsons, named Mahāpanthaka and Cūḷapanthaka. Mahāpanthaka, being the elder, used to accompany his grandfather to listen to religious discourses. Later, Mahāpanthaka joined the Buddhist religious Order and in course of time became an arahat. Cūḷapanthaka followed his brother and became a bhikkhu. But, because in a previous existence in the time of Kassapa Buddha Cūḷapanthaka had made fun of a bhikkhu who was very dull, he was born a dullard in the present existence. He could not even memorize one verse in four months. Mahāpanthaka was very disappointed with his younger brother and even told him that he was not worthy of the Order.

About that time, Jīvaka came to the monastery to invite the Buddha and the resident bhikkhus to his house for a meal. Mahāpanthaka, who was then in charge of assigning the bhikkhus to meal invitations, left out Cūḷapanthaka from the list. When Cūḷapanthaka learnt about this he felt very much frustrated and decided that he would return to the life of a householder. Knowing his intention, the Buddha took him along and made him sit in front of the Gandhakuṭi hall. He then gave a clean piece of cloth to Cūḷapanthaka and told him to sit there facing east and rub the piece of cloth. At the same time he was to repeat the word "Rajoharaṇaṁ", which means "taking on impurity." The Buddha then went to the residence of Jīvaka, accompanied by the bhikkhus.

Meanwhile, Cūḷapanthaka went on rubbing the piece of cloth, all the time muttering the word "Rajoharaṇaṁ". Very soon, the cloth became soiled. Seeing this change in the condition of the cloth, Cūḷapanthaka came to realize the impermanent nature of all conditioned things. From the house of Jīvaka, the Buddha through supernormal power learnt about the progress of Cūḷapanthaka. He sent forth his radiance so that (to Cūḷapanthaka) the Buddha appeared to be sitting in front of him, saying: "It is not the piece of cloth alone that is made dirty by the dust; within oneself also there exist the dust of passion (rāga), the dust of ill will (dosa), and the dust of ignorance (moha), i.e., the ignorance of the Four Noble Truths. Only by removing these could one achieve one's goal and attain arahatship". Cūḷapanthaka got the message and kept on meditating and in a short while attained arahatship, together with Analytical Insight. Thus, Cūḷapanthaka ceased to be a dullard.

At the house of Jīvaka, they were about to pour libation water as a mark of donation; but the Buddha covered the bowl with his hand and asked if there were any bhikkhus left at the monastery. On being answered that there were none, the Buddha replied that there was one and directed them to fetch Cūḷapanthaka from the monastery. When the messenger from the house of Jīvaka arrived at the monastery he found not only one bhikkhu, but a thousand identical bhikkhus. They all have been created by Cūḷapanthaka, who by now possessed supernormal powers The messenger was baffled and he turned back and reported the matter to Jīvaka. The messenger was sent to the monastery for the second time and was instructed to say that the Buddha summoned the bhikkhu by the name of Cūḷapanthaka. But when he delivered the message, a thousand voices responded, "I am Cūḷapanthaka." Again baffled, he turned back for the second time. Then he was sent to the monastery, for the third time. This time, he was instructed to get hold of the bhikkhu who first said that he was Cūḷapanthaka. As soon as he got hold of that bhikkhu all the rest disappeared, and Cūḷapanthaka accompanied the messenger to the house of Jīvaka. After the meal, as directed by the Buddha, Cūḷapanthaka delivered a religious discourse confidently and bravely, roaring like a young lion.

Later, when the subject of Cūḷapanthaka cropped up among the bhikkhus, the Buddha said that one who was diligent and steadfast in his striving would certainly attain arahatship.

Then the Buddha spoke in verse as follows:

Verse 25. Through diligence, mindfulness, discipline (with regard to moral precepts), and control of his senses, let the man of wisdom make of himself an island which no flood can overwhelm.

Verses 26 and 27

II (4) The Story of Bālanakkhatta Festival

While residing at the Jetavana monastery, the Buddha uttered Verses (26) and (27) of this book, in connection with the Bālanakkhatta festival.

At one time, the Bālanakkhatta festival was being celebrated in Sāvatthi. During the festival, many foolish young men smearing themselves with ashes and cowdung roamed about the city shouting and making themselves a nuisance to the public. They would also stop at the doors of others and leave only when given some money.

At that time there were a great many lay disciples of the Buddha, living in Sāvatthi. On account of these foolish young hooligans, they sent word to the Buddha, requesting him to keep to the monastery and not to enter the city for seven days. They sent alms-food to the monastery and they themselves kept to their own houses. On the eighth day, when the festival was over, the Buddha and his disciples were invited into the city for alms-food and other offerings. On being told about the vulgar and shameful behaviour of the foolish young men during the festival, the Buddha commented that it was in the nature of the foolish and the ignorant to behave shamelessly.

Then the Buddha spoke in verse as follows:

Verse 26. The foolish and the ignorant give themselves over to negligence; whereas the wise treasure mindfulness as a precious jewel.

Verse 27. Therefore, one should not be negligent, nor be addicted to sensual pleasures; for he who is established in mindfulness, through cultivation of Tranquillity and Insight Development Practice, experiences supreme happiness (i.e., realizes Nibbāna).

Verse 28

II (5) The Story of Thera Mahākassapa

While residing at the Jetavana monastery, the Buddha uttered Verse (28) of this book, with reference to Thera Mahākassapa.

On one occasion, while Thera Mahākassapa was staying at Pipphali cave, he spent his time developing the mental image of light (āloka kasiṇa) and trying to find out through Divine Vision, beings who were mindful and beings who were negligent, also those who were about to die and those who were about to be born.

From his monastery, the Buddha saw through his Divine Vision what Thera Mahākassapa was doing and wanted to warn him that he was wasting his time. So he sent forth his radiance and appeared seated before the thera and exhorted him thus: "My son Kassapa, the number of births and deaths of beings is innumerable and cannot be counted. It is not your concern to count them; it is the concern only of the Buddhas."

Then the Buddha spoke in verse as follows:

Verse 28. The wise one dispels negligence by means of mindfulness; he ascends the pinnacle of wisdom and being free from sorrow looks at the sorrowing beings. Just as one on the mountain top looks at those on the plain below, so also, the wise one (the arahat) looks at the foolish and the ignorant (worldlings).

Verse 29

II (6) The Story of the Two Companion Bhikkhus

While residing at the Jetavana monastery, the Buddha uttered Verse (29) of this book, with reference to two bhikkhus, who were friends.

Two bhikkhus, after obtaining a subject of meditation from the Buddha, went to a monastery in the forest. One of them, being negligent, spent his time warming himself by the fire and talking to young novices throughout the first watch of the night, and generally idling away his time. The other faithfully performed the duties of a bhikkhu. He walked in meditation during the first watch, rested during the second watch and again meditated during the last watch of the night. Thus, being diligent and ever mindful, the second bhikkhu attained arahatship within a short time.

At the end of the rainy season (vassa) both of them went to pay obeisance to the Buddha, and the Buddha asked them how they had spent their time during the vassa. To this, the lazy and negligent bhikkhu answered that the other bhikkhu had been idling away his time, just lying down and sleeping. The Buddha then asked, "But, what about you?" His reply was that he generally sat warming himself by the fire during the first watch of the night and then sat up without sleeping. But the Buddha knew quite well how the two bhikkhus had spent their time, so he said to the idle one: "Though you are lazy and negligent you claim to be diligent and ever mindful; but you have made the other bhikkhu appear to be lazy and negligent though he is diligent and ever mindful. You are like a weak and slow horse compared to my son who is like a strong, fleet-footed horse."

Then the Buddha spoke in verse as follows:

Verse 29. Mindful amongst the negligent, highly vigilant amongst the drowsy, the man of wisdom advances like a race-horse, leaving the jade behind.

Verse 30

II (7) The Story of Magha

While residing at the Kūṭāgāra monastery near Vesālī, the Buddha uttered Verse (30) of this book, with reference to Sakka, king of the devas.

On one occasion, a Licchavī prince, named Mahāli, came to listen to a religious discourse given by the Buddha. The discourse given was Sakkapañha Suttanta. The Buddha spoke of Sakka vividly in glowing terms;

so, Mahāli thought that the Buddha must have personally met Sakka. To make sure, he asked the Buddha, and the Buddha replied, "Mahāli, I do know Sakka; I also know what has made him a Sakka." He then told Mahāli that Sakka, king of the devas, was in a previous existence a young man by the name of Magha, in the village of Macala. The youth Magha and his thirty-two companions went about building roads and rest houses. Magha took upon himself also to observe seven obligations. These seven obligations are that throughout his life, (1) he would support his parents; (2) he would respect the elders ; (3) he would be gentle of speech; (4) he would avoid back-biting; (5) he would not be avaricious, but would be generous; (6) he would speak the truth; and (7) he would restrain himself from losing his temper.

It was because of his good deeds and right conduct in that existence that Magha was reborn as Sakka, king of the devas.

Then the Buddha spoke in verse as follows:

Verse 30. Through mindfulness (in doing meritorious deeds) Magha became king of the devas. Mindfulness is always praised, but negligence is always blamed.

At the end of the discourse Mahāli attained Sotāpatti Fruition.

Verse 31

II (8) The Story of a Certain Bhikkhu

While residing at the Jetavana monastery, the Buddha uttered Verse (31) of this book, with reference to a certain bhikkhu.

A certain bhikkhu, after obtaining a subject of meditation from the Buddha, went to the forest to meditate. Although he tried hard he made very little progress in his meditation practice. As a result, he became very depressed and frustrated. So, with the thought of getting further specific instructions from the Buddha, he set out for the Jetavana monastery On his way, he came across a big, blazing fire. He ran up to the top of a mountain and observed the fire from there. As the fire spread, it suddenly occurred to him that just as the fire burnt up everything, so also Magga Insight will burn up all etters of life, big and small.

Meanwhile, from the Gandhakuṭi hall in the Jetavana monastery, the Buddha was aware of what the bhikkhu was thinking. So, he transmitted his radiance and appeared to the bhikkhu and spoke to him. "My son," he said, "you are on the right line of thought; keep it up. All beings must burn up all fetters of life with Magga Insight."

Then the Buddha spoke in verse as follows:

Verse 31. A bhikkhu who takes delight in mindfulness and sees danger in negligence, advances like fire, burning up all fetters, great and small.

At the end of the discourse that bhikkhu attained arahatship then and there.

Verse 32

II (9) The Story of Thera Nigamavāsitissa

While residing at the Jetavana monastery, the Buddha uttered Verse (32) of this book, with reference to Thera Nigamavāsitissa.

Nigamavāsitissa was born and brought up in a small market town near Sāvatthi. After becoming a bhikkhu he lived a very simple life, with very few wants. For alms-food, he used to go to the village where his relatives were staying and took whatever was offered to him. He kept away from big occasions. Even when Anāthapiṇḍika and King Pasenadi of Kosala made offerings on a grand scale, the thera did not go.

Some bhikkhus then started talking about the thera that he kept close to his relatives and that he did not care to go even when people like Anāthapiṇḍika and King Pasenadi were making offerings on a grand scale, etc. When the Buddha was told about this, he sent for the thera and asked him. The thera respectfully explained to the Buddha that it was true he frequently went to his village, but it was only to get alms-food, that when he had received enough food, he did not go any further, and that he never cared whether the food was delicious or not. Whereupon, instead of blaming him, the Buddha praised him for his conduct in the presence of the other bhikkhus. He also told them that to live contentedly with only a few wants is in conformity with the practice of the Buddha and the Noble Ones (Ariyas), and that all bhikkhus should, indeed, be like Thera Tissa from the small market town. In this connection, he further related the story of the king of the parrots.

Once upon a time, the king of the parrots lived in a grove of fig trees on the banks of the Ganges river, with a large number of his followers. When the fruits were eaten, all the parrots left the grove, except the parrot king, who was well contented with whatever was left in the tree where he dwelt, be it shoot or leaf or bark. Sakka, knowing this and wanting to test the virtue of the parrot king, withered up the tree by his supernormal power. Then, assuming the form of geese, Sakka and his queen, Sujāta, came to where the parrot king was and asked him why he did not leave the old withered tree as the others had done and why he did not go to other trees which were still bearing fruits. The parrot king replied, "Because of a feeling of gratitude towards the tree I did not leave and as long as I could get just enough food to sustain myself I shall not forsake it. It would be ungrateful for me to desert this tree even though it be inanimate."

Much impressed by this reply, Sakka revealed himself. He took water from the Ganges and poured it over the withered fig tree and instantly, it was rejuvenated; it stood with branches lush and green, and fully decked with fruits. Thus, the wise even as animals are not greedy; they are contented with whatever is available.

The parrot king in the story was the Buddha himself; Sakka was Anuruddha.

Then the Buddha spoke in verse as follows:

Verse 32. A bhikkhu who takes delight in mindfulness and sees danger in negligence will not fall away[1]; he is, indeed, very close to Nibbāna.

At the end of the discourse Thera Tissa attained arahatship.

End of Chapter Two: Mindfulness

---

1. **will not fall away:** It means, will not fall away from Tranquillity and Insight Development Practice and is assured of attaining Magga and Phala. (The Commentary)

Chapter III

The Mind (Cittavagga)

Verses 33 and 34

III (1) The Story of Thera Meghiya

While residing on the Cālikā Mountain, the Buddha uttered Verses (33) and (34) of this book, with reference to Thera Meghiya.

At that time, Thera Meghiya was attending upon the Buddha. On one occasion, on his return from alms-round, the thera noticed a pleasant and beautiful mango grove, which he thought was an ideal spot for meditation. He asked the Buddha's permission to let him go there, but as the Buddha was alone at that time, he was told to wait for awhile until the arrival of some other bhikkhus. The thera was in a hurry to go and so he repeated his request again and again, until finally the Buddha told him to do as he wished.

Thus, Thera Meghiya set out for the mango grove, sat at the foot of a tree and practised meditation. He stayed there the whole day, but his mind kept wandering and he made no progress. He returned in the evening and reported to the Buddha how all the time he was assailed by thoughts associated with the senses, ill will and cruelty (kāma vitakka, byāpāda vitakka and vihiṁsa vitakka).

So, the Buddha told him that as the mind is easily excitable and fickle, one should control one's mind.

Then the Buddha spoke in verse as follows:

Verse 33. The mind is excitable and unsteady; it is difficult to control and to restrain. The wise one trains his mind to be upright as a fletcher straightens an arrow.

Verse 34. As a fish quivers when taken out of its watery home and thrown on to dry ground, so does the mind quiver when it is taken out of the sensual world to escape from the realm of Māra (i. e., kilesa vaṭṭa, round of moral defilements).

At the end of the discourse Thera Meghiya attained Sotāpatti Fruition.

Verse 35

III (2) The Story of a Certain Bhikkhu

While residing at the Jetavana monastery, the Buddha uttered Verse (35) of this book, with reference to a certain bhikkhu.

On one occasion, sixty bhikkhus, after obtaining a subject of meditation from the Buddha, went to Mātika village, at the foot of a mountain. There, Mātikamātā, mother of the village headman, offered them alms-food; she also built a monastery for them, so that they could stay in the village during the rainy season. One day she asked the group of bhikkhus to teach her the practice of meditation. They taught her how to meditate on the thirty-two constituents of the body leading to the awareness of the decay and dissolution of the body. Mātikamātā practised with diligence and attained the three Maggas and Phalas together with Analytical Insight and mundane supernormal powers, even before the bhikkhus did.

Rising from the bliss of the Magga and Phala she looked with the Divine Power of Sight (Dibbacakkhu) and saw that the bhikkhus had not attained any of the Maggas yet. She also learnt that those bhikkhus had enough potentiality for the attainment of arahatship, but that they needed proper food. So, she prepared good, choice food for them. With proper food and right effort, the bhikkhus developed right concentration and eventually attained arahatship.

At the end of the rainy season, the bhikkhus returned to the Jetavana monastery, where the Buddha was in residence. They reported to the Buddha that all of them were in good health and in comfortable circumstances and that they did not have to worry about food. They also mentioned about Mātikamātā who was aware of their thoughts and prepared and offered them the very food they wished for.

A certain bhikkhu, hearing them talking about Mātikamātā, decided that he, too, would go to that village. So, taking a subject of meditation from the Buddha he arrived at the village monastery. There, he found that everything he wished for was sent to him by Mātikamātā, the lay-devotee. When he wished her to come she personally came to the monastery, bringing along choice food with her. After taking the food, he asked her if she knew the thoughts of others, but she evaded his question and replied, "People who can read the thoughts of others behave in such and such a way." Then, the bhikkhu thought, "Should I, like an ordinary worldling, entertain any impure thoughts, she is sure to find out." He therefore got scared of the lay-devotee and decided to return to the Jetavana monastery. He told the Buddha that he could not stay in Mātika village because he was afraid that the lay-devotee might detect impure thoughts in him. The Buddha then asked him to observe just one thing; that is, to control his mind. The Buddha also told the bhikkhu to return to Mātika village monastery, and not to think of anything else, but the object of his meditation only. The bhikkhu went back. The lay-devotee offered him good food as she had done to others before, so that he might able to practise meditation without worry. Within a short time, he, too, attained arahatship.

With reference to this bhikkhu, the Buddha spoke in verse as follows:

Verse 35. The mind is difficult to control; swiftly and lightly, it moves and lands wherever it pleases. It is good to tame the mind, for a well-tamed mind brings happiness.

At the end of the discourse, many of those assembled attained Sotāpatti Fruition.

Verse 36

III (3) The Story of a Certain Disgruntled Bhikkhu

While residing at the Jetavana monastery, the Buddha uttered Verse (36) of this book, with reference to a young disgruntled bhikkhu who was the son of a banker.

Once, there lived in Sāvatthi, the son of a banker. This young man asked the bhikkhu, who used to come to his house for alms, what he should do to be liberated from the ills of life. The bhikkhu instructed him to divide his property into three parts; one part to do business with, one part to support the family and one part to give in charity. He did as he was told and again asked what else should be done next. So he was further instructed; first to take refuge in the Three

Gems[1] and to observe the five precepts; secondly, to observe the ten precepts; and thirdly, to renounce the world and enter the Buddhist religious Order. The young man complied with all these instructions and became a bhikkhu.

As a bhikkhu, he was taught the Abhidhamma[2] by one teacher and the Vinaya by another. Being taught in this way, he felt that there was too much to be learnt, that the disciplinary rules were too strict and too many, so much so that there was not enough freedom even to stretch out one's hands. He thought that it might be better to return to the life of a householder. As a result of doubt and discontent, he became unhappy and neglected his duties; he also became thin and emaciated. When the Buddha came to know about this, he said to the young bhikkhu, "If you can only control your mind, you will have nothing more to control; so guard your own mind."

Then the Buddha spoke in verse as follows:

Verse 36. The mind is very difficult to see, very delicate and subtle; it moves and lands wherever it pleases. The wise one should guard his mind, for a guarded mind brings happiness.

At the end of the discourse, the young bhikkhu and many others attained arahatship.

Verse 37

III (4) The Story of Thera Saṁgharakkhita

While residing at the Jetavana monastery, the Buddha uttered Verse (37) of this book, with reference to the nephew of Thera Saṁgharakkhita.

Once, there lived in Sāvatthi, a senior bhikkhu by the name of Saṁgharakkhita. When his sister gave birth to a son, she named the child after the thera and he came to be known as Saṁgharakkhita Bhāgineyya. The nephew Saṁgharakkhita, in due course, was admitted into the Order. While the young bhikkhu was staying in a village monastery he was offered two sets of robes, and he intended to offer one to his uncle, the thera.

1. **Three Gems:** The Three Gems are the Buddha, the Dhamma and the Saṁgha, (i. e., the Buddha, the Teaching of the Buddha, and the Buddhist religious Order).
2. **Abhidhamma:** the third great division of the Piṭaka comprising the Buddha's philosophical exposition of ultimate realities.

At the end of the vassa he went to his uncle to pay respect to him and offered the robe to the thera. But, the uncle declined to accept the robe, saying that he had enough. Although he repeated his request, the thera would not accept. The young bhikkhu felt disheartened and thought that since his uncle was so unwilling to share the requisites with him, it would be better for him to leave the Order and live the life of a layman.

From that point, his mind wandered and a train of thoughts followed. He thought that after leaving the Order he would sell the robe and buy a she-goat; that she-goat would breed quickly and soon he would make enough money to enable him to marry; his wife would give birth to a son. He would take his wife and child in a small cart to visit his uncle at the monastery. On the way, he would say that he would carry the child; she would tell him to drive the cart and not to bother about the child. He would insist and grab the child from her; between them the child would drop on the cart-track and the wheel would pass over the child. He would get so furious with his wife that he would strike her with the goading-stick.

At that time he was fanning the thera with a palmyra fan and he absent-mindedly struck the head of the thera with the fan. The thera, knowing the thoughts of the young bhikkhu, said, "You were unable to beat your wife; why have you beaten an old bhikkhu?" Young Saṁgharakkhita was very much surprised and embarassed at the words of the old bhikkhu; he also became extremely frightened. So he fled. Young bhikkhus and novices of the monastery chased him and finally took him to the presence of the Buddha.

When told about the whole episode, the Buddha said that the mind has the ability to think of an object even though it might be far away, and that one should strive hard for liberation from the bondage of passion, ill will and ignorance.

Then the Buddha spoke in verse as follows:

Verse 37. The mind wanders far and moves about alone; it is non-material; it lies in the cave (chamber) of the heart. Those who control their mind will be free from the bonds of Māra.

At the end of the discourse the young bhikkhu attained Sotāpatti Fruition.

Verses 38 and 39

III (5) The Story of Thera Cittahattha

While residing at the Jetavana monastery, the Buddha uttered Verses (38) and (39) of this book, with reference to Thera Cittahattha.

A man from Sāvatthi, after looking for his lost ox in the forest, felt very hungry and went to a village monastery, where he was given the remains of the morning meal. While taking his food, it occurred to him that even though he worked hard every day he could not get such good food and that it might be a good idea to become a bhikkhu. So he asked the bhikkhus to admit him into the Order. At the monastery, he performed the duties of a bhikkhu and as there was plenty of food he soon gained weight. After some time, he got weary of going round for alms-food and returned to the life of a lay man. A few days later, he felt that life at home was too strenuous and he went back to the monastery to be admitted as a bhikkhu for a second time. For a second time, he left the Order and returned to home-life. Again, he went back to the monastery for a third time and left it. This shuttling process went on for six times, and because he acted only according to his whims he was known as Thera Cittahattha.

While he was going back and forth between his home and the monastery, his wife became pregnant. One day, during his last stay at home, he happened to enter the bedroom while his wife was asleep. She was almost naked as the clothes she was wearing had partially fallen off. She was also snoring loudly through her nose and mouth and saliva was trickling down her mouth. Thus, with her mouth open and her bloated stomach, she looked just like a corpse. Seeing her thus, he instantly came to perceive the impermanent and unpleasant nature of the body, and he reflected, "I have been a bhikkkhu for several times and it is only because of this woman that I have not been able to remain as a bhikkhu." Hence, taking the yellow robe with him he left his home for the monastery for the seventh time. As he went along he repeated the words "impermanence" and "unpleasantness" (anicca and dukkha) and thus attained Sotāpatti Fruition on the way to the monastery.

On arrival at the monastery he asked the bhikkhus to admit him into the Order. They refused and said, "We cannot admit you as a bhikkhu. You have been shaving your head so often that your head is like a whetting stone." Still, he entreated them to admit him into the Order just once more and they complied. Within a few days, the bhikkhu Cittahattha attained arahatship together with Analytical Insight. Other bhikkhus, seeing him staying on for a long time in the monastery, were surprised and they asked him the reason why. To this, he replied, "I went home when I still had attachment in me, but now that attachment has been cut off." The bhikkhus, not believing him, approached the Buddha and reported the matter. To them, the Buddha said, "Thera Cittahattha was speaking the truth; he shifted between home and monastery before because at that time, his mind was not steadfast and he did not understand the Dhamma. But at this moment, Thera Cittahattha is already an arahat; he has discarded both good and evil."

Then the Buddha spoke in verse as follows:

Verse 38. If a man's mind is unsteady, if he is ignorant of the true Dhamma, and if his faith is wavering, then his knowledge will never be perfect.

Verse 39. If a man's mind is free from passion, if he is free from ill will, if he has abandoned both good and evil, and if he is vigilant, for such a man there is no danger.

Verse 40

III (6) The Story of Five Hundred Bhikkhus

While residing at the Jetavana monastery, the Buddha uttered Verse (40) of this book, with reference to five hundred bhikkhus.

Five hundred bhikkhus from Sāvatthi, after obtaining a subject of meditation from the Buddha, travelled for a distance of one hundred yojanas[1] away from Sāvatthi and came to a large forest grove, a suitable place for meditation practice. The guardian spirits of the trees dwelling in that forest thought that if those bhikkhus were staying in the forest, it would not be proper for them to

1. yojana: a measure of length about twelve miles.

live with their families in the trees. So they descended from the trees, thinking that the bhikkhus would stop there only for one night. But the bhikkhus were still there at the end of a fortnight; then it occurred to them that the bhikkhus might be staying there till the end of the vassa. In that case, they and their families would have to be living on the ground for a long time. So, they decided to frighten away the bhikkhus, by making ghostly sounds and frightful apparitions. They showed up with bodies without heads, and with heads without bodies, etc. The bhikkhus were very upset and left the place and returned to the Buddha, to whom they related everything. On hearing their account, the Buddha told them that this had happened because previously they went without any weapon and that they should go back there armed with a suitable weapon. So saying, the Buddha taught them the entire Metta Sutta (discourse on Loving-Kindness) beginning with the following stanza:

Karaṇiyamattha kusalena
Yanta santaṁ padaṁ abhisamecca
Sakko ujū ca suhujū ca
Suvaco c'assa mudu anatimānī.

[The above stanza may be translated as follows:

He who is skilled in (acquiring) what is good and beneficial, (mundane as well as supra-mundane), aspiring to attain Perfect Peace (Nibbāna) should act (thus): He should be efficient, upright, perfectly upright, compliant, gentle and free from conceit.]

The bhikkhus were instructed to recite the sutta from the time they came to the outskirts of the forest grove and to enter the monastery reciting the same. The bhikkhus returned to the forest grove and did as they were told. The guardian spirits of the trees receiving loving-kindness from the bhikkhus reciprocated by readily welcoming and not harming them. There were no more ghostly sounds and ungainly sights. Thus left in peace, the bhikkhus meditated on the body and came to realize its fragile and impermanent nature.

From the Jetavana monastery, the Buddha, by his supernormal power, learned about the progress of the bhikkhus and sent forth his radiance making them feel his presence. To them he said, "Bhikkhus just as you have realized, the body is, indeed, impermanent and fragile like an earthern jar."

Then the Buddha spoke in verse as follows:

Verse 40. Knowing that this body is (fragile) like an earthen jar, making one's mind secure like a fortified town, one should fight Māra with the weapon of Knowledge. (After defeating Māra) one should still continue to guard one's mind, and feel no attachment to that which has been gained (i.e., jhāna ecstasy and serenity gained through meditation).

At the end of the discourse, the five hundred bhikkhus attained arahatship.

Verse 41

III (7) The Story of Tissa, the Thera with a Stinking Body

While residing at the Jetavana monastery, the Buddha uttered Verse (41) of this book, with reference to Thera Tissa.

After taking a subject of meditation from the Buddha, Thera Tissa was diligently practising meditation when he was afflicted with a disease. Small boils appeared all over his body and these developed into big sores. When these sores burst, his upper and lower robes became sticky and stained with pus and blood, and his whole body was stinking. For this reason, he was known as Pūtigattatissa, Tissa the thera wit a stinking body.

As the Buddha surveyed the universe with the li t of his own intellect, the thera appeared in his vis n. He saw the sorrowful state of the thera, who had en abandoned by his resident pupils on account of his stinking body. At the same time, he also knew that Tissa would soon attain arahatship. So, the Buddha proceeded to the fire-shed, close to the place where the thera was staying. There, he boiled some water, and then going to where the thera was lying down, took hold of the edge of the couch. It was then only that th resident pupils gathered round the thera, and a instructed by the Buddha, they carried the thera t the fire-shed, where he was washed and bathed. While he was being bathed, his upper and lower robes were washed and dried. After the bath, the thera became fresh in body and mind and soon developed one-pointedness of concentration. Standing at the head of the couch, the Buddha said to him that this body when devoid of life would be as useless as a log and would be laid on the earth.

Then the Buddha spoke in verse as follows:

Verse 41. Before long, alas, this body, deprived of consciousness, will lie on the earth, discarded like a useless log!

At the end of the discourse Thera Tissa attained arahatship together with Analytical Insight, and soon passed away.

Verse 42

III (8) The Story of Nanda, the Herdsman

While on a visit to a village in the kingdom of Kosala, the Buddha uttered Verse (42) of this book, with reference to Nanda, the herdsman.

Nanda was a herdsman who looked after the cows of Anāthapiṇḍika. Although only a herdsman, he had some means of his own. Occasionally, he would go to the house of Anāthapiṇḍika and there he sometimes met the Buddha and listened to his discourses. Nanda requested the Buddha to pay a visit to his house. But the Buddha did not go to Nanda's house immediately, saying that it was not yet time.

After some time, while travelling with his followers, the Buddha went off his route to visit Nanda, knowing that the time was ripe for Nanda to receive his teaching properly. Nanda respectfully received the Buddha and his followers; he served them milk and milk products and other choice food for seven days. On the last day, after hearing the discourse given by the Buddha, Nanda attained Sotāpatti Fruition. As the Buddha was leaving that day, Nanda carrying the bowl of the Buddha, followed him for some distance. paid obeisance and turned back to go home.

At that instant, a hunter who was an old enemy of Nanda, shot him down. The bhikkhus who were following the Buddha, saw Nanda lying dead. They reported the matter to the Buddha, saying, "Venerable Sir, because you came here, Nanda who made great offerings to you and accompanied you on your return was killed as he was turning back to go home." To them, the Buddha replied, "Bhikkhus, whether I came here or not, there was no escape from death for him, as a wrongly directed mind can do oneself much greater harm than an enemy or a thief can."

Then the Buddha spoke in verse as follows:

Verse 42. A thief may harm a thief; an enemy may harm an enemy; but a wrongly directed mind can do oneself far greater harm.

Verse 43

III (9) The Story of Soreyya

While residing at the Jetavana monastery, the Buddha uttered Verse (43) of this book, with reference to Soreyya, the son of a rich man of Soreyya city.

On one occasion, Soreyya accompanied by a friend and some attendants was going out in a luxurious carriage for a bath. At that moment, Thera Mahākaccāyana was adjusting his robes outside the city, as he was going into the city of Soreyya for alms-food. The youth Soreyya, seeing the golden complexion of the thera, thought, "How I wish the thera were my wife, or else that the complexion of my wife were like that of his." As the wish arose in him, his sex changed and he became a woman. Very much ashamed, he got down from the carriage and ran away, taking the road to Taxila. His companions missing him, looked for him, but could not find him.

Soreyya, now a woman, offered her signet ring to some people going to Taxila, to allow her to go along with them in their carriage. On arrival at Taxila, her companions told a young rich man of Taxila about the lady who came along with them. The young rich man, finding her to be very beautiful and of a suitable age for him, married her. As a result of this marriage two sons were born; there were also two sons from the previous marriage of Soreyya as a man.

One day, a rich man's son from the city of Soreyya came to Taxila with five hundred carts. Lady-Soreyya recognizing him to be an old friend sent for him. The man from Soreyya city was surprised that he was invited, because he did not know the lady who invited him. He told the lady-Soreyya that he did not know her, and asked her whether she knew him. She answered that she knew him and also enquired after the health of her family and other people in Soreyya city. The man from Soreyya city next told her about the rich man's son who disappeared mysteriously while going out for a bath. Then the lady-Soreyya revealed her identity and related all that had happened, about the wrongful thoughts with regard to Thera Mahākaccāyana, about the change of sex, and her marriage to the young rich man of Taxila. The man from the city of Soreyya then advised the lady-Soreyya to ask pardon of the thera. Thera Mahākaccāyana was accordingly invited to the home of Soreyya and alms-food was offered to him. After the meal, the lady-Soreyya was brought to the presence of the thera, and the man from Soreyya told the thera that the lady was at one time the son of a rich man from Soreyya city. He then explained to the thera how Soreyya was turned into a female on account of his wrongful thoughts towards the respected thera. Lady-Soreyya then respectfully asked pardon of Thera Mahākaccāyana. The thera then said, "Get up, I forgive you." As soon as these words were spoken, the woman was changed back to a man. Soreyya then pondered how within a single existence and with a single body he had undergone change of sex and how sons were born to him, etc. And feeling very weary and repulsive of all these things, he decided to leave the household life and joined the Order under the thera.

After that, he was often asked, "Whom do you love more, the two sons you had as a man or the other two you had as a wife?" To them, he would answer that his love for those born of the womb was greater. This question was put to him so often, he felt very much annoyed and ashamed. So he stayed by himself and, with diligence, contemplated the decay and dissolution of the body. He soon attained arahatship together with the Analytical Insight. When the old question was next put to him he replied that he had no affection for any one in particular. Other bhikkhus hearing him thought he must be telling a lie. When reported about Soreyya giving a different answer, the Buddha said, "My son is not telling lies, he is speaking the truth. His answer now is different because he has now realized arahatship and so has no more affection for anyone in particular. By his well-directed mind my son has brought about in himself a well-being which neither the father nor the mother can bestow on him."

Then the Buddha spoke in verse as follows:

Verse 43. Not a mother, nor a father, nor any other relative can do more for the well-being of one than a rightly-directed mind can.

At the end of the discourse many attained Sotāpatti Fruition.

End of Chapter Three: The Mind.

Chapter IV

Flowers (Pupphavagga)

Verses 44 and 45

IV (1)The Story of Five Hundred Bhikkhus

While residing at the Jetavana monastery, the Buddha uttered Verses (44) and (45) of this book, with reference to five hundred bhikkhus.

Five hundred bhikkhus, after accompanying the Buddha to a village, returned to the Jetavana monastery. In the evening, while the bhikkhus were talking about the trip, especially the condition of the land, whether it was level or hilly, or whether the soil was clayey or sandy, red or black, etc., the Buddha came to them. Knowing the subject of their talk, he said to them, "Bhikkhus, the earth you are talking about is external to the body; it is better, indeed, to examine your own body and make preparations (for meditation practice)."

The Buddha then spoke in verse as follows:

Verse 44. Who shall examine this earth (i. e., this body), the world of Yama (i. e., the four Apāyas) and the world of man together with the world of devas? Who shall examine the well-taught Path of Virtue (Dhammapada) as an expert florist picks and chooses flowers?

Verse 45. The Ariya Sekha[1] shall examine this earth (i. e., the body), the world of Yama (i. e., the four Apāyas) and the world of man together with the world of devas. The Ariya Sekha shall examine the well-taught Path of Virtue (Dhammapada) as an expert florist picks and chooses flowers.

At the end of the discourse those five hundred bhikkhus attained arahatship.

---

1. **Sekha/Ariya Sekha:** one who practises the Dhamma and has entered the Path, but has not yet become an arahat.

Verse 46

IV (2) The Story of the Bhikkhu who Contemplates The Body as a Mirage

While residing at the Jetavana monastery, the Buddha uttered Verse (46) of this book, with reference to a certain bhikkhu.

On one occasion, a certain bhikkhu, after taking a subject of meditation from the Buddha, went to the forest. Although he tried hard he made little progress in his meditation; so he decided to go back to the Buddha for further instruction. On his way back he saw a mirage, which, after all, was only an illusive appearance of a sheet of water. At that instant, he came to realize that the body also was insubstantial like a mirage. Thus keeping his mind on the insubstantiality of the body he came to the bank of the river Aciravatī. While sitting under a tree close to the river, seeing big froths breaking up, he realized the impermanent nature of the body.

Soon, the Buddha appeared in his vision and said to him, "My son, just as you have realized, this body is impermanent like froth and insubstantial like a mirage."

Then the Buddha spoke in verse as follows:

Verse 46. One who knows that this body is impermanent like froth, and comprehends that it is insubstantial like a mirage will cut the flowers of Māra (i.e., the three kinds of vaṭṭa or rounds), and pass out of sight of the King of Death.

At the end of the discourse the bhikkhu attained arahatship.

Verse 47

IV (3) The Story of Viṭaṭūbha

While residing at the Jetavana monastery, the Buddha uttered Verse (47) of this book, with reference to Viṭaṭūbha, son of King Pasenadi of Kosala.

King Pasenadi of Kosala, wishing to marry into the clan of the Sakyans, sent some emissaries to Kapilavatthu with a request for the hand of one of the Sakyan princesses. Not wishing to offend King Pasenadi, the Sakyan princes replied that they would comply with his request, but instead of a Sakyan princess they sent a very beautiful girl born of King Mahānāma and a slave woman. King Pasenadi made that girl one of his chief queens and subsequently she gave birth to a son. This son was named Viṭaṭūbha. When the prince was sixteen years old, he was sent on a visit to King Mahānāma and the Sakyan princes. There he was received with some hospitality but all the Sakyan princes who were younger than Viṭaṭūbha had been sent away to a village, so that they would not have to pay respect to Viṭaṭūbha. After staying a few days in Kapilavatthu, Viṭaṭūbha and his company left for home. Soon after they left, a slave girl was washing with milk the place where Viṭaṭūbha had sat; she was also cursing him, shouting, "This is the place where that son of a slave woman had sat,......". At that moment, a member of Viṭaṭūbha's entourage returned to fetch something which he had left at the place and heard what the slave girl said. The slave girl also told him that Viṭaṭūbha's mother, Vāsabhakhattiyā, was the daughter of a slave girl belonging to Mahānāma.

When Viṭaṭūbha was told about the above incident, he became wild with rage and declared that one day he would wipe out the whole clan of the Sakyans. True to his word, when Viṭaṭūbha became king, he marched on the Sakyan clan and massacred them all, with the exception of a few who were with Mahānāma and some others. On their way home, Viṭaṭūbha and his army encamped on the sandbank in the river Aciravatī. As heavy rain fell in the upper parts of the country on that very night, the river swelled and rushed down with great force carrying away Viṭaṭūbha and his army into the ocean.

On hearing about these two tragic incidents, the Buddha explained to the bhikkhus that his relatives, the Sakyan princes, had in one of their previous existences, put poison into the river killing the fishes. It was as a result of that particular action that the Sakyan princes had to die en masse. Then, referring to the incident about Viṭaṭūbha and his army, the Buddha said, "As a great flood sweeps away all the villagers in a sleeping village, so also, Death carries away all the creatures hankering after sensual pleasures."

Then the Buddha spoke in verse as follows:

Verse 47. Like one who picks and chooses flowers, a man who has his mind attached to sensual pleasures is carried away by Death, just as a great flood sweeps away a sleeping village.

Verse 48

IV (4) The Story of Patipūjika Kumārī

While residing at the Jetavana monastery, the Buddha uttered Verse (48) of this book, with reference to Patipūjika Kumārī.

Patipūjika Kumārī was a lady from Sāvatthi. She married at the age of sixteen and had four sons. She was a virtuous as well as a generous lady, who loved to make offerings of food and other requisites to the bhikkhus. She would often go to the monastery and clean up the premises, fill the pots and jars with water and perform other services. Patipūjikā also possessed Jātissara Knowledge through which she remembered that in her previous existence she was one of the numerous wives of Mālabhārī, in the deva world of Tāvatiṁsa. She also remembered that she had passed away from there when all of them were out in the garden enjoying themselves, plucking and picking flowers. So, every time she made offerings to the bhikkhus or performed any other meritorious act, she would pray that she might be reborn in the Tāvatiṁsa realm as a wife of Mālabhārī, her previous husband.

One day, Patipūjikā fell ill and passed away that same evening. As she had so ardently wished, she was reborn in Tāvatiṁsa deva world as a wife of Mālabhārī. As one hundred years in the human world is equivalent to just one day in Tāvatiṁsa world, Mālabhārī and his other wives were still in the garden enjoying themselves and Patipūjikā was barely missed by them. So, when she rejoined them, Mālabhārī asked her where she had been the whole morning. She then told him about her passing away from Tāvatiṁsa, her rebirth in the human world, her marriage to a man and also about how she had given birth to four sons, her passing away from there and finally her return to Tāvatiṁsa.

When the bhikkhus learned about the death of Patipūjikā, they were stricken with grief. They went to the Buddha and reported that Patipūjikā, who was offering alms-food to them early in the morning, had passed away in the evening. To them the Buddha replied that the life of beings was very brief; and that before they could hardly be satiated in their sensual pleasures, they were overpowered by Death.

Then the Buddha spoke in verse as follows:

Verse 48. Like one who picks and chooses flowers, a man who has his mind attached to sensual pleasures and is insatiate in them is overpowered by Death.

Verse 49

IV (5) The Story of Kosiya, the Miserly Rich Man

While residing at the Jetavana monastery, the Buddha uttered Verse (49) of this book, with reference to the Chief Disciple Mahā Moggallāna and the miserly rich man, Kosiya.

In the village of Sakkāra, near Rājagaha, there lived a miserly rich man by the name of Kosiya, who was very reluctant to give away even the tiniest part of anything belonging to him. One day, to avoid sharing with others, the rich man and his wife were making some pancakes in the uppermost storey of their house, where no one would see them.

Early in the morning, on that day, the Buddha, through his supernormal power, saw the rich man and his wife in his vision, and knew that both of them would soon attain Sotāpatti Fruition. So he sent his Chief Disciple Mahā Moggallāna to the house of the rich man, with instructions to bring the couple to the Jetavana monastery in time for the midday meal. The Chief Disciple, by supernormal power, reached Kosiya's house in an instant and stood at the window. The rich man saw him and asked him to leave; the Venerable Mahā Moggallāna just stood there without saying anything. In the end, Kosiya said to his wife, "Make a very small pancake and give it to the bhikkhu." So she took just a little amount of dough and put it in the pan, and the cake filled up the whole pan. Kosiya thought his wife must have put in too much, so he took just a pinch of dough and put it into the pan; his pancake also swelled into a big one. It so happened that however little dough they might put in, they were unable to make small pancakes. At last, Kosiya asked his wife to offer one from the basket to the bhikkhu. When she tried to take out one from the basket it would not come off because all the pancakes were sticking together and could not be separated. By this time Kosiya has lost all appetite for pancakes and offered the whole basket of pancakes to Mahā Moggallāna. The Chief Disciple then delivered a discourse on charity to the rich man and his wife. He also told the couple about how the Buddha was waiting with five hundred bhikkhus at the Jetavana monastery in Sāvatthi, forty-five yojanas away from Rājagaha. Mahā Moggallāna, by his supernormal power, then took both Kosiya and his wife together with their basket of pancakes, to the presence of the Buddha. There, they offered the pancakes to the Buddha and the five hundred bhikkhus. At the end of the meal, the Buddha delivered a discourse on charity, and both Kosiya and his wife attained Sotāpatti Fruition.

Next evening, while the bhikkhus were talking in praise of Mahā Moggallāna, the Buddha came to them and said, "Bhikkhus, you should also dwell and act in the village like Mahā Moggallāna, receiving the offerings of the villagers without affecting their faith and generosity, or their wealth."

Then the Buddha spoke in verse as follows:

Verse 49. As the bee collects nectar and flies away without damaging the flower or its colour or its scent, so also, let the bhikkhu dwell and act in the village (without affecting the faith and generosity or the wealth of the villagers).

Verse 50

IV (6) The Story of the Ascetic Pāveyya

While residing at the Jetavana monastery, the Buddha uttered Verse (50) of this book, with reference to the ascetic Pāveyya and a rich lady.

A rich lady of Sāvatthi had adopted Pāveyya, an ascetic, as a son and was looking after his needs. When she heard her neighbours talking in praise of the Buddha, she wished very much to invite him to her house to offer him alms-food. So, the Buddha was invited and choice food was offered. As the Buddha was expressing appreciation (anumodanā), Pāveyya, who was in the next room, fumed with rage. He blamed and cursed the lady for venerating the Buddha. The lady heard him cursing and shouting and felt so ashamed that she could not concentrate on what the Buddha was saying. The Buddha told her not to be concerned about those curses and threats, but to concentrate only on her own good and bad deeds.

Then the Buddha spoke in verse as follows:

Verse 50. One should not consider the faults of others, nor their doing or not doing good or bad deeds. One should consider only whether one has done or not done good or bad deeds.

At the end of the discourse the rich lady attained Sotāpatti Fruition.

Verses 51 and 52

IV (7) The Story of Chattapāṇi, a Lay Disciple

While residing at the Jetavana monastery, the Buddha uttered Verses (51) and (52) of this book, with reference to the lay disciple Chattapāṇi and the tow queens of King Pasenadi of Kosala.

A lay disciple named Chattapāṇi who was an anāgāmī[1] lived in Sāvatthi. On one occasion, Chattapāṇi was with the Buddha at the Jetavana monastery, respectfully and attentively listening to a religious discourse, when King Pasenadi also came to the Buddha. Chattapāṇi did not stand up because he thought that by standing up, it might mean that he was paying respect to the king, but not paying due respect to the Buddha. The king took that as an insult and was very much offended. The Buddha knew exactly how the king was feeling; so he spoke in praise of Chattapāṇi, who was well-versed in the Dhamma and had also attained the Anāgāmi Fruition. On hearing this, the king was impressed and favourably inclined towards Chattapāṇi.

---

1. **anāgāmī:** one who has attained the third Magga.

When the king next met Chattapāṇi he said, "You are so learned; could you please come to the palace and give lessons on the Dhamma to my two queens?" Chattapāṇi declined but he suggested that the king should request the Buddha to assign a bhikkhu for this purpose. So, the king approached the Buddha in connection with this, and the Buddha directed the Venerable Ānanda to go regularly to the palace and teach the Dhamma to queen Mallikā and queen Vāsabhakhattiyā. After some time, the Buddha asked the Venerable Ānanda about the progress of the two queens. The Venerable Ānanda answered that although Mallikā was learning the Dhamma seriously, Vāsabhakhattiyā was not paying proper attention. On hearing this the Buddha said that the Dhamma could be of benefit only to those who learn it seriously with due respect and proper attention and then practise diligently what was taught.

Then the Buddha spoke in verse as follows:

Verse 51. Just as a beautiful flower, lacking in scent, cannot give the wearer the benefit of its scent, so also, the well-preached words of the Buddha cannot benefit one who does not practise the Dhamma.

Verse 52. Just as a flower, beautiful as well as fragrant, will give the wearer the benefit of its scent, so also, the well-preached words of the Buddha will benefit one who practises the Dhamma.

Verse 53

IV (8) The Story of Visākhā

While residing at the Pubbārāma monastery in Sāvatthi, the Buddha uttered Verse (53) of this book, with reference to Visākhā, the famous donor of the Pubbārāma monastery.

Visākhā was the daughter of a rich man of Bhaddiya, named Dhanañcaya, and his wife Sumanadevī, and the granddaughter of Meṇḍaka, one of the five extremely wealthy men of King Bimbisāra's dominions. When Visākhā was seven years old, the Buddha came on a tour to Bhaddiya. On that occasion, the rich man Meṇḍaka took Visākhā and her five hundred companions with him to pay homage to the Buddha. After hearing the discourse given by the Buddha, Visākhā, her grandfather and all her five hundred companions attained Sotāpatti Fruition.

When Visākhā came of age, she married Puṇṇavaḍḍhana, son of Migāra, a fairly rich man from Sāvatthi. One day, while Migāra was having his meal, a bhikkhu stopped for alms at his house; but Migāra completely ignored the bhikkhu. Visākhā, seeing this, said to the bhikkhu, "I am sorry, your reverence, my father-in--law only eats left-overs." On hearing this, Migāra flew into a rage and told her to leave his house. But Visākhā said she was not going away, and that she would send for the eight elderly rich men who were sent by her father to accompany her and to advise her. It was for them to decide whether she was guilty or not. When the elders came, Migāra said to them, "While I was having my rice-with-milk in a golden bowl, Visākhā said that I was taking only dirt and filth. For this offence, I'm sending her away." Thereupon, Visākhā explained as follows: "When I saw my father-in-law completely ignoring the bhikkhu standing for alms-food, I thought to myself that my father-in-law was not doing any meritorious deed in this existence, he was only eating the fruits of his past good deeds. So, I said, 'My father-in-law only eats left-overs.' Now Sirs, what do you think, am I guilty?" The elders decided that Visākhā was not guilty. Visākhā then said that she was one who had absolute and unshakable faith in the Teaching of the Buddha and so could not stay where the bhikkhus were not welcome; and also, that if she was not given permission to invite the bhikkhus to the house to offer alms-food and make other offerings, she would leave the house. So permission was granted her to invite the Buddha and his bhikkhus to the house.

The next day, the Buddha and his disciples were invited to the house of Visākhā. When alms-food was about to be offered, she sent word to her father-in-law to join her in offering food; but he did not come. When the meal was over, again she sent a message, this time requesting her father-in-law to join her in hearing the discourse that would soon be given by the Buddha. Her father-in-law felt that he should not refuse for a second time. But his ascetic teachers, the Niganṭhas, would not let him go; however, they conceded that he could listen from behind a curtain. After hearing the Buddha's discourse Migāra attained Sotāpatti Fruition. He felt very thankful to the Buddha and also to his daughter-in-law. Being so thankful, he declared that henceforth Visākhā would be like a mother to him, and Visākhā came to be known as Migāramātā.

Visākhā gave birth to ten sons and ten daughters, and ten sons and ten daughters each were born to everyone of her children and grand-children. Visākhā possessed an immensely valuable gem-encrusted cloak given by her father as a wedding present. One day, Visākhā went to the Jetavana monastery with her entourage. On arrival at the monastery, she found that her bejewelled cloak was too heavy. So, she took it off, wrapped it up in her shawl, and gave it to the maid to hold it and take care of it. The maid absent--mindedly left it at the monastery. It was the custom for the Venerable Ānanda to look after the things left by any one of the lay disciples. Visākhā sent the maid back to the monastery saying, "Go and look for the bejewelled cloak, but if the Venerable Ānanda had already found it and kept it in a place do not bring it back; I donate the bejewelled cloak to the Venerable Ānanda." But the Venerable Ānanda did not accept her donation. So Visākhā decided to sell the bejewelled cloak and donate the sale proceeds. But there was no one who could afford to buy that bejewelled cloak. So Visākhā bought it back for nine crores and one lakh. With this money, she built a monastery on the eastern side of the city; this monastery came to be known as Pubbārāma.

After the libation ceremony she called all her family to her and on that night she told them that all her wishes had been fulfilled and that she had nothing more to desire. Then reciting five verses of exultation she went round and round the monastery. Some bhikkhus hearing her, thought she was singing and reported to the Buddha that Visākhā was not like before, and that she was going round and round the monastery, singing. "Could it be that she had gone off her head?" they asked the Buddha. To this question, the Buddha replied, "Today, Visākhā had all her wishes of the past and present existences fulfilled and on account of that sense of achievement, she was feeling elated and contented; Visākhā was just reciting some verses of exultation ; she certainly had not gone off her head. Visākhā, throughout her previous existences, had always been a generous donor and an ardent promoter of the Doctrine of successive Buddhas. She was most strongly inclined to do good deeds and had done much good in her previous existences, just as an expert florist makes many garlands from a collection of flowers.

Then the Buddha spoke in verse as follows:

Verse 53. As from a collection of flowers many a garland can be made by an expert florist, so also, much good can be done (with wealth, out of faith and generosity) by one subject to birth and death.

Verses 54 and 55

IV (9) The Story of the Question Raised by the Venerable Ānanda

While residing at the Jetavana monastery, the Buddha uttered Verses (54) and (55) of this book, with reference to a question raised by the Venerable Ānanda.

While the Venerable Ānanda was sitting by himself one evening, the problem relating to scents and perfumes came to his mind and he pondered: "The scent of wood, the scent of flowers, and the scent of roots all spread with the current of wind but not against it. Is there no scent which would spread with the current of wind as well as against it? Is there no scent which would pervade every part of the world?" Without answering the question himself, the Venerable Ānanda approached the Buddha and solicited an answer from him. The Buddha said, "Ānanda, supposing, there is one who takes refuge in the Three Gems (the Buddha, the Dhamma, the Saṁgha), who observes the five moral precepts, who is generous and not avaricious; such a man is truly virtuous and truly worthy of praise. The reputation of that virtuous one would spread far and wide, and bhikkhus, brahmins and laymen all alike would speak in praise of him, wherever he lives."

Then the Buddha spoke in verse as follows:

Verse 54. The scent of flowers cannot go against the wind; nor the scent of sandalwood, nor of rhododendron, nor of jasmin (mallikā); only the reputation of good people can go against the wind. The reputation of the virtuous ones (sappurisa) is wafted abroad in all directions.

Verse 55. There are the scents of sandalwood, rhododendron, lotus and jasmin (vassikā); but the scent of virtue surpasses all scents.

Verse 56

IV (10) The Story of Thera Mahākassapa

While residing at the Veḷuvana monastery in Rājagaha, the Buddha uttered Verse (56) of this book, with reference to Thera Mahākassapa.

Arising from nirodhasamāpatti[1], Thera Mahākassapa entered a poor section of the city of Rājagaha for alms-food. His intention was to give a poor man an opportunity of gaining great merit as a result of offering alms-food to one who had just come out of nirodhasamāpatti. Sakka, king of the devas, wishing to take the opportunity of offering alms-food to Thera Mahākassapa, assumed the form of a poor old weaver and came to Rājagaha with his wife Sujāta in the form of an old woman. Thera Mahākassapa stood at their door; the poor old weaver took the bowl from the thera and filled up the bowl with rice and curry, and the delicious smell of the curry spread throughout the city. Then it occurred to the thera that this person must be no ordinary human being, and he came to realize that this must be Sakka himself. Sakka admitted the fact and claimed that he too was poor because he had had no opportunity of offering anything to anyone during the time of the Buddhas. So saying, Sakka and his wife Sujāta left the thera after paying due respect to him.

The Buddha, from his monastery, saw Sakka and Sujāta leaving and told the bhikkhus about Sakka offering alms-food to Thera Mahākassapa. The bhikkhus wondered how Sakka knew that Thera Mahākassapa had just come out of nirodhasamāpatti, and that it was the right and auspicious time for him to make offerings to the thera. This question was put up to

1. **Nirodhasamāpatti**: sustained deep mental absorption following the attainment of nirodha, i.e., temporary cessation of the four mental khandhas.

the Buddha, and the Buddha answered, "Bhikkhus, the reputation of a virtuous one as my son, Thera Mahākassapa, spreads far and wide; it reaches even the deva world. On account of his good reputation, Sakka himself has come to offer alms-food to him."

Then the Buddha spoke in verse as follows:

Verse 56. The scents of rhododendron and of sandalwood are very faint; but the scent (reputation) of the virtuous is the strongest; it spreads even to the abodes of the devas.

Verse 57

IV (11) The Story of Thera Godhika

While residing at the Veḷuvana monastery, the Buddha uttered Verse (57) of this book, with reference to Thera Godhika.

Thera Godhika was, on one occasion, diligently practising Tranquillity and Insight Development, on a stone slab on the side of Isigili mountain in Magadha. When he had achieved one-pointedness of the mind (jhāna) he became very ill; that impaired the effectiveness of his practice. In spite of his sickness, he kept on striving hard; but every time he was making some progress he was overcome by sickness. He was thus inflicted for six times. Finally, he made up his mind to overcome all obstacles and attain arahatship even if he were to die. So, without relaxing he continued to practise diligently; in the end he decided to give up his life by cutting his throat; at the point of death he attained arahatship.

When Māra learned that Thera Godhika had died, he tried to find out where the thera was reborn but failed to find him. So, assuming the likeness of a young man, Māra approached the Buddha and enquired where Thera Godhika was. The Buddha replied to him, "It will be of no benefit to you to learn of the destination of Thera Godhika; for having been freed of moral defilements he became an arahat. One like you, Māra, for all your power will not be able to find out where such arahats go after death."

Then the Buddha spoke in verse as follows:

Verse 57. Māra cannot find the path taken by those who are endowed with virtue, who live mindfully, and have been freed from moral defilements by Right Knowledge.

Verses 58 and 59

IV (12) The Story of Garahadinna

While residing at the Jetavana monastery, the Buddha uttered Verses (58) and (59) of this book, with reference to a rich man named Garahadinna and the miracle of the lotus flowers.

There were two friends named Sirigutta and Garahadinna in Sāvatthi. Sirigutta was a follower of the Buddha and Garahadinna was a follower of the Nigaṇṭhas, the ascetics who were hostile to the Buddhists. At the instance of the Nigaṇṭhas, Garahadinna often said to Sirigutta, "What benefit do you get by following the Buddha? Come, be a follower of my teachers." Having been told thus many times, Sirigutta said to Garahadinna, "Tell me, what do your teachers know?" To this, Garahadinna replied that his teachers knew everything; with their great power they knew the past, the present and the future and also the thoughts of others. So, Sirigutta invited the Nigaṇṭhas to his house for alms-food.

Sirigutta wanted to find out the truth about the Nigaṇṭhas, whether they really possessed the power of knowing other people's thoughts, etc. So he made a long, deep trench and filled it up with excreta and filth. Seats were then placed precariously over the trench; and big empty pots were brought in and covered up with cloth and banana leaves to make them appear as if they were full of rice and curries. When the Nigaṇṭhas arrived, they were requested to enter one by one, to stand near their respective seats, and to sit down simultaneously. As all of them sat down, the flimsy strings broke and the Nigaṇṭhas fell into the filthy trench. Then Sirigutta taunted them, "Why don't you know the past, the present and the future? Why don't you know the thoughts of others?" All the Nigaṇṭhas then fled in terror.

Garahadinna naturally was furious with Sirigutta and refused to talk to him for two weeks. Then, he decided that he would have his revenge on Sirigutta. He pretended that he was no longer angry, and one day asked Sirigutta to invite, on his behalf, the Buddha and his five hundred disciples to partake of alms-food. So Sirigutta went to the Buddha and invited him to the house of Garahadinna. At the same time, he told the Buddha about what he had done to the Niganṭhas, the teachers of Garahadinna. He also expressed his fear that this invitation might be a reprisal and so the invitation should be accepted only after due consideration.

The Buddha, with his supernormal power, knew that this would be the occasion for the two friends to attain Sotāpatti Fruition, and therefore accepted the invitation. Garahadinna made a trench, filled it with live coals and covered it with mats. He also kept some empty pots covered with cloth and banana leaves to make them appear as if filled with rice and curries. The next day, the Buddha came followed by five hundred bhikkhus in single file. When the Buddha stepped on the mat over the trench, the mat and live coals miraculously disappeared, and five hundred lotus flowers, each as large as a cart wheel, sprang up for the Buddha and his disciples to sit upon.

Seeing this miracle, Garahadinna was very much alarmed and he said rather incoherently to Sirigutta, "Help me, dear friend. Out of my desire for revenge, I have truly done a great wrong. My bad designs have had no effect at all on your Teacher. The pots in my kitchen are all empty. Please help me." Sirigutta then told Garahadinna to go and look at the pots. When Garahadinna found all the pots filled with food he was astounded and at the same time very much relieved and very happy. So the food was offered to the Buddha and his disciples. After the meal, the Buddha expressed his appreciation (anumodanā) of the meritorious act and then said, "Ignorant worldlings, lacking in knowledge, do not know the unique qualities of the Buddha, the Dhamma and the Saṁgha and so they are like the blind; but the wise, having knowledge, are like people with sight."

Then the Buddha spoke in verse as follows:

Verses 58, 59. As a sweet-smelling and beautiful lotus flower may grow upon a heap of rubbish thrown on the highway, so also, out of the rubbish heap of beings may appear a disciple of the Buddha, who with his wisdom shines forth far above the blind (ignorant) worldlings.

At the end of the discourse, both Garahadinna and Sirigutta attained Sotāpatti Fruition.

End of Chapter Four: Flowers.

Chapter V

The Fool (Bālavagga)

Verse 60

V (1) The Story of a Certain Person

While residing at the Jetavana monastery, the Buddha uttered Verse (60) of this book, with reference to a certain young man and King Pasenadi of Kosala.

One day King Pasenadi, while going out in the city, happened to see a beautiful young woman standing at the window of her house and he instantly fell in love with her. So the king tried to find ways and means of getting her. Finding that she was a married woman, he sent for her husband and made him serve at the palace. Later, the husband was sent on an impossible errand by the king. The young man was to go to a place, a yojana (twelve miles) away from Sāvatthi, bring back some Kumuda lotus flowers and some red earth called 'aruṇavatī' from the land of the dragons (nāgas) and arrive back at Sāvatthi the same evening, in time for the king's bath. The king's intention was to kill the husband if he failed to arrive back in time, and to take the wife for himself.

Hurriedly taking a food packet from his wife, the young man set out on his errand. On the way, he shared his food with a traveller. He also threw some rice into the water and said loudly, "O guardian spirits and dragons inhabiting this river! King Pasenadi has commanded me to get some Kumuda lotus flowers and aruṇavatī red earth for him. I have today shared my food with a traveller; I have also fed the fish in the river; I now share with you the benefits of the good deeds I have done today. Please get the Kumuda lotus and aruṇavatī red earth for me." The king of the dragons, hearing him, took the appearance of an old man and brought the lotus and the red earth.

On that evening, King Pasenadi, fearing that the young husband might arrive back in time, had the city-gates closed early. The young man, finding the city-gates closed, placed the red earth on the city-wall and stuck the flowers on the earth. Then he declared loudly,

"O citizens! Be my witnesses! I have today accomplished my errand in time as instructed by the king. King Pasenadi, without any justification, plans to kill me." After that, the young man left for the Jetavana monastery to take shelter and find solace in the peaceful atmosphere of the monastery.

Meanwhile, King Pasenadi, obsessed with sexual desire, could not sleep, and kept thinking out how he would get rid of the husband in the morning and take his wife. At about midnight, he heard some eerie sounds; actually, these were the doleful voices of four persons suffering in Lohakumbhī Niraya. Hearing those weird voices, the king was terrified. Early in the morning, he went to the Buddha, as advised by Queen Mallikā. When the Buddha was told about the four voices the king heard in the night, he explained to the king that those were the voices of four beings, who were the sons of rich men during the time of Kassapa Buddha, and that now they were suffering in Lohakumbhī Niraya because they had committed sexual misconduct with other people's wives. Then, the king came to realize the depravity of the deed and the severity of the punishment. So, he decided then and there that he would no longer covet another man's wife. "After all, it was on account of my intense desire for another man's wife that I was tormented and could not sleep the whole of last night," he reflected. Then King Pasenadi said to the Buddha, "Venerable Sir, now I know how long the night is for one who cannot sleep." The young man who was close at hand also said, "Venerable Sir, because I had travelled the full distance of a yojana yesterday, I, too, know how long the journey of a yojana is to one who is weary."

Combining their two statements, the Buddha spoke in verse as follows:

Verse 60. Long is the night to one who is wakeful; long is (the journey of) one yojana to the traveller who is tired; long is saṁsāra (round of rebirths) to the fool, who is ignorant of the true Dhamma (the Teaching of the Buddha).

At the end of the discourse, the young man attained Sotāpatti Fruition.

Verse 61

V (2) The Story of a Resident Pupil of Thera Mahākassapa

While residing at the Jetavana monastery, the Buddha uttered Verse (61) of this book, with reference to a resident pupil of Thera Mahākassapa.

When Thera Mahākassapa was residing near Rājagaha, he had two young bhikkhus staying with him. One of them was respectful, obedient and dutiful to the thera; but the other one was not. When the old thera chided the latter for his slackness in his duties, he was very much offended. On one occasion, he went to the house of a lay-disciple of the thera, and lied to them that the thera was ill. Thus, he got some choice food from them for the thera; but he ate the food on the way. When admonished by the thera for this he was extremely angry. The next day, when the thera was out on his alms-round, the young foolish bhikkhu stayed behind, broke the pots and pans and set fire to the monastery.

When a bhikkhu from Rājagaha told the Buddha about this, the Buddha said that it would have been much better for Thera Mahākassapa to live alone than to live with a foolish companion.

Then the Buddha spoke in verse as follows:

Verse 61. If a person seeking a companion cannot find one who is better than or equal to him, let him resolutely go on alone; there can be no companionship with a fool.

At the end of the discourse, the bhikkhu from Rājagaha attained Sotāpatti Fruition.

Verse 62

V (3) The Story of Ānanda, the Rich Man

While residing at the Jetavana monastery, the Buddha uttered Verse (62) of this book, with reference to a miserly rich man, named Ānanda.

There was once a very wealthy man named Ānanda in Sāvatthi. Although he possessed eighty crores, he was very reluctant to give anything in charity. To his son, Mūlasiri, he used to say, "Don't think the wealth we have now is very much. Do not give away anything from what you have, for you must make it grow. Otherwise, your wealth will dwindle away." This rich man had five pots of gold buried in his house and he died without revealing their location to his son.

Ānanda, the rich man, was reborn in a village of beggars, not far from Sāvatthi. From the time his mother was pregnant, the income of the beggars decreased; the villagers thought there must be a wicked and unlucky one amongst them. By dividing themselves up into groups and by the process of elimination, they came to the conclusion that the pregnant beggar woman must be the unfortunate one. Thus, she was driven out of the village. When her son was born, the son proved to be extremely ugly and repulsive. If she went out begging by herself, she would get as before, but if she went out with her son she would get nothing. So, when the boy could go out by himself, his mother placed a plate in his hand and left him. As he wandered about in Sāvatthi, he remembered his old house and his past existence. So he went into the house. When the sons of his son Mūlasiri saw him, they were frightened by his ugly looks and began to cry. The servants then beat him and threw him out of the house.

The Buddha who was on his alms-round saw the incident and asked the Venerable Ānanda to fetch Mūlasiri. When Mūlasiri came, the Buddha told him that the young beggar was his own father in his previous existence. But Mūlasiri could not believe it. So, the Buddha directed the beggar boy to show where he had buried his five pots of gold. Then only, Mūlasiri accepted the truth and from that time he became a devoted lay-disciple of the Buddha.

Then the Buddha spoke in verse as follows:

Verse 62. "I have sons, I have wealth"; with this (feeling of attachment) the fool is afflicted. Indeed, he himself is not his own, how can sons and wealth be his?

Verse 63

V (4) The Story of Two Pick-pockets

While residing at the Jetavana monastery, the Buddha uttered Verse (63) of this book, with reference to two pick-pockets.

On one occasion, two pick-pockets joined a group of lay-disciples going to the Jetavana monastery, where the Buddha was giving a discourse. One of them listened attentively to the discourse and soon attained Sotāpatti Fruition. However, the second thief did not attend to the discourse as he was bent on stealing only; and he managed to snatch a small sum of money from one of the lay-disciples. After the discourse they went back and cooked their meal at the house of the second thief, the one who managed to get some money. The wife of the second thief taunted the first thief, "You are so wise, you don't even have anything to cook at your house." Hearing this remark, the first thief thought to himself, "This one is so foolish that she thinks she is being very smart." Then, together with some relatives, he went to the Buddha and related the matter to him.

To the man, the Buddha spoke in verse as follows:

Verse 63. The fool who knows that he is a fool can, for that reason, be a wise man; but the fool who thinks that he is wise is, indeed, called a fool.

At the end of the discourse, all the relatives of the man attained Sotāpatti Fruition.

Verse 64

V (5) The Story of Thera Udāyi

While residing at the Jetavana monastery, the Buddha uttered Verse (64) of this book, with reference to Thera Udāyi, a pretentious bhikkhu.

Thera Udāyi would often go and sit on the platform from which learned theras delivered their discourses. On one occasion, some visiting bhikkhus, taking him for a very learned thera, put to him some questions on the five aggregates (khandhas). Thera Udāyi could not answer, because he did not know anything of the dhamma. The visiting bhikkhus were greatly astonished to find that one staying in the same monastery with the Buddha knew so very little about the khandhas and the āyatanas (sense-bases and sense-objects).

To them, the Buddha spoke in verse as follows:

Verse 64. A fool, even though he is associated with a wise man all his life, does not understand the Dhamma, just as a ladle does not know the taste of soup.

At the end of the discourse, all the visiting bhikkhus attained arahatship.

Verse 65

V (6) The Story of Thirty Bhikkhus from Pāveyyaka

While residing at the Jetavana monastery, the Buddha uttered Verse (65) of this book, with reference to thirty bhikkhus from Pāveyyaka.

Thirty youths from Pāveyyaka were, on one occasion, enjoying themselves with a prostitute in a forest, when the prostitute stole some of their valuable ornaments and ran away. While searching for her in the forest, they met the Buddha on the way. As the Buddha delivered them a discourse the youths attained Sotāpatti Fruition, and all of them joined the Order of the Buddha and followed him to the Jetavana monastery. While staying at the monastery, they strictly observed the austerity or purification practice (dhutaṅga). Later, when the Buddha delivered the Anamatagga Sutta (Discourse on Countless Existences), all those bhikkhus attained arahatship.

When other bhikkhus commented that Pāveyyaka bhikkhus were very quick in attaining arahatship, the Buddha replied to them in verse as follows:

Verse 65. An intelligent man, even though he is associated with a wise man only for a moment, quickly understands the Dhamma, just as the tongue knows the taste of soup.

Verse 66

V (7) The Story of Suppabuddha, the Leper

While residing at the Jetavana monastery, the Buddha uttered Verse (66) of this book, with reference to Suppabuddha, a leper.

Suppabuddha the leper, while sitting at the back of the crowd and listening attentively to the discourse given by the Buddha, attained Sotāpatti Fruition. When the crowd had dispersed, he followed the Buddha to the monastery as he wished to tell the Buddha about his attainment of Sotāpatti Fruition. Sakka, king of the devas, wishing to test the leper's faith in the Buddha, the Dhamma and the Saṁgha, appeared to him and said, "You are only a poor man, living on what you get by begging, with no one to fall back on. I can give you immense wealth if you deny the Buddha, the Dhamma and the Saṁgha and say that you have no use for them." To this, Suppabuddha replied, "I am certainly not a poor man, with no one to rely on. I am a rich man; I possess the seven attributes which the ariyas possess; I have faith (saddhā), morality (sīla), sense of shame to do evil (hirī), sense of fear to do evil (ottappa), learning (suta), generosity (cāga) and knowledge (paññā).

Then, Sakka went to the Buddha ahead of Suppabuddha and related the conversation between himself and Suppabuddha. To him the Buddha replied that it would not be easy even for a hundred or a thousand Sakkas to coax Suppabuddha away from the Buddha, the Dhamma and the Saṁgha. Soon after this, Suppabuddha arrived at the monastery and reported to the Buddha about his attainment of Sotāpatti Fruition. On his way back from the Jetavana monastery, Suppabuddha was gored to death by an infuriated cow, who, in fact, was an ogress assuming the form of a cow. This ogress was none other than the prostitute who was killed by Suppabuddha in one of his previous existences and who had vowed to have her revenge on him.

When the news of Suppabuddha's death reached the Jetavana monastery, the bhikkhus asked the Buddha where Suppabuddha was reborn and the Buddha replied to them that Suppabuddha was reborn in Tāvatiṁsa deva realm. The Buddha also explained to them that Suppabuddha was born a leper because, in one of his previous existences, he had spat upon a paccekabuddha.

Then the Buddha spoke in verse as follows:

Verse 66. With themselves as their own enemies, fools lacking in intelligence, move about doing evil deeds, which bear bitter fruits.

Verse 67

V (8) The Story of a Farmer

While residing at the Jetavana monastery, the Buddha uttered Verse (67) of this book, with reference to a farmer who handled poison.

One day, some thieves having stolen some valuables and cash from the house of a rich man came to a field. There, they divided the stolen property among themselves and dispersed; but a packet containing one thousand in cash, having dropped from one of the thieves, was left behind unnoticed.

Early in the morning on that day, the Buddha, on surveying the world with his supernormal power, perceived that a farmer, cultivating near that field, would attain Sotāpatti Fruition on that very day. So, the Buddha went there, accompanied by the Venerable Ānanda. The farmer on seeing the Buddha paid obeisance to him and continued to plough the field. The Buddha seeing the packet of money said to the Venerable Ānanda, "Ānanda, look at that very poisonous snake," and Ananda replied, "Venerable Sir, yes, it is, indeed, a very poisonous snake!" Then, both the Buddha and the Venerable Ānanda continued their way.

The farmer, hearing them, went to find out if there really was a snake and found the packet of money. He took the packet and hid it in a place. The owners of the property coming after the thieves came to the field, and tracing the footprints of the farmer, found the packet of money. They beat the farmer and took him to the king, who ordered his men to kill the farmer. On being taken to the cemetery, where he was to be killed, the farmer kept on repeating, "Ānanda, look at that very poisonous snake. Venerable Sir, I see the snake; it is, indeed, a very poisonous snake!" When the king's men heard the above dialogue between the Buddha and the Venerable Ānanda being repeated all the way, they were puzzled and took him to the king. The king surmised that the farmer was calling upon the Buddha as a witness; he was therefore taken to the presence of the Buddha. After hearing from the Buddha everything that had happened in the morning, the king remarked, "If he had not been able to call upon the Buddha as a witness of his innocence, this man would have been killed." To him, the Buddha replied, "A wise man should not do anything that he would repent after doing it."

Then the Buddha spoke in verse as follows:

Verse 67. That deed is not well done, if one has to repent for having done it, and if, with a tearful face, one has to weep as a result of that deed.

At the end of the discourse, the farmer attained Sotāpatti Fruition.

Verse 68

V (9) The Story of Sumana, the Florist

While residing at the Jetavana monastery, the Buddha uttered Verse (68) of this book, with reference to Sumana the florist.

A florist, named Sumana, had to supply King Bimbisāra of Rājagaha with jasmin flowers every morning. One day, as he was going to the king's palace he saw the Buddha, with a halo of light-rays radiating from him, coming into town for alms-food accompanied by many bhikkhus. Seeing the Buddha in his resplendent glory, the florist Sumana felt a strong desire to offer his flowers to the Buddha. Then and there, he decided that even if the king were to drive him out of the country or to kill him, he would not offer the flowers to the king for that day. Thus, he threw up the flowers to the sides, to the back and over and above the head of the Buddha. The flowers remained hanging in the air; those over the head formed a canopy of flowers and those at the back and the sides formed walls of flowers. These flowers followed the Buddha in this position as he moved on, and stopped when the Buddha stopped. As the Buddha proceeded, surrounded by walls of flowers, and a canopy of flowers, with the six-coloured rays radiating from his body, followed by a large entourage, thousands of people inside and outside of Rājagaha came out of their houses to pay obeisance to the Buddha. As for Sumana, his entire body was suffused with delightful satisfaction (Pīti).

The wife of the florist Sumana then went to the king and said that she had nothing to do with her husband failing to supply the king with flowers for that day. The king, being a Sotāpanna himself, felt quite happy about the flowers. He came out to see the wonderful sight and paid obeisance to the Buddha. The king also took the opportunity to offer alms-food to the Buddha and his disciples. After the meal, the Buddha returned in the Jetavana monastery and the king followed him for some distance. On arrival back at the palace King Bimbisāra sent for Sumana and offered him a reward of eight elephants, eight horses, eight male slaves, eight female slaves, eight maidens and eight thousand in cash.

At the Jetavana monastery, the Venerable Ānanda asked the Buddha what benefits Sumana would gain by his good deed done on that day. The Buddha answered that Sumana, having given to the Buddha without any consideration for his life, would not be born in any of the four lower worlds (Apāya) for the next one hundred thousand worlds and that eventually he would become a paccekabuddha. After that, as the Buddha entered the Perfumed Hall (Gandhakuṭi) the flowers dropped off of their own accord.

That night, at the end of the usual discourse, the Buddha spoke in verse as follows:

Verse 68. That deed is well done if one has not to repent for having done it, and if one is delightful and happy with the result of that deed.

Verse 69

V (10) The Story of Therī Uppalavaṇṇā

While residing at the Jetavana monastery, the Buddha uttered Verse (69) of this book, with reference to Therī Uppalavaṇṇā.

Once there was a young daughter of a rich man in Sāvatthi. Because she was so beautiful, with looks so tender and sweet, like a blue lotus flower, she was called "Uppalavaṇṇā", the blue lotus. The fame of her beauty spread far and wide and there were many suitors: princes, rich men and many others. But she decided that it would be better for her to become a bhikkhunī, a female member of the Buddhist Order. One day, after lighting a lamp, she kept her mind fixed on the flame and meditating on the fire kasiṇa (object of concentration) she soon achieved Magga Insight and finally attained arahatship.

Some time later, she moved to the 'Dark Forest' (Andhavana) and lived in solitude. While Therī Uppalavaṇṇā was out on her alms-round, Nanda, the son of her uncle, came to her monastery and hid himself underneath her couch. Nanda had fallen in love with Uppalavaṇṇā before she became a bhikkhunī; his intention obviously was to take her by force. When Uppalavaṇṇā returned she saw Nanda and said, "You fool! Do no harm, do not molest." But he would not be stopped. After satisfying himself, he left her. As soon as he stepped on the ground, the earth opened wide and he was swallowed up.

Hearing about this, the Buddha spoke in verse as follows:

Verse 69. As long as the evil deed does not bear fruit, the fool thinks it is sweet like honey; but when his evil deed does bear fruit, the fool suffers for it.

At the end of the discourse, many attained Sotāpatti Fruition.

The Buddha next sent for King Pasenadi of Kosala and told him about the dangers that bhikkhunīs living in forests had to face from irresponsible persons obsessed with sex. The king then promised to build monasteries for bhikkhunīs only in towns or close to the towns.

Verse 70

V (11) The Story of Thera Jambuka

While residing at the Jetavana monastery, the Buddha uttered Verse (70) of this book, with reference to Thera Jambuka.

Jambuka was the son of a rich man in Sāvatthi. Due to his past evil deeds he was born with very peculiar habits. As a child, he wanted to sleep on the floor with no proper bed, and to take his own excreta for food instead of rice. When he grew older, his parents sent him to the Ājīvakas, the naked ascetics. When those ascetics found out about his peculiar food habits they drove him away. At nights he ate human excreta and in the day time stood still on one leg and kept his mouth open. He used to say that he kept his mouth open because he only lived on air and that he stood on one leg because it would otherwise be too heavy for the earth to bear him. "I never sit down, I never go to sleep," he boasted and on account of this, he was known as Jambuka, a'jackal'.

Many people believed him and some would come to him with offerings of choice food. Then Jambuka would refuse and say, "I do not take any food except air." When pressed, he would take just a little of the food with the tip of a blade of grass and say, "Now go, this little will give you enough merit." In this way, Jambuka lived for fifty-five years, naked and taking only excreta.

One day, the Buddha saw in his vision that Jambuka was due to attain arahatship within a short time. So, in the evening, the Buddha went to where Jambuka was staying and asked for some place to spend the night. Jambuka pointed out to him a mountain--cave not far from the stone slab on which he himself was staying. During the first, second and third watches of the night, the Cātumahārājika devas, Sakka and Mahābrahmā came to pay homage to the Buddha in turn. On all the three occasions, the forest was lit up and Jambuka saw the light three times. In the morning, he walked over to the Buddha and enquired about the lights.

When told about the devas, Sakka and Mahābrahmā coming to pay homage to the Buddha, Jambuka was very much impressed, and said to the Buddha, "You must, indeed, be a wonderfully great person for the devas, Sakka and Mahābrahmā to come and pay homage to you. As for me, even though I have practised austerely for fifty-five years, living only on air and standing only on one leg, none of the devas, nor Sakka, nor Mahābrahmā has ever came to me." To him, the Buddha replied, "O Jambuka! You have been deceiving other people, but you cannot deceive me. I know that for fifty-five years you have been eating excreta and sleeping on the ground."

Furthermore, the Buddha explained to him how in one of his past existences during the time of Kassapa Buddha, Jambuka had prevented a thera from going with him to the house of a lay-disciple where alms-food was being offered and how he had also thrown away the food that was sent along with him for that thera. It was for those evil deeds that Jambuka had to be eating excreta and sleeping on the ground. Hearing that account, Jambuka was horrified and terror-stricken, and repented for having done evil and for having deceived other people. He went down on his knees and the Buddha gave him a piece of cloth to put on. The Buddha then proceeded to deliver a discourse; at the end of the discourse Jambuka attained arahatship and joined the Buddhist Order on the spot.

Soon after this, Jambuka's pupils from Aṅga and Magadha arrived and they were surprised to see their teacher with the Buddha. Thera Jambuka then explained to his pupils that he had joined the Buddhist Order and that he was now only a disciple of the Buddha. To them, the Buddha said that although their teacher had lived austerely by taking food very sparingly, it was not worth even one-sixteenth part of his present practice and achievement.

Then the Buddha spoke in verse as follows:

Verse 70. Even though, month after month, the fool (living in austerity) takes his food sparingly with the tip of a grass blade, he is not worth even one-sixteenth part of those who have comprehended the Truth (i.e., the ariyas).

Verse 71

V (12) The Story of Ahipeta[1]

While residing at the Jetavana monastery, the Buddha uttered Verse (71) of this book, with reference to a peta-ghost.

---

1. **Ahipeta** - Ahi + peta; ahi = snake + peta = peta-ghost, an ever-hungry spirit or ghost. In this instance a ghost with the head of a human being and the body of a snake.

The Chief Disciple Mahā Moggallāna was on one occasion going on an alms-round with Thera Lakkhaṇa in Rājagaha. On seeing something, he smiled but said nothing. When they were back at the monastery, Thera Mahā Moggallāna told Thera Lakkhaṇa that he smiled because he saw a peta-ghost with the head of a human being and the body of a snake. The Buddha then said that he himself had seen that very peta-ghost on the day he attained Buddhahood. The Buddha also explained that, a very long time ago, there was a paccekabuddha, who was respected by many. People going to his monastery had to traverse a field. The owner of the field, fearing that his field would be damaged by too many people going to and from the monastery, set fire to it. Consequently, the paccekabuddha had to move to some other place. The disciples of the paccekabuddha, being very angry with the land--owner, beat him and killed him. On his death he was reborn in Avīci Niraya. In his present existence, he was serving out the remaining term of the evil consequences (kamma), as a peta-ghost.

In conclusion, the Buddha said, "An evil deed does not bear fruit immediately, but it invariably follows the evil doer. There is no escape from the consequences of an evil deed."

Then the Buddha spoke in verse as follows:

Verse 71. An evil deed does not immediately bear fruit, just as the newly-drawn milk does not curdle at once; but it follows the fool burning him like live coal covered with ashes.

Verse (72)

V (13) The Story of Saṭṭhikūṭapeta

While residing at the Veḷuvana monastery, the Buddha uttered Verse (72) of this book with reference to a peta-ghost named Saṭṭhikūṭa.

The Chief Disciple Mahā Moggallāna saw this enormous peta-ghost while going on an alms-round with Thera Lakkhaṇa. In this connection, the Buddha explained that Saṭṭhikūṭa, in one of his previous existences, was very skilful in throwing stones at things. One day, he asked permission from his teacher to try out his skill. His teacher told him not to hit a cow, or a human being as he would have to pay compensation to the owner or to the relative, but to find a target which was ownerless or guardianless.

On seeing the paccekabuddha, the idiot, lacking in intelligence, thought the paccekabuddha, having no relative or guardian, would be an ideal target. So he threw a stone at the paccekabuddha who was on an alms-round. The stone entered from one ear and came out of the other. The paccekabuddha expired when he reached the monastery. The stone-thrower was killed by the disciples of the paccekabuddha and he was reborn in Avīci Niraya. Afterwards, he was reborn as a peta-ghost and had since been serving the remaining term of the evil consequences (kamma) of his evil deed. As a peta-ghost his enormous head was being continuously hit with red-hot hammers.

In conclusion, the Buddha said, "To a fool, his skill or knowledge is of no use; it can only harm him."

Then the Buddha spoke in verse as follows:

Verse 72. The skill of a fool can only harm him; it destroys his merit and his wisdom (lit., it severs his head).

Verses 73 and 74

V (14) The Story of Citta the Householder

While residing at the Jetavana monastery, the Buddha uttered Verses (73) and (74) of this book, with reference to Thera Sudhamma and Citta the householder.

Citta, a householder, once met Thera Mahānāma, one of the group of the first five bhikkhus (Pañcavaggis), going on an alms-round, and invited the thera to his house. There, he offered alms-food to the thera and after listening to the discourse given by him, Citta attained Sotāpatti Fruition. Later, Citta built a monastery in his mango grove. There, he looked to the needs of all bhikkhus who came to the monastery and Bhikkhu Sudhamma was installed as the resident bhikkhu.

One day, the two Chief Disciples of the Buddha, the Venerable Sāriputta and the Venerable Mahā Moggallāna, came to the monastery and after listening to the discourse given by the Venerable Sāriputta, Citta attained Anāgāmi Fruition. Then, he invited the two Chief Disciples to his house for alms-food the next day. He also invited Thera Sudhamma, but Thera Sudhamma refused in anger and said, "You invite me only after the other two." Citta repeated his invitation, but it was turned down. Nevertheless, Thera Sudhamma went to the house of Citta early on the following day. But when invited to enter the house, Thera Sudhamma refused and said that he would not sit down as he was going on his alms-round. But when he saw the things that were to be offered to the two Chief Disciples, he envied them so much that he could not restrain his anger. He abused Citta and said, "I do not want to stay in your monastery any longer," and left the house in anger.

From there, he went to the Buddha and reported everything that had happened. To him, the Buddha said, "You have insulted a lay-disciple who is endowed with faith and generosity. You'd better go back to him and own up your mistake." Sudhamma did as he was told by the Buddha, but Citta would not be appeased; so he returned to the Buddha for the second time. The Buddha, knowing that the pride of Sudhamma had dwindled by this time, said, "My son, a good bhikkhu should have no attachment; a good bhikkhu should not be conceited and say 'This is my monastery, this is my place, these are my lay-disciples,' etc., for in one with such thoughts, covetousness and pride will increase."

Then the Buddha spoke in verse as follows:

Verse 73. The foolish bhikkhu desires praise for qualities he does not have, precedence among bhikkhus, authority in the monasteries, and veneration from those unrelated to him.

Verse 74. "Let both laymen and bhikkhus think that things are done because of me; let them obey me in all matters, great and small." Such being the thoughts of the fool, his greed and his pride grow.

At the end of the discourse, Sudhamma went to the house of Citta, and this time they got reconciled; nd within a few days, Sudhamma attained arahatship.

Verse 75

V (15) The Story of Sāmaṇera Tissa of the Forest Monastery

While residing at the Jetavana monastery, the Buddha uttered Verse (75) of this book, with reference to Tissa, a sāmaṇera, who dwelt in a forest monastery.

Tissa was the son of a rich man from Sāvatthi. His father used to offer alms-food to the Chief Disciple Sāriputta in their house and so Tissa even as a child had met the Chief Disciple on many occasions. At the age of seven he became a novice (sāmaṇera) under the Chief Disciple Sāriputta. While he was staying at the Jetavana monastery, many of his friends and relatives came to see him, bringing presents and offerings. The sāmaṇera found these visits to be very tiresome; so after taking a subject of meditation from the Buddha, he left for a forest monastery. Whenever a villager offered him anything, Tissa would just say "May you be happy, may you be liberated from the ills of life," ("Sukhitā hotha, dukkhā muccatha"), and would go on his own way. While he stayed at the forest monastery, he ardently and diligently practised meditation, and at the end of three months he attained arahatship.

After the vassa, the Venerable Sāriputta accompanied by the Venerable Mahā Moggallāna and other senior disciples paid a visit to Sāmaṇera Tissa, with the permission of the Buddha. All the villagers came out to welcome the Venerable Sāriputta and his company of four thousand bhikkhus. They also requested the Venerable Sāriputta to favour them with a discourse, but the Chief Disciple declined; instead, he directed his pupil Tissa to deliver a discourse to the villagers. The villagers, however, said that their teacher Tissa could only say "May you be happy, may you be liberated from the ills of life," and asked the Chief Disciple to assign another bhikkhu in his place. But the Venerable Sāriputta insisted that Tissa should deliver a discourse on the dhamma, and said to Tissa, "Tissa, talk to them about the dhamma and show them how to gain happiness and how to be liberated from the ills of life."

Thus, in obedience to his teacher, Sāmaṇera Tissa went up the platform to deliver his discourse. He explained to the audience the meaning of the aggregates (khandhas), sense bases and sense objects (āyatanas), elements of the perpetuation of the Teaching (Bodhipakkhiya Dhamma), the Path leading to arahatship and Nibbāna, etc. Finally he concluded, "And thus, those who attain arahatship are liberated from all the ills of life and have Perfect Peace; all the rest will still wander about in the round of rebirths (saṁsāra)."

The Venerable Sāriputta praised Tissa for having expounded the dhamma so well. Dawn was approaching when he finished his exposition, and all the villagers were very much impressed. Some of them were surprised that Sāmaṇera Tissa knew the dhamma so well, but they were also dissatisfied with him because formerly he had talked so little about the dhamma to them; the others were happy and contented to find the sāmaṇera to be so learned and felt that they were very lucky to have him amongst them.

The Buddha, with his supernormal power, saw from the Jetavana monastery these two groups of villagers and appeared before them. His intention in coming to the village was to clear up the misunderstanding amongst the first group of villagers. The Buddha arrived while the villagers were preparing alms-food for the bhikkhus. So, they had the opportunity to offer alms-food to the Buddha as well. After the meal, the Buddha addressed the villagers, "O lay disciples, all of you are so lucky to have Sāmaṇera Tissa amongst you. It is on account of his presence here that I myself, my Chief Disciples, senior disciples and many other bhikkhus now pay you a visit." These words made them realize how fortunate they were to have Sāmaṇera Tissa with them and they were satisfied. The Buddha then delivered a discourse to the villagers and the bhikkhus, and consequently, many of them attained Sotāpatti Fruition.

After the discourse, the Buddha returned to the Jetavana monastery. In the evening, the bhikkhus said in praise of Tissa to the Buddha, "Venerable Sir, Sāmaṇera Tissa had performed a very difficult task; he was so well provided with gifts and offerings of all kinds here in Sāvatthi, yet he gave up all these to go and live austerely in a forest monastery." To them the Buddha replied, "Bhikkhus, a bhikkhu, whether in town or in village, should not live for the sake of gifts and offerings. If a bhikkhu renounces all good prospects of worldly gain and diligently practises the dhamma in solitude, he is sure to attain arahatship."

Then the Buddha spoke in verse as follows;

Verse 75. Indeed, the path that leads to worldly gain is one and the Path that leads to Nibbāna is another. Fully comprehending this, the bhikkhu, the disciple of the Buddha, should not take delight in worldly gain and honour, but devote himself to solitude, detachment and the realization of Nibbāna.

End of Chapter Five : The Fool.

Chapter VI

The Wise (Paṇḍita Vagga)

Verse 76

VI (1) The Story of Thera Rādha

While residing at the Jetavana monastery, the Buddha uttered Verse(76) of this book, with reference to Thera Rādha, who was at one time a poor old brahmin.

Rādha was a poor brahmin who stayed in the monastery doing small services for the bhikkhus. For his services he was provided with food and clothing and other needs, but was not encouraged to join the Order, although he had a strong desire to become a bhikkhu.

One day, early in the morning, when the Buddha surveyed the world with his supernormal power, he saw the poor old brahmin in his vision and knew that he was due for arahatship. So the Buddha went to the old man, and learned from him that the bhikkhus of the monastery did not want him to join the Order. The Buddha therefore called all the bhikkhus to him and asked them, "Is there any bhikkhu here who recollects any good turn done to him by this old man?" To this question, the Venerable Sāriputta replied, "Venerable Sir, I do recollect an instance when this old man offered me a spoonful of rice." "If that be so," the Buddha said, "shouldn't you help your benefactor get liberated from the ills of life?" Then the Venerable Sāriputta agreed to make the old man a bhikkhu and he was duly admitted to the Order. The Venerable Sāriputta guided the old bhikkhu and the old bhikkhu strictly followed his guidance. Within a few days, the old bhikkhu attained arahatship.

When the Buddha next came to see the bhikkhus, they reported to him how strictly the old bhikkhu followed the guidance of the Venerable Sāriputta. To them, the Buddha replied that a bhikkhu should be amenable to guidance like Rādha and should not resent when rebuked for any fault or failing.

Then the Buddha spoke in verse as follows:

Verse 76. One should follow a man of wisdom who rebukes one for one's faults, as one would follow a guide to some buried treasure. To one who follows such a wise man, it will be an advantage and not a disadvantage.

Verse 77

VI (2) The Story of Bhikkhus Assaji and Punabbasuka

While residing at the Jetavana monastery, the Buddha uttered Verse (77) of this book, with reference to bhikkhus Assaji and Punabbasuka.

Bhikkhus Assaji and Punabbasuka and their five hundred disciples were staying at Kīṭāgiri village. While staying there they made their living by planting flowering plants and fruit trees for gain, thus violating the rules of Fundamental Precepts for bhikkhus.

The Buddha hearing about these bhikkhus sent his two Chief Disciples, Sāriputta and Mahā Moggallāna, to stop them from committing further misconduct. To his two Chief Disciples the Buddha said, "Tell those bhikkhus not to destroy the faith and generosity of the lay disciples by misconduct and if anyone should disobey, drive him out of the monastery. Do not hesitate to do as I told you, for only fools dislike being given good advice and being forbidden to do evil."

Then the Buddha spoke in verse as follows:

Verse 77. The man of wisdom should admonish others; he should give advice and should prevent others from doing wrong; such a man is held dear by the good; he is disliked only by the bad.

Verse 78

VI (3) The Story of Thera Channa

While residing at the Jetavana monastery, the Buddha uttered Verse (78) of this book, with reference to Thera Channa.

Channa was the attendant who accompanied Prince Siddhattha when he renounced the world and left the palace on horseback. When the prince attained Buddhahood, Channa also became a bhikkhu. As a bhikkhu, he was very arrogant and overbearing because of his close connection to the Buddha. Channa used to say, "I came along with my Master when he left the palace for the forest. At that time, I was the only companion of my Master and there was no one else. But now, Sāriputta and Moggallāna are saying, 'we are the Chief Disciples,' and are strutting about the place."

When the Buddha sent for him and admonished him for his behaviour, he kept silent but continued to abuse and taunt the two Chief Disciples. Thus the Buddha sent for him and admonished him three times; still, he did not change. And again, the Buddha sent for Channa and said, "Channa, these two noble bhikkhus are good friends to you; you should associate with them and be on good terms with them."

Then the Buddha spoke in verse as follows:

Verse 78. One should not associate with bad friends, nor with the vile. One should associate with good friends, and with those who are noble.

In spite of repeated admonitions and advice given by the Buddha, Channa did as he pleased and continued to scold and abuse the bhikkhus. The Buddha, knowing this, said that Channa would not change during the Buddha's lifetime but after his demise (parinibbāna) Channa would surely change. On the eve of his parinibbāna, the Buddha called Thera Ānanda to his bedside and instructed him to impose the Brahma-punishment (Brahmadaṇḍa) to Channa; i.e., for the bhikkhus to simply ignore him and to have nothing to do with him.

After the parinibbāna of the Buddha, Channa, learning about the punishment from Thera Ānanda, felt a deep and bitter remorse for having done wrong and he fainted three times Then, he owned up his guilt to the bhikkhus and asked for pardon. From that moment, he changed his ways and outlook. He also obeyed their instructions in his meditation practice and soon attained arahatship.

Verse 79

VI (4) The Story of Thera Mahākappina

While residing at the Jetavana monastery, the Buddha uttered Verse (79) of this book, with reference to Thera Mahākappina.

Mahākappina was king of Kukkuṭavatī. He had a queen named Anojā; he also had one thousand ministers to help him rule the country. One day, the king accompanied by those one thousand ministers, was out in the park. There, they met some merchants from Sāvatthi. On learning about the Buddha, the Dhamma, and the Saṁgha from these merchants the king and his ministers immediately set out for Sāvatthi.

On that day, when the Buddha surveyed the world with his supernormal power, he saw in his vision, Mahākappina and his ministers coming towards Sāvatthi. He also knew that they were due for arahatship. The Buddha went to a place one hundred and twenty yojanas away from Sāvatthi to meet them. There, he waited for them under a banyan tree on the bank of the river Candabhaga. King Mahākappina and his ministers came to the place where the Buddha was waiting for them. When they saw the Buddha, with six-coloured rays radiating from his body, they approached the Buddha and paid homage to him. The Buddha then delivered a discourse to them. After listening to the discourse the king and all his ministers attained Sotāpatti Fruition, and they asked the Buddha to permit them to join the Order. The Buddha, reflecting on their past and finding that they had made offerings of yellow robes in a past existence, said to them, "Ehi bhikkhū", and they all became bhikkhus.

Meanwhile, Queen Anojā, learning about the king's departure for Savatthi, sent for the wives of the one thousand ministers, and together with them followed the king's trail. They too came to the place where the Buddha was and seeing the Buddha with a halo of six colours, paid homage to him. All this time, the Buddha by exercising his supernormal power had made the king and his ministers invisible so that their wives did not see them. The queen therefore enquired where the king and his ministers were. The Buddha told the queen and her party to wait for a while and that the king would soon come with his ministers. The Buddha then delivered another discourse; at the end of this discourse the king and his ministers attained arahatship; the queen and the wives of the ministers attained Sotāpatti Fruition. At that instant, the queen and her party saw the newly admitted bhikkhus and recognized them as their former husbands.

The ladies also asked permission from the Buddha to enter the Order of bhikkhunīs ; so they were directed to go ahead to Sāvatthi. There they entered the Order and very soon they also attained arahatship. The Buddha then returned to the Jetavana monastery accompanied by one thousand bhikkhus.

At the Jetavana monastery, Thera Mahākappina while resting during the night or during the day would often say, "Oh, what happiness !" (Aho Sukhaṁ). The bhikkhus, hearing him saying this so many times a day, told the Buddha about it. To them the Buddha replied, "My son Kappina having had the taste of the Dhamma lives happily with a serene mind ; he is saying these words of exultation repeatedly with reference to Nibbāna.

Then the Buddha spoke in verse as follows:

Verse 79. He who drinks in the Dhamma lives happily with a serene mind ; the wise man always takes delight in the Dhamma (Bodhipakkhiya Dhamma) expounded by the Noble Ones (ariyas).

Verse 80

VI (5) The Story of Sāmaṇera Paṇḍita

While residing at the Jetavana monastery, the Buddha uttered Verse (80) of this book, with reference to Sāmaṇera Paṇḍita.

Paṇḍita was a young son of a rich man of Sāvatthi. He became a sāmaṇera at the age of seven. On the eighth day after becoming a sāmaṇera, as he was following Thera Sāriputta on an alms-round, he saw some farmers channeling water into their fields and asked the thera, "Can water which has no consciousness be guided to wherever one wishes ?" The thera replied, "Yes, it can be guided to wherever one wishes." As they continued on their way, the sāmaṇera next saw some fletchers heating their arrows with fire and straightening them. Further on, he came across some carpenters cutting, sawing and planing timber to make it into things like cart-wheels. Then he pondered, "If water which is without consciousness can be guided to wherever one desires, if a crooked bamboo which is without consciousness can be straightened, and if timber which is without consciousness can be made into useful things, why should I, having consciousness, be unable to tame my mind and practise Tranquillity and Insight Meditation?"

Then and there he asked permission from the thera and returned to his own room in the monastery. There he ardently and diligently practised meditation, contemplating the body. Sakka and the devas also helped him in his meditation by keeping the monastery and its precincts very quiet and still. Before Meal time Sāmaṇera Paṇḍita attained Anāgāmi Fruition.

At that time Thera Sāriputta was bringing food to the sāmaṇera. The Buddha saw with his supernormal power that Sāmaṇera Paṇḍita had attained Anāgāmi Fruition and also that if he continued to practise meditation he would soon attain arahatship. So the Buddha decided to stop Sāriputta from entering the room, where the sāmaṇera was. The Buddha went to the door and kept Sāriputta engaged by putting some questions to him. While the conversation was taking place, the sāmaṇera attained arahatship. Thus, the sāmaṇera attained arahatship on the eighth day after becoming a novice.

In this connection, the Buddha said to the bhikkhus of the monastery, "When one is earnestly practising the Dhamma, even Sakka and the devas give protection and keep guard; I myself have kept Thera Sāriputta engaged at the door so that Sāmaṇera Paṇḍita should not be disturbed. The sāmaṇera, having seen the farmers irrigating their fields, the fletchers straightening their arrows, and carpenters making cart-wheels and other things, tames his mind and practises the dhamma; he has now become an arahat."

The Buddha then spoke in verse as follows:

Verse 80. Farmers (lit., makers of irrigation canals) channel the water; fletchers straighten the arrows; carpenters work the timber; the wise tame themselves.

Verse 81

VI (6) The Story of Thera Lakuṇḍaka Bhaddiya

While residing at the Jetavana monastery, the Buddha uttered Verse (81) of this book, with reference to Thera Bhaddiya.

Bhaddiya was one of the bhikkhus staying at the Jetavana monastery. Because of his short stature he was known as Lakuṇḍaka (the dwarf) to other bhikkhus. Lakuṇḍaka Bhaddiya was very good natured; even young bhikkhus would often tease him by pulling his nose or his ear, or by patting him on his head. Very often they would jokingly say, "Uncle, how are you? Are you happy, or are you bored with your life here as a bhikkhu?", etc. Lakuṇḍaka Bhaddiya never retaliated in anger, or abused them; in fact, even in his heart he did not get angry with them.

When told about the patience of Lakuṇḍaka Bhaddiya, the Buddha said, "An arahat never loses his temper, he has no desire to speak harshly or to think ill of others. He is like a mountain of solid rock; as a solid rock is unshaken, so also, an arahat is unperturbed by scorn or by praise."

Then the Buddha spoke in verse as follows:

Verse 81. As a mountain of rock is unshaken by wind, so also, the wise are unperturbed by blame or by praise.

Verse 82

VI (7) The Story of Kāṇamātā

While residing at the Jetavana monastery, the Buddha uttered Verse (82) of this book, with reference to the mother of Kāṇa (Kāṇamātā).

Kāṇamātā was a devoted lay disciple of the Buddha. Her daughter Kāṇa was married to a man from another village. As Kāṇa had been on a visit to her mother for some time, her husband sent a message for her to come home. Her mother told her to wait for one more day as she wanted to send along some sweetmeats with her for her husband. The next day, Kāṇamātā made some sweetmeats, but when four bhikkhus stood at her door for alms she offered some to them. The four bhikkhus told other bhikkhus about the sweetmeats from Kāṇamātā's house and they also came to stand at the door of Kāṇamātā. Kāṇamātā, as a devotee of the Buddha and his disciples, offered her sweetmeats to the bhikkhus as they came in, one after another. The result was that in the end there was none left for Kāṇa and she did not go home on that day. The same thing happened on the next two days; her mother made some sweetmeats, the bhikkhus stood at her door, she offered her sweetmeats to the bhikkhus, there was nothing left for her daughter to take home,and her daughter did not go home. On the third day, for the third time, her husband sent her a message, which was also an ultimatum stating that if she failed to come home the next day, he would take another wife. But on the next day also, Kāṇa was unable to go home because her mother offered all her sweetmeats to the bhikkhus. Kāṇa's husband then took another wife and Kāṇa became very bitter towards the bhikkhus. She used to abuse all bhikkhus so much so that the bhikkhus kept away from the house of Kāṇamātā.

The Buddha heard about Kāṇa and went to the house of Kāṇamātā; there Kāṇamātā offered him some rice gruel. After the meal, the Buddha sent for Kāṇa and asked her, "Did my bhikkhus take what was given them or what was not given them?" Kāṇa answered that the bhikkhus had taken only what was given them, and then added, "They were not in the wrong; only I was in the wrong." Thus, she owned up her fault and she also paid homage to the Buddha. The Buddha then gave a discourse. At the end of the discourse, Kāṇa attained Sotāpatti Fruition.

On the way back to the monastery, the Buddha met King Pasenadi of Kosala. On being told about Kāṇa and her bitter attitude towards the bhikkhus, King Pasenadi asked the Buddha whether he had been able to teach her the Dhamma and make her see the Truth (Dhamma). The Buddha replied, "Yes, I have taught her the Dhamma, and I have also made her rich in her next existence." Then the king promised the Buddha that he would make Kāṇa rich even in this existence. The king then sent his men with a palanquin to fetch Kāṇa. When she arrived, the king announced to his ministers, "Whoever can keep my daughter Kāṇa in comfort may take her." One of the ministers volunteered to adopt Kāṇa as his daughter, gave her all his wealth, and said to her, "You may give in charity as much as you like." Every day, Kāṇa made offerings to the bhikkhus at the four city-gates. When told about Kāṅa giving generously in charity, the Buddha said, "Bhikkhus, the mind of Kāṇa which was foggy and muddled was made clear and calm by my words."

Then the Buddha spoke in verse as follows:

Verse 82. Like a lake which is deep, clear and calm, the wise after listening to the Teaching (Dhamma) become serene.

Verse 83

VI (8) The Story of Five Hundred Bhikkhus

While residing at the Jetavana monastery, the Buddha uttered Verse (83) of this book, with reference to five hundred bhikkhus.

At the request of a brahmin from Verañjā, the Buddha was, on one occasion, staying at Verañjā with five hundred bhikkhus. While they were at Verañjā, the brahmin failed to look after them. The people of Varañjā, who were then facing a famine, could offer very little to the bhikkhus when they went on their rounds for alms-food. In spite of all these hardships, the bhikkhus were not disheartened; they were quite contented with the small amount of shrivelled grain which the horse-traders offered them daily. At the end of the vassa, after informing the brahmin from Verañjā, the Buddha returned to the Jetavana monastery, accompanied by the five hundred bhikkhus. The people of Sāvatthi welcomed them back with choice food of all kinds.

A group of people living with the bhikkhus, eating whatever was left over by the bhikkhus, ate greedily like true gluttons and went to sleep after their meals. On waking up, they were shouting, singing and dancing, thus making themselves a thorough nuisance. When the Buddha came in the evening to the congregation of bhikkhus, they reported to him about the behaviour of those unruly persons, and said, "These people living on the left-overs were quite decent and well-behaved when all of us were facing hardship and famine in Verañjā. Now that they have enough good food they are going about shouting, singing and dancing, and thus make themselves a thorough nuisance. The bhikkhus, however, behave themselves here just as they were in Verañjā".

To them the Buddha replied, "It is in the nature of the foolish to be full of sorrow and feel depressed when things go wrong, and to be full of gladness and feel elated when things go well. The wise, however, can withstand the ups and downs of life."

Then the Buddha spoke in verse as follows:

Verse 83. Indeed, the virtuous give up all (i.e., attachment to the five khandhas, etc.); the virtuous (lit., the tranquil) do not talk with sensual desire; when faced with joy or sorrow, the wise do not show elation or depression.

Verse 84

VI (9) The Story of Thera Dhammika

While residing at the Jetavana monastery, the Buddha uttered Verse (84) of this book, with reference to Thera Dhammika.

Dhammika lived in Sāvatthi with his wife. One day, he told his pregnant wife that he wished to become a bhikkhu; his wife pleaded with him to wait until after the birth of their child. When the child was born, he again requested his wife to let him go; again, she pleaded with him to wait until the child could walk. Then Dhammika thought to himself, "It will be useless for me to ask my wife for her approval to join the Order; I shall work for my own liberation." Having made a firm decision, he left his house to become a bhikkhu. He took a subject of meditation from the Buddha and practised meditation ardently and diligently and soon became an arahat.

Some years later, he visited his house in order to teach the Dhamma to his son and his wife. His son entered the Order and he too attained arahatship. The wife then thought, "Now that both my husband and my son have left the house, I'd better leave it, too." With this thought she left the house and became a bhikkhunī; eventually, she too attained arahatship.

At he congregation of the bhikkhus, the Buddha was told how Dhammika became a bhikkhu and attained arahatship, and how through him his son and his wife also attained arahatship. To them the Buddha said, "Bhikkhus, a wise man does not wish for wealth and prosperity by doing evil, whether it is for his own sake or for the sake of others. He only works for his own liberation from the round of rebirths (saṁsāra) by comprehending the Dhamma and living according to the Dhamma."

Then the Buddha spoke in verse as follows:

Verse 84. For his own sake or for the sake of others, he does no evil; nor does he wish for sons and daughters or for wealth or for a kingdom by doing evil; nor does he wish for success by unfair means; such a one is indeed virtuous, wise and just.

Verses 85 and 86

VI (10) The Story of Dhamma Listeners

While residing at the Jetavana monastery, the Buddha uttered Verses (85) and (86) of this book, with reference to a congregation of people who had come to listen to a religious discourse in Sāvatthi.

On one occasion, a group of people from Sāvatthi made special offerings to the bhikkhus collectively and they arranged for some bhikkhus to deliver discourses throughout the night, in their locality. Many in the audience could not sit up the whole night and they returned to their homes early; some sat through the night, but most of the time they were drowsy and half-asleep. There were only a few who listened attentively to the discourses.

At dawn, when the bhikkhus told the Buddha about what happened the previous night, he replied, "Most people are attached to this world; only a very few reach the other shore (Nibbāna)."

Then the Buddha spoke in verse as follows:

Verse 85. Few among men reach the other shore (Nibbāna); all the others only run up and down on this shore.

Verse 86. But those who practise according to the well-expounded Dhamma will reach the other shore (Nibbāna), having passed the realm of Death (i.e., saṁsāra), very difficult as it is to cross.

VI (11) Verses 87, 88 and 89

The Story of Five Hundred Visiting Bhikkhus

While residing at the Jetavana monastery, the Buddha uttered Verses (87), (88) and (89) of this book, with reference to five hundred visiting bhikkhus.

Five hundred bhikkhus who had spent the vassa in Kosala came to pay homage to the Buddha at the Jetavana monastery, at the end of the vassa.

The Buddha uttered the following three verses to suit their various temperaments.

Verse 87, 88. The man of wisdom, leaving the home of craving and having Nibbāna as his goal, should give up dark, evil ways and cultivate pure, good ones. He should seek great delight in solitude, detachment and Nibbāna, which an ordinary man finds so difficult to enjoy. He should also give up sensual pleasures, and clinging to nothing, should cleanse himself of all impurities of the mind.

Verse 89. Those, with mind well-developed in the seven Factors of Enlightenment (bojjhaṅgā), having rid themselves of all craving, rejoice in their abandonment of attachment. Such men, with all moral intoxicants eradicated, and powerful (with the light of Arahatta Maggañāṇa), have realized Nibbāna in this world (i.e., with khandha aggregates remaining).

End of Chapter Six : The Wise.

Chapter VII

The Arahat (Arahantavagga)

Verse 90

VII (1) The Story of the Question Asked by Jīvaka

While residing at the mango-grove monastery of Jīvaka, the Buddha uttered Verse (90) of this book, with reference to the question raised by Jīvaka to the Buddha.

Devadatta, on one occasion, tried to kill the Buddha by pushing a big rock from the peak of Gijjhakūṭa mountain (Vulture's Peak). The rock struck a ledge on the side of the mountain and a splinter struck the big toe of the Buddha. The Buddha was taken to the mango-grove monastery of Jīvaka. There, Jīvaka, the renowned physician, attended on the Buddha; he put some medicine on the toe of the Buddha and bandaged it. Jīvaka then left to see another patient in town, but promised to return and remove the bandage in the evening. When Jīvaka returned that night, the city-gates were already closed and he could not come to see the Buddha that night. He was very upset because if the bandage was not removed in time, the whole body would become very hot and the Buddha would be very ill.

Just about this time, the Buddha asked Thera Ānanda to remove the bandage from his big toe and found that the wound was completely healed. Jīvaka came to the monastery early next morning and asked the Buddha whether he felt great pain and distress the previous night. The Buddha replied, "Jīvaka! Ever since I attained Buddhahood there has been no pain and distress for me."

Then the Buddha spoke in verse as follows:

Verse 90. For him (an arahat) whose journey is ended, who is free from sorrow and from all (e.g. khandha aggregates), who has destroyed all fetters, there is no more distress.

At the end of the discourse many attained Sotāpatti Fruition.

Verse 91

VII (2) The Story of Thera Mahākassapa

While residing at the Veḷuvana monastery, the Buddha uttered Verse (91) of this book, with reference to Thera Mahākassapa.

The Buddha once spent the vassa at Rājagaha with a number of bhikkhus. About two weeks before the end of the vassa, the Buddha informed the bhikkhus that they would soon be leaving Rājagaha and told them to prepare for departure. Some bhikkhus stitched and dyed new robes, some washed the old robes. When some bhikkhus saw Mahākassapa washing his robes, they speculated, "There are so many people inside and outside Rājagaha who love and respect Thera Mahākassapa and are constantly looking to all his needs; is it possible that the thera would leave his lay devotees here and follow the Buddha elsewhere?"

At the end of fifteen days, on the eve of his departure, the Buddha thought that there might be some occasions like alms-food offering ceremonies, initiation of novices, funerals, etc., and so it would not be proper for all the bhikkhus to leave. So he decided that some bhikkhus should remain at the Veḷuvana monastery and that the most suitable person would be Thera Mahākassapa. Consequently, Thera Mahākassapa remained in Rājagaha with some junior bhikkhus.

Then the other bhikkhus said scornfully, "Mahākassapa has not accompanied the Buddha, just as we have predicted!" The Buddha heard their remark and said to them, "Bhikkhus! Do you wish to say that my son Kassapa is attached to his lay disciples of Rājagaha and to the things they offer him? You are very much mistaken. My son Kassapa remains here under my instruction; he is not attached to anything here."

Then the Buddha spoke in verse as follows:

Verse 91. The mindful strive diligently (in the Tranquillity and Insight Development Practice); they take no delight in the home (i.e., in the life of sensual pleasures); like swans (haṁsa) that forsake the muddy pool, they abandon all homelife (i.e., all cravings).

Verse 92

VII (3) The Story of Thera Belaṭṭhasīsa

While residing at the Jetavana monastery, the Buddha uttered Verse (92) of this book, with reference to Thera Belaṭṭhasīsa.

Thera Belaṭṭhasīsa, after going on an alms-round in the village, stopped on the way and took his food there. After the meal, he continued his round of alms for more food. When he had collected enough food he returned to the monastery, dried up the rice and hoarded it. Thus, there was no need for him to go on an alms-round every day; he then remained in jhāna concentration for two or three days. Arising from jhāna concentration he ate the dried rice he had stored up, after soaking it in water. Other bhikkhus thought ill of the thera on this account, and reported to the Buddha about his hoarding of rice. Since then, the hoarding of food by the bhikkhus has been prohibited.

As for Thera Belaṭṭhasīsa, since he stored up rice before the ruling on hoarding was made and because he did it not out of greed for food, but only to save time for meditation practice, the Buddha declared that the thera was quite innocent and that he was not to be blamed.

The Buddha then spoke in verse as follows:

Verse 92. Arahats do not hoard (anything); when taking food they reflect well over it (i,e., in accordance with the three pariññās).[1] They have as their object liberation from existence, that is, Nibbāna which is Void and Signless. Their destination, like the course of birds in the air, cannot be traced.

Verse 93

VII (4) The Story of Thera Anuruddha

While residing at the Jetavana monastery, the Buddha uttered Verse (93) of this book, with reference to Thera Anuruddha.

---

1. **Taking food in accordance with the three pariññās:** See footnote on pariññātabhojanā, verse 92 in the first part of this book.

Thera Anuruddha was one day looking for some discarded pieces of cloth in a rubbish heap to make into a robe as his old robe was getting soiled and torn. Jālinī, his wife of a previous existence, who was now in a deva world, saw him. Knowing that he was looking for some cloth, she took three pieces of good deva material and put them in the rubbish heap, making them barely visible. The thera found the pieces of cloth and took them to the monastery. While he was making the robe, the Buddha arrived with his Chief Disciples and senior disciples and they also helped stitch the robe.

Meanwhile, Jālinī, assuming the form of a young lady, came to the village and learnt about the arrival of the Buddha and his disciples and also how they were helping Thera Anuruddha. She urged the villagers to send good delicious food to the monastery and consequently there was more than enough for all. Other bhikkhus, seeing so much surplus, put the blame on the thera and said, "Thera Anuruddha should have asked his relatives and lay disciples to send just enough food; may be, he just wanted to show off that he had so many devotees." To those bhikkhus, the Buddha said, "Bhikkhus, do not think my son Anuruddha has asked his relatives and lay disciples to send rice gruel and other foods. My son the thera did not ask for anything; arahats do not talk about such things like food and clothing. The excessive amount of food brought to the monastery this morning was due to the promptings of a celestial being and not of a man."

Then the Buddha spoke in verse as follows:

Verse 93. The arahat is free from moral intoxicants (āsavas); he is not attached to food. He has as his object liberation from existence, i. e., Nibbāna which is Void and Signless. His path, like that of birds in the air, cannot be traced.

Verse 94

VII (5) The Story of Thera Mahākaccāyana

While residing at the Pubbārāma monastery, the Buddha uttered Verse (94) of this book, with reference to Thera Mahākaccāyana.

On a full moon day, which was also the end of the vassa, Sakka with a large company of devas came to pay homage to the Buddha, who was then in residence at Pubbārāma, the monastery built by Visākhā. At that time, the Buddha was being attended upon by the Chief Disciples and all the senior bhikkhus. Thera Mahākaccāyana, who spent the vassa in Avanti, had not yet arrived, and a seat was kept vacant for him. Sakka paid homage to the Buddha with flowers, incense and perfumes. On seeing a vacant seat he declared how he wished that Thera Mahākaccāyana would come so that he could pay obeisance to him also. At that instant Mahākaccāyana arrived; Sakka was very pleased and eagerly paid obeisance to him with flowers, incense and perfumes.

The bhikkhus were awed by Sakka paying obeisance to Mahākaccāyana, but some bhikkhus thought that Sakka was being partial to Mahākaccāyana. To them, the Buddha said, "One who is restrained in his senses is loved by both men and devas."

The Buddha then spoke in verse as follows:

Verse 94. The arahat whose sense-faculties are calm like horses well-tamed by the charioteer, who is free from pride and moral intoxicants— such an arahat is held dear even by the devas.

Verse 95

VII (6) The Story of Thera Sāriputta

While residing at the Jetavana monastery, the Buddha uttered Verse (95) of this book, with reference to the Chief Disciple Sāriputta and a young bhikkhu.

It was the end of the vassa; and Thera Sāriputta was about to set out on a journey with some followers. A young bhikkhu, who bore some grudge against the thera, approached the Buddha and falsely reported that Thera Sāriputta had abused him and beaten him. The Buddha therefore sent for the thera and questioned him, and Thera Sāriputta replied as follows: "Venerable Sir! How could a bhikkhu, who steadfastly keeps his mind on the body, set out on a journey without apologizing, after doing wrong to a fellow bhikkhu? I am like the earth, which feels no pleasure when flowers are cast on it, nor resentment when rubbish and excreta are piled upon it. I am also like the door-mat, the beggar, the bull with broken horns; I also feel abhorrence for the impurity of the body and am no longer attached to it."

When Thera Sāriputta spoke thus, the young bhikkhu felt very much distressed and wept bitterly, and admitted that he had lied about the Chief Disciple Sāriputta. Then the Buddha advised Thera Sāriputta to accept the apology of the young bhikkhu, lest a heavy punishment should fall on him and get his head crushed. The young bhikkhu then admitted that he had done wrong and respectfully asked for pardon. Thera Sāriputta pardoned the young bhikkhu and also asked to be forgiven if he also had done any wrong.

All those present talked in praise of Thera Sāriputta, and the Buddha said, "Bhikkhus, a bhikkhu like Sāriputta has no anger or ill will in him. Like the earth and the door-post, he is patient, tolerant, and firm; like the lake free from mud, he is serene and pure.

Then the Buddha spoke in verse as follows:

Verse 95. Like the earth, the arahat is patient and is not provoked to respond in anger; like the door-post he is firm; he is unperturbed by the ups and downs of life; he is serene and pure like a lake free from mud. For such an arahat there will be no more rebirth.

Verse 96

VII (7) The Story of a Sāmaṇera from Kosambī

While residing at the Jetavana monastery, the Buddha uttered Verse (96) of this book, with reference to a sāmaṇera, a pupil of Thera Tissa from Kosambī.

Once, a seven year old boy was made a sāmaṇera at the request of his father. Before his head was shaved the boy was given a subject of meditation. While he was being shaved, the boy had his mind fixed steadfastly on the object of meditation; as a result, he attained arahatship as soon as they finished shaving his head.

After some time, Thera Tissa, accompanied by the sāmaṇera, set out for Sāvatthi to pay homage to the Buddha. On the way, they spent one night in a village monastery. The thera fell asleep, but the young sāmaṇera sat up the whole night beside the bed of the old thera. Early in the morning, the old thera thought it was time to wake up the young sāmaṇera. So he roused up the sāmaṇera with a palm-leaf fan, and accidentally hit the eye of the sāmaṇera with the handle of the fan and damaged the eye. The sāmaṇera covered that eye with one hand and went about doing his duties of getting water for the thera to wash his face and clean his mouth, sweeping the floor of the monastery, etc. When the young sāmaṇera offered water with one hand to the thera, the thera chided him, and said that he should offer things with both hands. Only then, did the thera learn how the sāmaṇera lost his eye. At that instant, he realized that he had wronged a truly noble person. Feeling very sorry and humiliated, he made an apology to the sāmaṇera. But the sāmaṇera said that it was not the fault of the thera, nor his own fault, but that it was only the result of kamma, and so the thera was not to feel sad about it. But the thera could not get over the unfortunate incident.

Then they continued their journey to Sāvatthi and arrived at the Jetavana monastery where the Buddha was in residence. The thera then told the Buddha that the young sāmaṇera who came along with him was the most noble person he had ever met, and related all that had happened on their way. The Buddha listened to him, and replied, "My son, an arahat does not get angry with anyone; he is restrained in his senses and is perfectly calm and serene."

Then the Buddha spoke in verse as follows:

Verse 96 An arahat is calm in his mind, calm in his speech, and also in his deed; truly knowing the Dhamma, such an arahat is free from moral defilements and is unperturbed by the ups and downs of life.

Verse 97

VII (8) The Story of Thera Sāriputta

While residing at the Jetavana monastery, the Buddha uttered Verse (97) of this book, with reference to Thera Sāriputta.

Thirty bhikkhus from a village had arrived at the Jetavana monastery to pay homage to the Buddha. The Buddha knew that the time was ripe for those bhikkhus to attain arahatship. So, he sent for Sāriputta, and in the presence of those bhikkhus, he asked, "My son Sāriputta, do you accept the fact that by meditating on the senses one could realize Nibbāna?" Sāriputta answered, "Venerable Sir, in the matter of the realization of Nibbāna by meditating on the senses, it is not the I accept it because I have faith in you; it is only those who have not personally realized it that accept the fact from others." Sāriputta's answer was not properly understood by the bhikkhus; they thought, "Sāriputta has not given up wrong views yet; even now, he has no faith in the Buddha."

Then the Buddha explained to them the true meaning of Sāriputta's answer. "Bhikkhus, Sāriputta's answer is simply this; he accepts the fact that Nibbāna is realized by means of meditation on the senses, but his acceptance is due to his own personal realization and not merely because I have said it or somebody else has said it. Sāriputta has faith in me; he also has faith in the consequences of good and bad deeds."

Then the Buddha spoke in verse as follows:

Verse 97. He who is not credulous, who has realized the Unconditioned (Nibbāna), who has cut off the links of the round of rebirths, who has destroyed all consequences of good and bad deeds, who has discarded all craving, is indeed the noblest of all men (i.e., an arahat).

At the end of the discourse, all those bhikkhus attained arahatship.

Verse 98

VII (9) The Story of Thera Revata

While residing at the Jetavana monastery, the Buddha uttered Verse (98) of this book, with reference to Thera Revata of the Acacia (khadira) Forest.

Revata was the youngest brother of the Chief Disciple Sāriputta. He was the only one of the brothers and sisters of Sāriputta who had not left home for the homeless life. His parents were very anxious to get him married. Revata was only seven years old when his parents arranged a marriage for him to a young girl. At the wedding reception, he met an old lady who was one hundred and twenty years old, and he realized that all beings are subject to ageing and decay. So, he ran away from the house and went straight to a monastery, where there were thirty bhikkhus. Those bhikkhus had been requested earlier by Thera Sāriputta to make his brother a sāmaṇera if he should come to them. Accordingly, he was made a sāmaṇera and Thera Sāriputta was informed about it.

Sāmaṇera Revata took a subject of meditation from those bhikkhus and left for an acacia forest, thirty yojanas away from the monastery. At the end of the vassa, the sāmaṇera attained arahatship. Thera Sāriputta then asked permission from the Buddha to visit his brother, but the Buddha replied that he himself would go there. So the Buddha accompanied by Thera Sāriputta, Thera Sīvali and five hundred other bhikkhus set out to visit Sāmaṇera Revata.

The journey was long, the road was rough and the area was uninhabited by people; but the devas looked to all the needs of the Buddha and the bhikkhus on the way. At an interval of every yojana, a monastery and food were provided, and they travelled at the rate of a yojana a day. Revata, learning about the visit of the Buddha, also made arrangements to welcome him. By supernormal power he created a special monastery for the Buddha and five hundred monasteries for the other bhikkhus, and made them comfortable throughout their stay there.

On their return journey, they travelled at the same rate as before, and came to the Pubbārāma monastery on the eastern end of Sāvatthi at the end of the month. From there, they went to the house of Visākhā, who offered them alms-food. After the meal, Visākhā asked the Buddha if the place of Revata in the acacia forest was pleasant.

And the Buddha answered in verse as follows:

Verse 98. In a village or in a forest, in a valley or on a hill, wherever arahats dwell, that place is delightful.

Verse 99

VII (10) The Story of a Woman

While residing at the Jetavana monastery, the Buddha uttered Verse (99) of this book, with reference to a woman of doubtful character.

A bhikkhu, after taking a subject of meditation from the Buddha, was practising meditation in an old garden. A woman of doubtful character came into the garden and, seeing the bhikkhu, tried to attract his attention and seduce him. The thera got frightened; at the same time, his whole body was diffused with some kind of delightful satisfaction. The Buddha saw him from his monastery, and with his supernormal power, sent rays of light to him, and the bhikkhu received this message, which said, "My son, where worldlings seek sensual pleasures is not the place for bhikkhus; bhikkhus should take delight in forests where worldlings find no pleasure."

Then the Buddha spoke in verse as follows:

Verse 99. Forests are delightful, but the worldlings find no delight in them; only those who are free from passion will find delight in them, for they do not seek sensual pleasures.

End of Chapter Seven: The Arahat.

Chapter VIII

Verse 100

The Thousand (Sahassavagga)

VIII (1) The Story of Tambadāṭhika

While residing at the Jetavana monastery, the Buddha uttered Verse (100) of this book, with reference to Tambadāṭhika, the executioner of thieves.

Tambadāṭhika served the king as an executioner of thieves for fifty-five years; he had just retired from that post. One day, after preparing rice gruel at his house, he went to the river for a bath; he had intended to take the specially prepared rice gruel on his return. As he was about to take the rice gruel, Thera Sāriputta, who had just arisen from sustained absorption in Concentration (jhāna samāpatti), stood at his door for alms-food. Seeing the thera, Tambadāṭhika thought to himself, "Throughout my life, I have been executing thieves; now I should offer this food to the thera." So, he invited Thera Sāriputta to come in and respectfully offered the rice gruel.

After the meal, the thera taught him the Dhamma, but Tambadāṭhika could not pay attention, because he was so agitated as he recollected his past life as an executioner. When the thera knew this, he decided to ask Tambadāṭhika tactfully whether he killed the thieves because he wished to kill them or because he was ordered to do so. Tambadāṭhika answered that he was ordered to kill them by the king and that he had no wish to kill. Then the thera asked, "If that is so, would you be guilty or not?" Tambadāṭhika then concluded that, as he was not responsible for the evil deeds, he was not guilty. He, therefore, calmed down, and requested the thera to continue his exposition. As he listened to the Dhamma with proper attention, he came very close to attaining Sotāpatti Magga and reached as far as anuloma ñāṇa[1]. After the discourse, Tambadāṭhika accompanied Thera Sāriputta for some distance and then returned home. On his way home a cow (actually a demon in the guise of a cow) gored him to death.

---

1. **anuloma ñāṇa:** vipassanā insight which causes the nāmarūpa process of the yogī to become fully adapted for Magga Insight.

When the Buddha came to the congregation of the bhikkhus in the evening, they informed him about the death of Tambadāṭhika. When asked where Tambadāṭhika was reborn, the Buddha told them that although Tambadāṭhika had committed evil deeds throughout his life, because he comprehended the Dhamma after hearing it from Thera Sāriputta and had already attained anuloma ñāṇa before he died, he was reborn in the Tusita deva world. The bhikkhus wondered how such an evil-doer could have such great benefit after listening to the Dhamma just once. To them the Buddha said that the length of a discourse is of no consequence, for one single word of sense can produce much benefit.

Then the Buddha spoke in verse as follows:

Verse 100. Better than a thousand words that are senseless and unconnected with the realization of Nibbāna, is a single word of sense, if on hearing it one is calmed.

Verse 101

VIII (2) The Story of Bāhiyadārucīriya

While residing at the Jetavana monastery, the Buddha uttered Verse (101) of this book, with reference to Bāhiyadārucīriya.

A group of merchants went out to sea in a boat; their boat was wrecked at sea and all, except one, died. The only survivor got hold of a plank and eventually came to land at the port of Suppāraka. As he was naked, he tied the plank to his body, got hold of a bowl, and sat in a place where people could see him. Passers-by gave him rice and gruel; some took him for an arahat and talked in praise of him. Some brought clothes for him to wear but he refused, fearing that by wearing clothes, people would give less to him. Besides, because some said that he was an arahat, he mistakenly came to think that he really was one. Thus, because he was a man of wrong views who was wearing a piece of wood as his clothing, he came to be known as Bāhiyadārucīriya.

At about this time, Mahābrahmā, who had been his friend in one of his previous existences, saw him going astray and felt that it was his duty to put Bāhiya on the right path. So, Mahābrahmā came to him in the night and said to him, "Bāhiya, you are not an arahat yet, and what is more, you do not have the qualities that make one an arahat." Bāhiya looked up at Mahābrahmā and said, "Yes, I must admit that I am not an arahat, as you have said. I now realize that I have done a great wrong. But is there anyone else in this world now who is an arahat?" Mahābrahmā then told him that there lived in Sāvatthi Gotama Buddha, an arahat, who was perfectly self-enlightened.

Bāhiya, realizing the enormity of his guilt, felt very much distressed and ran all the way to Sāvatthi. Mahābrahmā helped him by his supernormal power, so that the whole stretch of one hundred and twenty yojanas was covered in one night. Bāhiya found the Buddha going on an alms-round with other bhikkhus and respectfully followed him. He pleaded with the Buddha to teach him the Dhamma, but the Buddha replied that since they were on an alms-round it was not yet time for a religious discourse. And again, Bāhiya pleaded, "Venerable Sir, one cannot know the danger to your life or to my life, so please talk to me about the Dhamma. The Buddha knew that Bāhiya had made the journey of one hundred and twenty yojanas in one night, and also that he was overwhelmed with joy at seeing the Buddha. That was why the Buddha did not want to talk about the Dhamma immediately but wanted him to calm down to enable him to take in the Dhamma properly. Still, Bāhiya persistently pleaded. So, while standing on the road, the Buddha said to Bāhiya, "Bāhiya, when you see an object, be conscious of just the visible object; when you hear a sound, be conscious of just the sound; when you smell or taste or touch something, be conscious of just the smell, the taste or the touch; and when you think of anything, be conscious of just the mind--object."

After hearing the above discourse, Bāhiya attained arahatship and he asked permission from the Buddha to join the Order. The Buddha told him to get the robes, the bowl and other requisites of a bhikkhu. On his way to get them, he was gored to death by a cow which was, in fact, an ogress in the likeness of a cow. When the Buddha and the other bhikkhus came out after having had their meal, they found Bāhiya lying dead on a rubbish heap. As instructed by the Buddha, the bhikkhus cremated the body of Bāhiya and had his bones enshrined in a stupa.

Back at the Jetavana monastery, the Buddha told the bhikkhus that Bāhiya had realized Nibbāna. He also told them that as far as speed was concerned in attaining Magga Insight (abhiññā) Bāhiya was the fastest, the best (etadaggaṁ). The bhikkhus were puzzled by the statement made by the Buddha and they asked him why and when Bāhiya became an arahat. To this, the Buddha replied, "Bāhiya attained arahatship while he listened to my instructions given to him on the road when we were on the alms-round." The bhikkhus wondered how one could attain arahatship after listening to just a few sentences of the Dhamma. So, the Buddha told them that the number of words or the length of a speech did not matter if it was beneficial to someone.

Then the Buddha spoke in verse as follows:

Verse 101. Better than a thousand verses that are senseless and unconnected with the realization of Nibbāna, is a single verse, if on hearing it one is calmed.

Verses 102 and 103

VIII (3) The Story of Therī kuṇḍalakesī

While residing at the Jetavana monastery, the Buddha uttered Verses (102) and (103) of this book, with reference to Therī kuṇḍalakesī.

Kuṇḍalakesī was the daughter of a rich man from Rājagaha. She had led a very secluded life; but one day, she happened to see a thief being led out to be killed and she immediately fell in love with him. Her parents had to pay for the freedom of the thief, and they married her off to him. Although she loved her husband very dearly, her husband being a thief, was only attracted to her property and her jewels. One day, he coaxed her to put on all her jewellery and led her to a mountain saying that he wanted to make some offerings to the guardian spirit of the mountain because that guardian spirit had saved his life when he was about to be killed. Kuṇḍalakesī went along with her husband, but when they reached their destination, the thief revealed that he intended to kill her and take her jewels. She pleaded with him to take her jewels, but to spare her life, but it was of no avail. She then realized that if she did not get rid of her husband, there would be no way of escape for her. She felt she must be cautious and crafty. So she said to her husband that as they would be together only for a few moments more, she wanted to pay respect to him for the last time. So saying, and going round the man respectfully, she pushed him off the crag, taking him unawares.

After this, she had no desire to return home. She left all her jewellery hanging on a tree, and went on her way, without any idea where she was going. She happened to come to a place of some paribbājikās (female wandering ascetics) and she herself became a paribbājikā. The paribbājikās taught her all their one thousand problems in sophistry; being intelligent she mastered all of them within a short time. Then her teachers told her to go out into the world and if she should find somebody who could answer all her questions, to become a pupil to him. Kuṇḍalakesī went throughout the length and breadth of Jambudīpa, openly challenging everyone else to compete with her. Accordingly, she came to be known as "Jambukaparibbājikā."

On one occasion, she came to Sāvatthi. Before entering the city for alms-food she made a mound of sand and stuck a branch of eugenia on it, her usual sign of invitation to all others to take up her challenge. Thera Sāriputta took up her challenge. Kuṇḍalakesī asked him a thousand questions and Thera Sāriputta answered them all. When his turn came, he asked her just this, "What is the one?(ekaṁ nāma kiṁ)." Kuṇḍalakesī could not answer, so she asked Thera Sāriputta to teach her the answer to the question. Thera Sāriputta replied that she should first become a bhikkhunī; so she became a bhikkhunī, by the name of Therī Kuṇḍalakesī. Within a few days, she became an arahat.

Soon after this, the bhikkhus asked the Buddha, "Could it be possible for Bhikkhunī Kuṇḍalakesī to become an arahat after listening to the Dhamma only a little?" They also added that this lady had fought and won a victory over her husband, who was a thief, before she became a paribbājikā.

Then the Buddha spoke in verse as follows:

Verse 102. Better than the recitation of a hundred verses that are senseless and unconnected with the realization of Nibbāna, is the recitation of a single verse of the Teaching (Dhamma), if on hearing it one is calmed.

Verse 103. A man may conquer a million men in battle, but one who conquers himself is, indeed, the greatest of conquerors.

Verses 104 and 105

VIII (4) The Story of the Brahmin Anatthapucchaka

While residing at the Jetavana monastery, the Buddha uttered Verses (104) and (105) of this book, with reference to Anatthapucchaka, a brahmin.

On one occasion, a brahmin by the name of Anatthapucchaka came to the Buddha and said to him, "Venerable Sir, I think that you know only the practices that are beneficial and not the practices that are unbeneficial." To him, the Buddha answered that he also knew the practices which were unbeneficial and harmful. Then the Buddha enumerated six practices which cause dissipation of wealth; they are: (1) sleeping until the sun has risen, (2) habitual idleness, (3) cruelty, (4) indulgence in intoxicants which causes drunkenness and negligence, (5) sauntering alone in streets at unearthly hours, and (6) sexual misconduct.

Further, the Buddha asked the brahmin how he earned his living, and the brahmin replied that he earned his living by playing dice, i.e., by gambling. Next, the Buddha asked him whether he won or lost. When the brahmin answered that he sometimes lost and sometimes won, the Buddha said to him, "To win in a game of dice is nothing compared to a victory over moral defilements."

Then the Buddha spoke in verse as follows:

Verses 104, 105. It is better indeed, to conquer oneself than to conquer others. Neither a deva, nor a gandhabba, nor Māra together with Brahmā can turn into defeat the victory of the man who controls himself.

Verse 106

VIII (5) The Story of Thera Sāriputta's Uncle

While residing at the Veḷuvana monastery, the Buddha uttered Verse (106) of this book, with reference to a brahmin, who was the maternal uncle of Thera Sāriputta.

On one occasion, Thera Sāriputta asked his uncle the brahmin whether he was doing any meritorious deeds. The brahmin answered that he was making offerings to the value of one thousand kahāpaṇas every month to the Nigaṇṭha ascetics, hoping to get to the Brahmā world in his next existence. Thera Sāriputta then explained to him that his teachers had given him false hopes and that they themselves did not know the way to the Brahmā world. So saying, he took his uncle the brahmin to the Buddha, and requested the Buddha to expound the Dhamma, which would surely take one to the Brahmā world.

The Buddha said to the brahmin, "Brahmin, an offering of a spoonful of alms-food to a bhikkhu would be much better than your present offering of one thousand kahāpaṇas to your teachers."

Then the Buddha spoke in verse as follows:

Verse 106. Month after month for a hundred years, one may make offerings (to ordinary people) to the value of a thousand kahāpaṇas; yet if, only for a moment one pays homage to a bhikkhu who has practised Insight Development, this homage is, indeed, better than a hundred years of making offerings (to ordinary people).

At the end of the discourse, the brahmin, who was the maternal uncle of Thera Sāriputta, attained Sotāpatti Fruition.

Verse 107

VIII (6) The Story of Thera Sāriputta's Nephew

While residing at the Veḷuvana monastery, the Buddha uttered Verse (107) of this book, with reference to Thera Sāriputta's nephew.

On one occasion, Thera Sāriputta asked his nephew, a brahmin, whether he was doing any meritorious deeds. His nephew answered that he had been sacrificing a goat in fire-worship every month, hoping to get to the Brahmā world in his next existence. Thera Sāriputta then explained to him that his teachers had given him false hopes and that they themselves did not know the way to the Brahmā world.

Then he took his nephew the young brahmin to the Buddha. There, the Buddha taught him the Dhamma that would lead one to the Brahmā world and said to the brahmin, "Young brahmin, paying homage to the bhikkhus for a moment would be far better than making sacrifices in fire-worship for a hundred years."

Then the Buddha spoke in verse as follows:

Verse 107. For a hundred years, a man may tend the sacred fire in the forest: yet if, only for a moment, one pays homage to a bhikkhu who has practised Insight Development, this homage is, indeed, better than a hundred years of making sacrifices (in fire--worship).

At the end of the discourse, the brahmin, who was Thera Sāriputta's nephew, attained Sotāpatti Fruition.

Verse 108

VIII (7) The Story of Thera Sāriputta's Friend

While residing at the Veḷuvana monastery, the Buddha uttered Verse (108) of this book, with reference to a friend of Thera Sāriputta.

On one occasion Thera Sāriputta asked his friend, a brahmin, whether he was doing any meritorious deeds and he replied that he had been making sacrificial offerings on a big scale, hoping to get to the Brahmā world in his next existence. Thera Sāriputta told him that his teachers had given him false hopes and that they themselves did not know the way to the Brahmā world. Then he took his friend to the Buddha, who showed him the way to the Brahmā world. To the friend of Thera Sāriputta, the Buddha said, "Brahmin, worshipping the Noble Ones (Ariyas) only for a moment is better than making sacrificial offerings, great and small, throughout the year."

Then the Buddha spoke in verse as follows:

Verse 108. In this world, one may make sacrificial offerings, great and small, all the year round, in order to gain merit; all these offerings are not worth a quarter of the merit gained by worshipping the Noble Ones (Ariyas) who walk the right path.

At the end of the discourse the brahmin attained Sotāpatti Fruition.

Verse 109

VIII (8) The Story of Āyuvaḍḍhanakumāra

While residing in a village monastery near Dīghalaṅghika, the Buddha uttered Verse (109) of this book, with reference to Āyuvaḍḍhanakumāra.

Once, there were two hermits who lived together practising religious austerities (tapacaraṇaṁ) for forty-eight years. Later, one of the two left the hermit life and got married. After a son was born, the family visited the old hermit and paid obeisance to him. To the parents the hermit said, "May you live long," but he said nothing to the child. The parents were puzzled and asked the hermit the reason for his silence. The hermit told them that the child would live only seven more days and that he did not know how to prevent his death, but Gotama Buddha might know how to do it.

So the parents took the child to the Buddha; when they paid obeisance to the Buddha, he also said, "May you live long" to the parents only and not to the child. The Buddha also predicted the impending death of the child. To prevent his death, the parents were told to build a pavilion at the entrance to the house, and put the child on a couch in the pavilion. Then some bhikkhus were sent there to recite the parittas[1] for seven days. On the seventh day the Buddha himself came to that pavilion; the devas from all over the universe also came. At that time the ogre

1. parittas: religious stanzas that are usually recited for protection against harmful influences.

Avaruddhaka was at the entrance, waiting for a chance to take the child away. But as more powerful devas arrived the ogre had to step back and make room for them so that he had to stay at a place two yojanas away from the child. That whole night, recitation of parittas continued, thus protecting the child. The next day, the child was taken up from the couch and made to pay obeisance to the Buddha. This time, the Buddha said, "May you live long" to the child. When asked how long the child would live, the Buddha replied that he would live up to one hundred and twenty years. So the child was named Āyuvaḍḍhana.

When the child grew up, he went about the country with a company of five hundred fellow devotees. One day, they came to the Jetavana monastery, and the bhikkhus, recognizing him, asked the Buddha, "For beings is there any means of gaining longevity?" To this question the Buddha answered, "By respecting and honouring the elders and those who are wise and virtuous, one would gain not only longevity, but also beauty, happiness and strength."

Then the Buddha spoke in verse as follows:

Verse 109. For one who always respects and honours those who are older and more virtuous, four benefits, viz., longevity, beauty, happiness and strength, will increase.

At the end of the discourse, Āyuvaḍḍhana and his five hundred companions attained Sotāpatti Fruition.

Verse 110

VIII (9) The Story of Sāmaṇera Saṁkicca

While residing at the Jetavana monastery, the Buddha uttered Verse (110) of this book, with reference to Sāmaṇera Saṁkicca.

On one occasion, thirty bhikkhus each took a subject of meditation from the Buddha and left for a large village, one hundred and twenty yojanas away from Sāvatthi. At that time, five hundred robbers were staying in a thick jungle, and they wanted to make an offering of human flesh and blood to the guardian spirits of the forest. So they came to the village monastery and demanded that one of the bhikkhus be given up to them for sacrifice to the guardian spirits. From the eldest to the youngest, each one of the bhikkhus volunteered to go. With the bhikkhus, there was also a young sāmaṇera by the name of Saṁkicca, who was sent along with them by Thera Sāriputta. This sāmaṇera was only seven years old, but had already attained arahatship. Saṁkicca said that Thera Sāriputta, his teacher, knowing this danger in advance, had purposely sent him to accompany the bhikkhus, and that he should be the one to go with the robbers. So saying, he went along with the robbers. The bhikkhus felt very bad for having let the young sāmaṇera go. The robbers made preparations for the sacrifice; when everything was ready, their leader came to the sāmaṇera, who was then seated, with his mind fixed on jhāna concentration. The leader of the robbers lifted his sword and struck hard at the young sāmaṇera, but the blade of the sword curled up without cutting the flesh. He straightened up the blade and struck again; this time, it bent upwards right up to the hilt without harming the sāmaṇera. Seeing this strange happening, the leader of the robbers dropped his sword, knelt at the feet of the sāmaṇera and asked his pardon. All the five hundred robbers were amazed and terror-stricken; they repented and asked permission from Saṁkicca to become bhikkhus. He complied with their request.

The young sāmaṇera accompanied by five hundred new bhikkhus returned to the village monastery and the thirty bhikkhus felt very much relieved and happy on seeing him. Then Saṁkicca and the five hundred bhikkhus continued on their way to pay respect to Thera Sāriputta, his teacher, at the Jetavana monastery. After seeing Thera Sāriputta they went to pay homage to the Buddha. When told what had happened, the Buddha said, "Bhikkhus, if you rob or steal and commit all sorts of evil deeds, your life would be useless, even if you were to live a hundred years. Living a virtuous life even for a single day is much better than a hundred years of a life of depravity."

Then the Buddha spoke in verse as follows:

Verse 110. Better than a hundred years in the life of an immoral person who has no control over his senses, is a day in the life of a virtuous person who cultivates Tranquillity and Insight. Development Practice.

At the end of the discourse, the five hundred bhikkhus attained arahatship.

Verse 111

VIII (10) The Story of Khāṇu-Koṇḍañña

While residing at the Jetavana monastery, the Buddha uttered Verse (111) of this book, with reference to Khāṇu Koṇḍañña.

Thera Koṇḍañña, after taking a subject of meditation from the Buddha, went into the jungle to practise meditation and there attained arahatship. Coming back to pay homage to the Buddha, he stopped on the way because he was very tired. He sat on a large stone-slab, his mind fixed in jhāna concentration. At that moment five hundred robbers after looting a large village came to the place where the thera was. Taking him for a tree stump they put their bundles of loot all over and around the body of the thera. When day broke they realized that what they took to be a tree stump was, in fact, a living being. Then again, they thought it was an ogre and ran away in fright.

The thera revealed to them that he was only a bhikkhu and not an ogre and told them not to get frightened. The robbers were awed by his words, and asked his pardon for having wronged him. Soon afterwards, all the robbers requested the thera to admit them into the Order. From that time, Thera Koṇḍañña came to be known as "Khāṇu Kaṇḍañña" (tree-stump Koṇḍañña).

The thera accompanied by the new bhikkhus went to the Buddha and told him all that had happened. To them the Buddha said, "To live for a hundred years in ignorance, doing foolish things, is useless; now that you have seen the Truth and have become wise, your life of one day as a wise man is much more worthwhile."

Then the Buddha spoke in verse as follows:

Verse 111. Better than a hundred years in the life of an ignorant person, who has no control over his senses, is a day in the life of a wise man who cultivates Tranquillity and Insight Development Practice.

Verse 112

VIII (11) The Story of Thera Sappadāsa

While residing at the Jetavana monastery, the Buddha uttered Verse (112) of this book, with reference to Thera Sappadāsa.

Once a bhikkhu was not feeling happy with the life of a bhikkhu; at the same time he felt that it would be improper and humiliating for him to return to the life of a householder. So he thought it would be better to die. So thinking, on one occasion, he put his hand into a pot where there was a snake but the snake did not bite him. This was because in a past existence the snake was a slave and the bhikkhu was his master. Because of this incident the bhikkhu was known as Thera Sappadāsa. On another occasion, Thera Sappadāsa took a razor to cut his throat; but as he placed the razor on his throat he reflected on the purity of his morality practice throughout his life as a bhikkhu and his whole body was suffused with delightful satisfaction (pīti) and bliss (sukha). Then detaching himself from pīti, he directed his mind to the development of Insight Knowledge and soon attained arahatship, and he returned to the monastery.

On arrival at the monastery, other bhikkhus asked him where he had been and why he took the knife along with him. When he told them about his intention to take his life, they asked him why he did not do so. He answered, "I originally intended to cut my throat with this knife, but I have now cut off all moral defilements with the knife of Insight Knowledge." The bhikkhus did not believe him; so they went to the Buddha and asked, "Venerable Sir, this bhikkhu claims that he has attained arahatship as he was putting the knife to his throat to kill himself. Is it possible to attain Arahatta Magga within such a short time?" To them the Buddha said, "Bhikkhus! Yes, it is possible; for one who is zealous and strenuous in the practice of Tranquillity and Insight Development, arahatship can be gained in an instant. As the bhikkhu walks in meditation, he can attain arahatship even before his raised foot touches the ground."

Then the Buddha spoke in verse as follows:

Verse 112. Better than a hundred years in the life of a person who is idle and inactive, is a day in the life of one who makes a zealous and strenuous effort (in Tranquillity and Insight Development Practice).

Verse 113

VIII (12) The Story of Therī Paṭācārā

While residing at the Jetavana monastery, the Buddha uttered Verse (113) of this book, with reference to Paṭācārā.

Paṭācārā was the daughter of a rich man from Sāvatthi. She was very beautiful and was guarded very strictly by her parents. But one day, she eloped with a young male attendant of the family and went to live in a village, as a poor man's wife. In due course she became pregnant and as the time for confinement drew near, she asked permission from her husband to return to her parents in Sāvatthi, but her husband discouraged her. So, one day, while her husband was away, she set out for the home of her parents. Her husband followed her and caught up with her on the way and pleaded with her to return with him; but she refused. It so happened that as her time was drawing so near, she had to give birth to a son in one of the bushes. After the birth of her son she returned home with her husband.

Then, she was again with child and as the time for confinement drew near, taking her son with her, she again set out for the home of her parents in Sāvatthi. Her husband followed her and caught up with her on the way; but her time for delivery was coming on very fast and it was also raining hard. The husband looked for a suitable place for confinement and while he was clearing a little patch of land, he was bitten by a poisonous snake, and died instantaneously. Paṭācārā waited for her husband, and while waiting for his return she gave birth to her second son. In the morning, she searched for her husband, but only found his dead body. Saying to herself that her husband died on account of her, she continued on her way to her parents.

Because it had rained incessantly the whole night, the river Aciravatī was in spate; so it was not possible for her to cross the river carrying both her sons. Leaving the elder boy on this side of the river, she crossed the stream with her day-old son and left him on the other bank. She then came back for the elder boy. While she was still in the middle of the river, a large hawk hovered over the younger child taking it for a piece of meat. She shouted to frighten away the bird, but it was all in vain; the child was carried away by the hawk. Meanwhile, the elder boy heard his mother shouting from the middle of the stream and thought she was calling out to him to come to her. So he entered the stream to go to his mother, and was carried away by the strong current. Thus, Paṭācārā lost her two sons as well as her husband.

So she wept and lamented loudly, "A son is carried away by a hawk, another son is carried away by the current, my husband is also dead, bitten by a poisonous snake!" Then, she saw a man from Sāvatthi and she tearfully asked after her parents. The man replied that due to a violent storm in Sāvatthi the previous night, the house of her parents had fallen down and that both her parents, together with her three brothers, had died, and had been cremated on one funeral pyre. On hearing this tragic news, Paṭācārā went stark mad. She did not even notice that her clothes had fallen off from her and that she was half-naked. She went about the streets, shouting out her woes.

While the Buddha was giving a discourse at the Jetavana monastery, he saw Paṭācārā at a distance; so he willed that she should come to the congregation. The crowd seeing her coming tried to stop her, saying "Don't let the mad woman come in." But the Buddha told them not to prevent her coming in. When Paṭācārā was close enough to hear him, he told her to be careful and to keep calm. Then, she realized that she did not have her skirt on and shamefacedly sat down. Someone gave her a piece of cloth and she wrapped herself up in it. She then told the Buddha how she had lost her sons, her husband, her brothers and her parents.

The Buddha said to her, "Paṭācārā, have no fear; you have now come to one who can protect you and guide you. Throughout this round of existences (saṁsāra), the amount of tears you have shed on account of the death of your sons, husbands, parents and brothers is voluminous; it is even more than the waters of the four oceans." Thus the Buddha expounded to her the Anamatagga Sutta, which dealt with countless existences, and she felt relieved. Then, the Buddha added that one should not think too much about those who were gone, but that one should purify oneself and strive to realize Nibbāna. On hearing this exhortation from the Buddha, Paṭācārā attained Sotāpatti Fruition.

Then, Paṭācārā became a bhikkhunī. One day, she was cleaning her feet with water from a water-pot. As she poured the water for the first time, it flowed only a short distance and disappeared; then she poured for the second time and the water went a little farther, but the water she poured for the third time went the farthest. As she looked at the flow and the disappearance of water poured out successively for three times, she came to perceive clearly the three stages in the life of beings. The Buddha seeing her through supernormal power from the Jetavana monastery sent forth his radiance and appeared to her in person. He then said to her, "Paṭācārā, you are now on the right track, and you now have the true perception of the aggregates (khandhas). One who does not perceive the impermanence, unsatisfactoriness and insubstantiality of the aggregates is useless, even if he were to live for a hundred years.

Then the Buddha spoke in verse as follows:

Verse 113. Better than a hundred years in the life of a person who does not perceive the arising and the dissolving of the five aggregates (khandhas), is a day in the life of one who perceives the arising and dissolving of the five aggregates.

At the end of the discourse, Paṭācārā attained arahatship.

Verse 114

VIII (13) The Story of Therī Kisāgotamī

While residing at the Jetavana monastery, the Buddha uttered Verse (114) of this book, with reference to Kisāgotamī.

Kisāgotamī was the daughter of a rich man from Sāvatthi; she was known as Kisāgotamī because of her slim body. Kisāgotamī was married to a rich young man and a son was born to them. The boy died when he was just a toddler and Kisāgotamī was stricken with grief. Carrying the dead body of her son, she went about asking for medicine that would restore her son to life from everyone she happened to meet. People began to think that she had gone mad. But a wise man seeing her condition thought that he should be of some help to her. So, he said to her, "The Buddha is the person you should approach, he has the medicine you want; go to him." Thus, she went to the Buddha and asked him to give her the medicine that would restore her dead son to life.

The Buddha told her to get some mustard seeds from a house where there had been no death. Carrying her dead child in her bosom, Kisāgotamī went from house to house, with the request for some mustard seeds. Everyone was willing to help her, but she could not find a single house where death had not occurred. Then, she realized that hers was not the only family that had faced death and that there were more people dead than living. As soon as she realized this, her attitude towards her dead son changed; she was no longer attached to the dead body of her son.

She left the corpse in the jungle and returned to the Buddha and reported that she could find no house where death had not occurred. Then the Buddha said, "Gotamī, you thought that you were the only one who had lost a son. As you have now realized, death comes to all beings; before their desires are satiated death takes them away." On hearing this, Kisāgotamī fully realized the impermanence, unsatisfactoriness and insubstantiality of the aggregates and attained Sotāpatti Fruition.

Soon afterwards, Kisāgotamī became a bhikkhunī. One day, as she was lighting the lamps she saw the flames flaring up and dying out, and suddenly she clearly perceived the arising and the perishing of beings. The Buddha, through supernormal power, saw her from his monastery, and sent forth his radiance and appeared to her in person. Kisāgotamī was told to continue meditating on the impermanent nature of all beings and to strive hard to realize Nibbāna.

Then the Buddha spoke in verse as follows:

Verse 114. Better. than a hundred years in the life of a person who does not perceive the Deathless (Nibbāna), is a day in the life of one who perceives the Deathless (Nibbāna).

At the end of the discourse Therī Kisāgotamī attained arahatship.

Verse 115

VIII (14) The Story of Therī Bahuputtikā

While residing at the Jetavana monastery, the Buddha uttered Verse (115) of this book, with reference to Bahuputtikā, a mother of many children.

Once in Sāvatthi, there lived a couple, with their seven sons and seven daughters. All the children got married and the family was doing quite well. Then, the father died and the mother kept all the property without giving anything to the children. Her sons and daughters wanted the inheritance, so they said, to their mother, "What benefit do we get from our property? Can't we make it multiply? Can't we look after our mother?" They said such things again and again so their mother thought that her children would look after her, and she finally divided up the property without leaving anything for herself.

After the division of the property, she first went to stay with her eldest son, but her daughter-in-law complained and said, "She has come and stayed with us, as if she has given us two shares!", and such other things. So, Bahuputtikā went to stay with her second son, and the same things were said. Thus, she went from one son to another, from one daughter to the next; but none of them was willing to take her on for a long stretch of time and none paid her due respect.

The old lady was hurt and felt bitter against her children; she left her family and became a bhikkhunī. Because she was a mother of many children she came to be known as Bahuputtikā. Bahuputikā realized that she became a bhikkhunī only in her old age and that she must not be negligent, but must make use of the remaining period of her life to the utmost. So, for the whole night, she meditated on the Dhamma taught by the

Buddha. The Buddha seeing her from the Jetavana monastery, through supernormal power, sent forth the radiance and appeared seated in front of her. Then the Buddha said to her, "The life of one who does not practise the Dhamma taught by me is useless, even if he were to live for a hundred years."

Then the Buddha spoke in verse as follows:

Verse 115. Better than a hundred years in the life of a person who does not comprehend the Noble Dhamma (Dhammamuttamaṁ), is a day in the life of one who comprehends the Noble Dhamma.

End of Chapter Eight: The Thousand.

Chapter IX

Evil (Pāpavagga)

Verse 116

IX (1) The Story of Cūḷekasāṭaka

While residing at the Jetavana monastery, the Buddha uttered Verse (116) of this book, with reference to a brahmin couple by the name of Cūḷekasāṭaka.

There was once a brahmin couple in Sāvatthi, who had only one outer garment between the two of them. Because of this they were also known as Ekasāṭaka. As they had only one outer garment, both of them could not go out at the same time. So, the wife would go to listen to the discourse given by the Buddha during the day and the husband would go at night. One night, as the brahmin listened to the Buddha, his whole body came to be suffused with delightful satisfaction and he felt a strong desire to offer the outer garment he was wearing to the Buddha. But he realized that if he were to give away the only outer garment he had, there would be none left for him and his wife. So he wavered and hesitated. Thus, the first and the second watches of the night passed. Came the third watch and he said to himself, "If I am so miserly and hesitant, I will not be able to avoid falling to the four Lower Worlds (apāyas); I shall now offer my outer garment to the Buddha." So saying, he placed the piece of cloth at the feet of the Buddha and cried out "I have won" three times.

King Pasenadi of Kosala, who was among the audience, heard those words and ordered a courtier to investingate. Learning about the brahmin's offering to the Buddha, the king commented that the brahmin had done something which was not easy to do and so should be rewarded. The king ordered his men to give the brahmin a piece of cloth as a reward for his faith and generosity. The brahmin offered that piece of cloth also to the Buddha and he was rewarded by the king with two pieces of cloth. Again, the brahmin offered the two pieces of cloth to the Buddha and he was rewarded with four. Thus, he offered to the Buddha whatever was given him by the king, and each time the king doubled his reward. When finally.

the reward came up to thirty-two pieces of cloth, the brahmin kept one piece for himself and another for his wife, and offered the remaining thirty pieces to the Buddha.

Then, the king again commented that the brahmin had truly performed a very difficult task and so must be rewarded fittingly. The king sent a messenger to the palace to bring two pieces of velvet cloth, each of which was worth one hundred thousand, and gave them to the brahmin. The brahmin made those two pieces of valuable cloth into two canopies and kept one in the Perfumed Chamber where the Buddha slept and the other in his own house above the place where a bhikkhu was regularly offered alms-food. When the king next went to the Jetavana monastery to pay homage to the Buddha, he saw the velvet canopy and recognized it as the offering made by the brahmin and he was very pleased. This time, he made a reward of seven kinds in fours (sabbacatukka), viz., four elephants, four horses, four female slaves, four male slaves, four errand boys, four villages and four thousands in cash.

When the bhikkhus heard about this, they asked the Buddha, "How is it that, in the case of this brahmin, a good deed done at present bears fruit immediately?" To them the Buddha replied, "If the brahmin had offered his outer garment in the first watch of the night, he would have been rewarded with sixteen of each kind; if he had made his offering during the middle watch, he would have been rewarded with eight of each kind; since he had made his offering only during the last watch of the night, he was rewarded with only four of each kind. So, when one wants to give in charity, one should do so quickly; if one procrastinates, the reward comes slowly and only sparingly. Also, if one is too slow in doing good deeds, one may not be able to do it at all, for the mind tends to take delight in doing evil.

Then the Buddha spoke in verse as follows:

Verse 116. One should make haste in doing good deeds; one should restrain one's mind from evil; for the mind of one who is slow in doing good tends to take delight in doing evil

Verse 117

IX (2) The Story of Thera Seyyasaka

While residing at the Jetavana monastery, the Buddha uttered Verse (117) of this book, with reference to Thera Seyyasaka.

Once there was a thera by the name of Seyyasaka, who was in the habit of masturbating. When the Buddha heard about this, he rebuked the thera for doing something that would lead one farther away from the attainment of Magga and Phala. At the same time, the Buddha laid down the discipline prohibiting such indulgence in sexual pleasures, i.e., Saṁghādisesa Āpatti, offences which require penance and suspension from the Order. Then, the Buddha added, "This kind of offence can only lead to evil results in this world as well as in the next."

Then the Buddha spoke in verse as follows:

Verse 117. If a man does evil, he should not do it again and again; he should not take delight in it; the accumulation of evil leads to dukkha.

Verse 118

IX (3) The Story of Lājadevadhītā

While residing at the Jetavana monastery, the Buddha uttered Verse (118) of this book, with reference to Lājā, a female deva.

At one time Thera Mahākassapa stayed in the Pippali cave and remained in sustained absorption in concentration (samāpatti) for seven days. Soon after he had arisen from samāpatti, wishing to give someone a chance of offering something to a thera just arisen from samāpatti, he looked out and found a young maid frying corn in a field-hut. So he stood at her door for alms-food and she put all the pop corn into the bowl of the thera. As she turned back after offering pop corn to the thera, she was bitten by a poisonous snake and died. She was reborn in Tāvatiṁsa deva world and was known as Lājā (pop corn) devadhītā.

Lājā realized that she was reborn in Tāvatiṁsa because she had offered pop corn to Thera Mahākassapa and felt very grateful to him. Then she concluded that she should keep on doing some services to the thera in order to make her good fortune more enduring. So, every morning she went to the monastery of the thera, swept the premises, filled up water pots, and did other services. At first, the thera thought that young sāmaṇeras had done those services; but one day, he found out that a female deva had been performing those services. So he told her not to come to the monastery any more, as people might start talking if she kept on coming to the monastery. Lājadevadhītā was very upset; she pleaded with the thera and cried, "Please do not destroy my riches, my wealth." The Buddha heard her cries and sent forth the radiance from his chamber and said to the female deva, "Devadhītā, it is the duty of my son Kassapa to stop your coming to the monastery; to do good deeds is the duty of one who is anxious to gain merit."

Then the Buddha spoke in verse as follows:

Verse 118. If a man does what is good, he should do it again and again; he should take delight in it; the accumulation of merit Leads to happiness.

At the end of the discourse, Lājadevadhītā attained Sotāpatti Fruition.

Verses 119 and 120

IX (4) The Story of Anātnapiṇḍika

While residing at the Jetavana monastery, the Buddha uttered Verses (119) and (120) of this book, with reference to Anāthapiṇḍika, the famous rich man of Sāvatthi.

Anāthapiṇḍika was the donor of the Jetavana monastery, which was built at a cost of fifty-four crores. He was not only generous but also truly devoted to the Buddha. He would go to the Jetavana monastery and pay homage to the Buddha thrice daily. In the mornings he would bring along rice gruel, in the day-time some suitable rich food or medicine and in the evenings some flowers and incense. After some time Anāthapiṇḍika became poor, but being a sotāpanna he was not shaken by misfortune, and he continued to do his daily acts of charity. One night, the spirit guarding the gate to the house of Anāthapiṇḍika appeared to him in person, and said, "I am the guardian of your gate. You have been offering your property to Samaṇa Gotama with no thoughts of your future. That is why you are now a poor man. Therefore, you should make no more offerings to Samaṇa Gotama and should look after your own business affairs and get rich again".

Anāthapiṇḍika drove the guardian spirit out of his house for saying such things, and as Anāthapiṇḍika was a sotāpanna the guardian spirit could not disobey him and so had to leave the premises. He had nowhere to go and wanted to return but was afraid of Anāthapiṇḍika. So, he approached Sakka, king of the devas. Sakka advised him first to do a good turn to Anāthapiṇḍika, and after that, to ask his pardon. Then Sakka continued, "There are about eighteen crores taken as loans by some traders which are not yet repaid to Anāthapiṇḍika; another eighteen crores buried by the ancestors of Anāthapiṇḍika, which have been washed away into the ocean, and another eighteen crores, which belong to no one, buried in a certain place. Go and recover all these wealth by your supernatural power and fill up the rooms of Anāthapiṇḍika. Having done so, you may ask his pardon". The guardian spirit did as instructed by Sakka, and Anāthapiṇḍika again became rich.

When the guardian spirit told Anāthapiṇḍika about the information and instructions given by Sakka, about the recovery of his riches from underneath the earth, from within the ocena and from the debtors, he was struck with awe. Then Anāthapiṇḍika took the guardian spirit to the Buddha. To both of them the Buddha said, "One may not enjoy the benefits of a good deed, or suffer the consequences of a bad deed for a long time; but time will surely come when his good or bad deed will bear fruit and ripen".

Then the Buddha spoke in verse as follows:

Verse 119. Even an evil person may still find happiness so long as his evil deed does not bear fruit; but when his evil deed does bear fruit he will meet with evil consequences.

Verse 120. Even a good person may still meet with suffering so long as his good deed does not bear fruit; but when it does bear fruit he will enjoy the benefits of his good deed.

At the end of the discourse, the guardian spirit of the gate of Anāthapiṇḍika's house attained Sotāpatti Fruition."

Verse 121

IX (5) The Story of a Careless Bhikkhu

While residing at the Jetavana monastery, the Buddha uttered Verse (121) of this book, with reference to a bhikkhu who was careless in the use of furniture belonging to the monastery.

This bhikkhu, after using any piece of furniture, such as a couch, a bench or a stool belonging to the monastery, would leave it outside in the compound, thus exposing it to rain and sun and also to white ants. When other bhikkhus chided him for his irresponsible behaviour, he would retort, "I do not have the intention to destroy those things; after all, very little damage has been done," and so on and so forth and he continued to behave in the same way. When the Buddha came to know about this, he sent for the bhikkhu and said to him, "Bhikkhu, you should not behave in this way; you should not think lightly of an evil, however small it may be, because it will become big if you do it habitually."

Then the Buddha spoke in verse as follows:

Verse 121. One should not think lightly of doing evil, imagining. "A little will not affect me"; just as a water-jar is filled up by falling drops of rain, so also, the fool is filled up with evil, by accumulating it little by little.

Verse 122

IX (6) The Story of Biḷālapādaka

While residing at the Jetavana monastery, the Buddha uttered Verse (122) of this book, with reference to Biḷālapādaka, a rich man.

Once, a man from Sāvatthi, having heard a discourse given by the Buddha, was very much impressed, and decided to practise what was taught by the Buddha. The exhortation was to give in charity not only by oneself but also to get others to do so and that by so doing one would gain much merit and have a large number of followers in the next existence. So, that man invited the Buddha and all the resident bhikkhus in the Jetavana monastery for alms-food the next day. Then he went round to each one of the houses and informed the residents that alms-food would be offered the next day to the Buddha and other bhikkhus and so to contribute according to their wishes. The rich man Biḷālapādaka seeing the man going round from house to house disapproved of his behaviour and felt a strong dislike for him and murmured to himself, "O this wretched man! Why did he not invite as many bhikkhus as he could himself offer alms, instead of going round coaxing people?" So he asked the man to bring his bowl and into this bowl, he put only a little rice, only a little butter, only a little molass. These were taken away separately and not mixed with what others had given. The rich man could not understand why his things were kept separately; and he thought perhaps that man wanted others to know that a rich man like him had contributed very little and so put him to shame. Therefore, he sent a servant to find out.

The promoter of charity put a little of everything that was given by the rich man into various pots of rice and curry and sweetmeats so that the rich man may gain much merit. His servant reported what he had seen; but Biḷālapādaka did not get the meaning and was not sure of the intention of the promoter of charity. However, the next day he went to the place where alms-food was being offered. At the same time, he took a knife with him, intending to kill the chief promoter of charity, if he were to reveal in public just how little a rich man like him had contributed.

But this promoter of charity said to the Buddha, "Venerable Sir, this charity is a joint offering of all; whether one has given much or little is of no account; each one of us has given in faith and generosity; so may all of us gain equal merit." When he heard those words, Biḷālapādaka realized that he had wronged the man and pondered that if he were not to own up his mistake and ask the promoter of charity to pardon him, he would be reborn in one of the four lower worlds (apāyas). So he said, "My friend, I have done you a great wrong by thinking ill of you; please forgive me." The Buddha heard the rich man asking for pardon, and on enquiry found out the reason. So, the

Buddha said, "My disciple, you should not think lightly of a good deed, however small it may be, for small deeds will become big if you do them habitually."

Then the Buddha spoke in verse as follows:

Verse 122. One should not think lightly of doing good, imagining "A little will not affect me"; just as a water-jar is filled up by falling drops of rain, so also, the wise one is filled up with merit, by accumulating it little by little.

At the end of the discourse, Biḷālapādaka the rich man attained Sotāpatti Fruition.

Verse 123

IX (7) The Story of Mahādhana

While residing at the Jetavana monastery, the Buddha uttered Verse (123) of this book, with reference to Mahādhana the merchant.

Mahadhāna was a rich merchant from Sāvatthi. On one occasion, five hundred robbers were planning to rob him, but they did not get the chance to rob him. In the meantime, they heard that the merchant would soon be going out with five hundred carts loaded with valuable merchandise. The merchant Mahādhana also invited the bhikkhus who would like to go on the same journey to accompany him, and he promised to look to their needs on the way. So, five hundred bhikkhus accompanied him. The robbers got news of the trip and went ahead to lie in wait for the caravan of the merchant. But the merchant stopped at the outskirts of the forest where the robbers were waiting. The caravan was to move on after camping there for a few days. The robbers got the news of the impending departure and made ready to loot the caravan; the merchant, in his turn, also got news of the movements of the bandits and he decided to return home. The bandits now heard that the merchant would go home; so they waited on the homeward way. Some villagers sent word to the merchant about the movements of the bandits, and the merchant finally decided to remain in the village for some time. When he told the bhikkhus about his decision, the bhikkhus returned to Sāvatthi by themselves.

On arrival at the Jetavana monastery, they went to the Buddha and informed him about the cancellation of their trip. To them, the Buddha said, "Bhikkhus, Mahādhana keeps away from the journey beset with bandits; one who does not want to die keeps away from poison; so also, a wise bhikkhu, realizing that the three levels of existence[1] are like a journey beset with danger, should strive to keep away from doing evil."

Then the Buddha spoke in verse as follows:

Verse 123. Just as a wealthy merchant with few attendants avoids a dangerous road, just as one who desires to go on living avoids poison, so also, one should avoid evil.

At the end of the discourse, those five hundred bhikkhus attained Sotāpatti Fruition.

Verse 124

IX (8) The Story of Kukkuṭamitta

While residing at the Veḷuvana monastery, the Buddha uttered Verse (124) of this book, with reference to the hunter Kukkuṭamitta and his family.

At Rājagaha there was once a rich man's daughter who had attained Sotāpatti Fruition as a young girl. One day, Kukkuṭamitta, a hunter, came into town in a cart to sell venison. Seeing Kukkuṭamitta the hunter, the rich young lady fell in love with him immediately; she followed him, married him and lived with him in a small village. As a result of that marriage, seven sons were born to them and in course of time, all the sons got married. One day, the Buddha surveyed the world early in the morning with his supernormal power and found that the hunter, his seven sons and their wives were due for attainment of Sotāpatti Fruition. So, the Buddha went to the place where the hunter had set his trap in the forest. He put his footprint close to the

---

1. **The three levels of existence are:**
   - (a) **Kāmabhava**, the level of sensuous existence; comprising the eleven realms of sense-desire;
   - (b) **Rūpabhava**, the level of fine material existence; comprising sixteen of the realms of Brahmās;
   - (c) **Arūpabhava**, the level of non-material existence; comprising four realms of the upper Brahmās.

trap and seated himself under the shade of a bush, not far from the trap.

When the hunter came, he saw no animal in the trap; he saw the footprint and surmised that someone must have come before him and let out the animal. So, when he saw the Buddha under the shade of the bush, he took him for the man who had freed the animal from his trap and flew into a rage. He took out his bow and arrow to shoot at the Buddha, but as he drew his bow, he became immobilized and remained fixed in that position like a statue. His sons followed and found their father; they also saw the Buddha at some distance and thought he must be the enemy of their father. All of them took out their bows and arrows to shoot at the Buddha, but they also became immobilized and remained fixed in their respective postures. When the hunter and his sons failed to return, the hunter's wife followed them into the forest, with her seven daughters-in-law. Seeing her husband and all her sons with their arrows aimed at the Buddha, she raised both her hands and shouted, "Do not kill my father."

When her husband heard her words, he thought, "This must be my father-in-law", and her sons thought, "This must be our grandfather"; and thoughts of loving-kindness came into them. Then the lady said to them, "Put away your bows and arrows and pay obeisance to my father". The Buddha realized that, by this time, the minds of the hunter and his sons had softened and so he willed that they should be able to move and to put away their bows and arrows. After putting away their bows and arrows, they paid obeisance to the Buddha and the Buddha expounded the Dhamma to them. In the end, the hunter, his seven sons and seven daughters-in-law, all fifteen of them, attained Sotāpatti Fruition.

Then the Buddha returned to the monastery and told Thera Ānanda and other bhikkhus about the hunter Kukkuṭamitta and his family attaining Sotāpatti Fruition in the early part of the morning. The bhikkhus then asked the Buddha, "Venerable Sir, is the wife of the hunter, who is a sotāpanna, also not guilty of taking life, if she has been getting things like nets, bows and arrows for her husband when he goes out hunting?" To this question her Buddha answered, "Bhikkhus, the sotāpannas do not kill, they do not wish others to get killed. The wife of the hunter was only obeying her husband in getting things for him. Just as the hand that has no wound is not affected by poison, so also, because she has no intention to do evil she is not doing any evil."

Then the Buddha spoke in verse as follows:

Verse 124. If there is no wound on the hand, one may handle poison; poison does not affect one who has no wound; there can be no evil for one who has no evil intention.

Verse 125

IX (9) The Story of Koka the Huntsman

While residing at the Jetavana monastery, the Buddha uttered Verse (125) of this book, with reference to Koka the huntsman.

One morning, as Koka was going out to hunt with his pack of hounds, he met a bhikkhu entering the city for alms-food. He took that as a bad omen and grumbled to himself, "Since I have seen this wretched one, I don't think I would get anything today," and he went on his way. As expected by him he did not get anything. On his way home also he again saw the same bhikkhu returning to the monastery after having had his alms-food in the city, and the hunter became very angry. So he set his hounds on the bhikkhu. Swiftly, the bhikkhu climbed up a tree to a level just out of reach of the hounds. Then the hunter went to the foot of the tree and pricked the heels of the bhikkhu with the tip of his arrow. The bhikkhu was in great pain and was not able to hold his robes on; so the robes slipped off his body on to the hunter who was at the foot of the tree.

The dogs seeing the yellow robe thought that the bhikkhu had fallen off the tree and pounced on the body, biting and pulling at it furiously. The bhikkhu, from his shelter in the tree, broke a dry branch and threw it at the dogs. Then the dogs discovered that they had been attacking their own master instead of the bhikkhu, and ran away into the forest. The bhikkhu came down from the tree and found that the hunter had died and felt sorry for him. He also wondered whether he could be held responsible for the death, since the hunter had died for having been covered up by his yellow robes.

So, he went to the Buddha to clear up his doubt. The Buddha said, "My son, rest assured and have no doubt; you are not responsible for the death of the hunter; your morality (sīla) is also not soiled on account of that death. Indeed, that huntsman did a great wrong to one whom he should do no wrong and so had come to this grievous end."

Then the Buddha spoke in verse as follows:

Verse 125. If one wrongs a person who should not be wronged, one who is pure and is free from moral defilements, viz., an arahat, the evil falls back upon that fool, like fine dust thrown against the wind.

At the end of the discourse the bhikkhu attained arahatship.

Verse 126

IX (10) The Story of Thera Tissa

While residing at the Jetavana monastery, the Buddha uttered Verse (126) of this book, with reference to Thera Tissa.

Once, there was a gem polisher and his wife in Sāvatthi; there was also a thera, who was an arahat. Every day, the couple offered alms-food to the thera. One day, while the gem polisher was handling meat, a messenger of King Pasenadi of Kosala arrived with a ruby, which was to be cut and polished and sent back to the king. The gem polisher took the ruby with his hand which was covered with blood, put it on a table and went into the house to wash his hands. The pet crane of the family seeing the blood stained ruby and taking it for a piece of meat picked it up and swallowed it in the presence of the thera. When the gem polisher returned, he found that the ruby was missing. He asked his wife and his son and they answered that they had not taken it. Then, he asked the thera and the thera said that he did not take it; but he was not satisfied. As there was no one else in the house, the gem polisher concluded that it must be the thera who had taken the precious ruby: so he told his wife that he must torture the thera to get admission of theft.

But his wife replied, "This thera had been our guide and teacher for the last twelve years, and we have never seen him doing anything evil; please do not accuse the thera. It would be better to take the king's punishment than to accuse a noble one." But her husband paid no heed to her words; he took a rope and tied up the thera and beat him many times with a stick, as a result of which the thera bled profusely from the head, ears and nose, and dropped on the floor. The crane, seeing blood and wishing to take it, came close to the thera. The gem polisher, who was by then in a great rage, kicked the crane with all his might and the bird died instantaneously. Then, the thera said, "Please see whether the crane is dead or not," and the gem polisher replied, "You too shall die like this crane." When the thera was sure the crane had died, he said softly, "My disciple, the crane swallowed the ruby."

Hearing this, the gem polisher cut up the crane and found the ruby in the stomach. Then, the gem polisher realized his mistake and trembled with fear. He pleaded with the thera to pardon him and also to continue standing at his door for alms. To him the thera replied, "My disciple, it is not your fault, nor is it mine. This has happened on account of what has been done in our previous existences; it is just our debt in saṁsāra; I feel no ill will towards you. As a matter of fact, this has happened because I have entered a house. From today, I would not enter any house; I would only stand at the door." Soon after saying this, the thera expired as a result of his injuries.

Later, the bhikkhus asked the Buddha where the various characters in the above episode were reborn, and the Buddha answered, "The crane was reborn as the son of the gem polisher; the gem polisher was reborn in niraya; the wife of the gem polisher was reborn in one of the deva worlds; and the thera, who was already an arahat when he was living, realized Parinibbāna."

Then the Buddha spoke in verse as follows:

Verse 126. Some are reborn as human beings, the wicked are reborn in a place of continuous torment (niraya), the righteous go to the deva world, and those who are free from moral intoxicants (viz., the arahats) realize Nibbāna.

Verse 127

IX (11) The Story of Three Groups of Persons

While residing at the Jetavana monastery, the Buddha uttered Verse (127) of this book, with reference to questions raised by three groups of bhikkhus concerning three extraordinary incidents.

The first group : A group of bhikkhus were on their way to pay homage to the Buddha and they stopped at a village on the way. Some people were cooking alms-food for those bhikkhus when one of the houses caught fire and a ring of fire flew up into the air. At that moment, a crow came flying, got caught in the ring of fire and dropped dead in the central part of the village. The bhikkhus seeing the dead crow observed that only the Buddha would be able to explain for what evil deed this crow had to die in this manner. After taking alms-food they continued on their journey to pay homage to the Buddha, and also to ask about the unfortunate crow.

The second group : Another group of bhikkhus were travelling in a boat; they too were on their way to pay homage to the Buddha. When they were in the middle of the ocean the boat could not be moved. So, lots were drawn to find out who the unlucky one was; three times the lot fell on the wife of the skipper. Then the skipper said sorrowfully, "Many people should not die on account of this unlucky woman; tie a pot of sand to her neck and throw her into the water so that I would not see her." The woman was thrown into the sea as instructed by the skipper and the ship could move on. On arrival at their destination, the bhikkhus disembarked and continued on their way to the Buddha. They also intended to ask the Buddha due to what evil kamma the unfortunate woman was thrown overboard.

The third group : A group of seven bhikkhus were also on their way to pay homage to the Buddha. On the way, they enquired at a monastery whether there was any suitable place for them to take shelter for the night in the neighbourhood. They were directed to a cave, and there they spent the night; but in the middle of the night, a large boulder slipped off from above and effectively closed the entrance. In the morning, the bhikkhus from the nearby monastery coming to the cave saw what had happened and they went to bring people from seven villages. With the help of these people they tried to move the boulder, but it was of no avail. Thus, the seven bhikkhus were trapped in the cave without food or water for seven days. On the seventh day, the boulder moved miraculously by itself, and the bhikkhus came out and continued their way to the Buddha. They also intended to ask the Buddha due to what previous evil deed they were thus shut up for seven days in a cave.

The three groups of travellers met on the way and together they went to the Buddha. Each group related to the Buddha what they had seen or experienced on their way and the Buddha answered their questions.

The Buddha's answer to the first group: "Bhikkhus, once there was a farmer who had an ox. The ox was very lazy and also very stubborn. It could not be coaxed to do any work; it would just lie down chewing the cud or else go to sleep. The farmer lost his temper many times on account of this lazy, stubborn animal; so in anger, he tied a straw rope round the neck of the ox and set fire to it, and the ox died. On account of this evil deed the farmer had suffered for a long time in niraya, and in serving out the remaining part of his punishment, he had been burnt to death in the last seven existences."

The Buddha's answer to the second group: "Bhikkhus, once there was a woman who had a pet dog. She used to take the dog along with her wherever she went and young boys of the city poked fun at her. She was very angry and felt so ashamed that she planned to kill the dog. She filled a pot with sand, tied it round the neck of the dog and threw it into the water; and the dog was drowned. On account of this evil deed that woman had suffered for a long time in niraya and in serving the remaining part of her punishment, she had been thrown into the water to drown in the last one hundred existences."

The Buddha's answer to the third group: "Bhikkhus, once, seven cowherds saw an iguana going into a mound and they closed all the seven outlets of the mound with twigs and branches of trees. After closing the outlets they went away, completely forgetting the iguana that was trapped in the mound. Only after seven days, they remembered what they had done and hurriedly returned to the scene of their mischief and let out the iguana. On account of this evil deed, those seven had been imprisoned together for seven days without any food, in the last fourteen existences."

Then, a bhikkhu remarked, "O indeed! There is no escape from evil consequences for one who has done evil, even if he were in the sky, or in the ocean, or in a cave." To him, the Buddha said, "Yes, Bhikkhu! You are right; even in the sky or anywhere else, there is no place which is beyond the reach of evil consequences."

Then the Buddha spoke in verse as follows:

Verse 127. Not in the sky, nor in the middle of the ocean, nor in the cave of a mountain, nor anywhere else, is there a place, where one may escape from the consequences of an evil deed.

At the end of the discourse all the bhikkhus attained Sotāpatti Fruition.

Verse 128

IX (12) The Story of King Suppabuddha

While residing at the Nigrodhārāma monastery, the Buddha uttered Verse (128) of this book, with reference to King Suppabuddha.

King Suppabuddha was the father of Devadatta and father-in-law of Prince Siddhattha who later became Gotama Buddha. King Suppabuddha was very antagonistic to the Buddha for two reasons. First, because as prince Siddhattha he had left his wife Yasodharā, the daughter of King Suppabuddha, to renounce the world; and secondly, because his son Devadatta, who was admitted into the Order by Gotama Buddha, had come to regard the Buddha as his arch enemy. One day, knowing that the Buddha would be coming for alms-food, he got himself drunk and blocked the way. When the Buddha and the bhikkhus came, Suppabuddha refused to make way, and sent a message saying, "I cannot give way to Samaṇa Gotama, who is so much younger than me." Finding the road blocked, the

Buddha and the bhikkhus turned back. Suppabuddha then sent someone to follow the Buddha secretly and find out what the Buddha said, and to report to him.

As the Buddha turned back, he said to Ānanda, "Ānanda, because King Suppabuddha had refused to give way to me, on the seventh day from now he would be swallowed up by the earth, at the foot of the steps leading to the pinnacled hall of his palace." The king's spy heard these words and reported to the king. And the king said that he would not go near those steps and would prove the words of the Buddha to be wrong. Further, he instructed his men to remove those steps, so that he would not be able to use them; he also kept some men on duty, with instructions to hold him back should he go in the direction of the stairs.

When the Buddha was told about the king's instructions to his men, he said, "Bhikkhus! Whether King Suppabuddha lives in a pinnacled tower, or up in the sky, or in an ocean, or in a cave, my word cannot go wrong; King Suppabuddha will be swallowed up by the earth at the very place I have told you."

Then the Buddha spoke in verse as follows:

Verse 128. Not in the sky, nor in the middle of the ocean, nor in the cave of a mountain, nor anywhere else, is there a place where one cannot be oppressed by Death.

On the seventh day, about the time of the alms meal the royal horse got frightened for some unknown reason and started neighing loudly and kicking about furiously. Hearing frightening noises from his horse, the king felt that he must handle his pet horse and forgetting all precautions, he started towards the door. The door opened of its own accord, the steps which had been pulled down earlier were also there, his men forgot to stop him from going down. So the king went down the stairs and as soon as he stepped on the earth, it opened and swallowed him up and dragged him right down to Avīci Niraya.

End of Chapter Nine: Evil.

Chapter X

Punishment (Daṇḍavagga)

Verse 129

X (1) The Story of a Group of Six Bhikkhus

While residing at the Jetavana monastery, the Buddha uttered Verse (129) of this book, with reference to a group of six bhikkhus (chabbaggī) who picked a quarrel with another group comprising seventeen bhikkhus.

Once, seventeen bhikkhus were cleaning up a building in the Jetavana monastery-complex with the intention of occupying it, when another group comprising six bhikkhus arrived on the scene. The group of six said to the first group, "We are senior to you, so you had better give way to us; we will take this place." The group of seventeen did not give in, so the chabbaggis beat up the other group who cried out in pain. The Buddha learning about this reprimanded them and laid down the disciplinary rule forbidding bhikkhus to beat others.

Then the Buddha spoke in verse as follows:

Verse 129. All are afraid of the stick, all fear death. Putting oneself in another's place, one should not beat or kill others.

Verse 130

X(2) The Story of a Group of Six Bhikkhus

While residing at the Jetavana monastery, the Buddha uttered Verse (130) of this book, with reference to a group of six bhikkhus.

After coming to blows the first time, the same two groups of bhikkhus quarrelled again over the same building. As the rule prohibiting beating others had already been laid down, the group of six threatened the other group with upraised hands. The group of seventeen, who were junior to the chabbaggis, cried out in fright. The Buddha hearing about this laid down the disciplinary rule forbidding the raising of hands in threat.

Then the Buddha spoke in verse as follows:

Verse 130. All are afraid of the stick, all hold their lives dear. Putting oneself in another's place, one should not beat or kill others.

Verses 131 and 132

X (3) The Story of Many Youths

While residing at the Jetavana monastery, the Buddha uttered Verses (131) and (132) of this book, with reference to a number of youths.

Once, the Buddha was out on an alms-round at Sāvatthi when he came across a number of youths beating a snake with sticks. When questioned, the youths answered that they were beating the snake because they were afraid that the snake might bite them. To them the Buddha said, "If you do not want to be harmed, you should also not harm others: if you harm others, you will not find happiness in your next existence."

Then the Buddha spoke in verse as follows:

Verse 131. He who seeks his own happiness by oppressing others, who also desire to have happiness, will not find happiness in his next existence.

Verse 132. He who seeks his own happiness by not oppressing others, who also desire to have happiness, will find happiness in his next existence.

At the end of the discourse all the youths attained Sotāpatti Fruition.

Verses 133 and 134

X (4) The Story of Thera Koṇḍadhāna

While residing at the Jetavana monastery, the Buddha uttered Verses (133) and (134) of this book, with reference to Thera Koṇḍadhāna.

Since the day Koṇḍadhāna was admitted to the Order, the image of a female was always following him. This image was seen by others, but Koṇḍadhāna himself did not see it and so did not know about it.

When he was out on an alms-round, people would offer two spoonfuls to him, saying, "This is for you, Venerable Sir, and this is for your female companion." Seeing the bhikkhu going about with a woman, people went to King Pasenadi of Kosala and reported about the bhikkhu and the woman. They said to the king, "O king! Drive out the bhikkhu, who is lacking in moral virtues, from your kingdom." So the king went to the monastery where that bhikkhu was staying and surrounded it with his men.

Hearing noises and voices, the bhikkhu came out and stood at the door, and the image also was there not far from the bhikkhu. Knowing that the king had come, the bhikkhu went into the room to wait for him. When the king entered the room, the image was not there. The king asked the bhikkhu where the woman was and he replied that he saw no woman. The king wanted to make sure and he asked the bhikkhu to leave the room for a while. The bhikkhu left the room, but when the king looked out, again he saw the woman near the bhikkhu. But when the bhikkhu came back to the room the woman was nowhere to be found. The king concluded that the woman was not real and so the bhikkhu must be innocent. He therefore invited the bhikkhu to come to the palace every day for alms-food.

When other bhikkhus heard about this, they were puzzled and said to the bhikkhu, "O bhikkhu with no morals! Now that the king, instead of driving you out of his kingdom, has invited you for alms-food, you are doomed!". The bhikkhu on his part retorted, "Only you are the ones without morals; only you are doomed because you are the ones who go about with women!"

The bhikkhus then reported the matter to the Buddha. The Buddha sent for Koṇḍadhāna and said to him, "My son, did you see any woman with the other bhikkhus that you have talked to them thus ? You have not seen any woman with them as they have seen one with you. I see that you do not realize that you have been cursed on account of an evil deed done by you in a past existence. Now listen, I shall explain to yon why you have an image of a woman following you about.

"You were a deva in your last existence. During that time, there were two bhikkhus who were very much attached to each other. But you tried to create trouble between the two, by assuming the appearance of a woman and following one of the bhikkhus. For that evil deed you are now being followed by the image of a woman. So, my son, in future do not argue with other bhikkhus any more; keep silent like a gong with the rim broken off and you will realize Nibbāna."

Then the Buddha spoke in verse as follows:

Verse 133. Do not speak harshly to anyone; those who are thus spoken to will retort. Malicious talk is indeed the cause of trouble (dukkha) and retribution will come to you.

Verse 134. If you can keep yourself calm and quiet, like a broken gong which is no longer resonant, you are sure to realize Nibbāna, there will be no harshness in you.

Verse 135

X (5) The Story of Some Ladies Observing the Moral Precepts

While residing at the Pubbārāma monastery, the Buddha uttered Verse (135) of this book, with reference to five hundred ladies.

Once, five hundred ladies from Sāvatthi came to the Pubbārāma monastery to keep the Uposatha Sīla vows. The donor of the monastery, the well-renowned Visākhā, asked different age groups of ladies why they had come to keep the sabbath. She got different answers from different age groups for they had come to the monastery for different reasons. The old ladies came to the monastery to keep the sabbath because they hoped to gain the riches and glories of the devas in their next existence; the middle-aged ladies had come to the monastery because they did not want to stay under the same roof with the mistresses of their respective husbands. The young married ladies had come because they wanted their first born to be a son, and the young unmarried ladies had come because they wanted to get married to good husbands.

Having had these answers, Visākhā took all the ladies to the Buddha. When she told the Buddha about the various answers of the different age groups of ladies, the Buddha said, "Visākhā! Birth, ageing and death are always actively working in beings; because one is born, one is subject to ageing and decay, and finally to death. Yet, they do not wish to strive for liberation from the round of existences (saṁsāra); they still wish to linger in saṁsāra."

Then the Buddha spoke in verse as follows:

Verse 135. As with a stick the cowherd drives his cattle to the pasture, so also, Ageing and Death drive the life of beings.

Verse 136

X (6) The Story of the Boa Constrictor Peta

While residing at the Jetavana monastery, the Buddha uttered Verse (136) of this book, with reference to a boa constrictor peta[1].

Once, as Thera Mahā Moggallāna was coming down the Gijjhakūṭa hill with Thera Lakkhaṇa he saw a boa constrictor peta and smiled, but he did not say anything. When they were back at the Jetavana monastery, Thera Mahā Moggallāna told Lakkhaṇa, in the presence of the Buddha, about the boa constrictor peta, with its long body burning in flames. The Buddha also said he himself had also seen that very peta soon after he had attained Buddhahood, but that he did not say anything about it because people might not believe him and thus they would be doing a great wrong to the Buddha. So out of compassion for these beings, the Buddha had kept silent. Then he continued, "Now that I have a witness in Moggallāna, I will tell you about this boa constrictor peta. This peta was a thief during the time of Kassapa Buddha. As a thief and a cruel-hearted man, he had set fire to the house of a rich man seven times And not satisfied with that, he also set fire to the perfumed hall donated by the same rich man to Kassapa Buddha, while Kassapa Buddha was out on an alms-round. As a result of those evil deeds he had suffered for a long time in niraya. Now,

1. peta: an always hungry spirit or ghost.

while serving out his term of suffering as a peta, he is being burnt with sparks of flames going up and down the length of his body. Bhikkhus, fools when doing evil deeds do not know them as being evil; but they cannot escape the evil consequences."

Then the Buddha spoke in verse as follows:

Verse 136. A fool while doing evil deeds does not know them as being evil; but that fool suffers for his evil deeds like one who is burnt by fire.

Verses 137, 138, 139 and 140

X (7) The Story of Thera Mahā Moggallāna

While residing at the Jetavana monastery, the Buddha uttered Verses (137), (138), (139) and (140) of this book, with reference to Thera Mahā Moggallāna.

Once, the Nigaṇṭha ascetics planned to kill Thera Mahā Moggallāna because they thought that by doing away with Thera Mahā Moggallāna the fame and fortune of the Buddha would also be diminished. So they hired some assassins to kill Thera Mahā Moggallāna who was staying at Kāḷasilā near Rājagaha at that time. The assassins surrounded the monastery; but Thera Mahā Moggallāna, with his supernormal power, got away first through a key hole, and for the second time through the roof. Thus, they could not get hold of the thera for two whole months. When the assassins again surrounded the monastery during the third month, Thera Mahā Moggallāna, recollecting that he had yet to pay for the evil deeds done by him during one of his past existences, did not exercise his supernormal power. So he was caught and the assassins beat him up until all his bones were utterly broken. After that, they left his body in a bush, thinking that he had passed away. But the thera, through his jhānic power, revived himself and went to see the Buddha at the Jetavana monastery. When he informed the Buddha that he would soon realize parinibbāna at Kāḷasilā, near Rājagaha, the Buddha told him to go only after expounding the Dhamma to the congregation of bhikkhus, as that would be the last time they would see him. So, Thera Mahā Moggallāna expounded the Dhamma and left after paying obeisance seven times to the Buddha.

The news of the passing away of Thera Mahā Moggallāna at the hands of assassins spread like wild fire. King Ajātasattu ordered his men to investigate and get hold of the culprits. The assassins were caught and they were burnt to death. The bhikkhus felt very sorrowful over the death of Thera Mahā Moggallāna, and could not understand why such a personage like Thera Mahā Moggallāna should die at the hands of assassins. To them the Buddha said, "Bhikkhus! Considering that Moggallāna had lived a noble life in this existence, he should not have met with such a death. But in one of his past existences, he had done a great wrong to his own parents, who were both blind. In the beginning, he was a very dutiful son, but after his marriage, his wife began to make trouble and she suggested that he should get rid of his parents. He took his blind parents in a cart into a forest, and there he killed them by beating them and making them believe that it was some thief who was beating them. For that evil deed he suffered in niraya for a long time; and in this existence, his last, he has died at the hands of assassins. Indeed, by doing wrong to those who should not be wronged, one is sure to suffer for it."

Then the Buddha spoke in verse as follows:

Verse 137. He who does harm with weapons to those who are harmless and should not be harmed will soon come to any of these ten evil consequences:

Verses 138, 139, 140. He will be subject to severe pain, or impoverishment, or injury to the body (i.e., loss of limbs), or serious illness (e.g., leprosy), or lunacy, or misfortunes following the wrath of the king, or wrongful and serious accusations, or loss of relatives, or destruction of wealth, or the burning down of his houses by fire or by lightning After the dissolution of his body, the fool will be reborn in the plane of continuous suffering (niraya).

Verse 141

X (8) The Story of Bhikkhu Bahubhaṇḍika

While residing at the Jetavana monastery, the Buddha uttered Verse (141) of this book, with reference to Bahubhaṇḍika, a bhikkhu with many possessions.

Once there was a rich man in Sāvatthi. After the death of his wife, he decided to become a bhikkhu. But before he entered the Order, he built a monastery, which included a kitchen and a store room. He also brought his own furniture, utensils and a large stock of rice, oil, butter and other provisions. Whatever dishes he wanted was cooked for him by his servants. Thus, even as a bhikkhu he was living in comfort, and because he had so many things with him, he was known as 'Bahubhandika.' One day, other bhikkhus took him to the Buddha, and in his presence told the Buddha about the many things he had brought along with him to the monastery, and also how he was still leading the luxurious life of a rich man. So, the Buddha said to Bahubhaṇḍika, "My son, I have been teaching all of you to live an austere life; why have you brought so much property with you?" When reprimanded even this much, that bhikkhu lost his temper and said angrily, "Indeed, Venerable Sir! I will now live as you wish me to." So saying, he cast off his upper robe.

Seeing him thus, the Buddha said to him, "My son, in your last existence you were an ogre; even as an ogre you had a sense of shame and a sense of fear to do evil. Now that you are a bhikkhu in my Teaching, why do you have to throw away the sense of shame, and the sense of fear to do evil?" When he heard those words, the bhikkhu realized his mistake; his sense of shame and fear to do evil returned, and he respectfully paid obeisance to the Buddha and asked that he should be pardoned. The Buddha then said to him, "Standing there without your upper robe is not proper; just discarding your robe etc., does not make you an austere bhikkhu; a bhikkhu must also discard his doubt."

Then the Buddha spoke in verse as follows:

Verse 141. Not going naked, nor having matted hair, nor smearing oneself with mud, nor fasting, nor sleeping on bare ground, nor covering oneself with dust, nor striving by squatting can purify a being, who has not yet overcome doubt.

At the end of the discourse many attained Sotāpatti Fruition.

Verse 142

X (9) The Story of Santati the Minister

While residing at the Jetavana monastery, the Buddha uttered Verse (142) of this book, with reference to Santati, the minister of King Pasenadi of Kosala.

On one occasion, Santati the minister returned after suppressing a rebellion on the border. King Pasenadi was so pleased with him that he honoured the minister with the gift of the riches and glory of a ruler together with a dancing girl to entertain him for seven days. For seven days, the king's minister enjoyed himself to his heart's content, getting intoxicated with drink and infatuated with the young dancer. On the seventh day, riding the ornamented royal elephant, he went down to the riverside for a bath. On the way, he met the Buddha going on an alms-round, and being drunk, he just bowed casually, as a sign of respect to the Buddha. The Buddha smiled, and Ānanda asked the Buddha why he smiled. So, the Buddha said to Ānanda, "Ānanda, this minister will come to see me this very day and after I have given him a short discourse will become an arahat. Soon after becoming an arahat he will realize parinibbāna."

Santati and his party spent the whole day at the riverside, bathing, eating, drinking and thus thoroughly enjoying themselves. In the evening the minister and his party went to the garden to have more drinks and to be entertained by the dancer. The dancer, on her part, tried her best to entertain the minister. For the whole week she was living on reduced diet to keep herself trim. While dancing, she suffered a severe stroke and collapsed, and at that instant she died with her eyes and mouth wide open. The minister was shocked and deeply distressed. In agony, he tried to think of a refuge and remembered the Buddha. He went to the Buddha, accompanied by his followers, and related to him about the grief and anguish he suffered on account of the sudden death of the dancer. He then said to the Buddha, "Venerable Sir! Please help me get over my sorrow; be my refuge, and let me have the peace of mind." To him the Buddha replied, "Rest assured my son, you have come to One, who could help you, One who could be a constant solace to you and who will be your refuge. The tears you have shed due to the death of this dancer throughout the round of rebirths is more than the waters of all the oceans." The Buddha then instructed the minister in verse. The meaning of the verse is as follows.

> "In the past there has been in you clinging (upādāna) due to craving; get rid of it. In future, do not let such clinging occur in you. Do not also harbour any clinging in the present; by not having any clinging, craving and passion will be calmed in you and you will realize Nibbāna."

After hearing the verse, the minister attained arahatship. Then, realizing that his life span was at an end, he said to the Buddha, "Venerable Sir! Let me now realize parinibbāna, for my time has come." The Buddha consenting, Santati rose to a height of seven toddy-palms into the sky and there, while meditating on the element of fire (tejo kasiṇa), he passed away realizing parinibbāna. His body went up in flames, his blood and flesh burnt up and the bone relics (dhātu) fell through the sky and dropped on the clean piece of cloth which was spread by the bhikkhus as instructed by the Buddha.

At the congregation, the bhikkhus asked the Buddha, "Venerable Sir! The minister had realized parinibbāna dressed in full regalia; is he a samaṇa on a brāhmaṇa?" To them, the "Buddha replied Bhikkhus! My son can be called both a samaṇa and a brāhmaṇa."

Then the Buddha spoke in verse as follows:

Verse 142. Though he is gaily decked, if he is calm, free from moral defilements, and has his senses controlled, if he is established in Magga Insight, if he is pure and has laid aside enmity (lit., weapons) towards all beings, he indeed is a brāhmaṇa, a samaṇa, and a bhikkhu.

Verses 143 and 144

X (10) The Story of Thera Pilotikatissa

While residing at the Jetavana monastery, the Buddha uttered Verses (143) and (144) of this book, with reference to Thera Pilotikatissa.

Once, Thera Ānanda saw a shabbily dressed youth going round begging for food; he felt pity for the youth and made him a sāmaṇera. The young sāmaṇera left his old clothes and his begging plate on the fork of a tree. When he became a bhikkhu he was known as Pilotikatissa. As a bhikkhu, he did not have to worry about food and clothing as he was in affluent circumstances. Yet, sometimes he did not feel happy in his life as a bhikkhu and thought of going back to the life of a lay man. Whenever he had this feeling, he would go back to that tree where he had left his old clothes and his plate. There, at the foot of the tree, he would put this question to himself, "Oh shameless one! Do yon want to leave the place where you are fed well and dressed well? Do you still want to put on these shabby clothes and go begging again with this old plate in your hand?" Thus, he would rebuke himself, and after calming down, he would go back to the monastery.

After two or three days, again, he felt like leaving the monastic life of a bhikkhu, and again, he went to the tree where he kept his old clothes and his plate. After asking himself the same old question and having been reminded of the wretchedness of his old life, he returned to the monastery. This was repeated many times. When other bhikkhus asked him why he often went to the tree where he kept his old clothes and his plate, he told them that he went to see his teacher.[1] Thus keeping his mind on his old clothes as the subject of meditation, he came to realize the true nature of the aggregates of the khandhas (i. e., anicca, dukkha, anatta), and eventually he became an arahat. Then, he stopped going to the tree. Other bhikkhus noticing that Pilotikatissa had stopped going to the tree where he kept his old clothes and his plate asked him, "Why don't you go to your teacher any more?" To them, he answered, "When I had the need, I had to go to him; but there is no need for me to go to him now." When the bhikkhus heard his reply, they took him to see the Buddha. When they came to his presence they said, "Venerable Sir! This bhikkhu claims that he has attained arahatship; he must be telling lies." But the Buddha refuted them, and said, "Bhikkhus! Pilotikatissa is not telling lies, he speaks the truth. Though he had relationship with his teacher

1. **teacher**: here refers to Pilotika's old clothes and his begging plate: they are like a teacher to him because they imbued him with a deep sense of shame and put him on the right track.

previously, now he has no relationship whatsoever with his teacher. Thera Pilotikatissa has instructed himself to differentiate right and wrong causes and to discern the true nature of things. He has now become an arahat, and so there is no further connection between him and his teacher."

Then the Buddha spoke in verse as follows:

Versa 143. Rare in this world is the kind of person who out of a sense of shame restrains from doing evil and keeps himself awake like a good horse that gives no cause to be whipped.

Verse 144. Like a good horse stirred at a touch of the whip, be diligent and get alarmed by endless round of rebirths (i. e., saṁsāra). By faith, morality, effort, concentration, discernment of the Dhamma, be endowed with knowledge and practice of morality, and with mindfulness, leave this immeasurable dukkha (of saṁsāra) behind.

Verse 145

X (11) The Story of Sāmaṇera[1] Sukha

While residing at the Jetavana monastery, the Buddha uttered Verse (145) of this book, with reference to a sāmaṇera named Sukha.

Sukha was made a sāmaṇera at the age of seven years by Thera Sāriputta. On the eighth day after being made a sāmaṇera he followed Thera Sāriputta on his alms-round. While doing the round they came across some farmers irrigating their fields, some fletchers straightening their arrows and some carpenters making things like cart-wheels, etc. Seeing these, he asked Thera Sāriputta whether these inanimate things could be guided to where one wished or be made into things one wished to make, and the thera answered him in the affirmative. The young sāmaṇera then pondered that if that were so, there could be no reason why a person could not tame his mind and practise Tranquillity and Insight Meditation.

So, he asked permission from the thera to return to the monastery. There, he shut himself up in his

1. This story is the same as that of Sāmaṇera Paṇḍita (Verse 80).

room and practised meditation in solitude, Sakka and the devas also helped him in his practice by keeping the monastery very quiet. That same day, the eighth day after his becoming a sāmaṇera, Sukha attained arahatship. In connection with this, the Buddha said to the congregation of bhikkhus, "When a person earnestly practises the Dhamma, even Sakka and the devas give protection and help. I myself have kept Sāriputta at the entrance so that Sukha should not be disturbed. The sāmaṇera, having seen the farmers irrigating their fields, the fletchers straightening their arrows and the carpenters making cart-wheels and other things, trains his mind and practises the Dhamma. Thus, he has now become an arahat."

Then the Buddha spoke in verse as follows:

Verse 145. Farmers (lit., makers of irrigation canals) channel the water; fletchers straighten the arrows; carpenters work the timber; the wise tame themselves.

End of Chapter Ten: Punishment

Chapter XI
Ageing (Jarāvagga)
Verse 146
XI (1) The Story of the Companions of Visākhā

While residing at the Jetavana monastery, the Buddha uttered Verse (146) of this book, with reference to companions of Visākhā.

Five hundred men from Sāvatthi, wishing to make their wives to be generous, kind-hearted and virtuous like Visākhā, sent them to Visākhā to be her constant companions. During a bacchanalian festival which lasted for seven days, the wives of those men took all the drinks left by their husbands and got drunk in the absence of Visākhā. For this misbehaviour they were beaten by their husbands. On another occasion, saying that they wished to listen to the Buddha's discourse, they asked Visākhā to take them to the Buddha and secretly took small bottles of liquor hidden in their clothes.

On arrival at the monastery, they drank all the liquor they had brought and threw away the bottles. Visākhā requested the Buddha to teach them the Dhamma. By that time, the women were getting intoxicated and felt like singing and dancing. Māra, taking this opportunity made them bold and shameless, and soon they were boisterously singing, dancing, clapping and jumping about in the monastery. The Buddha saw the hand of Māra in the shameless behaviour of these women and said to himself, "Māra must not be given the opportunity." So, the Buddha sent forth dark-blue rays from his body and the whole room was darkened; the women were frightened and began to get sober. Then, the Buddha vanished from his seat and stood on top of Mt.Meru, and from there he sent forth white rays and the sky was lit up as if by a thousand moons. After thus manifesting his powers, the Buddha said to those five hundred women, "You ladies should not have come to my monastery in this unmindful state. Because you have been negligent Māra has had the opportunity to make you behave shamelessly, laughing and singing loudly, in my monastery. Now, strive to put out the fire of passion (rāga) which is in you".

Then the Buddha spoke in verse as follows:

Verse 146. Why is there laughter? Why is there joy although (the world) is always burning? Shrouded in darkness why not seek the light?

At the end of the discourse those five hundred women attained Sotāpatti Fruition.

Verse 147

XI (2) The Story of Sirimā

While residing at the Jetavana monastery, the Buddha uttered Verse (147) of this book, with reference to Sirimā the courtesan.

Once, there lived in Rājagaha, a very beautiful courtesan by the name of Sirimā. Every day Sirimā offered alms-food to eight bhikkhus. One of these bhikkhus happened to mention to other bhikkhus how beautiful Sirimā was and also that she offered very delicious food to the bhikkhus every day. On hearing this, a young bhikkhu fell in love with Sirimā even without seeing her. The next day, the young bhikkhu went with the other bhikkhus to the house of Sirimā. Sirimā was not well on that day, but since she wanted to pay obeisance to the bhikkhus, she was carried to their presence. The young bhikkhu, seeing Sirimā, thought to himself, "Even though she is sick, she is very beautiful!" And he felt a strong desire for her.

That very night, Sirimā died. King Bimbisāra went to the Buddha and reported to him that Sirimā, the sister of Jīvaka, had died. The Buddha told King Bimbisāra to take the dead body to the cemetery and keep it there for three days without burying it, but to have it protected from crows and vultures. The king did as he was told. On the fourth day, the dead body of the beautiful Sirimā was no longer beautiful or desirable; it got bloated and maggots came out from the nine orifices. On that day, the Buddha took his bhikkhus to the cemetery to observe the body of Sirimā. The king also came with his men. The young bhikkhu, who was so desperately in love with Sirimā, did not know that Sirimā had died. When he learnt that the Buddha and the bhikkhus were going to see Sirimā, he joined them. At the cemetery, the corpse of Sirimā was surrounded by the bhikkhus headed by the Buddha, and also by the king and his men.

The Buddha then asked the king to get a town crier announce that Sirimā would be available on payment of one thousand in cash per night. But nobody would take her for one thousand, or for five hundred, or for two hundred and fifty, or even if she were to be given free of charge. Then the Buddha said to the audience, "Bhikkhus! Look at Sirimā. When she was living, there were many who were willing to give one thousand to spend one night with her; but now none would take her even if given without any payment. The body of a person is subject to deterioration and decay."

Then the Buddha spoke in verse as follows:

Verse 147. Look at this dressed up body, a mass of sores, supported (by bones), sickly, a subject of many thoughts (of sensual desire). Indeed, that body is neither permanent nor enduring.

At the end of the discourse, the young bhikkhu attained Sotāpatti Fruition.

Verse 148

XI (3) The Story of Therī Uttarā

While residing at the Jetavana monastery, the Buddha uttered Verse (148) of this book, with reference to Therī Uttarā.

Therī Uttarā, who was one hundred and twenty years old, was one day returning from her alms-round when she met a bhikkhu and requested him to accept her offering of alms-food. The inconsiderate bhikkhu accepted all her alms-food; so she had to go without food for that day. The same thing happened on the next two days. Thus Therī Uttarā was without food for three successive days and she was feeling weak. On the fourth day, while she was on her alms-round, she met the Buddha on the road where it was narrow. Respectfully, she paid obeisance to the Buddha and stepped back. While doing so, she accidentally stepped on her own robe and fell on the ground, injuring her head. The Buddha went up to her and said, "Your body is getting very old and infirm, it is ready to crumble, it will soon perish."

Then the Buddha spoke in verse as follows :

Verse 148. This body is worn out with age, it is the seat of sickness, it is subject to decay. This putrid body disintegrates; life, indeed, ends in death.

At the end of the discourse, Therī Uttarā attained Sotāpatti Fruition.

Verse 149

XI (4) The Story of Adhimānika Bhikkhus

While residing at the Jetavana monastery, the Buddha uttered Verse (149) of this book, with reference to some bhikkhus who over-estimated themselves.

Five hundred bhikkhus, after taking a subject of meditation from the Buddha, went into the woods. There, they practised meditation ardently and diligently and soon attained deep mental absorption (jhāna) and they thought that they were free from sensual desires and, therefore, had attained arahatship. Actually, they were only over-estimating themselves. Then, they went to the Buddha, with the intention of informing the Buddha about what they thought was their attainment of arahatship.

When they arrived at the outer gate of the monastery, the Buddha said to the Venerable Ānanda, "Those bhikkhus will not benefit much by coming to see me now; let them go to the cemetery first and come to see me only afterwards." The Venerable Ānanda then delivered the message of the Buddha to those bhikkhus, and they reflected, "The Enlightened One knows everything; he must have some reason in making us go to the cemetery first." So they went to the cemetery.

There, when they saw the putrid corpses they could look at them as just skeletons, and bones, but when they saw some fresh dead bodies they realized, with horror, that they still had some sensual desires awakening in them. The Buddha saw them from his perfumed chamber and sent forth the radiance; then he appeared to them and said, "Bhikkhus! Seeing these bleached bones, is it proper for you to have any sensual desire in you?"

Then the Buddha spoke in verse as follows:

Verse 149. Like gourds thrown away in autumn are these dove-grey bones; what pleasure is there in seeing them?

At the end of the discourse, those five hundred bhikkhus attained arahatship.

Verse 150

XI (5) The Story of Therī Rūpanandā (Janapadakalyāṇī)

While residing at the Jetavana manastery, the Buddha uttered Verse (150) of this book, with reference to Janapadakalyāṇī.

Princess Janapadakalyāṇī was the daughter of Gotamī, the step-mother of Gotama the Buddha; because she was very beautiful she was also known as Rūpanandā. She was married to Nanda, a cousin of the Buddha. One day she pondered, "My elder brother who could have become a Universal Monarch has renounced the world to become a bhikkhu; he is now a Buddha. Rāhulā, the son of my elder brother, and my own husband Prince Nanda have also become bhikkhus. My mother Gotamī has also become a bhikkhunī, and I am all alone here!" So saying, she went to the monastery of some bhikkhunīs and became a bhikkhunī herself. Thus, she had become a bhikkhunī not out of faith but only in imitation of others and because she felt lonely.

Rūpanandā had heard from others that the Buddha often taught about the impermanence, unsatisfactoriness and insubstantiality of the khandhas. So she thought he would talk deprecatingly about her good looks if he should see her; and thus thinking, she kept away from the Buddha. But other bhikkhunīs, coming back from the monastery, kept talking in praise of the Buddha; so, one day, she decided to accompany other bhikkhunīs to the monastery.

The Buddha saw her and reflected, "A thorn can only be taken out with a thorn; Rūpanandā being very attached to her body and being very proud of her beauty, I must take the pride and attachment out of her through beauty." So with his supernormal power, he caused an image of a very beautiful lady of about sixteen years of age to be seated near him, fanning him. This young girl was visible only to Rūpanandā and the Buddha. When Rūpanandā saw the girl, she realized that compared to that girl, she herself was just like an old, ugly crow compared to a beautiful white swan. Rūpanandā had a good look at the girl and she felt that she liked her very much. Then, she looked again and was surprised to find that the girl had grown to the age of about twenty. Again and again, she looked at the figure beside the Buddha and every time she noticed that the girl had grown older and older. Thus, the girl turned into a grown-up lady, then into a middle-aged lady, an old lady, a decrepit and a very old lady successively. Rūpanandā also noticed that with the arising of a new image, the old image disappeared, and she came to realize that there was a continuous process of change and decay in the body. With the coming of this realization, her attachment to the body diminished. Meanwhile, the figure near the Buddha had turned into an old, decrepit lady, who could no longer control her bodily functions, and was rolling in her own excreta. Finally, she died, her body got bloated, pus and maggots came out of the nine openings and crows and vultures were trying to snatch at the dead body.

Having seen all these, Rūpanandā pondered, "This young girl has grown old and decrepit and died in this very place under my own eyes. In the same way, my body will also grow old and wear out; it will be subject to disease and I will also die." Thus, she came to perceive the true nature of the khandhas. At this point, the Buddha talked about the impermanence, the unsatisfactoriness and the insubstantiality of the khandhas, and Rūpanandā attained Sotāpatti Fruition.

Then the Buddha spoke in verse as follows:

Verse 150. This body (lit., the city) is built up with bones which are covered with flesh and blood; within this dwell (lit., are deposited) decay and death, pride and detraction (of others' virtues and reputation).

At the end of the discourse, Rūpanandā attained arahatship.

Verse 151

XI (6) The Story of Queen Mallikā

While residing at the Jetavana monastery, the Buddha uttered Verse (151) of this book, with reference to Mallikā, queen of King Pasenadi of Kosala.

One day, Mallikā went into the bathroom to wash her face, hands and feet. Her pet dog also came in; as she was bending to wash her feet, the dog tried to have sex with her, and the queen appeared to be amused and somewhat pleased. The king saw this strange incident through the window from his bedroom. When the queen came in, he said angrily to the queen, "Oh, you wicked woman! What were you doing with that dog in the bathroom? Do not deny what I saw with my own eyes." The queen replied that she was only washing her face, her hands and her feet, and so was doing nothing wrong. Then she continued, "But, that room is very strange. If anyone went into that room, to one looking from this window there would appear to be two. If you do not believe me, O King, please go into that room and I will look through this window."

So, the king went into the bathroom. When he came out, Mallikā asked the king why he misbehaved with a she-goat in that room. The king denied it, but the queen insisted that she saw them with her own eyes. The king was puzzled, but being dim-witted, he accepted the queen's explanation, and concluded that the bathroom was, indeed, very strange.

From that time, the queen was full of remorse for having lied to the king and for having brazenly accused him of misbehaving with a she-goat. Thus, even when she was approaching death, she forgot to think about the great, unrivalled charities she had shared with her husband and only remembered that she had been unfair to him. As a result of this, when she died she was reborn in niraya. After her burial, the king intended to ask the Buddha where she was reborn. The Buddha wished to spare his feelings, and also did not want him to lse faith in the Dhamma. So he willed that this question should not be put to him, and King Pasenadi forgot to ask the Buddha.

However, after seven days in niraya, the queen was reborn in the Tusitā deva world On that day, the

Buddha went to King Pasenadi's palace for alms-food; he indicated that he wished to rest in the coach-shed where the royal carriages were kept. After offering alms--food, the king asked the Buddha where queen Mallikā was reborn and the Buddha replied, "Mallikā has been reborn in the Tusitā deva world." Hearing this, the king was very pleased, and said, "Where else could she have been reborn? She was always thinking of doing good deeds, always thinking what to offer to the Buddha on the next day. Venerable Sir! Now that she is gone, I, your humble disciple, hardly know what to do." To him the Buddha said, "Look at these carriages of your father and your grandfather; these are all worn down and lying useless; so also is your body, which is subject to death and decay. Only the Dhamma of the Virtuous is not subject to decay."

Then the Buddha spoke in verse as follows:

Verse 151. The much ornamented royal carriages do wear out, the body also grows old, but the Dhamma of the Virtuous does not decay. Thus, indeed, say the Virtuous among themselves.

Verse 152

XI (7) The Story of Thera Lāḷudāyī

While residing at the Jetavana monastery, the Buddha uttered Verse (152) of this book, with reference to Lāḷudāyī, a thera with little intelligence.

Lāḷudāyī was a bhikkhu who was dim-witted and very absent-minded. He could never say things which were appropriate to the occasion, although he tried hard. Thus, on joyful and auspicious occasions he would talk about sorrow, and on sorrowful occasions he would talk about joy and gladness. Besides, he never realized that he had been saying things which were inappropriate to the occasion. When told about this, the Buddha said, "One like Lāḷudāyī who has little knowledge is just like an ox."

Then the Buddha spoke in verse as follows:

Verse 152. This man of little learning grows old like an ox; only his flesh grows but not his wisdom.

Verses 153 and 154

XI (8) The Story Concerning the "Words of Exultation of the Buddha"

These two verses are expressions of intense and sublime joy felt by the Buddha at the moment of attainment of Supreme Enlightenment (Bodhi ñāṇa or Sabbaññuta ñāṇa). These verses were repeated at the Jetavana monastery at the request of the Venerable Ānanda.

Prince Siddhattha, of the family of Gotama, son of King Suddhodana and Queen Māyā of the kingdom of the Sakyans, renounced the world at the age of twenty-nine and became an ascetic in search of the Dhamma (Truth). For six years, he wandered about the valley of the Ganges, approaching famous religious leaders, studying their doctrines and methods. He lived austerely and submitted himself strictly to rigorous ascetic discipline; but he found all these traditional practices to be unsound. He was determined to find the Truth in his own way, and by avoiding the two extremes of excessive sensual indulgence and self-mortification,[1] he found the Middle Path which would lead to Perfect Peace, Nibbāna. This Middle Path (Majjhimapaṭipadā) is the Noble Path of Eight Constituents, viz., Right view, Right thought, Right speech, Right action, Right livelihood, Right effort, Right mindfulness and Right concentration.

Thus, one evening, seated under a Bo tree on the bank of the Nerañjarā river, Prince Siddhattha Gotama attained Supreme Enlightenment (Bodhi ñāṇa or Sabbaññuta ñāṇa) at the age of thirty-five. During the first watch of the night, the prince attained the power of recollection of past existences (Pubbenivāsānussati ñāṇa) and during the second watch he attained the divine power of sight (Dibbacakkhu ñāṇa). Then, during the third watch of the night he contemplated the Doctrine of Dependent Origination (Paṭiccasamuppāda) in the order of arising (anuloma) as well as in the order of cessation (paṭiloma). At the crack of dawn, Prince Siddhattha Gotama by his own intellect and insight fully and completely comprehended the Four Noble Truths. The Four Noble Truths are: The Noble Truth of Dukkha (Dukkha Ariya Sacca), the Noble Truth of

---

1. Kāmasukhallikānuyoga and Attakilamathānuyoga.

the Cause of Dukkha (Dukkha Samudaya Ariya Sacca), the Noble Truth of the Cessation of Dukkha (Dukkha Nirodha Ariya Sacca), and the Noble Truth of the Path Leading to the Cessation of Dukkha (Dukkha Nirodha Gāminī Paṭipadā Ariya Sacca). There also appeared in him, in all their purity, the knowledge of the nature of each Noble Truth (Sacca ñāṇa), knowledge of the performance required for each Noble Truth (Kicca ñāṇa), and the knowledge of the completion of the performance required for each Noble Truth (Kata ñāṇa); and thus, he attained the Sabbaññuta ñāṇa (also called Bodhi ñāṇa) of a Buddha. From that time, he was known as Gotama the Buddha.

In this connection, it should be noted that only when the Four Noble Truths, under their three aspects (therefore, the twelve modes), had become perfectly clear to him that the Buddha acknowledged in the world of Men, the world of Devas and that of Brahmās, that he had attained the Supreme Enlightenment and therefore had become a Buddha.

At the moment of the attainment of Buddhahood, the Buddha uttered the following two verses:

Verse 153. I, who have been seeking the builder of this house (body), failing to attain Enlightenment (Bodhi ñāṇa or Sabbaññuta ñāṇa) which would enable me to find him, have wandered through innumerable births in saṁsāra. To be born again and again is, indeed, dukkha!

Verse 154. Oh house-builder! You are seen, you shall build no house (for me) again. All your rafters are broken, your roof-tree is destroyed. My mind has reached the Unconditioned (i.e., Nibbāna); the end of craving (Arahatta Phala) has been attained.

Verses 155 and 156

XI (9) The Story of the Son of Mahādhana

While residing at the Migadāya wood, the Buddha uttered Verses (155) and (156) of this book, with reference to the son of Mahādhana, a rich man from Bārāṇasī.

The son of Mahādhana did not study while he was young; when he came of age he married the daughter of a rich man, who, like him, also had no education. When the parents on both sides died, they inherited eighty crores from each side and so were very rich. But both of them were ignorant and knew only how to spend money and not how to keep it or to make it grow. They just ate and drank and had a good time, squandering their money. When they had spent all, they sold their fields and gardens and finally their house. Thus, they became very poor and helpless; and because they did not know how to earn a living they had to go begging. One day, the Buddha saw the rich man's son leaning against a wall of the monastery, taking the left-overs given him by the sāmaṇeras; seeing him, the Buddha smiled.

The Venerable Ānanda asked the Buddha why he smiled, and the Buddha replied, "Ānanda, look at this son of a very rich man; he had lived a useless life, an aimless life of pleasure. If he had learnt to look after his riches in the first stage of his life he would have been a top-ranking richman; or if he had become a bhikkhu, he could have been an arahat, and his wife could have been an anāgamī. If he had learnt to look after his riches in the second stage of his life he would have been a second rank rich man, or if he had become a bhikkhu he could have been an anāgāmī, and his wife could have been a sakadāgāmī. If he had learnt to look after his riches in the third stage of his life he would have been a third rank rich man, or if he had become a bhikkhu he could have been a sakadāgāmī, and his wife could have been a sotāpanna. However, because he had done nothing in all the three stages of his life he had lost all his worldly riches, he had also lost all opportunities of attaining any of the Maggas and Phalas.

Then the Buddha spoke in verse as follows:

Verse 155. They, who in youth have neither led the Life of Purity nor have acquired wealth, waste away in dejection like decrepit herons on a drying pond deplete of fish.

Verse 156. They, who in youth have neither led the Life of Purity nor have acquired wealth, lie helplessly like arrows that have lost momentum, moaning and sighing after the past.

End of Chapter Eleven : Ageing.

Chapter XII
Self (Attavagga)

Verse 157
XII (1) The Story of Bodhirājakumāra

While residing at the Bhesakaḷā wood, the Buddha uttered Verse (157) of this book, with reference to Prince Bodhi (Bodhirājakumāra).

Once, Prince Bodhi built a magnificent palace for himself. When the palace was finished he invited the Buddha for alms-food. For this special occasion, he had the building decorated and perfumed with four kinds of scents and incense. Also, a long length of cloth was spread on the floor, starting from the threshold to the interior of the room. Then, because he had no children, the prince made a solemn asseveration that if he were to have any children the Buddha should step on the cloth. When the Buddha came, Prince Bodhi respectfully requested the Buddha three times to enter the room. But the Buddha, instead of moving, only looked at Ānanda. Ānanda understood him and so asked Prince Bodhi to remove the cloth from the door-step. Then only, the Buddha entered the palace. The prince then offered delicious and choice food to the Buddha. After the meal, the prince asked the Buddha why he did not step on the cloth. The Buddha in turn asked the prince whether he had not spread the cloth making a solemn asseveration that if he were to be blessed with a child, the Buddha would step on it; and the prince replied in the affirmative. To him, the Buddha said that he and his wife were not going to have any children because of their past evil deeds. The Buddha then related their past story.

In one of their past existences, the prince and his wife were the sole survivors of a shipwreck. They were stranded on a deserted island, and there they lived by eating birds' eggs, fledglings and birds, without any feeling of remorse at any time. For that evil deed, they would not be blessed with any children. If they had felt even a slight remorse for their deed at any stage of their lives, they could have a child or two in this existence. Then turning to the prince, the

Buddha said, "One who loves himself should guard himself in all stages of life, or at least, during one stage in his life."

Then the Buddha spoke in verse as follows:

Verse 157. If one knows that one is dear to oneself, one should protect oneself well. During any of the three watches (of life) the wise man should be on guard (against evil).

At the end of the discourse, Bodhirājakumāra attained Sotāpatti Fruition.

Verse 158

XII (2) The Story of Thera Upananda Sakyaputta

While residing at the Jetavana monastery, the Buddha uttered Verse (158) of this book, with reference to Upananda, a thera of the Sakyan Clan.

Upananda was a very eloquent preacher. He used to preach to others not to be greedy and to have only a few wants and would talk eloquently on the merits of contentment and frugality (appicchatā) and austere practices (dhūtaṅgas). However, he did not practise what he taught and took for himself all the robes and other requisites that were given up by others.

On one occasion, Upananda went to a village monastery just before the vassa. Some young bhikkhus, being impressed by his eloquence, asked him to spend the vassa in their monastery. He asked them how many robes each bhikkhu usually received as donation for the vassa in their monastery and they told him that they usually received one robe each. So he did not stop there, but he left his slippers in that monastery. At the next monastery, he learned that the bhikkhus usually received two robes each for the vassa; there he left his staff. At the next monastery, the bhikkhus received three robes each as donation for the vassa; there he left his water bottle. Finally, at the monastery where each bhikkhu received four robes, he decided to spend the vassa.

At the end of the vassa, he claimed his share of robes from the other monasteries where he had left his personal effects. Then he collected all his things in a cart and came back to his old monastery. On his way.

he met two young bhikkhus who were having a dispute over the share of two robes and a valuable velvet blanket which they had between them. Since they could not come to an amicable settlement, they asked Upananda to arbitrate. Upananda gave one robe each to them and took the valuable velvet blanket for having acted as an arbitrator.

The two young bhikkhus were not satisfied with the decision but they could do nothing about it. With a feeling of dissatisfaction and dejection, they went to the Buddha and reported the matter. To them the Buddha said, "One who teaches others should first teach himself and act as he has taught."

Then the Buddha spoke in verse as follows:

Verse 158. One should first establish oneself in what is proper; then only one should teach others. A wise man should not incur reproach.

At the end of the discourse the two young bhikkhus attained Sotāpatti Fruition.

Verse 159

XII (3) The Story of Thera Padhānikatissa

While residing at the Jetavana monastery, the Buddha uttered Verse (159) of this book, with reference to Thera Padhānikatissa.

Thera Padhānikatissa, after taking a subject of meditation from the Buddha, left for the forest with five hundred other bhikkhus. There, he told the bhikkhus to be ever mindful and diligent in their meditation practice. After thus exhorting others he himself would lie down and go to sleep. The young bhikkhus did as they were told. They practised meditation during the first watch of the night and when they were about to go to bed, Padhānikatissa would get up and tell them to go back to their practice. When they returned after meditation practice during the second and third watches also he would say the same thing to them.

As he was always acting in this way, the young bhikkhus never had peace of mind, and so they could not concentrate on meditation practice or even on recitation of the texts. One day, they decided to investigate if their teacher was truly zealous and vigilant as he posed himself to be. When they found out that their teacher Padhānikatissa only exhorted others but was himself sleeping most of the time, they remarked, "We are ruined, our teacher knows only how to scold us, but he himself is just wasting time, doing nothing." By this time, as the bhikkhus were not getting enough rest, they were tired and worn out. As a result, none of the bhikkhus made any progress in their meditation practice.

At the end of the vassa, they returned to the Jetavana monastery and reported the matter to the Buddha. To them the Buddha said, "Bhikkhus! One who wants to teach others should first teach himself and conduct himself properly."

Then the Buddha spoke in verse as follows:

Verse 159. One should act as one teaches others; only with oneself thoroughly tamed should one tame others. To tame oneself is, indeed, difficult.

At the end of the discourse those five hundred bhikkhus attained arahatship.

Verse 160

XII (4) The Story of the Mother of Kumārakassapa

While residing at the Jetavana monastery, the Buddha uttered Verse (160) of this book, with reference to the mother of Kumārakassapa.

Once, a young married woman asked permission from her husband to become a bhikkhunī. Through ignorance, she went to join some bhikkhunīs who were the pupils of Devadatta. This young woman was pregnant before she became a bhikkhunī, but she was not aware of the fact at that time. But in due course, the pregnancy became obvious and the other bhikkhunīs took her to their teacher Devadatta. Devadatta ordered her to go back to the household life. She then said to the other bhikkhunīs, "I have not intended to become a bhikkhunī under your teacher Devadatta; I have come here by mistake. Please take me to the Jetavana monastery, take me to the Buddha." Thus she came to the Buddha. The Buddha knew that she was pregnant before she became a bhikkhunī and was therefore innocent; but he was not going to handle the case. The Buddha sent for King Pasenadi of Kosala, Anāthapiṇḍika, the famous rich man, and Visākhā, the famous donor of the Pubbārāma monastery, and many other persons. He then told Thera Upāli to settle the case in public.

Visākhā took the young girl behind a curtain; she examined her and reported to Thera Upāli that the girl was already pregnant when she became a bhikkhunī. Thera Upāli then declared to the audience that the girl was quite innocent and therefore had not soiled her morality (sīla). In due course, a son was born to her. The boy was adopted by King Pasenadi and was named Kumārakassapa. When the boy was seven years old, on learning that his mother was a bhikkhunī, he also became a sāmaṇera under the tutelage of the Buddha. When he came of age he was admitted to the Order; as a bhikkhu, he took a subject of meditation from the Buddha and went to the forest. There, he practised meditation ardently and diligently and within a short time attained arahatship. However, he continued to live in the forest for twelve more years.

Thus his mother had not seen him for twelve years and she longed to see her son very much. One day, seeing him, the mother bhikkhunī ran after her son weeping and calling out his name. Seeing his mother, Kumārakassapa thought that if he were to speak pleasantly to his mother she would still be attached to him and her future would be ruined. So for the sake of her future (realization of Nibbāna) he was deliberately stern and spoke harshly to her: "How is it, that you, a member of the Order, could not even cut off this affection for a son?" The mother thought that her son was very cruel to her, and she asked him what he meant. Kumārakassapa repeated what he had said before. On hearing his answer, the mother of Kumārakassapa reflected: "O yes, for twelve years I have shed tears for this son of mine. Yet, he has spoken harshly to me. What is the use of my affection for him?" Then, the futility of her attachment to her son dawned upon her, and then and there, she decided to cut off her attachment to her son. By cutting off her attachment entirely, the mother of Kumārakassapa attained arahatship on the same day.

One day, at the congregation of bhikkhus, some bhikkhus said to the Buddha, "Venerable Sir! If the mother of Kumārakassapa had listened to Devadatta, she as well as her son would not have become arahats. Surely, Devadatta had tried to do them a great wrong; but you, Venerable Sir, are a refuge to them!" To them the Buddha said, "Bhikkhus! In trying to reach the deva world, or in trying to attain arahatship, you cannot depend on others, you must work hard on your own."

Then the Buddha spoke in verse as follows:

Verse 160. One indeed is one's own refuge; how can others be a refuge to one? With oneself thoroughly tamed, one can attain a refuge (i.e., Arahatta Phala), which is so difficult to attain.

Verse 161

XII (5) The Story of Mahākāla Upāsaka

While residing at the Jetavana monastery, the Buddha uttered Verse (161) of this book, with reference to Mahākāla, a lay disciple.

On a certain sabbath day, Mahākāla, a lay disciple, went to the Jetavana monastery. On that day, he kept the sabbath by observing the eight moral precepts (Uposatha sila) and listened to the discourses on the Dhamma throughout the night. It so happened that on that same night, some thieves broke into a house; and the owners on waking up went after the thieves. The thieves ran away in all directions. Some ran in the direction of the monastery. It was then nearing dawn, and Mahākāla was washing his face at the pond close to the monastery. The thieves dropped their stolen property in front of Mahākāla and ran on. When the owners arrived, they saw Mahākāla with the stolen property. Taking him for one of the thieves they shouted at him, threatened him and beat him hard. Mahākāla died on the spot. Early in the morning, when some young bhikkhus and sāmaṇeras from the monastery came to the pond to fetch water, they saw the dead body and recognized it.

On their return to the monastery, they reported what they had seen and said to the Buddha, "Venerable Sir! The lay disciple who was at this monastery listening to the religious discourses all through the night has met with a death which he does not deserve." To them the Buddha replied, "Bhikkhus! If you judge from the good deeds he has done in this existence, he has indeed met with a death he does not deserve. But the fact is that he has only paid for the evil he had done in a past existence. In one of his previous existences, when he was a courtier in the palace of the king, he fell in love with another man's wife and had beaten her husband to death. Thus, evil deeds surely get one into trouble; they even lead one to the four apāyas."

Then the Buddha spoke in verse as follows:

Verse 161. The evil done by oneself, arising in oneself, and caused by oneself, destroys the foolish one, just as a diamond grinds the rock from which it is formed.

Verse 162

XII (6) The Story of Devadatta

While residing at the Jetavana monastery, the Buddha uttered Verse (162) of this book, with reference to Devadatta.

One day, some bhikkhus were talking amongst themselves when the Buddha came in and asked the subject of their talk. They answered that they were talking about Devadatta and then continued as follows: "Venerable Sir! Devadatta is, indeed, a man without morality; he is also very avaricious. He has tried to gain fame and fortune by getting the confidence of Ajātasattu by unfair means. He has also tried to convince Ajātasattu that by getting rid of his father, he (Ajātasattu) would immediately become a powerful king. Having been thus misled by Devadatta, Ajātasattu killed his father, the noble king, Bimbisāra. Devadatta has even attempted three times to kill you, our most Venerable Teacher. Devadatta is, indeed, very wicked and incorrigible!"

After listening to the bhikkhus, the Buddha told them that Devadatta had tried to kill him not only now but also in his previous existences. The Buddha then narrated the story of a deer-stalker.

"Once, while King Brahmadatta was reigning in Bārāṇasī, the future Buddha was born as a deer, and Devadatta was then a deer-stalker. One day, the deer-stalker saw the footprints of a deer under a tree. So, he put up a bamboo platform in the tree and waited with the spear ready for the deer. The deer came but he came very cautiously. The deer-stalker saw him hesitating, and threw some fruits of the tree to coax him. But that put the deer on guard; he looked more carefully and saw the deer-stalker in the tree. He pretended not to see the deer-stalker and turned away slowly. From some distance, he addressed the tree thus: 'O tree! You always drop your fruits vertically, but today you have broken the law of nature and have dropped your fruits slantingly. Since you have violated the natural law of trees, I am now leaving you for another tree.'

"Seeing the deer turning away, the dear-stalker dropped his spear to the ground and said, 'Yes, you can now move on; for today, I have been wrong in my calculations.' The deer who was the Buddha-to-be replied, 'O hunter! You have truly miscalculated today, but your evil kamma will not make any mistake; it will certainly follow you.' Thus, Devadatta had attempted to kill me not only now but also in the past, yet he had never succeeded." Then the Buddha continued, "Bhikkhus! Just as a creeper strangles the tree to which it clings, so also, those without morality, being overwhelmed by lust, are finally thrown into niraya."

Then the Buddha spoke in verse as follows:

Verse 162. As the creeper (māluvā) strangles the sal tree, so also, a really immoral person (overwhelmed by Craving) does to himself just what his enemy wishes him to do.

At the end of the discourse, many people attained Sotāpatti Fruition.

Verse 163

XII (7) The Story of Schism in the Order

While residing at the Veḷuvana monastery, the Buddha uttered Verse (163) of this book, with reference to Devadatta, who committed the offence of causing a schism in the Order of the bhikkhus.

On one occasion, while the Buddha was giving a discourse in the Veḷuvana monastery, Devadatta came to him and suggested that since the Buddha was getting old, the duties of the Order should be entrusted to him (Devadatta); but the Buddha rejected his proposal and also rebuked him and called him a "spittle swallower" (Kheḷāsika). From that time, Devadatta felt very bitter towards the Buddha. He even tried to kill the Buddha three times, but all his attempts failed. Later, Devadatta tried another tactic. This time, he came to the Buddha and proposed five rules of discipline for the bhikkhus to observe throughout their lives. He proposed (i) that the bhikkhus should live in the forest; (ii) that they should live only on food received on alms-rounds; (iii) that they should wear robes made only from pieces of cloth collected from rubbish heaps; (iv) that they should reside under trees; and (v) that they should not take fish or meat. The Buddha did not have any objections to these rules and made no objections to those who were willing to observe them, but for various valid considerations, he was not prepared to impose these rules of discipline on the bhikkhus in general.

Devadatta claimed that the rules proposed by him were much better than the existing rules of discipline, and some new bhikkhus agreed with him. One day, the Buddha asked Devadatta if it was true that he was trying to create a schism in the Order, and he admitted that it was so. The Buddha warned him that it was a very serious offence, but Devadatta paid no heed to his warning. After this, as he met Thera Ānanda on his alms-round in Rājagaha, Devadatta said to Thera Ānanda, "Ānanda, from today I will observe the sabbath (Uposatha), and perform the duties of the Order separately, independent of the Buddha and his Order of bhikkhus." On his return from the alms-round, Thera Ānanda reported to the Buddha what Devadatta had said.

On hearing this, the Buddha reflected, "Devadatta is committing a very serious offence; it will send him to Avīci Niraya. For a virtuous person, it is easy to do good deeds and difficult to do evil; but for an evil one, it is easy to do evil and difficult to do good deeds. Indeed, in life it is easy to do something which is not beneficial, but it is very difficult to do something which is good and beneficial."

Then the Buddha spoke in verse as follows:

Verse 163. It is easy to do things that are bad and unbeneficial to oneself, but it is, indeed, most difficult to do things that are beneficial and good.

Then, on the Uposatha day, Devadatta, followed by five hundred Vajjian bhikkhus, broke off from the Order, and went to Gayāsīsa. However, when the two Chief Disciples, Sāriputta and Moggallāna, went to see the bhikkhus who had followed Devadatta and talked to them they realized their mistakes and most of them returned with the two Chief Disciples to the Buddha.

Verse 164

XII (8) The Story of Thera Kāla

While residing at the Jetavana monastery, the Buddha uttered Verse (164) of this book, with reference to Thera Kāla.

Once in Sāvatthi, an elderly woman was looking after a thera named Kāla, like her own son. One day, hearing from her neighbours about the virtues of the Buddha, she wished very much to go to the Jetavana monastery and listen to the discourses given by the Buddha. So she told Thera Kāla about her wishes; but the thera advised her against it. Three times she spoke to him about her wishes but he always dissuaded her. But one day, in spite of his dissuasions, the lady decided to go. After asking her daughter to look to the needs of Thera Kāla she left the house. When Thera Kāla came on his usual round of alms-food, he learned that the lady of the house had left for the Jetavana monastery. Then he reflected, "It is quite possible that the lady of this house is losing her faith in me." So, he made haste and quickly followed her to the monastery. There, he found her listening to the discourse being given by the Buddha. He approached the Buddha respectfully, and said, "Venerable Sir! This woman is very dull; she will not be able to understand the sublime Dhamma; please teach her only about charity (dāna) and morality (sīla)."

The Buddha knew very well that Thera Kāla was talking out of spite and with an ulterior motive. So he said to Thera Kāla, "Bhikkhu! Because you are foolish and because of your wrong view, you scorn my Teaching. You yourself are your own ruin; in fact, you are only trying to destroy yourself."

Then the Buddha spoke in verse as follows:

Verse 164. The foolish man who, on account of his wrong views, scorns the teaching of homage--worthy Noble Ones (Ariyas) who live according to the Dhamma is like the bamboo which bears fruit for its own destruction.

At the end of the discourse the elderly lady attained Sotāpatti Fruition.

Verse 165

XII (9) The Story of Cūḷakāla Upāsaka

While residing at the Jetavana monastery, the Buddha uttered Verse (165) of this book, with reference to Cūḷakāla, a lay disciple.

Cūḷakāla, a lay disciple, observed the Uposatha precepts on a certain sabbath day and spent the night at the Jetavana monastery, listening to religious discourses all through the night. Early in the morning, as he was washing his face at the pond near the monastery, some thieves dropped a bundle near him. The owners seeing him with the stolen property took him for a thief and beat him hard. Fortunately, some slave girls who had come to fetch water testified that they knew him and that he was not the thief. So Cūḷakāla was let off.

When the Buddha was told about it, he said to Cūḷakāla, "You have been let off not only because the slave girls said that you were not the thief but also because you did not steal and was therefore innocent. Those who do evil go to niraya, but those who do good are reborn in the deva worlds or else realize Nibbāna."

Then the Buddha spoke in verse as follows:

Verse 165. By oneself indeed is evil done and by oneself is one defiled; by oneself is evil not done and by oneself is one purified. Purity and impurity depend entirely on oneself; no one can purify another.

At the end of the discourse Cūḷakāla the lay disciple attained Sotāpatti Fruition.

Verse 166

XII (10) The Story of Thera Attadattha

While residing at the Jetavana monastery, the Buddha uttered Verse (166) of this book, with reference to Thera Attadattha.

When the Buddha declared that he would realize parinibbāna in four months' time, many puthujjana bhikkhus[1] were apprehensive and did not know what to do; so they kept close to the Buddha. Attadattha, however, did not go to the Buddha and, having resolved to attain arahatship during the lifetime of the Buddha, was striving hard in the meditation practice. Other bhikkhus, not understanding him, took him to the Buddha and said, "Venerable Sir, this bhikkhu does not seem to love and revere you as we do; he only keeps to himself." The thera then explained to them that he was striving hard to attain arahatship before the Buddha realized parinibbāna and that was the only reason why he had not come to the Buddha.

The Buddha then said to the bhikkhus, "Bhikkhus, those who love and revere me should act like Attadattha. You are not paying me homage by just offering flowers, perfumes and incense and by coming to see me; you pay me homage only by practising the Dhamma I have taught you, i. e., the Lokuttara Dhamma."

Then the Buddha spoke in verse as follows:

Verse 166. For the sake of another's benefit, however great it may be, do not neglect one's own (moral) benefit. Clearly perceiving one's own benefit one should make every effort to attain it.

At the end of the discourse Thera Attadattha attained arahatship.

End of Chapter Twelve: Self.

---

1. **Puthujjana bhikkhus:** bhikkhus who have not yet attained any Magga.

Chapter XIII
The World (Lokavagga)

Verse 167
XIII (1) The Story of a Young Bhikkhu

While residing at the Jetavana monastery, the Buddha uttered Verse (167) of this book, with reference to a young bhikkhu.

Once, a young bhikkhu accompanied an older bhikkhu to the house of Visākhā. After taking rice gruel, the elder bhikkhu left for another place, leaving the young bhikkhu behind at the house of Visākhā. The granddaughter of Visākhā was filtering some water for the young bhikkhu, and when she saw her own reflection in the big water pot she smiled. Seeing her thus smiling, the young bhikkhu looked at her and he also smiled. When she saw the young bhikkhu looking at her and smiling at her, she lost her temper, and cried out angrily, "You, a shaven head! Why are you smiling at me?" The young bhikkhu reported, "You are a shaven head yourself; your mother and your father are also shaven heads!" Thus, they quarrelled, and the young girl went weeping to her grandmother. Visākhā came and said to the young bhikkhu, "Please do not get angry with my granddaughter. But, a bhikkhu does have his hair shaved, his finger nails and toe nails cut, and putting on a robe which is made up of cut pieces, he goes on alms-round with a bowl which is rimless. What this young girl said was, in a way, quite right, is it not?" The young bhikkhu replied, "It is true, but why should she abuse me on that account?" At this point, the elder bhikkhu returned; but both Visākhā and the old bhikkhu failed to appease the young bhikkhu and the young girl.

Soon after this, the Buddha arrived and learned about the quarrel. The Buddha knew that time was ripe for the young bhikkhu to attain Sotāpatti Fruition. Then, in order to make the young bhikkhu more responsive to his words, he seemingly sided with him and said to Visākhā, "Visākhā, what reason is there for your granddaughter to address my son as a shaven head just because he has his head shaven? After all, he' had his head shaven to enter my Order, didn't he?'

Hearing these words, the young bhikkhu went down on his knees, paid obeisance to the Buddha, and said, "Venerable Sir! You alone understand me; neither my teacher nor the great donor of the monastery understands me." The Buddha knew that the bhikkhu was then in a receptive mood and so he said, "To smile with sensual desire is ignoble; it is not right and proper to have ignoble thoughts."

Then the Buddha spoke in verse as follows:

Verse 167. Do not follow ignoble ways, do not live in negligence, do not embrace wrong views, do not be the one to prolong saṁsāra (lit., the world).

At the end of the discourse, the young bhikkhu attained Sotāpatti Fruition.

Verses 168 and 169

XIII (2) The Story of King Suddhodana

While residing at the Nigrodhārāma monastery, the Buddha uttered Verses (168) and (169) of this book, with reference to King Suddhodana, father of Gotama Buddha.

When the Buddha revisited Kapilavatthu for the first time he stayed at the Nigrodhārāma monastery. There, he expounded the Dhamma to his relatives. King Suddhodana thought that Gotama Buddha, who was his own son, would go to no other place, but would surely come to his palace for alms-food the next day; but he did not specifically invite the Buddha to come for alms-food. However, the next day, he prepared alms-food for twenty thousand bhikkhus. On that morning the Buddha went on his alms-round with a retinue of bhikkhus, as was the custom of all the Buddhas.

Yasodharā, wife of Prince Siddhattha before he renounced the world, saw the Buddha going on an alms-round, from the palace window. She informed her father-in-law, King Suddhodana, and the King went in great haste to the Buddha. The king told the Buddha that for a member of the royal Khattiya family, to go round begging for food from door to door was a disgrace. Whereupon the Buddha replied that it was the custom of all the Buddhas to go round for alms-food from house to house, and therefore it was right and proper for him to keep up the tradition.

The Buddha then spoke in verse as follows:

Verse 168. Do not neglect the duty of going on alms-round; observe proper practice (in going on alms-round). One who observes proper practice lives happily both in this world and in the next.

Verse 269. Observe proper practice (in going on alms-round); do not observe improper practice. One who observes proper practice lives happily both in this world and in the next.

At the end of the discourse the father of Gotama Buddha attained Sotāpatti Fruition.

Verse 170

XIII (3) The Story of Five Hundred Bhikkhus

While residing at the Jetavana monastery, the Buddha uttered Verse (170) of this book, with reference to five hundred bhikkhus.

On one occasion, five hundred bhikkhus, after taking a subject of meditation from the Buddha, went into the forest to practise meditation. But they made very little progress; so they returned to the Buddha to ask for a more suitable subject of meditation. On their way to the Buddha, seeing a mirage they meditated on it. As soon as they entered the compound of the monastery, a storm broke out; as big drops of rain fell, bubbles were formed on the ground and soon disappeared. Seeing those bubbles, the bhikkhus reflected "This body of ours is perishable like the bubbles", and perceived the impermanent nature of the aggregates (khandhas).

The buddha saw them from his perfumed chamber and sent forth the radiance and appeared in their vision.

Then the Buddha spoke in verse as follows:

Verse 170. If a man looks at the world (i.e., the five khandhas) in the same way as one looks at a bubble or a mirage, the King of Death will not find him.

At the end of the discourse those five hundred bhikkhus attained arahatship.

Verse 171

XIII (4) The Story of Prince Abhaya

While residing at the Veḷuvana monastery, the Buddha uttered Verse (171) of this book, with reference to Prince Abhaya (Abhayarājakumāra).

On one occasion, Prince Abhaya triumphantly returned after suppressing a rebellion at the frontier; King Bimbisāra was so pleased with him that for seven days, Abhaya was given the glory and honour of a ruler, together with a dancing girl to entertain him. On the last day, while the dancer was entertaining the prince and his company in the garden, she had a severe stroke; she collapsed and died on the spot. The prince was shocked and very much distressed. Sorrowfully, he went to the Buddha to find solace. To him the Buddha said, "O prince, the tears you have shed all through the round of rebirths cannot be measured. This world of aggregates (i. e., khandhas) is the place where fools flounder."

Then the Buddha spoke in verse as follows:

Verse 171. Come, look at this world (i.e., the five khandhas), which is like an ornamented royal carriage. Fools flounder in this world of the khandhas; but the wise are not attached to it.

Verse 172.

XIII (5) The Story of Thera Sammajjana

While residing at the Jetavana monastery, the Buddha uttered Verse (172) of this book, with reference to Thera Sammajjana.

Thera Sammajjana spent most of his time sweeping the precincts of the monastery. At that time, Thera Revata was also staying at the monastery; unlike Sammajjana, Thera Revata spent most of his time in meditation or deep mental absorption. Seeing Thera Revata's behaviour, Thera Sammajjana thought the other thera was just idling away his time. Thus, one day Sammajjana went to Thera Revata and said to him, 'You are being very lazy, living on the food offered out of faith and generosity; don't you think you should sometimes sweep the floors or the compound or some other place?" To him, Thera Revata replied, "Friend, a bhikkhu should not spend all his time sweeping. He should sweep early in the morning, then go out on the alms-round. After the meal, contemplating his body he should try to perceive the true nature of the aggregates, or else, recite the texts until nightfall. Then he can do the sweeping again if he so wishes." Thera Sammajjana strictly followed the advice given by Thera Revata and soon attained arahatship.

Other bhikkhus noticed some rubbish piling up in the compound and they asked Sammajjana why he was not sweeping as much as he used to, and he replied, "When I was not mindful, I was all the time sweeping; but now I am no longer unmindful." When the bhikkhus heard his reply they were sceptical; so they went to the Buddha and said, "Venerable Sir! Thera Sammajjana falsely claims himself to be an arahat; he is telling lies." To them the Buddha said, "Sammajjana has indeed attained arahatship; he is telling the truth."

Then the Buddha spoke in verse as follows:

Verse 172. He, who has been formerly unmindful, but is mindful later on, lights, up the world (with the light of Magga Insight as does the moon freed from clouds.

Verse 173

XIII (6) The Story of Thera Aṅgulimāla

While residing at the Jetavana monastery, the Buddha uttered Verse (173) of this book, with reference to Thera Aṅgulimāla.

Aṅgulimāla was the son of the head-priest in the court of King Pasenadi of Kosala. His original name was Ahiṁsaka. When he was of age, he was sent to Taxila, a renowned university town. Ahiṁsaka was intelligent and was also obedient to his teacher. So he was liked by the teacher and his wife; as a result, other pupils were jealous of him. So they went to the teacher and falsely reported that Ahiṁsaka was having an affair with the teacher's wife. At first, the teacher did not believe them, but after being told a number of times he believed them; and so he vowed to have revenge on the boy. To kill the boy would reflect badly on him; so he thought of a plan which was worse than murder. He told Ahiṁsaka to kill one thousand men or women and in return he promised to gave the boy priceless knowledge. The boy wanted to have this knowledge, but was very reluctant to take life. However, he agreed to do as he was told.

Thus, he kept on killing people, and not to lose count, he threaded a finger each of everyone he killed and wore them like a garland round his neck. In this way, he was known as Aṅgulimāla, and became the terror of the countryside. The king himself heard about the exploits of Aṅgulimāla, and he made preparations to capture him. When Mantānī, the mother of Aṅgulimāla, heard about the king's intention, out of love for her son, she went into the forest in a desperate bid to save her son. By this time, the chain round the neck of Aṅgulimāla had nine hundred and ninety-nine fingers in it, just one finger short of one thousand.

Early in the morning on that day, the Buddha saw Aṅgulimāla in his vision, and reflected that if he did not intervene, Aṅgulimāla who was on the look out for the last person to make up the one thousand would see his mother and might kill her. In that case, Aṅgulimāla would have to suffer in niraya endlessly. So out of compassion, the Buddha left for the forest where Aṅgulimāla was.

Aṅgulimāla, after many sleepless days and nights, was very tired and near exhaustion. At the same time, he was very anxious to kill the last person to make up his full quota of one thousand and so complete his task. He made up his mind to kill the first person he met. Suddenly, as he looked out he saw the Buddha and ran after him with his knife raised. But the Buddha could not be reached while he himself was completely exhausted. Then, looking at the Buddha, he cried out, "O bhikkhu, stop! stop!" and the Buddha replied, "I have stopped, only you have not stopped." Aṅgulimāla did not get the significance of the words of the Buddha, so he asked, "O bhikkhu! Why do you say that you have stopped and I have not stopped?"

The Buddha then said to him, "I say that I have stopped, because I have given up killing all beings, I have given up ill-treating all beings, and because I have established myself in universal love, patience, and knowledge through reflection. But, you have not given up killing or ill-treating others and you are not yet established in universal love and patience. Hence, you are the one who has not stopped." On hearing these words from the mouth of the Buddha, Aṅgulimāla reflected, "These are the words of a wise man. This bhikkhu is so very wise and so very brave; he must be the ruler of the bhikkhus. Indeed, he must be the Buddha himself! He must have come here specially to make me see the light." So thinking, he threw away his weapon and asked the Buddha to admit him to the Order of the bhikkhus. Then and there, the Buddha made him a bhikkhu.

Aṅgulimāla's mother looked for her son everywhere in the forest shouting out his name, but failing to find him she returned home. When the king and his men came to capture Aṅgulimāla, they found him at the monastery of the Buddha. Finding that Aṅgulimāla had given up his evil ways and had become a bhikkhu, the king and his men went home. During his stay at the monastery, Aṅgulimāla ardently and diligently practised meditation, and within a short time he attained arahatship.

Then, one day, while he was on an alms-round, he came to a place where some people were quarrelling among themselves. As they were throwing stones at one another, some stray stones hit Thera Aṅgulimāla on the head and he was seriously injured. Yet, he managed to come back to the Buddha, and the Buddha said to him, "My son Aṅgulimāla! You have done away with evil. Have patience. You are paying in this existence for the deeds you have done. These deeds would have made you suffer for innumerable years in niraya." Soon afterwards, Aṅgulimāla passed away peacefully; he had realized parinibbāna.

Other bhikkhus asked the Buddha where Aṅgulimāla was reborn, and when the Buddha replied "My son has realized parinibbāna", they could hardly believe it. So they asked him whether it was possible that a man who had killed so many people could have realized parinibbāna. To this question, the Buddha replied, "Bhikkhus! Aṅgulimāla had done much evil because he did not have good friends. But later, he found good friends and through their help and good advice he had been steadfast and mindful in his practice of the dhamma. Therefore, his evil deeds have been overwhelmed by good (i e., Arahatta Magga).

Then the Buddha spoke in verse as follows:

Verse 173. He who overwhelms with good the evil that he has done lights up this world (with the light of Magga Insight), as does the moon freed from clouds.

Verse 174

XIII (7) The Story of the Weaver-Girl

While residing at the monastery near Aggāvaḷa shrine in the country of Āḷavī, the Buddha uttered Verse (174) of this book, with reference to a young maiden, who was a weaver.

At the conclusion of an alms-giving ceremony in Āḷavī, the Buddha gave a discourse on the impermanence of the aggregates (khandhas). The main points the Buddha stressed on that day may be expressed as follows:

"My life is impermanent; for me, death only is permanent. I must certainly die; my life ends in death. Life is not permanent; death is permanent."

The Buddha also exhorted the audience to be always mindful and to strive to perceive the true nature of the aggregate . He also said, "As one who is armed with a stick or a spear is prepared to meet an enemy (e.g., a poisonous snake), so also, one who is ever mindful of death will face death mindfully. He would then leave this world for a good destination (sugati)." Many people did not take the above exhortation seriously, but a young girl of sixteen who was a weaver clearly understood the message. After giving the discourse, the Buddha returned to the Jetavana monastery.

After a lapse of three years, when the Buddha surveyed the world, he saw the young weaver in his vision, and knew that time was ripe for the girl to attain Sotāpatti Fruition. So the Buddha came to the country of Āḷavī to expound the dhamma for the second time. When the girl heard that the Buddha had come again with five hundred bhikkhus, she wanted to go and listen to the discourse which would be given by the Buddha. However, her father had also asked her to wind some thread spools which he needed urgently, so she promptly wound some spools and took them to her father. On the way to her father, she stopped for a moment at the outer fringe of the audience, who had come to listen to the Buddha.

Meanwhile, the Buddha knew that the young weaver would come to listen to his discourse; he also knew that the girl would die when she got to the weaving shed. Therefore, it was very important that she should listen to the Dhamma on her way to the weaving shed and not on her return. So, when the young weaver appeared on the fringe of the audience, the Buddha looked at her. When she saw him looking at her, she dropped her basket and respectfully approached the Buddha. Then, he put four questions to her and she answered all of them. The questions and answers are as given below.

Question (1). Where have you come from?
Answer (1). I do not know.
Question (2). Where are you going?
Answer (2). I do not know.
Question (3). Don't you know?
Answer (3). Yes, I do know.
Question (4). Do you know?
Answer (4). I do not know, Venerable Sir.

Hearing her answers, the audience thought that the young weaver was being very disrespectful. Then, the Buddha asked her to explain what she meant by her answers, and she explained.

"Venerable Sir! Since you know that I have come from my house, I interpreted that, by your first question, you meant to ask me from what past existence I have come here. Hence my answer, 'I do not know.' The second question means, to what future existence I would be going from here; hence my answer, 'I do not know.' The third question means whether I do not know that I would die one day; hence my answer, 'Yes, I do know.' The last question means whether I know when I would die; hence my answer, 'I do not know.'

The Buddha was satisfied with her explanation and he said to the audience, "Most of you might not understand clearly the meaning of the answers given by the young weaver. Those who are ignorant are in darkness, they are just like the blind."

Then the Buddha spoke in verse as follows:

Verse 174. Blind are the people of this world: only a few in this world see clearly (with Insight). Just as only a few birds escape from the net, so also, only a few get to the world of the devas, (and Nibbāna).

At the end of the discourse, the young weaver attained Sotāpatti Fruition.

Then, she continued on her way to the weaving shed. When she got there, her father was asleep on the weaver's seat. As he woke up suddenly, he accidently pulled the shuttle, and the point of the shuttle struck the girl at her breast. She died on the spot, and her father was broken-hearted. With eyes full of tears he went to the Buddha and asked the Buddha to admit him to the Order of the bhikkhus. So, he became a bhikkhu, and not long afterwards, attained arahatship.

Verse 175

XIII (8) The Story of Thirty Bhikkhu

While residing at the Jetavana monastery, the Buddha uttered Verse (175) of this book, with reference to thirty bhikkhus.

Once, thirty bhikkhus came to pay homage to the Buddha. When they came in, the Venerable Ānanda, who was then attending on the Buddha, left the room and waited outside. After some time, Thera Ānanda went in, but he did not find any of the bhikkhus. So, he asked the Buddha where all those bhikkhus had gone. The Buddha Then replied, Ānanda, all those bhikkhus, after hearing my discourse, had attained arahatship, and with their supernormal powers, they left travelling through space."

Then the Buddha spoke in verse as follows:

Verse 175. Swans travel in the sky; those with supernormal powers travel through space; the wise having conquered Māra together with his army, go out of this world (i. e., realize Nibbāna).

Verse 176

XIII (9) The Story of Ciñcamāṇavikā

While residing at the Jetavana monastery, the Buddha uttered Verse (176) of this book, with reference to Ciñcamāṇavikā.

As the Buddha went on teaching the Dhamma, more and more people came flocking to him, and the ascetics of other faiths found their following to be dwindling. So they made a plan that would harm the reputation of the Buddha. They called the very beautiful Ciñcamāṇavikā, a devoted pupil of theirs, to them and said to her, "If you have our interests in your heart, please help us and put Samaṇa Gotama to shame." Ciñcamāṇavikā agreed to comply.

That same evening, she took some flowers and went in the direction of the Jetavana monastery. When people asked her where she was going, she replied, "What is the use of you knowing where I am going?" Then she would go to the place of other ascetics near the Jetavana monastery and would come back early in the morning to make it appear as if she had spent the night at the Jetavana monastery. When asked, she would reply, "I spent the night with Samaṇa Gotama at the Perfumed Chamber of the Jetavana monastery." After three or four months had passed, she wrapped up her stomach with some cloth to make her look pregnant. Then, after eight or nine months, she wrapped up her stomach with a round piece of thin wooden plank; she also beat up her plams and feet to make them swollen, and pretended to be feeling tired and worn out. Thus, she assumed a perfect picture of a woman in an advanced stage of pregnancy. Then, in the evening, she went to the Jetavana monastery to confront the Buddha.

The Buddha was then expounding the Dhamma to a congregation of bhikkhus and laymen. Seeing him teaching on the platform, she accused the Buddha thus: "O you big Samaṇa! You only preach to others. I am now pregnant by you, yet you do nothing for my confinement. You only know how to enjoy yourself!" The Buddha stopped preaching for a while and said to her, "Sister, only you and I know whether you are speaking the truth or not," and Ciñcamāṇavikā replied, "Yes, you are right, how can others know what only you and I know?"

At that instant, Sakka, king of the devas, became aware of the trouble being brewed at the Jetavana monastery, so he sent four of his devas in the form of young rats. The four rats got under the clothes of Ciñcamāṇavikā and bit off the strings that fastened the wooden plank round her stomach. As the strings broke, the wooden plank dropped, cutting off the front part of her feet. Thus, the deception of Ciñcamāṇavikā was uncovered, and many from the crowd cried out in anger, "Oh you wicked woman! A liar and a cheat! How dare you accuse our noble Teacher!" Some of them spat on her and drove her out. She ran fast as she could, and when she had gone some distance the earth cracked and fissured and she was swallowed up.

The next day, while the bhikkhus were talking about Ciñcamāṇavikā, the Buddha came to them and said, "Bhikkhus, one who is not afraid to tell lies, and who does not care what happens in the future existence, will not hesitate to do any evil.

Then the Buddha spoke in verse as follows.

Verse 176. For one who transgresses the Truth, and is given to lying, and who is unconcerned with the life hereafter, there is no evil that he dare not do.

Verse 177

XIII (10) The Story of the Unrivalled Alms-Giving

While residing at the Jetavana monastery, the Buddha uttered Verse (177) of this book, with reference to the unrivalled alms-giving of King Pasenadi of Kosala.

Once, the king offered alms to the Buddha and other bhikkhus on a grand scale. His subjects, in competition with him, organized another alms-giving ceremony on a grander scale than that of the king. Thus, the king and his subjects kept on competing in giving alms. Finally, Queen Mallikā thought of a plan; to implement this plan, she asked the king to have a grand pavilion built. Next, she asked for five hundred white umbrellas and five hundred tame elephants; those five hundred elephants were to hold the five hundred white umbrellas over the five hundred bhikkhus. In the middle of the pavilion, they kept ten boats which were filled with perfumes and incense. There were also two hundred and fifty princesses, who kept fanning the five hundred bhikkhus. Since the subjects of the king had no princesses, nor white umbrellas, nor elephants, they could no longer compete with the king. When all preparations were made, alms-food was offered. After the meal, the king made an offering of all the things in the pavilion, which were worth fourteen crores.

At the time, two ministers of the king were present. Of those two, the minister named Juṇha was very pleased and praised the king for having offered alms so generously to the Buddha and his bhikkhus. He also reflected that such offerings could only be made by a king. He was very glad because the king would share the merit of his good deeds with all beings. In short, the minister Juṇha rejoiced with the king in his unrivalled charity. The minister Kāḷa, on the other hand, thought that the king was only squandering, by giving away fourteen crores in a single day, and that the bhikkhus would just go back to the monastery and sleep.

After the meal, the Buddha looked over at the audience and knew how Kāḷa the minister was feeling. Then, he thought that if he were to deliver a lengthy discourse of appreciation, Kāḷa would get more dissatisfied, and in consequence would have to suffer more in his next existence. So, out of compassion for Kāḷa, the Buddha delivered only a short discourse and returned to the Jetavana monastery. The king had expected a lengthy discourse of appreciation, and so he was very sad because the Buddha had been so brief. The king wondered if he had failed to do something which should have been done, and so he went to the monastery.

On seeing the king, the Buddha said, "Great King! You should rejoice that you have succeeded in making the offering of the unrivalled charity (asadisadāna). Such an opportunity comes very rarely; it comes only once during the appearance of each Buddha. But your minister Kāḷa had felt that it was a waste, and was not at all appreciative. So, if I had given a lengthy discourse, he would get more and more dissatisfied and uncomfortable, and in consequence, he would suffer much more in the present existence as well as in the next. That was why I preached so briefly. Then the

Buddha added, "Great King! Fools do not rejoice in the charities given by others and go to the lower worlds. The wise rejoice in other people's charities, and through appreciation, they share in the merit gained by others and go to the abode of the devas".

Then the Buddha spoke in verse as follows:

Verse 177. Indeed, misers do not go to the abode of the devas; fools do not praise charity; but the wise rejoice in charity and so gain happiness in the life hereafter.

Verse 178

XIII (11) The Story of Kāla, son of Anāthapiṇḍika

While residing at the Jetavana monastery, the Buddha uttered Verse (178) of this book, with reference to Kāla, son of Anāthapiṇḍika, the well renowned rich man of Sāvatthi.

Kāla, son of Anāthapiṇḍika, always kept away whenever the Buddha and his company of bhikkhus came to their house. Anāthapiṇḍika was afraid that if his son kept on behaving in this way, he would be reborn in one of the lower worlds (apāyas). So, he enticed his son with the promise of money. He promised to give one hundred if the youth consented to go to the monastery and keep sabbath for one day. So, the youth went to the monastery and returned home early the next day, without listening to any religious discourses. His father offered him rice gruel, but instead of taking his food, he first demanded to have the money.

The next day, the father said to his son, "My son, if you learn a stanza of the Text from the Buddha, I will give you one thousand on your return." So, Kāḷa went to the monastery again, and told the Buddha that he wanted to learn something. The Buddha gave him a short stanza to learn by heart; at the same time he willed that the youth would not be able to memorize it. Thus, the youth had to repeat a single stanza many times, but because he had to repeat it so many times, in the end, he came to perceive the full meaning of the Dhamma and attained Sotāpatti Fruition.

Early on the next morning, he followed the Buddha and the bhikkhus to his own house. But on that day, he was silently wishing, "I wish my father would not give me the one thousand in the presence of the Buddha. I do not wish the Buddha to know that I kept the sabbath just for the sake of money." His father offered rice gruel to the Buddha and the bhikkhus, and also to him. Then, his father brought one thousand, and told Kāla to take the money but surprisingly he refused. His father pressed him to take it, but he still refused. Then, Anāthapiṇḍika said to the Buddha, "Venerable Sir, my son is quite changed; he now behaves in a very pleasant manner." Then he related to the Buddha how he had enticed the youth with money to go to the monastery and keep sabbath and to learn some religious texts. To him the Buddha replied, "Anāthapiṇḍika! Today, your son has attained Sotāpatti Fruition, which is much better than the riches of the Universal Monarch or that of the devas or that of the brahmās."

Then the Buddha spoke in verse as follows:

Verse 178. Far better than sovereignty over the earth, or far better than going to the abodes of the devas, or far better than ruling supreme over the entire universe, is (the attainment of) Sotāpatti Fruition.

End of Chapter Thirteen : The World.

Chapter XIV

The Buddha (Buddhavagga)

Verses 179 and 180

XIV (1) The Story of the Three Daughters of Māra

The Buddha first uttered Verses (179) and (180) of this book while residing near the Bodhi tree, with reference to the three daughters of Māra. He repeated these verses to the brahmin Māgandiya while journeying through the Kuru country.

Māgandiya the brahmin and his wife lived in the kingdom of the Kurus with their daughter Māgandiyā who was exceedingly beautiful. She was so beautiful that her father rudely turned down all her suitors. One day, early in the morning, when the Buddha surveyed the world, he found that time was ripe for the brahmin Māgandiya and his wife to attain Anāgāmi Fruition. So, taking his bowl and the robes, the Buddha set out for the place where the brahmin usually went to offer fire sacrifice.

The brahmin, seeing the Buddha, promptly decided that the Buddha was the very person who was worthy of his daughter. He pleaded with the Buddha to wait there and hurriedly went off to fetch his wife and daughter. The Buddha left his footprint and went to another place, close at hand. When the brahmin and his family came, they found only the footprint. Seeing the footprint, the wife of the brahmin remarked that it was the footprint of one who was free from sensual desires. Then, the brahmin saw the Buddha and he offered his daughter in marriage to him.

The Buddha did not accept nor did he refuse the offer, but first, he related to the brahmin how the daughters of Māra tempted him soon after his attainment of Buddhahood. To the beautiful Taṇhā, Aratī and Ragā, the daughters of Māra, the Buddha had said, "It is no use tempting one who is free from craving, clinging and passion, for he cannot be lured by any temptation whatsoever."

Then the Buddha spoke in verse as follows:

Verse 179. The Buddha, whose conquest (of moral defilements) is complete, in whom there cannot arise any further defilements in this world, —that Buddha of infinite range of wisdom, who is trackless, by what track will you lead him?

Verse 180. The Buddha, in whom there is no craving, which like a net would bring him back to any existence (in saṁsāra),—that Buddha of infinite range of wisdom, who is trackless, by what track will you lead him?

Then, the Buddha continued, "Brahmin Māgandiya, even when I saw those peerless daughters of Māra, I felt no sensual desire in me. After all, what is this body of your daughter? It is full of urine and filth; I don't like to touch it even with my foot!" On hearing those words of the Buddha, both the brahmin and his wife attained Anāgāmi Fruition. Later, they joined the Order and eventually both of them attained arahatship.

Verse 181

XIV (2) The Story of the Buddha's Return from the Tāvatiṁsa Deva World

On return from the Tāvatiṁsa deva world, the Buddha uttered Verse (181) of this book at Saṅkassanagara, in reply to Thera Sāriputta's words of welcome.

On one occasion, while at Sāvatthi, the Buddha performed the Miracle of the Pairs in answer to the challenge of the ascetics of various sects. After this, the Buddha went to the Tāvatiṁsa deva world; his mother who had been reborn in the Tusita deva world as a deva known as Santusita also came to the Tāvatiṁsa deva world. There the Buddha expounded the Abhidhamma to the devas and the brahmās throughout the three months of the vassa. As a result, Santusita deva attained Sotāpatti Fruition; so did numerous other devas and brahmās.

During that period Thera Sāriputta spent the vassa at Saṅkassanagara, thirty yojanas away from Sāvatthi. During his stay there, as regularly instructed by the

Buddha, he taught the Abhidhamma to the five hundred bhikkhus staying with him and covered the whole course by the end of the vassa.

Towards the end of the vassa, Thera Mahā Moggallāna went to the Tāvatiṁsa deva world to see the Buddha. Then, he was told that the Buddha would return to the human world on the full moon day at the end of the vassa to the place where Thera Sāriputta was spending the vassa.

As promised, the Buddha came with the six coloured rays shining forth from his body to the city-gate of Saṅkassanagara, on the night of the full moon day of the month of Assayuja when the moon was shining brightly. He was accompanied by a large following of devas on one side and a large following of brahmās on the other. A large gathering headed by Thera Sāriputta welcomed the Buddha back to this world; and the whole town was lit up. Thera Sāriputta was awed by the grandeur and glory of the whole scene of the Buddha's return. He respectfully approached the Buddha and said, "Venerable Sir! We have never seen or even heard of such magnificent and resplendent glory. Indeed, Venerable Sir, you are loved, respected and revered alike by devas, brahmās and men!" To him the Buddha said, "My son Sāriputta, the Buddhas who are endowed with unique qualities are truly loved by men and devas alike."

Then the Buddha spoke in verse as follows:

Verse 181. The wise who practise jhāna concentration and Insight Meditation take delight in the peace of liberation from sensual pleasures and moral defilements. Such wise and mindful ones, who truly comprehend the Four Noble Truths (i.e., arahats and Buddhas), are held dear also by the devas.

At the end of the discourse the five hundred bhikkhus who were the pupils of Thera Sāriputta attained arahatship and a great many from the congregation attained Sotāpatti Fruition.

Verse 182

XIV (3) The Story of Erakapatta the Nāga King

While residing near Bārāṇasī, the Buddha uttered Verse (182) of this book, with reference to Erakapatta, a king of nāgas (dragons).

Once there was a nāga king by the name of Erakapatta. In one of his past existences during the time of Kassapa Buddha he had been a bhikkhu for a long time. Through worry (kukkucca) over a minor offence he had committed during that time, he was reborn as a nāga. As a nāga, he waited for the appearance of a Buddha. Erakapatta had a very beautiful daughter, and he made use of her as a means of finding the Buddha. He made it known that whoever could answer her questions could claim her for a wife. Twice every month, Erakapatta made her dance in the open and sing out her questions. Many suitors came to answer her questions hoping to claim her, but no one could give the correct answer.

One day, the Buddha saw a youth named Uttara in his vision. He also knew that the youth would attain Sotāpatti Fruition in connection with the questions put by the daughter of Erakapatta the nāga. By then the youth was already on his way to see Erakapatta's daughter. The Buddha stopped him and taught him how to answer the questions. While he was being taught, Uttara attained Sotāpatti Fruition. Now that Uttara had attained Sotāpatti Fruition, he had no desire for the nāga princess. However, Uttara still went to answer the questions for the benefit of numerous other beings.

The first four questions were:

(1) Who is a ruler?
(2) Is one who is overwhelmed by the mist of moral defilements to be called a ruler?
(3) What ruler is free from moral defilements?
(4) What sort of person is to be called a fool?

The answers to the above questions were:

(1) He who controls the six senses is a ruler.
(2) One who is overwhelmed by the mist of moral defilments is not to be called a ruler; he who is free from craving is called a ruler.

(3) The ruler who is free from craving is free from moral defilements.

(4) A person who hankers after sensual pleasures is called a fool.

Having had the correct answers to the above, the nāga princess sang out questions regarding the floods (oghas) of sensual desire, of renewed existence, of false doctrine and of ignorance, and how they could be overcome. Uttara answered these questions as taught by the Buddha.

When Erakapatta heard these answers he knew that a Buddha had appeared in this world. So he asked Uttara to take him to the Buddha. On seeing the Buddha, Erakapatta related to the Buddha how he had been a bhikkhu during the time of Kassapa Buddha, how he had accidentally caused a grass blade to be broken off while travelling in a boat, and how he had worried over that little offence for having failed to do the act of exoneration as prescribed, and finally how he was reborn as a nāga. After hearing him, the Buddha told him how difficult it was to be born in the human world, and to be born during the appearance of the Buddhas or during the time of their Teaching.

Then the Buddha spoke in verse as follows:

Verse 182. Hard to gain is birth as man; hard is the life of mortals; hard to get is the opportunity of hearing the Ariya Dhamma (Teaching of the Buddhas); hard it is for a Buddha to appear.

The above discourse benefited numerous beings. Erakapatta being an animal could not attain Sotāpatti Fruition then and there.

Verses 183, 184 and 185

XIV (4) The Story of the Question Raised by Thera Ānanda

While residing at the Jetavana monastery, the Buddha uttered Verses (183), (184) and (185) of this book, with reference to the question raised by Thera Ānanda regarding Fundamental Instructions to bhikkhus by the preceding Buddhas.

On one occasion, Thera Ānanda asked the Buddha whether the Fundamental Instructions to bhikkhus given by the preceding Buddhas were the same as those of the Buddha himself. To him the Buddha replied that the instructions given by all the Buddhas are as given in the following verses:

Verse 183. Not to do evil, to cultivate merit, to purify one's mind—this is the Teaching of the Buddhas.

Verse 184. The best moral practice is patience and forbearance; "Nibbāna is Supreme", said the Buddhas. A bhikkhu does not harm others; one who harms others is not a bhikkhu.

Verse 185. Not to revile, not to do any harm, to practise restraint according to the Fundamental Instructions for the bhikkhus, to be moderate in taking food, to dwell in a secluded place, to devote oneself to higher concentration—this is the Teaching of the Buddhas.

Verses 186 and 187

XIV (5) The Story of a Dissatisfied Young Bhikkhu

While residing at the Jetavana monastery, the Buddha uttered Verses (186) and (187) of this book, with reference to a young bhikkhu who was unhappy with his life as a bhikkhu.

Once, there was a young bhikkhu at the Jetavana monastery; one day his teacher sent him to another monastery to study. While he was away, his father became seriously ill and died without seeing him. But his father left for him one hundred kahāpaṇas with his brother, the boy's uncle. On his return, his uncle told him about his father's death and about the one hundred kahāpaṇas left to him. At first, he said that he had no need of the money. Later, he thought that it might be better to return to lay-life, and as a result, he got dissatisfied with the life of a bhikkhu. Gradually, he began to lose interest in his life and was also losing weight. When other bhikkhus knew about this, they took him to the Buddha.

The Buddha asked him whether it was true that he was feeling unhappy with his life as a bhikkhu and whether he had any capital to start the life of a layman. He answered that it was true and that he had one hundred kahāpaṇas to start his life with. Then the Buddha explained to him that he would need to get food, clothing, household utensils, two oxen, ploughs, pickaxes, knives, etc., so that his one hundred in cash would hardly meet the expenses. The Buddha then told him that for human beings there could never be enough, not even for Universal Monarchs who could call for a shower of coins or gems or any amount of wealth and treasures at any moment. Further, the Buddha related the story of Mandātu the Universal Monarch who enjoyed the glory of the devas both in the Cātumahārājika and Tāvatiṁsa realms for a long time. After spending a long time in Tāvatiṁsa, one day, Mandātu wished that he were the sole ruler of Tāvatiṁsa, instead of sharing it with Sakka. But this time, his wish could not be fulfilled and instantly he became old and decrepit; he returned to the human world and died soon after.

Then the Buddha spoke in verse as follows:

Verses 186, 187. Not by a shower of coins can sensua desires be satiated; sensual desires give little pleasure and are fraught with evil consequences (dukkha). Knowing this, the wise man, who is the disciple of the Buddha, does not find delight even in the pleasures of the devas, but rejoices in the cessation of craving (i.e., Nibbāna).

At the end of the discourse the young bhikkhu attained Sotāpatti Fruition.

Verses 188 to 192

XIV (6) The Story of Aggidatta

While residing at the Jetavana monastery, the Buddha uttered Verses (188) to (192) of this book, with reference to Aggidatta, a brahmin.

Aggidatta was the head priest during the time of King Mahākosala, father of King Pasenadi. After the death of King Mahākosala, Aggidatta gave away his property in charity, and after that he left his home and became a non-Buddhist ascetic. He lived with his ten thousand followers in a place near the border of the three kingdoms of Aṅga, Magadha and Kuru, not far from a mound of sand where a powerful nāga was staying. To his followers and the people of these three kingdoms, Aggidatta used to exhort: "Pay homage to forests, mountains, parks and gardens, and trees; by doing so, you will be liberated from all ills of life."

One day, the Buddha saw Aggidatta and his followers in his vision and realized that the time was ripe for them to attain arahatship. So the Buddha sent Thera Mahā Moggallāna to Aggidatta and his followers and told him that he himself would follow afterwards. Thera Mahā Moggallāna went to the place of Aggidatta and his followers and asked them to give him shelter for one night. They first turned down his request, but finally they agreed to let him stop at the mound of sand, the home of the nāga. The nāga was very antagonistic to Thera Mahā Moggallāna, and there followed a duel between the nāga and the thera; on both sides, there was a display of power by emitting smoke and flames. However, in the end, the nāga was subdued. He coiled himself round the mound of sand, and raised his head spreading it out like an umbrella over Thera Mahā Moggallāna, thus showing respect for him. Early in the morning, Aggidatta and the other ascetics came to the mound of sand to find out whether Thera Mahā Moggallāna was still alive; they had expected to see him dead. When they found the nāga tamed, and meekly holding his head like an umbrella over Thera Mahā Moggallāna, they were very much astounded.

Just then, the Buddha arrived and Thera Mahā Moggallāna got up from his seat on the mound and paid obeisance to the Buddha. Thera Mahā Moggallāna then proclaimed to the audience of ascetics, "This is my Teacher, the supreme Buddha, and I am but a humble pupil of this great Teacher!" Hearing him, the ascetics who had been very much impressed even by the power of Thera Mahā Moggallāna were awed by the greater power of the Buddha. The Buddha then asked Aggidatta what he taught his followers and the residents of the neighbourhood. Aggidatta replied that he had taught them to pay homage to mountains, forests, parks and gardens, and trees, and that by doing so, they would be liberated from all ills of life. The Buddha's reply to Aggidatta was, "Aggidatta, people go to mountains, forests, gardens and parks, and trees for refuge when they are threatened with danger, but these things cannot offer them any protection. Only those who take refuge in the Buddha, the Dhamma and the Saṁgha are liberated from the round of rebirths (saṁsāra).

Then the Buddha spoke in verse as follows:

Verse 188. When threatened with danger, men go to many a refuge,— to mountains and forests, to parks and gardens, and to sacred trees.

Verse 189. But such a refuge is not a safe refuge, not the best refuge. One is not liberated from all evil consequences of existence (dukkha) for having come to such a refuge.

Verse 190, 191. One, who takes refuge in the Buddha, the Dhamma and the Saṁgha, sees with Magga Insight the Four Noble Truths, viz., Dukkha, the Cause of Dukkha, the Cessation of Dukkha, and the Noble Path of Eight Constituents which leads to the Cessation of Dukkha.

Verse 192. This, indeed, is the safe refuge; this is the best refuge. Having come to this refuge, one is liberated from all dukkha.

At the end of the discourse Aggidatta and all his followers attained arahatship. All of them entered the Order of the bhikkhus. On that day, when the disciples of Aggidatta from Aṅga, Magadha and Kuru came to pay respect to him, they saw their teacher and his followers garbed as bhikkhus and they were puzzled and wondered, "Who is the more powerful? Our teacher or Samaṇa Gotama? Our teacher must be more powerful because Samaṇa Gotama has come to our teacher." The Buddha knew what they were thinking; Aggidatta also felt that he must set their minds at rest. So, he paid obeisance to the Buddha in the presence of his disciples, and said, "Venerable Sir! You are my teacher, I am but a disciple of yours." Thus, the audience came to realize the supremacy of the Buddha.

Verse 193

XIV (7) The Story of the Question Raised by Thera Ānanda

While residing at the Jetavana monastery, the Buddha uttered Verse (193) of this book, with reference to the question raised by Thera Ānanda.

One day, Thera Ānanda pondered thus: "Our Teacher has told us that thoroughbreds of elephants are born only among Chaddanta and Uposatha breeds, that thoroughbreds of horses are born only among the Sindh breed, that thoroughbreds of cattle are born only among the Usabha breed. Thus, he had talked to us only about the thoroughbreds of elephants, horses, and cattle, but not of the noblest of men (purisājañño)."

After reflecting thus, Thera Ānanda went to the Buddha, and put to him the question of the noblest of men. To him the Buddha replied, "Ānanda, the noblest of men is not born everywhere, he is born only among Khattiyamahāsāla and Brāhmaṇamahāsāla, the wealthy clans of Khattiya and Brāhmaṇa."

Then the Buddha spoke in verse as follows:

Verse 193. It is hard to find the noblest of men; he is not born everywhere nor in every clan. To whatever clan such a wise man is born, that clan prospers.

Verse 194

XIV (8) The Story of Many Bhikkhus

While residing at the Jetavana monastery, the Buddha uttered Verse (194) of this book, with reference to many bhikkhus.

Once, five hundred bhikkhus were discussing the question "What constitutes happiness?" These bhikkhus realized that happiness meant different things to different people. Thus, they said, "To some people to have the riches and glory like that of a king's is happiness, to some people sensual pleasure is happiness, but to others to have good rice cooked with meat is happiness." While they were talking, the Buddha came in. After learning the subject of their talk, the Buddha said, "Bhikkhus, all the pleasures you have mentioned do not get you out of the round of rebirths. In this world, these constitute happiness: the arising of a Buddha, the opportunity to hear the Teaching of the Sublime Truth, and the harmony amongst the bhikkhus."

Then the Buddha spoke in verse as follows:

Verse 194. Happy is the arising of a Buddha; happy is the exposition of the Ariya Dhamma; happy is the harmony amongst the Saṁgha; happy is the practice of those in harmony.

At the end of the discourse the five hundred bhikkhus attained arahatship.

Verses 195 and 196

XIV (9) The Story of the Golden Stupa of Kassapa Buddha

While travelling from Sāvatthi to Bārāṇasī, the Buddha uttered Verses (195) and (196) of this book, with reference to a brahmin and the golden stupa of Kassapa Buddha.

On one occasion, while the Buddha and his followers were on a journey to Bārāṇasī they came to a field where there was a spirit-shrine. Not far from the shrine, a brahmin was ploughing the field; seeing the brahmin the Buddha sent for him. When he arrived, the brahmin made obeisance to the shrine but not to the Buddha. To him the Buddha said, "Brahmin, by paying respect to the shrine you are doing a meritorious deed." That made the brahmin happy. After thus putting him in a favourable frame of mind, the Buddha, by his supernormal power, brought forth the golden stupa of Kassapa Buddha and let it remain visible in the sky. The Buddha then explained to the brahmin and the other bhikkhus that there were four classes of persons worthy of a stupa. They are: the Buddhas (Tathāgatas) who are homage-worthy and perfectly self-enlightened, the Paccekabuddhas, the Ariya disciples, and the Universal Monarchs. He also told them about the three types of stupas erected in honour of these four classes of persons. The stupas where corporeal relics are enshrined are known as Sarīradhātu cetiya; the stupas and figures made in the likeness of the above four personages are known as Uddissa cetiya; and the stupas where personal effects like robes, bowls, etc. of those revered personages are enshrined are known as Paribhoga cetiya. The Bodhi tree is also included in the Paribhoga cetiya. The Buddha then stressed the importance of paying homage to those who are worthy of veneration.

Then the Buddha spoke in verse as follows:

Verse 195. He pays homage to those who are worthy of veneration, whether they are the Buddhas or their disciples who have overcome obstacles (to Insight Development) and have rid themselves of sorrow and lamentation.

Verse 196. The merit gained by such a person who pays homage to those who have been freed from moral defilements and have nothing to fear, cannot be measured by anyone, as this much or that much.

At the end of the discourse the brahmin attained Sotāpatti Fruition. The stupa of Kassapa Buddha remained visible for seven more days, and people kept on coming to the stupa to pay homage and obeisance. At the end of seven days, as willed by the Buddha, the stupa disappeared, and in the place of the shrine erected to the spirits, there appeared miraculously, a big stone stupa.

End of Chapter Fourteen: The Buddha.

Chapter XV

Happiness (Sukhavagga)

Verse 197 to 199

XV (1) The Story of the Pacification of the Relatives of the Buddha

The Buddha uttered Verse (197) to (199) of this book, in the Sakyan country, with reference to his relatives who were quarrelling over the use of the water from the Rohinī river.

Kapilavatthu the town of the Sakyans and Koliya the town of the Kolyans were situated on either side of the Rohinī river. The cultivators of both towns worked the fields watered by the Rohinī river, One year, they did not have enough rain and finding that the paddy and other crops were beginning to shrivel up, cultivators on both sides wanted to divert the water from the Rohinī river to their own fields. Those living in Koliya said that there was not enough water in the river for both sides, and that if only they could channel the water just once more to their fields that would be enough for the paddy to mature and ripen. On the other hand, people from Kapilavatthu argued that, in that case, they would be denied the use of the water and their crops would surely fail, and they would be compelled to buy from other people. They said that they were not prepared to go carrying their money and valuables to the opposite bank of the river in exchange for food.

Both sides wanted the water for their own use only and there was much ill will between them due to abusive language and accusations on both sides. The quarrel that started between the cultivators came to the ears of the ministers concerned, and they reported the matter to their respective rulers, and both sides prepared to go to war.

The Buddha, surveying the world with his supernormal powers, saw his relatives on both sides of the river coming out to meet in battle and he decided to stop them. All alone, he went to them by going through the sky, and stopped immediately above the middle of the river. His relatives seeing him, powerfully and yet peacefully sitting above them in the sky, laid aside all their weapons and paid obeisance to the Buddha. Then, the Buddha said to them, "For the sake of some water, which is of little value, you should not destroy your lives which are of so much value and priceless. Why have you taken this stupid action? If I had not stopped you today, your blood would have been flowing like a river by now. You live hating your enemies, but I have none to hate; you are ailing with moral defilements, but I am free from them; you are striving to have sensual pleasures, but I do not strive for them."

Then the Buddha spoke in verse as follows:

Verse 197. Indeed we live very happily, not hating anyone among those who hate; among men who hate we live without hating anyone.

Verse 198. Indeed we live very happily, in good health among the ailing; among men who are ailing we live in good health.

Verse 199. Indeed we live very happily, not striving (for sensual pleasures) among those who strive (for them); among those who strive (for them) we live without striving.

At the end of the discourse many people attained Sotāpatti Fruition.

Verse 200

XV (2) The Story of Māra

The Buddha uttered Verse (200) of this book in a brahmin village known as Pañcasālā (village of five halls), with reference to Māra.

On one occasion, the Buddha saw in his vision that five hundred maidens from Pañcasālā village were due to attain Sotāpatti Fruition. So he went to stay near that village. The five hundred maidens went to the riverside to have a bath; after the bath they returned to the village fully dressed up, because it was a festival day. About the same time, the Buddha entered Pañcasālā village for alms-food but none of the villagers offered him anything because they had been possessed by Māra.

On his return the Buddha met Māra, who promptly asked him whether he had received much alms-food.

The Buddha saw the hand of Māra in his failure to get any alms-food on that day and replied, "You wicked Māra! It was you who turned the villagers against me. Because they were possessed by you they did not offer any alms-food to me. Am I not right?" Māra made no reply to that question, but he thought that it would be fun to entice the Buddha back to the village and get the villagers to insult the Buddha by making fun of him. So he suggested, "O Buddha, why don't you go back to the village again? This time, you are sure to get some food."

Just then, the five hundred village maidens arrived on the scene and paid obeisance to the Buddha. In their presence, Māra taunted the Buddha, "O Buddha, since you received no alms-food this morning, you must be feeling the pangs of hunger!" To him the Buddha replied, "O wicked Māra, even though we do not get any food, like the Ābhassara brahmās who live only on the delightful satisfaction (pīti) and bliss (sukha) of jhāna, we shall live on the delightful satisfaction and bliss of the Dhamma."

Then the Buddha spoke in verse as follows:

Verse 200. Indeed we live very happily, without any anxiety (i.e., without greed, ill will and ignorance); like the Ābhassara brahmās we shall live on delightful satisfaction (pīti) as our food.

At the end of the discourse, the five hundred maidens attained Sotāpatti Fruition.

Verse 201

XV (3) The Story of the Defeat of the King of Kosala

While residing at the Jetavana monastery, the Buddha uttered Verse (201) of this book, with reference to the King of Kosala who was defeated in battle by Ajātasattu, his own nephew.

In fighting against Ajātasattu, the King of Kosala was defeated three times. Ajātasattu was the son of King Bimbisāra and Queen Vedehī, the sister of the King of Kosala. The King of Kosala was ashamed and very much depressed over his defeat. Thus his lamentation: "What a disgrace! I cannot even conquer this boy who still smells of mother's milk. It is better that

I should die." Feeling depressed and very much ashamed, the king refused to take food, and kept to his bed. The news about the king's distress spread like wild fire and when the Buddha came to learn about it, he said, "Bhikkhus! In one who conquers, enmity and hatred increase ; one who is defeated suffers pain and distress."

Then the Buddha spoke in verse as follows:

Verse 201. Conquest begets enmity ; the conquered live in misery ; the peaceful live happily having renounced conquest and defeat.

Verse 202

XV (4) The Story of a Young Bride

While residing at the Jetavana monastery, the Buddha uttered Verse (202) of this book at the house of a lay-disciple, with reference to a young bride.

On the day a young woman was to be wedded to a young man, the parents of the bride invited the Buddha and eighty of his disciples for alms-food. Seeing the girl as she moved about the house, helping with the offering of alms-food, the bridegroom was very much excited, and he could hardly attend to the needs of the Buddha and the other bhikkhus. The Buddha knew exactly how the young bridegroom was feeling and also that time was ripe for both the bride and the bridegroom to attain Sotāpatti Fruition.

By his supernormal power, the Buddha willed that the bride would not be visible to the bridegroom. When the young man could no longer see the young woman, he could pay full attention to the Buddha, and his love and respect for the Buddha grew stronger in him. Then the Buddha said to the young man, "O young man, there is no fire like the fire of passion ; there is no evil like anger and hatred ; there is no ill like the burden of the five aggregates of existence (khandhas); there is no bliss like the Perfect Peace of Nibbāna."

Then the Buddha spoke in verse as follows:

Verse 202. There is no fire like passion ; there is no evil like hatred ; there is no ill like (the burden of) khandhas ; there is no bliss that surpasses the Perfect Peace (i.e., Nibbāna).

At the end of the discourse both the bride and bridegroom attained Sotāpatti Fruition.

Verse 203

XV (5) The Story of a Lay-Disciple

The Buddha uttered Verse (203) of this book at the village of Āḷavī, with reference to a lay-disciple.

One day, the Buddha saw in his vision that a poor man would attain Sotāpatti Fruition at the village of Āḷavī. So he went to that village, which was thirty yojanas away from Sāvatthi. It so happened that on that very day the man lost his ox. So, he had to be looking for the ox. Meanwhile, alms-food was being offered to the Buddha and his disciples in a house in the village of Āḷavī. After the meal, people got ready to listen to the Buddha's discourse; but the Buddha waited for the young man. Finally, having found his ox, the man came running to the house where the Buddha was. The man was tired and hungry, so the Buddha directed the donors to offer food to him. Only when the man had been fed, the Buddha gave a discourse, expounding the Dhamma step by step and finally leading to the Four Noble Truths. The lay-disciple attained Sotāpatti Fruition at the end of the discourse.

Afterwards, the Buddha and his disciples returned to the Jetavana monastery. On the way, the bhikkhus remarked that it was so surprising that the Buddha should have directed those people to feed the young man before he gave the discourse. On hearing their remarks, the Buddha said, "Bhikkhus! What you said is true, but you do not understand that I have come here, all this distance of thirty yojanas, because I knew that he was in a fitting condition to take in the Dhamma. If he were feeling very hungry, the pangs of hunger might have prevented him from taking in the Dhamma fully. That man had been out looking for his ox the whole morning, and was very tired and also very hungry. Bhikkhus! After all, there is no ailment which is so difficult to bear as hunger."

Then the Buddha spoke in verse as follows:

Verse 203. Hunger is the greatest ailment, khandhas are the greatest ill. The wise, knowing them as they really are, realize Nibbāna, the greatest bliss.

Verse 204

XV (6) The Story of King Pasenadi of Kosala

While residing at the Jetavana monastery, the Buddha uttered Verse (204) of this book, with reference to King Pasenadi of Kosala.

One day, King Pasenadi of Kosala went to the Jetavana monastery after having his full morning meal. It was said that the king had eaten one quarter basket (about half a bushel) of rice with meat curry on that day; so while listening to the Buddha's discourse he felt very sleepy and was nodding most of the time. Seeing him nodding, the Buddha advised him to take a little less rice everyday and to decrease the amount on a sliding scale to the minimum of one-sixteenth part of the original amount he was taking. The king did as he was told and found that by eating less he became thin, but he felt very much lighter and enjoyed much better health. When he told the Buddha about this, the Buddha said to him, "O king! Health is a great boon; contentment is a great wealth; a close and trusted friend is the best relative; Nibbāna is the greatest bliss."

Then the Buddha spoke in verse as follows:

Verse 204. Health is the greatest gift, contentment is the greatest wealth, a trusted friend is the best relative, Nibbāna is the greatest bliss.

Verse 205

XV (7) The Story of Thera Tissa

The Buddha uttered Verse (205) of this book at Vesālī, with reference to Thera Tissa.

When the Buddha declared that in four months' time he would realize parinibbāna, many puthujjana bhikkhus were apprehensive. They were at a loss and did not know what to do, and so they kept close to the Buddha. But Thera Tissa, having resolved that he would attain arahatship in the life-time of the Buddha did not go to him, but left for a secluded place to practise meditation. Other bhikkhus, not understanding his behaviour, took him to the Buddha and said, "Venerable Sir! This bhikkhu does not seem to cherish and honour you; he only keeps to himself instead of coming to your presence." Thera Tissa then explained to them that he was striving hard to attain arahatship before the Buddha realized parinibbāna, and that was the only reason why he had not come to see the Buddha.

Having heard his explanation, the Buddha said to the bhikkhus, "Bhikkhus! Those who love and respect me should act like Tissa. You are not paying homage to me by just offering me flowers, perfumes and incense You pay homage to me only by practising the Lokuttara Dhamma, i.e., Insight Meditation."

Then the Buddha spoke in verse as follows:

Verse 205. Having had the taste of solitude and the taste of Perfect Peace of Nibbāna, one who drinks in the joy of the essence of the Dhamma is free from fear and evil.

At the end of the discourse Thera Tissa attained Sotāpatti Fruition.

Verses 206, 207 and 208

XV (8) The Story of Sakka

While residing at the village of Veḷuva, the Buddha uttered Verses (206), (207) and (208) of this book, with reference to Sakka, king of the devas.

About ten months before the Buddha realized parinibbāna, the Buddha was spending the vassa at Veḷuva village neae Vesāli. While he was staying there, he suffered from dysentry. When Sakka learned that the Buddha was ailing, he came to Veḷuva village so that he could personally nurse the Buddha during his sickness. The Buddha told him not to worry about his health as there were many bhikkhus near him; but Sakka did not listen to him and kept on nursing the Buddha until he recovered.

The bhikkhus were surprised and awe-struck to find Sakka himself attending on the Buddha. When the Buddha heard their remarks he said, "Bhikkhus! There is nothing surprising about Sakka's love and devotion to me. Once, when the former Sakka was growing old and was about to pass away, he came to see me. Then, I expounded the Dhamma to him. While listening to the Dhamma, he attained Sotāpatti Fruition; then he passed away and was reborn as the present Sakka. All these happened to him simply because he listened to the Dhamma expounded by me. Indeed, bhikkhus, it is good to see the Noble Ones (ariyas); it is a pleasure to live with them; to live with fools is, indeed, painful."

Then the Buddha spoke in verse as follows:

Verse 206. It is good to see the Noble Ones (ariyas); to live with them is always a pleasure; not seeing fools is also always a pleasure.

Verse 207. He who walks in the company of fools has to grieve for a long time. Association with fools is ever painful, as living with an enemy; association with the wise is a pleasure, as living with relatives.

Verse 208. Therefore one should follow a resolute, intelligent, learned, persevering and dutiful ariya; follow such a virtuous and wise man, as the moon follows the path of the stars.

End of Chapter Fifteen: Happiness.

Chapter XVI

Affection (Piyavagga)

Verses 209, 210 and 211

XVI (1) The Story of Three Ascetics

While residing at the Jetavana monastery, the Buddha uttered Verses (209), (210) and (211) of this book, with reference to a trio, consisting of a father, a mother and a son.

Once in Sāvatthi, the only son of a family first became a bhikkhu; the father followed suit and finally, the mother also became a bhikkhunī. They were so attached to one another that they rarely stayed apart. The family stayed in the monastery as if they were in their own house, talking and eating together, thus making themselves a nuisance to others. Other bhikkhus reported their behaviour to the Buddha and he called them to his presence, and said to them, "Once you have joined the Order, you should no longer stay together like a family. Not seeing those who are dear, and seeing those who are not dear to one, are both painful; so you should not hold any being or anything dear to you".

Then the Buddha spoke in verse as follows:

Verse 209. He who does what should not be done and fails to do what should be done, who forsakes the noble aim of life (i. e., Morality, Concentration and Insight) and grasps at sensual pleasure, covets the benefits gained by those who exert themselves (in meditation).

Verse 210. Do not associate with those who are dear, and never with those who are not dear to you; not seeing the dear ones is painful, and seeing those who are not dear to you is also painful.

Verse 211. Therefore, one should hold nothing dear; separation from the loved ones is painful; there are no fetters for those who do not love or hate.

Verse 212

XVI (2) The Story of a Rich Householder

While residing at the Jetavana monastery, the Buddha uttered Verse (212) of this book, with reference to a rich householder who had lost his son.

Once, a householder was feeling very distressed over the death of his son. He often went to the cemetery and wept there. Early one morning, the Buddha saw the rich householder in his vision. So, taking a bhikkhu along with him, the Buddha went to the house of that man. There, he asked the man why he was feeling so unhappy. Then, the man related to the Buddha about the death of his son and about the pain and sorrow he was suffering. To him the Buddha said, "My disciple, death does not occur only in one place. All beings that are born must die one day; indeed, life ends in death. You must ever be mindful of the fact that life ends in death. Do not imagine that only your beloved son is subject to death. Do not be so distressed or be so shaken. Sorrow and fear arise out of affection."

Then the Buddha spoke in verse as follows:

Verse 212. Affection begets sorrow, affection begets fear. For him who is free from affection there is no sorrow; how can there be fear for him?

At the end of the discourse, the rich householder attained Sotāpatti Fruition.

Verse 213

XVI (3) The Story of Visākhā

While residing at the Jetavana monastery, the Buddha uttered Verse (213) of this book, with reference to Visākhā, the renowned donor of the Pubbārāma monastery.

One day, a granddaughter of Visākhā named Sudattā died and Visākhā felt very deeply about her loss and was sorrowing over the child's death. So she went to the Buddha; when the Buddha saw her, he said, "Visākhā, don't you realize that many people die in Sāvatthi every day? If you were to regard all of them as you regard your own grandchild you would have to be endlessly weeping and mourning. Let not the death of a child affect you too much. Sorrow and fear arise out of endearment."

Then the Buddha spoke in verse as follows:

Verse 213. Endearment begets sorrow, endearment begets fear. For him who is free from endearment there is no sorrow; how can there be fear for him?

Verse 214

XVI (4) The Story of Licchavī Princes

While residing at the Kūṭāgāra monastery in Vesālī, the Buddha uttered Verse (214) of this book, with reference to the Licchavī princes.

On one festival day, the Buddha entered the town of Vesālī, accompanied by a retinue of bhikkhus. On their way, they met some Licchavī princes, who had come out elegantly dressed up. The Buddha seeing them in full regalia said to the bhikkhus, "Bhikkhus, those who have not been to the Tāvatiṁsa deva world should have a good look at these Licchavī princes." The princes were then on their way to a pleasure garden. There, they quarrelled over a prostitute and soon came to blows. As a result, some of them had to be carried home, bleeding. As the Buddha returned with the bhikkhus after his meal in the town, they saw the wounded princes being carried home.

In connection with the above incident the bhikkhus remarked, "For the sake of a woman, these Licchavī princes are ruined." To them the Buddha replied, "Bhikkhus, sorrow and fear arise out of enjoyment of sensual pleasures and attachment to them."

Then the Buddha spoke in verse as follows:

Verse 214. Attachment (to sensual pleasures) begets sorrow, attachment begets fear. For him who is free from attachment there is no sorrow; how can there be fear for him?

Verse 215

XVI (5) The Story of Anitthigandha Kumāra

While residing at the Jetavana monastery, the Buddha uttered Verse (215) of this book, with reference to a youth, named Anitthigandha.

Anitthigandha lived in Sāvatthi. He was to marry a beautiful young girl from the city of Sāgala, in the country of the Maddas. As the bride was coming from her home to Sāvatthi, she became ill and died on the way. When the bridegroom learned about the tragic death of his bride he was broken-hearted.

At this juncture, the Buddha knowing that time was ripe for the young man to attain Sotāpatti Fruition went to his house. The parents of the young man offered alms-food to the Buddha. After the meal, the Buddha asked his parents to bring the young man to his presence. When he came, the Buddha asked him why he was in such pain and distress and the young man related the whole story of the tragic death of his young bride. Then the Buddha said to him, "O Anitthigandha! Lust begets sorrow; it is due to lust for things and lust for sensual pleasures that sorrow and fear arise."

Then the Buddha spoke in verse as follows:

Verse 215. Lust begets sorrow, lust begets fear. For him who is free from lust there is no sorrow; how can there be fear for him?

At the end of the discourse Anitthigandha attained Sotāpatti Fruition.

Verse 216

XVI (6) The Story of a Brahmin

While residing at the Jetavana monastery, the Buddha uttered Verse (216) of this book, with reference to a brahmin who was a farmer.

The brahmin lived in Sāvatthi, and he was a non--Buddhist. But the Buddha knew that the brahmin would attain Sotāpatti Fruition in the near future. So the Buddha went to where the brahmin was ploughing his field and talked to him. The brahmin became friendly and was thankful to the Buddha for taking an interest in him and his work in the field. One day, he said to the Buddha, "Samaṇa Gotama, when I have gathered my rice from this field, I will first offer you some before I take it. I will not eat my rice until I have given you some." However, the Buddha knew beforehand that the brahmin would not have the opportunity to harvest the rice from his field that year, but he kept silent.

Then, on the night before the brahmin was to harvest his rice, there was a heavy downpour of rain which washed away the entire crop of rice. The brahmin was very much distressed, because he would no longer be able to offer any rice to his friend, the Samaṇa Gotama.

The Buddha went to the house of the brahmin and the brahmin talked to him about the great disaster that had befallen him. In reply, the Buddha said, "Brahmin, you do not know the cause of sorrow, but I know. If sorrow and fear arise, they arise because of craving."

Then the Buddha spoke in verse as follows:

Verse 216. Craving begets sorrow, craving begets fear. For him who is free from craving there is no sorrow; how can there be fear for him?

At the end of the discourse the brahmin attained Sotāpatti Fruition.

Verse 217

XVI (7) The Story of Five Hundred Boys

While residing at the Veḷuvana monastery, the Buddha uttered Verse (217) of this book, with reference to five hundred boys.

On one festival day, the Buddha entered the city of Rājagaha for alms-food, accompanied by a number of bhikkhus. On their way, they met five hundred boys going to a pleasure garden. The boys were carrying some baskets of pan-cakes but they did not offer anything to the Buddha and his bhikkhus. But the Buddha said to his bhikkhus, "Bhikkhus, you shall eat those pan-cakes today; the owner is coming close behind us. We shall proceed only after taking some of these pan-cakes." After saying this, the Buddha and his bhikkhus rested under the shade of a tree. Just at that moment Thera Kassapa came along, and the boys seeing him paid obeisance to him and offered all their pan-cakes to the thera.

The thera then told the boys, "My teacher the Exalted One is resting underneath a tree over there accompanied by some bhikkhus; go and make an offering of your pan-cakes to him and the bhikkhus." The boys did as they were told. The Buddha accepted their offering of pan-cakes. Later, when the bhikkhus remarked that the boys were very partial to Thera Kassapa, the Buddha said to them, "Bhikkhus, all bhikkhus who are like my son Kassapa are liked by both devas and men. Such bhikkhus always receive ample offerings of the four requisites of bhikkhus."

Then the Buddha spoke in verse as follows:

Verse 217. He who is endowed with Virtue and Insight, who is established in the Dhamma, who has realized the Truth and performs his own duties, is loved by all men.

At the end of the discourse the five hundred boys attained Sotāpatti Fruition.

Verse 218

XVI (8) The Story of an Anāgāmi Thera

While residing at the Jetavana monastery, the Buddha uttered Verse (218) of this book, with reference to a thera who was an Anāgāmī.

On one occasion, the pupils of the thera asked him whether he had attained any of the maggas; but he did not say anything although he had attained the Anāgāmi Magga, the third magga. He kept silent because he had resolved not to talk about his attainment until he had attained arahatship. But the thera passed away without attaining arahatship, and also without saying anything about his attainment of Anāgāmi Magga Insight.

His pupils thought their teacher had passed away without attaining any of the maggas and they felt sorry for him. They went to the Buddha and asked him where their teacher was reborn. The Buddha replied, "Bhikkhus! Your teacher, who was an Anāgāmī before he passed away, is now reborn in the abodes of the Brahmās (Suddhāvāsa Brahmaloka). He did not reveal his attainment of Anāgāmi Magga because he felt ashamed that he had achieved only that much, and he was ardently striving to attain arahatship. Your teacher is now freed from the attachment to the sensual world (kāmaloka) and would certainly rise to higher realms."

Then the Buddha spoke in verse as follows:

Verse 218. He who has developed a desire for the Ineffable (i.e., Nibbāna), whose mind reaches the same, and is no longer attached to the sensual world (kāmaloka), is called one who is bound upstream (uddhaṁsoto).

At the end of the discourse those bhikkhus attained arahatship.

Verses 219 and 220

XVI (9) The Story of Nandiya

While residing at the Isipatana wood, the Buddha uttered Verses (219) and (220) of this book, with reference to Nandiya.

Nandiya was a rich man from Bārāṇasī. After listening to the Buddha's discourse on the benefits of building monasteries for bhikkhus, Nandiya built the Mahāvihāra monastery at Isipatana. The building was pinnacled and fully furnished. As soon as the monastery was offered to the Buddha, a mansion came up for Nandiya at the Tāvatiṁsa deva world.

One day, when Thera Mahā Moggallāna visited the Tāvatiṁsa deva world he saw the mansion which was meant for the donor of the Mahāvihāra monastery at Isipatana. On his return from the Tāvatiṁsa deva world, Thera Mahā Moggallāna asked the Buddha, "Venerable Sir! For those who perform meritorious deeds, do they have mansions and other riches prepared in the deva world even while they are still living in this world?" To him the Buddha said, "My son, why do you ask? Have you not yourself seen the mansion and riches waiting for Nandiya in the Tāvatiṁsa deva world? The devaș await the coming of the good and generous ones, as relatives await the return of one who is long absent. When the good ones die, they are welcomed joyously to the abode of the devas."

Then the Buddha spoke in verse as follows:

Verse 219. A man who has long been absent and has returned home safely from a distance is welcomed with joy by relatives, friends and well-wishers on his return.

Verse 220. In the same way, his good deeds will receive him who has done good when he goes from this world to the other, as relatives receive a dear one on his return.

End of Chapter Sixteen: Affection.

Chapter XVII

Anger (Kodhavagga)

Verse 221

XVII (1) The Story of Princess Rohinī

While residing at the Nigrodārāma monastery, the Buddha uttered Verse (221) of this book, with reference to Princess Rohinī, sister of Thera Anuruddha.

On one occasion, Thera Anuruddha visited Kapilavatthu. While he was staying at the monastery there, all his relatives, with the exception of his sister Rohinī, came to see him. On learning from them that Rohinī did not come because she was suffering from leprosy, he sent for her. Covering her head in shame, Rohinī came when she was sent for. Thera Anuruddha told her to do some meritorious deed and he suggested that she should sell some of her clothing and jewellery; and with the money raised, to build a refectory for the bhikkhus. Rohinī agreed to do as she was told. Thera Anuruddha also asked his other relatives to help in the construction of the hall. Further, he told Rohinī to sweep the floor and fill the water-pots every day even while the construction was still going on. She did as she was instructed and she began to get better.

When the hall was completed, the Buddha and his bhikkhus were invited for alms-food. After the meal, the Buddha asked for the donor of the building and alms-food, but Rohinī was not there. So the Buddha sent for her and she came. The Buddha asked her whether she knew why she was inflicted with this dreaded disease and she answered that she did not know. So the Buddha told her that she had the dreadful disease because of an evil deed she had done out of spite and anger, in one of her past existences. As explained by the Buddha, Rohinī was, at one time, the chief queen of the king of Bārāṇasī. It so happened that the king had a favourite dancer and the chief queen was very jealous of her. So the queen wanted to punish the dancer. Thus one day, she had her attendants put some itching powder made from cow-hage pods in the dancer's bed, her blankets, etc. Next, they called the dancer, and as though in jest, they threw some itching powder on her. The girl itched all over and was in great pain and discomfort. Thus itching unbearably, she ran to her room and her bed, which made her suffer even more.

As a result of that evil deed Rohinī had become a leper in this existence. The Buddha then exhorted the congregation not to act foolishly in anger and not to bear any ill will towards others.

Then the Buddha spoke in verse as follows:

Verse 221. Give up anger, abandon conceit, overcome all fetters. Ills of life (dukkha) do not befall one who does not cling to mind and body and is free from moral defilements.

At the end of the discourse, many in the congregation attained Sotāpatti Fruition. Princess Rohinī also attained Sotāpatti Fruition, and at the same time her skin disease disappeared, and her complexion became fair, smooth and very attractive.

Verse 222

XVII (2) The Story of a Bhikkhu

While residing at the Aggāḷava stupa in the city of Āḷavī, the Buddha uttered Verse (222) of this book, with reference to a bhikkhu.

Once, a bhikkhu from Āḷavī wanted to build a monastery for himself and so he began to cut down a tree. The deva dwelling in that tree (rukkha devatā) tried to stop him, saying that she and her infant son had nowhere to go. Failing to stop the bhikkhu she put her son on a branch, hoping that it would stop him from felling the tree. By then, the bhikkhu was already swinging his axe and he could not stop it in time and unintentionally cut off an arm of the child. Seeing her child being harmed in this way, the mother flew in a rage and was about to kill the bhikkhu. As she raised her hands to strike the bhikkhu, she suddenly checked herself and thought: "If I were to kill a bhikkhu, I would be killing one who observes the moral precepts (sīla); in that case, I would surely suffer in niraya. Other guardian devas of the trees would be following my example and other bhikkhus would also be killed. But this bhikkhu has a master; I must go and see his master." So she went weeping to the Buddha and related all that had happened.

To her the Buddha said, "O rukkha devatā! You have done well to control yourself."

Then the Buddha spoke in verse as follows:

Verse 222. He who restrains his rising anger as a skilful charioteer checks a speeding chariot,—him I call a true charioteer; other charioteers only hold the reins.

At the end of the discourse the deva attained Sotāpatti Fruition, and for her dwelling place she was offered a tree near the Perfumed Chamber of the Buddha. After this incident, the Buddha forbade bhikkhus to cut vegetation, such as grass, plants, shrubs and trees.

Verse 223

XVII (3) The Story of Uttarā the Lay-Disciple

While residing at the Veḷuvana monastery, the Buddha uttered Verse (223) of this book, with reference to Uttarā, a female lay-disciple.

Uttarā was the daughter of a farm labourer named Puṇṇa and his wife. Puṇṇa worked for a rich man named Sumana, in Rājagaha. One day, Puṇṇa and his wife offered alms-food to Thera Sāriputta soon after his arising from sustained deep mental absorption (nirodha samāpatti), and as a result of that good deed they suddenly became very rich. Puṇṇa came upon gold in the field he was ploughing, and the king officially declared him a royal banker. On one occasion, the family of Puṇṇa offered alms-food to the Buddha and the bhikkhus for seven days, and on the seventh day, after hearing the Buddha's discourse, all the three members of the family attained Sotāpatti Fruition.

Later, Uttarā the daughter of Puṇṇa married the son of the rich man Sumana. That family being non--Buddhist, Uttarā did not feel happy in her husband's home. So, she told her father, "My father, why have you put me in this cage? Here, I do not see any bhikkhu and I have no chance to offer anything to any bhikkhu." Her father felt sorry for her and sent her fifteen thousand in cash. With this money, after getting permission from her husband, Uttarā engaged a courte san to look to the needs of her husband. So it was arranged that Sirimā, a well-known and very beautiful courtesan, was to take her place as a wife for fifteen days.

During that time, Uttarā offered alms-food to the Buddha and the bhikkhus. On the fifteenth day, as she was busy preparing food in the kitchen, her husband saw her from the bedroom window and smiled, and then muttered to himself, "How foolish she is! She does not know how to enjoy herself. She is tiring herself out with this alms-giving ceremony!" Sirimā saw him smile, and forgetting that she was only a paid substitute wife felt very jealous of Uttarā. Being unable to control herself, Sirimā went into the kitchen and got a ladleful of boiling butter with the intention of pouring it over the head of Uttarā. Uttarā saw her coming, but she bore no ill will towards Sirimā. She reflected that because Sirimā had stood in for her, she had been able to listen to the dhamma, make offerings of alms-food for fifteen days, and perform other acts of charity. Thus she was quite thankful to Sirimā. Suddenly, she realized that Sirimā had come very close to her and was going to pour boiling-hot butter over her; so she made this asseveration: "If I bear any ill will towards Sirimā may this boiling-hot butter burn me; if I have no ill will towards her may it not burn me."

As Uttarā had no ill will towards Sirimā, the boiling butter poured over her head by Sirimā was just like cold water. Then Sirimā thought the butter must have gone cold; and as she went for another ladleful of boiling butter, the attendants of Uttarā fell upon her and beat her hard. Uttarā stopped her attendants and instructed them to rub Sirimā with medicinal ointment.

Then, Sirimā remembered her true position and she regretted that she had done wrong to Uttarā and asked Uttarā to forgive her. To her Uttarā replied, "I have my father; I shall ask him whether I should accept your apology." Sirimā then said that she would readily go and apologize to the rich man, the father of Uttarā. Uttarā then explained to Sirimā, "Sirimā, when I said 'My father', I did not mean my real father, who had brought me into this round of rebirths. I was referring to my father the Buddha, who had helped me break the chain of rebirths, who had taught me the Dhamma, the Noble Truths." Sirimā then expressed her wish to see the Buddha. So it was arranged that

Sirimā should offer alms-food to the Buddha and the bhikkhus on the following day at the house of Uttarā.

After the meal, the Buddha was told everything that had happened between Sirimā and Uttarā. Sirimā then owned up that she had done wrong to Uttarā and entreated the Buddha that she should be forgiven, for otherwise Uttarā would not forgive her. The Buddha then asked Uttarā how she felt in her mind when Sirimā poured boiling butter on her head, and Uttarā answered, "Venerable Sir, because I owed so much to Sirimā I had resolved not to lose my temper, not to bear any ill will towards her. I sent forth my love towards her". The Buddha then said, "Well done, well done, Uttarā! By not bearing any ill will you have been able to conquer one who has done you wrong through hate. By not abusing, you should conquer one who abuses you; by being generous you should conquer one who is stingy; by speaking the truth you should conquer one who tells lies."

Then the Buddha spoke in verse as follows:

Verse 223. Conquer the angry one by not getting angry (i. e., by loving-kindness); conquer the wicked by goodness; conquer the stingy by generosity, and the liar by speaking the truth.

At the end of the discourse Sirimā and five hundred ladies attained Sotāpatti Fruition.

Verse 224

XVII (4) The Story of the Question Raised by Thera Mahā Moggallāna

While residing at the Jetavana monastery, the Buddha uttered Verse (224) of this book, with reference to the question raised by Thera Mahā Moggallāna.

Once, Thera Mahā Moggallāna visited the deva world and found many devas living in luxurious mansions. He asked them for what good deed they were reborn in the deva world and they gave him different answers. One of them was reborn in the deva world not because he gave away much wealth in charity or because he had listened to the dhamma, but just because he always spoke the truth. The second one was a female deva who was reborn in the deva world because she did not get angry with her master and had no ill will towards him even though he often beat her and abused her. For keeping her temper and abandoning hatred she was reborn in the deva world. Then, there were others who were reborn in the deva world because they had offered little things like a stick of sugar cane, a fruit, or some vegetables to a bhikkhu or to someone else.

On his return from the deva world, Thera Mahā Moggallāna asked the Buddha whether it was possible to gain such great benefits by just speaking the truth, or by restraining one's actions, or by giving small amounts of such trifling things like fruits and vegetables. To him the Buddha answered, "My son, why do you ask? Have you not seen for yourself and heard what the devas said? You should not have any doubt. Little deeds of merit surely lead one to the world of the devas."

Then the Buddha spoke in verse as follows:

Verse 224. One should speak the truth, one should not yield to anger, one should give when asked even if it is only a little. By means of these three one may go to the world of the devas.

Verse 225

XVII (5) The Story of the Brahmin who had been the 'Father of the Buddha'

While residing at the Añjana wood, near Sāketa, the Buddha uttered Verse (225) of this book, with reference to a brahmin, who claimed that the Buddha was his son.

Once, the Buddha accompanied by some bhikkhus entered the town of Sāketa for alms-food. The old brahmin, seeing the Buddha, went to him and said, "O son, why have you not allowed us to see you all this long time? Come with me and let your mother also see you." So saying, he invited the Buddha to his house. On reaching the house, the wife of the brahmin said the same things to the Buddha and introduced the Buddha as "Your big brother" to her children, and made them pay obeisance to him. From that day, the couple offered alms-food to the Buddha every day, and having heard the religious discourses, both the brahmin and his wife attained Anāgāmi Fruition in due course.

The bhikkhus were puzzled why the brahmin couple said the Buddha was their son; so they asked the Buddha. The Buddha then replied, "Bhikkhus, they called me son because I was a son or a nephew to each of them for one thousand five hundred existences in the past." The Buddha continued to stay there, near the brahmin couple, for three more months and during that time, both the brahmin and his wife attained arahatship, and then realized parinibbāna.

The bhikkhus, not knowing that the brahmin couple had already become arahats, asked the Buddha where they were reborn. To them the Buddha answered: "Those who have become arahats are not reborn anywhere; they have realized Nibbāna."

Then the Buddha spoke in verse as follows:

Verse 225. The arahats, who do not harm others and are always restrained in their actions, go to the deathless Nibbāna, where there is no sorrow.

Verse 226

XVII (6) The Story of Puṇṇā the Slave Girl

While residing at the Gijjhakūṭa mountain, the Buddha uttered Verse (226) of this book, with reference to a slave girl in Rājagaha.

One night, Puṇṇā the slave girl was up pounding rice for her master. As she got tired she rested for a while. While resting, she saw Thera Dabba leading some bhikkhus to their respective monasteries on their return from listening to the Dhamma. The girl seeing them up so late, pondered, "I have to be up at this late hour because I am so poor and have to work hard. But, why are these good people up at this late hour? May be a bhikkhu is sick, or are they being troubled by a snake?"

Early in the morning the next day, Puṇṇā took some broken rice, soaked it in water and made a pan-cake out of it. Then, intending to eat it at the riverside she took her cheap, coarse pan-cake along with her. On the way, she saw the Buddha coming on an alms-round. She wanted to offer her pan-cake to the Buddha, but she was not sure whether the Buddha would condescend to eat such cheap, coarse pan-cake. The

Buddha knew her thoughts. He accepted her pan-cake and asked Thera Ānanda to spread the small mat on the ground. The Buddha sat on the mat and ate the pan-cake offered by the slave girl. After eating, the Buddha called Puṇṇā to him and answered the question which was troubling her. Said the Buddha to the slave girl, "Puṇṇā, you cannot go to sleep because you are poor and so have to work hard. As for my sons the bhikkhus, they do not go to sleep because they have to be always vigilant and ever mindful."

Then the Buddha spoke in verse as follows:

Verse 226. In those who are ever vigilant, who by day and by night train themselves in the three sikkhas (i.e., sīla, samādhi and paññā), and who have their mind directed towards Nibbāna, moral intoxicants become extinct.

At the end of the discourse Puṇṇā attained Sotāpatti Fruition.

Verses 227 to 230

XVII (7) The Story of Atula the Lay-disciple

While residing at the Jetavana monastery, the Buddha uttered Verses (227) to (230) of this book, with reference to Atula and his companions.

Once, Atula and his companions numbering five hundred, wishing to listen to words of dhamma, went to Thera Revata. The thera however was very aloof like a lion; he did not say anything to them. They were very much dissatisfied and so they went to Thera Sāriputta. When Thera Sāriputta learned why they had come, he expounded exhaustively on the Abhidhamma. He also was not to their liking, and they grumbled that Thera Sāriputta had been too lengthy and too profound. Next, Atula and his party approached Thera Ānanda. Thera Ānanda expounded to them the bare essentials of the Dhamma. This time, they remarked that Thera Ānanda had been too breif and too sketchy. Finally they came to the Buddha and said to him, "Venerable Sir, we have come to listen to your teaching. We have been to other teachers before we come here, but we are not satisfied with any of them. Thera Revata did not bother to teach us and he just kept silent;

Thera Sāriputta was too exhaustive and the Dhamma he taught us was too difficult for us. As for Thera Ānanda, he was too brief and too sketchy. We do not like any of their discourses."

To them the Buddha said, "My disciples, blaming others is not something new. There is no one in this world who is never blamed; people would blame even a king, or even a Buddha. To be blamed or to be praised by a fool is of no consequence; one is truly blamed only when he is blamed by a wise man, and truly praised only when praised by a wise man."

Then the Buddha spoke in verse as follows:

Verse 227. It is not new, O Atula! It has always been done from ancient times. They blame one who is silent, they blame one who speaks much, they blame one who speaks little. There is no one in this world who is not blamed.

Verse 228. There never has been, there never will be, nor is there now, anyone who is always blamed or always praised.

Verses 229, 230. If the wise praise him day after day, knowing him to be truly faultless, wise and endowed with knowledge and virtue, who would blame him, who is like a nikkha of pure gold? The devas praise him; he is praised even by the great Brahmās.

At the end of the discourse Atula anh his companions attained Sotāpatti Fruition.

Verses 231, 232, 233 and 234

XVII (8) The Story of a Group of Six Bhikkhus

While residing at the Veḷuvana monastery, the Buddha uttered Verses (231) to (234) of this book, with reference to a group of six bhikkhus.

Six bhikkhus wearing wooden sandals, and each holding a staff with both hands, were walking to and fro on a big stone slab, making much noise. The Buddha hearing the noises asked Thera Ānanda what was going on, and Thera Ānanda told him about the six bhikkhus. The Buddha then prohibited the bhikkhus from wearing wooden sandals. He further exhorted the bhikkhus to restrain themselves both in words and deeds.

Then the Buddha spoke in verse as follows:

Verse 231. Guard against evil deeds, control your body. Giving up evil deeds, cultivate good deeds.

Verse 232. Guard against evil speech, control your speech. Giving up evil speech, cultivate good speech.

Verse 233. Guard against evil thoughts, control your mind. Giving up evil thoughts, cultivate good thoughts.

Verse 234. The wise are controlled in deed, they are controlled in speech, they are controlled in thought. Indeed, they are perfectly self-controlled.

End of Chapter Seventeen: Anger.

Chapter XVIII
Impurities (Malavagga)

Verses 235 to 238

XVIII (1) The Story of the Son of a Butcher

While residing at the Jetavana monastery, the Buddha uttered Verses (235) to (238) of this book, with reference to the son of a butcher.

Once in Sāvatthi, there was a man who had been a butcher for fifty-five years. All this time, he slaughtered cattle and sold the meat and everyday he took meat curry with his rice. One day, he left some meat with his wife to cook it for the family, and then left for the riverside to have his bath. During his absence, a friend coaxed his wife to sell that particular piece of meat to him. As a result, there was no meat curry for the butcher on that day. But as the butcher never took his meal without meat curry, he hurriedly went to the back of his house, where an ox was standing. He promptly cut off the tongue of the ox and baked it over a fire. When having his meal, the butcher had a bite of the tongue of the ox, but as he did so his own tongue was cut off and fell into his plate of rice. Thus the ox and the butcher were in the same plight, both of them having had their tongues cut off. The butcher was in great pain and agony, and he went about agitatedly on his knees, with blood dripping profusely from his mouth. Then the butcher died and was reborn in the Avīci Niraya.

The butcher's wife was greatly disturbed and she was anxious for her son to get away to some other place, lest this evil should befall him too. So she sent her son to Taxila. At Taxila, he acquired the art of a goldsmith. Later, he married the daughter of his master and some children were born to them. When their sons came of age he returned to Sāvatthi. The sons were endowed with faith in the Buddha and were religiously inclined. They were anxious about their father, who had grown old with no thought of religion or of his future existence. So one day, they invited the Buddha and the bhikkhus to their house for alms-food. After the meal they said to the Buddha, "Venerable Sir, we are making this offering to you today on behalf of our father. Kindly give a discourse specially for him. So the Buddha said, "My disciple! You are getting old; but you have not made any provisions of merit for your journey to the next existence; you should now find a support for yourself."

Then the Buddha spoke in verse as follows:

Verse 235. You are now like a withered leaf; the messengers of death are near you; you are about to set out on a long journey; (yet), you have no provisions (for the journey).

Verse 236. Make a firm support for yourself; hasten to strive hard, and be wise. Having removed impurities and being free from moral defilements you shall enter the abodes of the ariyas (i.e., Suddhāvāsa brahmā realm).

Verse 237. Now you are of advanced age; you are going to the presence of the King of Death and you cannot stop on the way; (yet) you have no provisions (for the journey).

Verse 238. Make a firm support for yourself; hasten to strive hard, and be wise. Having removed impurities and being free from moral defilements you will no longer be subject to rebirth and decay.

At the end of the discourse the father of the donors of alms-food (i.e., the son of the butcher) attained Anāgāmi Fruition.

Verse 239

XVIII (2) The Story of a Brahmin

While residing at the Jetavana monastery, the Buddha uttered Verse (239) of this book, with reference to a brahmin.

Once, a brahmin saw a group of bhikkhus rearranging their robes as they were preparing to enter the city for alms-food. While he was looking, he found that the robes of some of the bhikkhus touched the ground and got wet because of dew on the grass. So he cleared that patch of ground. The next day, he found that as the robes of the bhikkhus touched bare ground, the robes got dirty. So he covered that patch of ground with sand. Then again, he observed that the bhikkhus would sweat when the sun was shining and that they got wet when it was raining. So finally, he built a rest house for the bhikkhus at the place where they gathered before entering the city for alms-food.

When the building was finished, he invited the Buddha and the bhikkhus for alms-food. The brahmin explained to the Buddha how he had performed this meritorious deed step by step. To him the Buddha replied, "O Brahmin! The wise perform their acts of merit little by little, and gradually and constantly they remove the impurities of moral defilements."

Then the Buddha spoke in verse as follows:

Verse 239. By degrees, little by little, from moment to moment, a wise man removes his own impurities (moral defilements), as a smith removes the dross of silver or gold.

At the end of the discourse the brahmin attained Sotāpatti Fruition.

Verse 240

XVIII (3) The Story of Thera Tissa

While residing at the Jetavana monastery, the Buddha uttered Verse (240) of this book, with reference to Thera Tissa.

Once there was a thera named Tissa in Sāvatthi. One day, he received a set of fine robes and was very pleased. He intended to wear those robes the next day. But that very night he died and because he was attached to the fine set of robes, he was reborn as a louse and lived within the folds of the robes. As there was no one to inherit his belongings, it was decided that this particular set of robes should be shared by other bhikkhus. When the bhikkhus were preparing to share out among themselves, the louse was very much agitated and cried out, "They are destroying my robes!" This cry was heard by the Buddha by means of his divine power of hearing. So he sent someone to stop the bhikkhus and instructed them to dispose of the robes only at the end of seven days. On the eighth day, the set of the robes which belonged to Thera Tissa was shared out by the bhikkhus.

Later, the Buddha was asked by the bhikkhus why he had told them to wait for seven days before sharing out the robes of Thera Tissa. To them the Buddha replied, "My sons, Tissa had his mind attached to this particular set of robes at the time of his death, and so he was reborn as a louse and stayed in the folds of the robes. When you all were preparing to share out the robes, Tissa the louse was very much in agony and was running about to and fro in the folds of the robes. If you had taken the robes at that time Tissa the louse would have felt very bitter against you and he would have to go to niraya. But now, Tissa has been reborn in the Tusita deva world, and that is why I have allowed you to take the robes. Indeed, bhikkhus, attachment is very dangerous; as rust corrodes iron from which it is formed, so also, attachment destroys one and sends one to niraya. A bhikkhu should not indulge too much in the use of the four requisites or be very much attached to them."

Then the Buddha spoke in verse as follows:

Verse 240. Just as rust is formed from iron, and corrodes the iron from which it is formed, so also, his own deeds lead the transgressor to a lower plane of existence (duggati).

Verse 241

XVIII (4) The Story of Lāludāyi

While residing at the Jetavana monastery, the Buddha uttered Verse (241) of this book, with reference to Thera Lāludāyi.

In Sāvatthi, people coming back after hearing the discourses given by Thera Sāriputta and Thera Mahā Moggallāna were always full of praise for the two Chief Disciples. On one occasion, Lāludāyi, hearing their praises, said to those people that they would be saying the same about him after listening to his discourses. So Lāludāyi was asked to deliver a discourse; he climbed on to the platform but he could not say anything. So he asked the audience to let another bhikkhu take the turn first and that he would take the next turn. In this way, he put off three times.

The audience lost patience with him and shouted, "You big fool! When we praised the two Chief

Disciples you were vainly boasting that you could preach like them. Why don't you preach now?" So Lāludāyi ran away and the crowd chased him. As he was frightened and was not looking where he was going, he fell into a latrine pit.

When the Buddha was told about this incident, he said, "Lāludāyi had learned very little of the Dhamma; he does not recite the religious texts regularly; he has not memorized anything. Whatever little he has learned gets rusty by not reciting."

Then the Buddha spoke in verse as follows:

Verse 241. Non-recitation is the taint of learning; non--maintenance is the taint of houses; indolence is the taint of beauty; unmindfulness is the taint of one who keeps watch.

Verses 242 and 243

XVIII (5) The Story of a Man Whose Wife Committed Adultery

While residing at the Veḷuvana monastery, the Buddha uttered Verses (242) and (243) of this book, with reference to a man whose wife committed adultery.

Once, the wife of a man committed adultery. He was so ashamed on account of his wife's misbehaviour that he dared not face anyone; he also kept away from the Buddha. After some time, he went to the Buddha and the Buddha asked him why he had been absent all that time and he explained everything. On learning the reason for his absence, the Buddha said, "My disciple, women are just like a river, or a road, or a liquor shop or a rest house, or a water-pot stand at the roadside; they associate with all sorts of people. Indeed, sexual misconduct is the cause of ruin for a woman."

Then the Buddha spoke in verse as follows:

Verse 242. Sexual misconduct is the taint of a woman; stinginess is the taint of a giver; evil ways are indeed taints in this world as well as in the next.

Verse 243. A taint worse than these is ignorance (of the Truth), which is the greatest of taints. O bhikkhus, abandon this taint and be taintless.

At the end of the discourse many people attained Sotāpatti Fruition.

Verses 244 and 245

XVIII (6) The Story of Cūḷasāri

While residing at the Jetavana monastery, the Buddha uttered Verses (244) and (245) of this book, with reference to a bhikkhu named Cūḷasāri who practised medicine.

One day, Cūḷasāri came back after ministering to a patient. On his way he met Thera Sāriputta and related to him how he went to treat a patient and had been given some delicious food for his services. He also begged Thera Sāriputta to accept some of the food from him. Thera Sāriputta did not say anything to him but continued on his way. Thera Sāriputta refused to accept food from that bhikkhu because that bhikkhu had transgressed the law prohibiting bhikkhus from practising medicine. Other bhikkhus reported about this to the Buddha and he said to them, "Bhikkhus! A bhikkhu who is shameless is coarse in thought, word and deed. He is arrogant like a crow, he would find a living by unlawful means and live in comfort. On the other hand, life for a bhikkhu who has a sense of shame is not easy."

Then the Buddha spoke in verse as follows:

Verse 244. Life is easy for one who is shameless and bold as a crow, who slanders others and is pretentious, aggressive and corrupt.

Verse 245. Life is hard for one with a sense of shame, who always seeks purity, who is free from attachment, who is modest and who sees clearly what is proper livelihood.

At the end of the discourse many people attained Sotāpatti Fruition.

Verses 246, 247 and 248

XVIII (7) The Story of Five Lay-Disciples

While residing at the Jetavana monastery, the Buddha uttered Verses (246), (247) and (248) of this book, with reference to five lay-disciples.

On one occasion five lay-disciples were keeping sabbath at the Jetavana monastery. Most of them were observing only one or two of the five moral precepts (sīla). Each one of them observing a particular precept claimed that the precept observed by him was the most difficult and there were a lot of arguments. In the end, they came to the Buddha with this problem. To them the Buddha said, "You should not consider any individual precept as being easy or unimportant. Each and every one of the precepts must be strictly observed. Do not think lightly of any of the precepts; none of them is easy to observe."

Then the Buddha spoke in verse as follows:

Verses 246, 247. He who destroys life, tells lies, takes what is not given him, commits adultery and takes intoxicating drinks, digs up his own roots even in this very life.

Verse 248. Know this, O man! Not restraining oneself is evil; do not let greed and ill will subject you to prolonged misery.

At the end of the discourse the five lay-disciples atained Sotāpatti Fruition.

Verses 249 and 250

XVIII (8) The Story of Tissa

While residing at the Jetavana monastery, the Buddha uttered Verses (249) and (250) of this book, with reference to Tissa, a young bhikkhu.

Tissa, a young bhikkhu, had a very bad habit of disparaging other people's charities and good deeds. He even criticized the charities given by such renowned donors like Anāthapiṇḍika and Visākhā. Besides, he boasted that his relatives were very rich and were like a well where anyone could come for water. Hearing him boast thus, other bhikkhus were very sceptical; so they decided to find out the truth.

Some young bhikkhus went to the village from where he came and made enquiries. They found out that Tissa's relatives were all poor and that all this time Tissa had only been making a vain boast. When the Buddha was told about this, he said, "Bhikkhus, a bhikkhu who is displeased with others receiving gifts and offerings can never attain Magga and Phala."

Then the Buddha spoke in verse as follows:

Verse 249. People give according to their faith and their devotion; one who is displeased with others receiving food and drink cannot attain concentration (samādhi) by day or by night.

Verse 250. He who has this feeling of displeasure cut off, uprooted and removed, will surely attain concentration (samādhi) by day or by night.

Verse 251

XVIII (9) The Story of Five Lay-disciples

While residing at the Jetavana monastery, the Buddha uttered Verse (251) of this book, with reference to five lay-disciples.

On one accasion, five lay-disciples were present while the Buddha was expounding the Dhamma at the Jetavana monastery. One of them was asleep while sitting, the second one was drawing lines with his fingers on the ground, the third was trying to shake a tree, the fourth was looking up at the sky. The fifth was the only one who was respectfully and attentively listening to the Buddha. Thera Ānanda, who was near the Buddha fanning him saw the different behaviour of the five disciples and said to the Buddha, "Venerable Sir! While you were expounding the Dhamma like big drops of rain falling from the sky, only one out of those five people were listening attentively." Then Thera Ānanda described the different behaviour of the other four to the Buddha and asked why they were behaving thus.

The Buddha then explained to Thera Ānanda, "Ānanda, these people could not get rid of their old habits. In their past existences, the first one was a snake; as a snake usually coils itself up and goes to sleep, so also, this man goes to sleep while listening to the Dhamma. The one who was scratching the earth with his hand was an earthworm, the one who was shaking the tree was a monkey, the one who was gazing up at the sky was an astronomer and the one who was listening attentively to the Dhamma was a learned astrologer. In this connection, Ānanda, you must remember that one must be attentive to be able to understand the Dhamma and that there are many people who cannot follow what was being said."

Thera Ānanda then asked the Buddha, "Venerable Sir! What are the things that prevent people from being able to take in the Dhamma? And the Buddha replied, "Ānanda, passion (rāga), ill will (dosa) and ignorance (moha) are the three things that prevent people from taking in the Dhamma. Passion burns one; there is no fire like passion. The world may burn up when seven suns rise in the sky, but that happens very rarely. Passion burns always and without any break."

Then the Buddha spoke in verse as follows:

Verse 251. There is no fire like passion, there is no grip like ill will, there is no net like ignorance, there is no river like craving.

At the end of the discourse the one who was listening attentively attained Sotāpatti Fruition.

Verse 252

XVIII (10) The Story of Meṇḍaka the Rich Man

While residing near the town of Baddiya, the Buddha uttered Verse (252) of this book, with reference to the renowned rich man Meṇḍaka and his family.

Once, during his tour of Aṅga and Uttara regions, the Buddha saw in his vision that time was ripe for Meṇḍaka, his wife, his son, his daughter-in-law, his granddaughter and his servant, to attain Sotāpatti Fruition. Seeing the prospect of these six people attaining Sotāpatti Fruition, the Buddha went to the town of Baddiya.

Meṇḍaka was an extremely rich man. It was said that he found a large number of life-size golden statues of goats in his backyard. For this reason, he was known as Meṇḍaka (a goat) the rich man. Again, it was also said that during the time of Vipassī Buddha he had donated a monastery for Vipassī Buddha and a congregation hall complete with a platform for the preacher. On completion of these buildings he made offerings of alms-food to Vipassī Buddha and the bhikkhus for four months. Then, in yet another of his past existences, when he was a rich man in Bārāṇasī, there was a famine throughout the region. One day, they had cooked a meal just enough for the members of the family when a paccekabuddha stood at the door for alms-food. Then and there he offered all the food. But due to his great faith and generosity, the rice pot was later found to be miraculously filled up again; so also were his granaries.

Meṇḍaka and his family, hearing that the Buddha was coming to Baddiya, went to pay homage to him. After hearing the discourse given by the Buddha, Meṇḍaka, his wife Candapadumā, his son Danañcaya, his daughter-in-law Sumanadevī, his granddaughter Visākhā and the servant Puṇṇa attained Sotāpatti Fruition. Meṇḍaka then told the Buddha how, on his way, some ascetics had spoken ill of the Buddha and had tried to dissuade him from coming to see him. The Buddha then said, "My disciple, it is natural for people not to see one's own faults, and to exaggerate other people's faults and failings."

Then the Buddha spoke in verse as follows:

Verse 252. It is easy to see the faults of others, but difficult to see one's own. A man broadcasts the faults of others like winnowing chaff in the wind, but hides his own faults as a crafty fowler covers himself.

Verse 253

XVIII (11) The Story of Thera Ujjhānasaññi

While residing at the Jetavana monastery, the Buddha uttered Verse (253) of this book, with reference to Thera Ujjhānasaññi.

Thera Ujjhānasaññi was always finding fault with and speaking ill of others. Other bhikkhus reported about him to the Buddha. The Buddha replied to them, "Bhikkhus, if someone finds fault with another so as to teach him in good ways it is not an act of evil and is therefore not to be blamed. But, if someone is always finding fault with others and speaking ill of them just out of spite and malice, he will not attain concentration and mental absorption (jhāna). He will not be able to understand the Dhamma, and moral intoxicants (āsavas) will increase in him.

Then the Buddha spoke in verse as follows:

Verse 253. In one who constantly sees the faults of others and is always disparaging them, moral intoxicants (āsavas) increase; he is far from extinction of moral intoxicants (i.e., he is far from attainment of arahatship).

Verses 254 and 255

XVIII (12) The Story of Subhadda the Wandering Ascetic

Verses (254) and (255) of this book were uttered by the Buddha in the Sal Grove of the Malla princes near Kusinārā, just before the parinibbāna (passing away) of the Buddha, in reply to the questions raised by Subhadda, the wandering ascetic (paribbājaka).

Subhadda the wandering ascetic was staying at Kusinārā when he heard that the parinibbāna of Gotama Buddha would take place in the last watch of that night. Subhadda had three questions which had been troubling him for a long time. He had already put these questions to other religious leaders, namely, Pūraṇa Kassapa, Makkhali Gosāla, Ajita Kesakambala, Pakudha Kaccāyana, Sañcaya Belaṭṭhaputta and Nigaṇṭha Nāṭaputta, but their answers did not satisfy him. He had not yet asked Gotama Buddha, and he felt that only the Buddha could answer his questions. So, he hurried off to the Sal Grove, but the Venerable Ānanda did not allow him to see the Buddha, because the Buddha was by that time very weak. The Buddha overheard their conversation and consented to see Subhadda. Subhadda asked three questions. They are: (1) Are there any tracks in the sky? (2) Are there any ariya bhikkhus (samaṇas) outside the Teaching of the Buddha? and (3) Is there any conditioned thing (saṅkhāra) that is permanent? The Buddha's answer to all the above questions was negative.

Then the Buddha spoke in verse as follows:

Verse 254. In the sky there is no track; outside the Buddha's Teaching there is no ariya bhikkhu (samaṇa). All beings take delight in fetters (i.e., craving, pride and wrong view) that prolong saṁsāra; all the Buddhas are free from these fetters.

Verse 255. In the sky there is no track; outside the Buddha's Teaching there is no ariya bhikkhu (samaṇa). There is no conditioned thing that is permanent; all the Buddhas are unperturbed (by craving, pride and wrong view).

At the end of the discourse Subhadda attained Anāgāmi Fruition and as requested by him the Buddha admitted him to the Order of the bhikkhus. Subhadda was the last one to become a bhikkhu in the life time of the Buddha. Eventually, Subhadda attained arahatship.

End of Chapter Eighteen: Impurities.

Chapter XIX

The Just or the Righteous (Dhammaṭṭhavagga)

Verses 256 and 257

XIX (1) The Story of the Julge

While residing at the Jetavana monastery, the Buddha uttered Verses (256) and (257) of this book, with reference to some judges who were corrupt.

One day, some bhikkhus were returning from their round of alms-food when it rained and they went into a law court to take shelter. While they were there, they found out that some judges, having taken bribes, were deciding cases arbitrarily. They reported the matter to the Buddha and the Buddha replied, "Bhikkhus! In deciding cases, if one is influenced by affection or by monetary consideration, he cannot be called 'the just', or 'a judge who abides by the law.' If one weighs the evidence intelligently and decides a case impartially, then he is to be called, 'the just' or 'a judge who abides by the law.'"

Then the Buddha spoke in verse as follows:

Verse 256. He is not just if he decides a case arbitrarily; the wise man should decide after considering both what is right and what is wrong.

Verse 257. The wise man who decides not arbitrarily but in accordance with the law is one who safeguards the law; he is to be called 'one who abides by the law (dhammaṭṭho).'

Verse 258

XIX (2) The Story of a Group of Six Bhikkhus

While residing at the Jetavana monastery, the Buddha uttered Verse (258) of this book, with reference to a group of six bhikkhus.

Once, there was a group of six bhikkhus who made trouble at the place of eating either in the monastery or in the village. One day, while some sāmaṇeras wer, having their alms-food, the group of six bhikkhus came in and said boastfully to the sāmaṇeras, "Look! We only are the wise." Then they started throwing things about, leaving the place of eating in disorder. When the Buddha was told about this, he said, "Bhikkhus! I do not say that one who talks much, abuses and bullies others is a wise man. Only he who is free from hatred, and harms no one is a wise man."

Then the Buddha spoke in verse as follows:

Verse 258. He is not a wise man just because he talks much; only he who is peaceful, free from enmity, and does no harm to others, is to be called 'a wise man.'

Verse 259

XIX (3) The Story of Ekudāna the Arahat

While residing at the Jetavana monastery, the Buddha uttered Verse (259) of this book, with reference to a bhikkhu who was an arahat.

This bhikkhu lived in a grove near Sāvatthi. He was known as Ekudāna, because he knew only one stanza of exultation (udāna) by heart. But the thera fully understood the meaning of the Dhamma as conveyed by the stanza. On each sabbath day, he would exhort others to listen to the Dhamma, and he himself would recite the one stanza he knew. Every time he had finished his recitation, the guardian spirits (devas) of the forests praised him and applauded him resoundingly. On one sabbath day, two learned theras, who were well-versed in the Tipiṭaka, accompanied by five hundred bhikkhus came to his place. Ekudāna asked the two theras to preach the Dhamma. They enquired if there were many who wished to listen to the Dhamma in this out of the way place. Ekudāna answered in the affirmative and also told them that even the guardian spirits of the forests usually came, and that they usually praised and applauded at the end of discourses.

So, the two learned theras took turns to preach the Dhamma, but when their discourses ended, there was no applause from the guardian spirits of the forests. The two learned theras were puzzled; they even doubted the words of Ekudāna. But Ekudāna insisted that the guardian spirits used to come and always applauded at the end of each discourse. The two theras then pressed Ekudāna to do the preaching himself. Ekudāna held the fan in front of him and recited the usual stanza. At the end of the recitation, the guardian spirits applauded as usual. The bhikkhus who had accompanied the two learned theras complained that the devas inhabiting the forests were very partial.

They reported the matter to the Buddha on arrival at the Jetavana monastery. To them the Buddha said, "Bhikkhus! I do not say that a bhikkhu who has learnt much and talks much of the Dhamma is "one who is versed in the Dhamma, (Dhammadhara)." One who has learnt very little and knows only one stanza of the Dhamma, but fully comprehends the Four Noble Truths, and is ever mindful is the one who is truly versed in the Dhamma."

Then the Buddha spoke in verse as follows:

Verse 259. He is not "one versed in the Dhamma (Dhammadhara)" just because he talks much. He who hears only a little but comprehends the Dhamma, and is not unmindful is, indeed, "one versed in the Dhamma."

Verses 260 and 261

XIX (4) The Story of Thera Bhaddiya

While residing at the Jetavana monastery, the Buddha uttered Verses (260) and (261) of this book, with reference to Thera Bhaddiya. He was also known as Lakuṇḍaka Bhaddiya because he was very short in stature.

One day, thirty bhikkhus came to pay obeisance to the Buddha. The Buddha knew that time was ripe for those thirty bhikkhus to attain arahatship. So he asked them whether they had seen a thera as they came into the room. They answered that they did not see a thera but they saw only a young sāmaṇera as they came in. Whereupon, the Buddha said to them, "Bhikkhus! That person is not a sāmaṇera, he is a senior bhikkhu although he is small-built and very unassuming. I do say that one is not a thera just because he is old and looks like a thera; only he who comprehends the Four Noble Truths and does not harm others is to be called a thera."

Then the Buddha spoke in verse as follows:

Verse 260. He is not a thera just because his head is grey; he who is ripe only in years is called "one grown old in vain."

Verse 261. Only a wise man who comprehends the Four Noble Truths and the Dhamma, who is harmless and virtuous, who restrains his senses and has rid himself of moral defilements is indeed called a thera.

At the end of the discourse those thirty bhikkhus attained arahatship.

Verses 262 and 263

XIX (5) The Story of Some Bhikkhus

While residing at the Jetavana monastery, the Buddha uttered Verses (262) and (263) of this book, with reference to some bhikkhus who were very envious of other bhikkhus.

At the monastery, young bhikkhus and sāmaṇeras were in the habit of attending on older bhikkhus who were their teachers. They washed and dyed the robes, or else performed other small services for their teachers. Some bhikkhus noticing these services envied those senior bhikkhus, and so they thought out a plan that would benefit them materially. Their plan was that they would suggest to the Buddha that young bhikkhus and sāmaṇeras should be required to come to them for further instruction and guidance even though they had been taught by their respective teachers. When they went to the Buddha with this proposal, the Buddha, knowing full well their motive, turned it down. To them the Buddha said, "Bhikkhus! I do not say that you are good-hearted just because you can talk eloquently. Only he who has got rid of covetousness and all that is evil by means of Arahatta Magga is to be called a good-hearted man."

Then the Buddha spoke in verse as follows:

Verse 262. Not by fine talk, nor by good looks could one be a good-hearted man, if he were envious, miserly and crafty.

Vrese 263. A wise man who has cut off, uprooted and removed these and has rid himself of moral defilements is indeed called a good-hearted man.

Verses 264 and 265

XIX (6) The Story of Bhikkhu Hatthaka

While residing at the Jetavana monastery, the Buddha uttered Verses (264) and (265) of this book, with reference to a bhikkhu named Hatthaka.

Bhikkhu Hatthaka was in the habit of challenging ascetics of non-Buddhist faiths to meet him in a certain place to debate on religious matters. He would then go out by himself to the self-appointed place. When nobody appeared he would boast, "Look, those wandering ascetics dare not meet me, they have been beaten by me!", and such other things. The Buddha called Hatthaka to him and said, "Bhikkhu! Why do you behave in this way? One who says such things cannot become a samaṇa in spite of his shaven head. Only one who has rid himself of all evil is to be called a samaṇa."

Then the Buddha spoke in verse as follows:

Verse 264. Not by a shaven head does a man become a samaṇa, if he lacks morality and austere practices and tells lies. How could he who is full of covetousness and greed be a samaṇa?

Verse 265. He who has totally subdued all evil, great and small, is called a samaṇa because he has overcome all evil.

Verses 266 and 267

XIX (7) The Story of a Brahmin

While residing at the Jetavana monastery, the Buddha uttered Verses (266) and (267) of this book, with reference to a brahmin.

Once, there was a brahmin who was in the habit of going round for alms. One day, he thought, "Samaṇa Gotama has declared that one who lives by going round for alms is a bhikkhu. That being so, I should also be called a bhikkhu." So thinking, he went to the Buddha and said to him that he (the brahmin) should also be called a bhikkhu, because he also went round for alms-food. To him the Buddha replied, "Brahmin, I do not say that you are a bhikkhu simply because you go round for alms-food. One who professes a wrong faith and acts accordingly is not to be called a bhikkhu. Only he who lives meditating on the impermanence, unsatisfactoriness, and insubstantiality of the aggregates is to be called a bhikkhu."

Then the Buddha spoke in verse as follows:

Verse 266. He does not become a bhikkhu merely because he stands at the door for alms. He cannot become a bhikkhu because he acts according to a faith which is not in comformity with the Dhamma.

Verse 267. In this world, he who lays aside both good and evil, who leads the life of purity, and lives meditating on the khandha aggregates is indeed called a bhikkhu.

Verses 268 and 269

XIX (8) The Story of the Followers of Non-Buddhist Doctrines

While residing at the Jetavana monastery, the Buddha uttered Verses (268) and (269) of this book, with reference to some non-Buddhist ascetics.

To those who offered them food or other things, those ascetics would say words of blessing. They would say, "May you be free from danger, may you prosper and get rich, may you live long," etc. At that time, the followers of the Buddha did not say anything after receiving something from their lay-disciples. This was because during the first twenty years after the Buddha's attainment of Buddhahood they were instructed to remain silent on receiving offerings. Since the followers of the Buddha were silent when ascetics of other doctrines were saying things which were pleasing to their disciples, people began to compare the two groups.

When the Buddha heard about this, he permitted the bhikkhus to say words of blessing to their disciples after receiving offerings. As a result of that, more and more people invited the followers of the Buddha for alms. Then, the ascetics of other doctrines remarked with disdain: "We adhere to the practice of the muni and keep silent, whereas the followers of Samaṇa Gotama go about talking exuberantly in the eating places." On hearing those disparaging remarks, the Buddha said, "Bhikkhus! There are some who keep silent because they are ignorant and timid, and some who keep silent because they do not want to share their profound knowledge with others. Thus, one does not become a muni simply by keeping silent. Only one who has overcome evil is to be called a muni."

Then the Buddha spoke in verse as follows:

Verses 268, 269. Not by silence does one become a muni, if one is dull and ignorant. Like one holding a pair of scales, the wise one takes what is good and rejects what is evil. For this reason he is a muni. He who understands both internal and external aggregates is also, for that reason, called a muni.

Verse 270

XIX (9) The Story of a Fisherman Named Ariya

While residing at the Jetavana monastery, the Buddha uttered Verse (270) of this book, with reference to a fisherman named Ariya.

Once, there was a fisherman who lived near the north gate of Sāvatthi. One day through his supernormal power, the Buddha found that time was ripe for the fisherman to attain Sotāpatti Fruition. So on his return from the alms-round, the Buddha, followed by the bhikkhus, stopped near the place where Ariya was fishing. When the fisherman saw the Buddha, he threw away his fishing gear and came and stood near the Buddha. The Buddha then proceeded to ask the names of his bhikkhus in the presence of the fisherman, and finally, he asked the name of the fisherman. When the fisherman replied that his name was Ariya, the Buddha said that the Noble Ones (ariyas) do not harm any living being, but since the fisherman was taking the lives of fish he was not worthy of his name.

Then the Buddha spoke in verse as follows:

Verse 270. He who harms living beings is, for that reason, not an ariya (a Noble One); he who does not harm any living being is called an ariya.

At the end of the discourse the fisherman attained Sotāpatti Fruition.

Verses 271 and 272

XIX (10) The Story of Some Bhikkhus

While residing at the Jetavana monastery, the Buddha uttered Verses (271) and (272) of this book, with reference to some bhikkhus.

Once, there were some bhikkhus who were endowed with virtue; some of them had strictly observed the austere practices (dhūtaṅga), some had wide knowledge of the Dhamma, some had achieved mental absorption (jhāna), some had achieved Anāgāmi Phala, etc. All of them thought that since they had achieved that much, it would be quite easy for them to attain Arahatta Phala. With this thought they went to the Buddha.

The Buddha asked them, "Bhikkhus, have you attained Arahatta Phala?" Then they replied that they were in such a condition that it would not be difficult for them to attain Arahatta Phala at any time. To them the Buddha said, "Bhikkhus! Just because you are endowed with morality (sīla), just because you have attained Anāgāmi Phala, you should not be complacent and think that there is just a little more to be done; unless you have eradicated all moral intoxicants (āsavas), you must not think that you have realized perfect bliss of Arahatta Fruition."

Then the Buddha spoke in verse as follows:

Verses 271, 272. Not by mere moral practice, nor by much learning, nor by acquiring concentration, nor by dwelling in seclusion, nor by assuring oneself "I enjoy the bliss of Anāgāmi Fruition that is not enjoyed by common worldlings (puthujjanas)" should the bhikkhu rest content without attaining the extinction of moral intoxicants (āsavas) [i.e., without attaining arahatship].

At the end of the discourse all those bhikkhus attained arahatship.

End of Chapter Nineteen: The Just or the Righteous.

Chapter XX

The Path (Maggavagga)

Verses 273 to 276

XX (1) The Story of Five Hundred Bhikkhus

While residing at the Jetavana monastery, the Buddha uttered Verses (273) to (276) of this book, with reference to five hundred bhikkhus.

Five hundred bhikkhus, after accompanying the Buddha to a village, returned to the Jetavana monastery. In the evening they talked about the trip, especially the nature of the land, whether it was level or hilly, clayey or stony, etc. The Buddha came to them in the midst of their conversation and said to them, "Bhikkhus, the path you are talking about is external to you; a bhikkhu should only be concerned with the path of the Noble Ones (ariyas) and strive to do what should be done for the attainment of the Ariya Path (Magga) that leads to the realization of the Perfect Peace (Nibbāna)."

Then the Buddha spoke in verse as follows:

Verse 273. Of paths, the Path of Eight Constituents is the noblest; of truths, the Four Noble Truths are the noblest; of the dhammas, the absence of craving (i.e., Nibbāna) is the noblest; of the two-legged beings, the All-Seeing Buddha is the noblest.

Verse 274. This is the only Path, and there is none other for the purity of vision. Follow this Path; it will bewilder Māra.

Verse 275. Following this Path, you will make an end of dukkha. Having myself known the Path which can lead to the removal of the thorns of moral defilements, I have shown you the Path.

Verse 276. You yourselves should make the effort; the Tathāgatas (Buddhas) only can show the way. Those who practise the Tranquillity and Insight Meditation are freed from the bond of Māra.

At the end of the discourse those five hundred ...ikkhus attained arahatship.

Verses 277, 278 and 279

XX (2), (3) and (4) Stories Relating to Anicca, Dukkha and Anatta

While residing at the Jetavana monastery, the Buddha uttered Verses (277), (278) and (279) of this book, with reference to three groups of five hundred bhikkhus each.

On Impermanence (Anicca)

Five hundred bhikkhus, after receiving their subject of meditation from the Buddha, went into the forest to practise meditation, but they made little progress. So, they returned to the Buddha to ask for another subject of meditation which would suit them better. On reflection, the Buddha found that those bhikkhus had, during the time of Kassapa Buddha, meditated on impermanence. So, he said, "Bhikkhus, all conditioned phenomena are subject to change and decay and are therefore impermanent."

Then the Buddha spoke in verse as follows:

Verse 277. "All conditioned phenomena are impermanent"; when one sees this with Insight-wisdom, one becomes weary of dukkha (i. e., the khandhas). This is the Path to Purity.

At the end of the discourse those five hundred bhikkhus attained arahatship.

On Dukkha

The story is the same as the story on Anicca. Here, the Buddha on reflection found that another group of five hundred bhikkhus had meditated on dukkha. So, he said, "Bhikkhus, all khandha aggregates are oppressive and unsatisfactory; thus all khandhas are dukkha."

Then the Buddha spoke in verse as follows:

Verse 278. "All conditioned phenomena are dukkha"; when one sees this with Insight-wisdom, one becomes weary of dukkha (i. e., the khandhas). This is the Path to Purity.

At the end of the discourse those five hundred bhikkhus attained arahatship.

On Insubstantiality or Non-Self (Anatta)

The story is the same as the stories on Anicca and Dukkha. Here, the Buddha on reflection found that still another group of five hundred bhikkhus had meditated on insubstantiality or non-self (anatta). So, he said, "Bhikkhus, all khandha aggregates are insubstantial; they are not subject to one's control."

Then the Buddha spoke in verse as follows:

Verse 279. "All phenomena (dhammas) are without Self"; when one sees this with Insight-wisdom, one becomes weary of dukkha (i. e., the khandhas). This is the Path to Purity.

At the end of the discourse all those five hundred bhikkhus attained arahatship.

Verse 280

XX (5) The Story of Thera Tissa the Idle One

While residing at the Jetavana monastery, the Buddha uttered Verse (280) of this book, with reference to Tissa, a lazy bhikkhu.

Once, five hundred young men were admitted into the Order by the Buddha in Sāvatthi. After receiving a subject of meditation from the Buddha, all the new bhikkhus except one went to the forest to practise meditation. They practised zealously and vigilantly so that in due course all of them attained arahatship. When they returned to the monastery to pay homage to him, the Buddha was very pleased and satisfied with their achievement. Bhikkhụ Tissa who stayed behind did not try hard and therefore achieved nothing.

When Tissa found that the relationship between the Buddha and those bhikkhus was very cordial and intimate, he felt rather neglected, and regretted that he had wasted all that time. So he resolved to practise meditation throughout the night. As he was walking in meditation on that night, he slipped and broke a thigh bone. Other bhikkhus hearing his cry went to help him. On hearing about the above incident the Buddha said, "Bhikkhus, one who does not strive when he should be striving but idle away his time will not attain mental absorption (jhāna) and Magga Insight."

Then the Buddha spoke in verse as follows:

Verse 280. The idler who does not strive when he should be striving, who though young and strong is given to idleness, whose thoughts are weak and wandering, will not attain Magga Insight which can only be perceived by wisdom.

Verse 281

XX (6) The Story of a Swine-Peta

While residing at the Veḷuvana monastery, the Buddha uttered Verse (281) of this book, with reference to a swine-peta.

Once Thera Mahā Moggallāna was coming down the Gijjhakūṭa hill with Thera Lakkhaṇa when he saw a miserable, ever-hungry peta, with the head of a swine and the body of a human being. On seeing the peta, Thera Mahā Moggallāna smiled but did not say anything. Back at the monastery, Thera Mahā Moggallāna, in the presence of the Buddha, talked about the swine-peta with its mouth swarming with maggots. The Buddha also said that he himself had seen that very peta soon after his attainment of Buddhahood, but that he did not say anything about it because people might not believe him and thus they would be doing wrong to him. Then the Buddha proceeded to relate the story about the swine-peta.

During the time of Kassapa Buddha, this particular peta was a bhikkhu who often expounded the Dhamma. On one occasion, he came to a monastery where two bhikkhus were staying together. After staying with those two for some time, he found that he was doing quite well because people liked his expositions. Then it occurred to him that it would be even better if he could make the other two bhikkhus leave the place and have the monastery all to himself. Thus, he tried to set one against the other. The two bhikkhus quarrelled and left the monastery in different directions. On account of this evil deed, that bhikkhu was reborn in Avīci Niraya and he was serving out the remaining part of his term of suffering as a swine-peta with its mouth swarming with maggots. Then the Buddha exhorted, "A bhikkhu should be calm and well-restrained in thought, word and deed."

Then the Buddha spoke in verse as follows:

Verse 281. One should be careful in speech, be well-restrained in mind, and physically, too, one should do no evil. One should purify these three courses of action and accomplish the practice of the Path of Eight Constituents made known by the Buddhas.

Verse 282

XX (7) The Story of Thera Poṭṭhila

While residing at the Jetavana monastery, the Buddha uttered Verse (282) of this book, with reference to Thera Poṭṭhila.

Poṭṭhila was a senior bhikkhu who knew the Piṭaka well and was actually teaching the Dhamma to five hundred bhikkhus. Because he knew the Piṭaka, he was also very conceited. The Buddha knew his weakness and wanted him to mend his ways and put him on the right path. So, whenever Poṭṭhila came to pay obeisance, the Buddha would address him as 'Useless Poṭṭhila'. When Poṭṭhila heard these remarks, he pondered over those words of the Buddha and came to realize that the Buddha had made those unkind remarks because he, Poṭṭhila, had not made any serious effort to practise meditation and had not achieved any of the Maggas or even any level of mental absorption (jhāna).

Thus, without telling anyone Thera Poṭṭhila left for a monastery at a place twenty yojanas away from the Jetavana monastery. At that monastery there were thirty bhikkhus. First, he went to the most senior bhikkhu and humbly requested him to be his mentor; but the thera, wishing to humble him, asked him to go to the next senior bhikkhu, who in his turn sent him on to the next. In this way, he was sent from one to the other until he came to a seven year old arahat sāmaṇera. The young sāmaṇera accepted him as a pupil only after ascertaining that Poṭṭhila would obediently follow his instructions. As instructed by the sāmaṇera, Thera Poṭṭhila kept his mind firmly fixed on the true nature of the body; he was very ardent and vigilant in his meditation.

The Buddha saw Poṭṭhila in his vision and through supernormal power made Poṭṭhila feel his presence and encouraged him to be steadfast and ardent.

Then the Buddha spoke in verse as follows:

Verse 282. Indeed, wisdom is born of meditation; without meditation wisdom is lost. Knowing this twofold path of gain and loss of wisdom, one should conduct oneself so that wisdom may increase.

At the end of the discourse Poṭṭhila attained arahatship.

Verses 283 and 284

XX (8) The Story of Five Old Bhikkhus

While residing at the Jetavana monastery, the Buddha uttered Verses (283) and (284) of this book, with reference to five old bhikkhus.

Once, in Sāvatthi, there were five friends who became bhikkhus only in their old age. These five bhikkhus were in the habit of going together to their old homes for alms-food. Of the former wives of those five, one lady in particular, by the name of Madhurapācikā, was a good cook and she looked after them very well. Thus, the five bhikkhus went mostly to her house. But one day, Madhurapācikā fell ill and died suddenly. The old bhikkhus felt their loss very deeply and together they cried praising her virtues and lamenting their loss.

The Buddha called those bhikkhus to him and said, "Bhikkhus! You all are feeling pain and sorrow because you are not free from greed, hatred, and ignorance (rāga, dosa, moha), which are like a forest. Cut down this forest and you will be freed from greed, hatred and ignorance."

Then the Buddha spoke in verse as follows:

Verse 283. O bhikkhus, cut down the forest of craving, not the real tree; the forest of craving breeds danger (of rebirth). Cut down the forest of craving as well as its undergrowth and be free from craving.

Verse 284. So long as craving of man for woman is not cut down and the slightest trace of it remains, so long is his mind in bondage as the calf is bound to its mother.

At the end of the discourse the five old bhikkhus attained Sotāpatti Fruition.

Verse 285

XX (9) The Story of a Thera who had been a Goldsmith

While ,residing at the Jetavana monastery, the Buddha uttered Verse (285) of this book, with reference to a bhikkhu, a pupil of Thera Sāriputta.

Once, a young, handsome son of a goldsmith was admitted into the Order by Thera Sāriputta. The young bhikkhu was given loathsomeness of the dead body as the subject of meditation by Thera Sāriputta. After taking the subject of meditation he left for the forest and practised meditation there; but he made very little progress. So he returned twice to Thera Sāriputta for further instructions. Still, he made no progress. So Thera Sāriputta took the young bhikkhu to the Buddha, and related everything about the young bhikkhu.

The Buddha knew that the young bhikkhu was the son of a goldsmith, and also that he had been born in the family of goldsmiths during his past five hundred existenses. Therefore the Buddha changed the subject of meditation for the young bhikkhu; instead of loathsomeness, he was instructed to meditate on pleasantness. With his supernormal power, the Buddha created a beautiful lotus flower as big as a cart-wheel and told the young bhikkhu to stick it on the mound of sand just outside the monastery. The young bhikkhu, concentrating on the big, beautiful, fragrant lotus flower, was able to get rid of the hindrances. He was filled with delightful satisfaction (pīti), and step by step he progressed until he reached as far as the fourth level of mental absorption (jhāna).

The Buddha saw him from his perfumed chamber and with his supernormal power made the flower wither instantly. Seeing the flower wither and change its colour, the bhikkhu perceived the impermanent nature of the flower and of all other things and beings. That led to the realization of the impermanence, unsatisfactoriness and the insubstantiality of all conditioned things. At that instant, the Buddha sent forth his radiance and appeared as if in person to the young bhikkhu and instructed him to get rid of craving (taṇhā).

Then the Buddha spoke in verse as follows:

Verse 285. Cut off your craving as one plucks an autumn lily with the hand. Nibbāna has been expounded on by the Buddha; cultivate that Path which leads to it.

At the end of the discourse the young bhikkhu attained arahatship.

Verse 286

XX (10) The Story of Mahādhana, a Merchant

While residing at the Jetavana monastery, the Buddha uttered Verse (286) of this book, with reference to Mahādhana, a merchant from Bārāṇasī.

Once, a merchant from Bārāṇasi came to a festival in Sāvatthi with five hundred carts fully loaded with textiles and other merchandise. When he reached a river bank near Sāvatthi the river was in spate; so he could not cross the river. He was held up for seven days as it was raining hard and the water did not subside. By that time, he was already late for the festival, and there was no need for him to cross the river.

Since he had come from a long distance he did not want to return home with his full load of merchandise. So he decided to spend the rainy season, the cold season and the hot season in that place and said so to his assistants. The Buddha while going on an alms-round knew the decision of the merchant and he smiled. Ānanda asked the Buddha why he smiled and the Buddha replied, "Ānanda, do you see that merchant? He is thinking that he would stay here and sell his goods the whole year. He is not aware that he would die here in seven days' time. What should be done should be done today. Who would know that one would die tomorrow? We have no date fixed with the King of Death. For one who is mindful by day or by night, who is not disturbed by moral defilements and is energetic, to live for just one night is a well-spent life.

Then the Buddha sent Ānanda to Mahādhana, the merchant. Ānanda explained to Mahādhana that time was running out for him, and that he should practise mindfulness instead of being negligent. On learning about his impending death, Mahādhana was alarmed and frightened. So, for seven days, he invited the Buddha and other bhikkhus for alms-food. On the seventh day, the Buddha expounded a discourse in appreciation (anumodanā).

Then the Buddha spoke in verse as follows:

Verse 286. "Here will I live in the rainy season; here will I live in the cold season and the hot season", so imagines the fool, not realizing the danger (of approaching death).

At the end of the discourse Mahādhana the merchant attained Sotāpatti Fruition. He followed the Buddha for some distance and returned. On his return, he had a severe headache and passed away soon after. Mahādhana was reborn in the Tusita deva world.

Verse 287

XX (11) The Story of Kisāgotamī[1]

While residing at the Jetavana monastery, the Buddha uttered Verse (287) of this book, with reference to Kisāgotamī, the daughter of a rich man from Sāvatthi.

Kisāgotamī came to the Buddha as she was stricken with grief due to the death of her only son. To her the Buddha said, "Kisāgotamī, you think you are the only one who has lost a son. Death comes to all beings; before their desires are satiated Death takes them away."

Then the Buddha spoke in verse as follows:

Verse 287. The man who dotes on his children and his herds of cattle, whose mind longs for and is attached to sensual pleasures, is carried away by Death even as a sleeping village is swept away by a great flood.

At the end of the discourse Kisāgotamī attained Sotāpatti Fruition.

---

1. This story has been given in Verse 114 (Chapter VIII, Story No. 13).

Verses 288 and 289

XX (12) The Story of Paṭācārā[1]

While residing at the Jetavana monastery, the Buddha uttered Verses (288) and (289) of this book, with reference to Paṭācārā, the daughter of a rich man from Sāvatthi.

As Paṭācārā had lost her husband and her two sons, as well as her parents and three brothers almost at the same time, she was driven to near insanity. When she approached the Buddha, he said to her, "Paṭācārā, sons and daughters cannot look after you; so even if they are alive they do not exist for you. The wise man observes morality (sīla) and clears (the obstacles to) the Path leading to Nibbāna."

Then the Buddha spoke in verse as follows:

Verse 288. Not sons, nor parents, nor close relatives can protect one assailed by Death; indeed, neither kith nor kin can give protection.

Verse 289. Knowing this, the wise man restrained by morality should quickly clear (the obstacles to) the Path leading to Nibbāna.

At the end of the discourse Paṭācārā attained Sotāpatti Fruition.

End of Chapter Twenty: The Path.

---

1. This story has been given in Verse 113 (Chapter VIII, Story No. 12).

Chapter XXI

Miscellaneous (Pakiṇṇakavagga)

Verse 290

XXI (1) The Story of the Buddha's Former Deeds

While residing at the Jetavana monastery, the Buddha uttered Verse (290) of this book, with reference to the power and glory of the Buddha as witnessed by many people on his visit to Vesālī.

Once, a famine broke out in Vesālī. It began with a serious drought. Because of drought, there was almost a total failure of crops and many people died of starvation. This was followed by an epidemic of diseases and as people could hardly cope with the disposal of the corpses there was a lot of stench in the air. This stench attracted the ogres. The people of Vesālī were facing the dangers of destruction by famine, disease and also by the ogres. In their grief and sorrow they tried to look for a refuge. They thought of going for help from various sources but finally, they decided to invite the Buddha. So a mission headed by Mahāli, the Licchavī prince, and the son of the chief brahmin were sent to King Bimbisāra to request the Buddha to pay a visit to Vesālī and help them in their distress. The Buddha knew that this visit would be of much benefit to many people, so he consented to go to Vesālī.

Accordingly, King Bimbisāra repaired the road between Rājagaha and the bank of the river Gaṅgā. He also made other preparations and set up special resting-places at an interval of every yojana. When everything was ready, the Buddha set out for Vesālī with five hundred bhikkhus. King Bimbisāra also accompanied the Buddha. On the fifth day they came to the bank of the river Gaṅgā and King Bimbisāra sent word to the Licchavī princes. On the other side of the river, the Licchavī princes had repaired the road between the river and Vesālī and had set up resting-places as had been done by King Bimbisāra on his side of the river. The Buddha went to Vesālī with Licchavī princes but King Bimbisāra stayed behind.

As soon as the Buddha reached the other bank of the river heavy rains fell in torrents, thus cleansing up

Vesālī. The Buddha was put up in the rest-house which was specially prepared for him in the central part of the city. Sakka, king of the devas, came with his followers to pay obeisance to the Buddha, and the ogres fled. That same evening the Buddha delivered the Ratana Sutta and asked the Venerable Ānanda to go round between the threefold walls of the city with the Licchavī princes and recite it. The Venerable Ānanda did as he was told. As the protective verses (parittas) were being recited, many of those who were sick recovered and followed the Venerable Ānanda to the presence of the Buddha. The Buddha delivered the same Sutta and repeated it for seven days. At the end of the seven days, everything was back to normal in Vesālī. The Licchavī princes and the people of Vesālī were very much relieved and were overjoyed. They were also very grateful to the Buddha. They paid obeisance to the Buddha and made offerings to him on a grand and lavish scale. They also accompanied the Buddha on his return journey until they came to the bank of the Gaṅgā at the end of three days.

On arrival at the river bank, King Bimbisāra was waiting for the Buddha; so also were the devas and the brahmās and the king of the Nāgas with their respective entourage. All of them paid obeisance and made offerings to the Buddha. The devas and the brahmās paid homage with umbrellas, flowers, etc., and sang in praise of the Buddha. The Nāgas had come with barges made of gold, silver and rubies to invite the Buddha to the realm of the Nāgas; they had also strewn the surface of the water with five hundred kinds of lotuses. This was one of the three occasions in the life of the Buddha when human beings, devas and brahmās came together to pay homage to the Buddha. The first occasion was when the Buddha manifested his power and glory by the miracle of the pairs, emitting rays of light and sprays of water; and the second was on his return from the Tāvatiṁsa deva world after expounding the Abhidhamma.

The Buddha, wishing to honour the Nāgas, then paid a visit to the realm of the Nāgas accompanied by the bhikkhus. The Buddha and his entourage went in the five hundred barges brought by the Nāgas. After his visit to the realm of the Nāgas, the Buddha returned to Rājagaha accompanied by King Bimbisāra. They arrived at Rājagaha on the fifth day. Two days after their arrival at Rājagaha, while the bhikkhus were talking about the amazing grandeur and glory of the trip to and from Vesālī, the Buddha arrived on the scene. On learning the subject of their talk, the Buddha said to them, "Bhikkhus, that I have been revered so much by brahmās, devas and human being alike and that they have made offerings on such a grand and lavish scale to me on this occasion is not due to the power I now possess; it is simply because I had done some small meritorious deeds in one of my previous existences that I now enjoy such great benefits". Then the Buddha related the story of one of his past existences, when he was a brahmin by the name of Saṅkha.

Once there was a brahmin named Saṅkha who lived in the city of Taxila. He had a son named Susīma. When Susīma was sixteen years old, he was sent by his father to another brahmin to study astrology. His teacher taught him all that should be learnt, but Susīma was not fully satisfied. So, his teacher directed him to approach the paccekabuddhas who were then staying in Isipatana. Susīma went to Isipatana, but the paccekabuddhas told him that he must first become a bhikkhu. Thus, he became a bhikkhu, and was instructed how to conduct himself as a bhikkhu. Sasīma diligently practised meditation and he soon comprehended the Four Noble Truths, acquired Bodhi ñāṇa, and became a paccekabuddha himself. But as a result of his previous kamma Susīma did not live long; he realized parinibbāna soon afterwards.

Saṅkha, the father of Susīma, came in search of his son, but when he arrived he only found the stupa where the relics of his son were enshrined. The brahmin felt very much distressed at the loss of his son. He proceeded to clean up the precincts of the stupa, by clearing away grass and weeds; then he covered up the ground with sand and sprinkled it with water. Next, he went into the nearby woods for some wild flowers and stuck them on the wet ground. In that way, he offered his services and paid respect to the paccekabuddha who was once his son. It was because of that good deed done in that previous existence of his that the Buddha gained such benefits, that he was showered with such lavish offerings, that he was shown such deep reverence and great devotion on that particular occasion.

Then the Buddha spoke in verse as follows:

Verse 290. If by giving up small pleasures great happiness is to be found, the wise should give up small pleasures seeing (the prospect of) great happiness.

Verse 291

XXI (2) The Story of the Woman Who Ate up the Eggs of a Hen

While residing at the Jetavana monastery, the Buddha uttered Verse (291) of this book, with reference to a feud between a woman and a hen.

Once, there lived a woman in a village near Sāvatthi. She had a hen in her house; every time the hen laid an egg she would eat it up. The hen was very much hurt and angry and made a vow to have vengeance on the woman and made a wish that it should be reborn as some being that would be in a position to kill the offspring of that woman. The hen's wish was fulfilled as it was reborn as a cat and the woman was reborn as a hen in the same house. The cat ate up the eggs of the hen. In their next existence the hen became a leopard and the cat became a deer. The leopard ate up the deer as well as its offspring. Thus, the feud continued for five hundred existences of the two beings. At the time of the Buddha one of them was born as a woman and the other an ogress.

On one occasion, the woman was returning from the house of her parents to her own house near Sāvatthi. Her husband and her young son were also with her. While they were resting near a pond at the roadside, her husband went to have a bath in the pond. At that moment the woman saw the ogress and recognized her as her old enemy. Taking her child she fled from the ogress straight to the Jetavana monastery where the Buddha was expounding the Dhamma and put her child at the feet of the Buddha. The ogress who was in hot pursuit of the woman also came to the door of the monastery, but the guardian spirit of the gate did not permit her to enter. The Buddha, seeing her, sent the Venerable Ānanda to bring the ogress to his presence When the ogress arrived, the Buddha reprimanded both the woman and the ogress for the long chain of feud between them. He also added, "If you two had not come to me today, your feud would have continued endlessly. Enmity cannot be appeased by enmity; it can only be appeased by loving-kindness."

Then the Buddha spoke in verse as follows:

Verse 291. He who seeks his own happiness by inflicting pain on others, being entangled by bonds of enmity, cannot be free from enmity.

At the end of the discourse the ogress took refuge in the three Gems, viz., the Buddha, the Dhamma and the Saṁgha, and the woman attained Sotāpatti Fruition.

Verses 292 and 293

XXI (3) The Story of the Baddiya Bhikkhus

While residing near the town of Baddiya, the Buddha uttered Verses (292) and (293) of this book, with reference to some bhikkhus.

Once, some bhikkhus who were staying in Baddiya made some ornate slippers out of some kinds of reeds and grasses. When the Buddha was told about this he said, "Bhikkhus, you have entered the Buddhist Order for the sake of attaining Arahatta Phala. Yet, you are now striving hard only in making slippers and decorating them."

Then the Buddha spoke in verse as follows:

Verse 292. In those who leave undone what should indeed be done but do what should not be done, who are conceited and unmindful, moral intoxicants increase.

Verse 293. In those who always make a good effort in meditating on the body, who do not do what should not be done but always do what should be done, who are also mindful and endowed with clear comprehension, moral intoxicants come to an end.

At the end of the discourse, those bhikkhus attained arahatship.

Verses 294 and 295

XXI (4) The Story of Thera Bhaddiya, the Short One

While residing at the Jetavana monastery, the Buddha uttered Verses (294) and (295) of this book, with reference to Thera Bhaddiya who was also known as Lakuṇḍaka Bhaddiya because of his short stature.

On one occasion, some bhikkhus came to visit and pay homage to the Buddha at the Jetavana monastery. While they were with the Buddha, Lakuṇḍaka Bhaddiya happened to pass by not far from them. The Buddha called their attention to the short thera and said to them, "Bhikkhus, look at that thera. He has killed both his father and his mother, and having killed his parents he goes about without any dukkha." The bhikkhus could not understand the statement made by the Buddha. So, they entreated the Buddha to make it clear to them and the Buddha explained the meaning to them.

In the above statement, the Buddha was referring to an arahat, who had eradicated craving, conceit, wrong beliefs, and attachment to sense bases and sense objects. The Buddha had made the statement by means of metaphors. Thus, the terms 'mother' and 'father' are used to indicate craving and conceit respectively. The Eternity-belief (Sassatadiṭṭhi) and Annihilation-belief (Ucchedadiṭṭhi) are likened to two kings, attachment is likened to a revenue officer and the sense bases and sense objects (the ajjhatta and bahiddha āyatanas) are likened to a kingdom.

After explaining the meaning to them, the Buddha spoke in verse as follows:

Verse 294. Having killed mother (i,e., Craving), father (i.e., Conceit), and the two kings (i.e., Eternity--belief and Annihilation-belief), and having destroyed the kingdom (i.e., the sense bases and sense objects) together with its revenue officer (i.e., attachment), the brāhmaṇa (i.e., the arahat) goes free from dukkha.

Verse 295. Having killed mother, father, the two brahmin kings and having destroyed the hindrances of which the fifth (i.e., doubt) is like a tiger-infested journey, the brāhmaṇa (i.e., the arahat) goes free from dukkha.

At the end of the discourse the visiting bhikkhus attained arahatship.

Verses 296, 297, 298, 299, 300 and 301

XXI (5) The Story of a Wood-Cutter's Son

While residing at the Jetavana monastery, the Buddha uttered Verses (296) to (301) of this book, with reference to the son of a wood-cutter.

Once in Rājagaha, a wood-cutter went into the woods with his son to cut some firewood. On their return home in the evening, they stopped near a cemetery to have their meal. They also took off the yoke from the two oxen to enable them to graze nearby; but the two oxen went away without being noticed by them. As soon as they discovered that the oxen were missing, the wood-cutter went to look for them, leaving his son with the cart of firewood. The father entered the town, looking for his oxen. When he returned to his son it was getting late and the city-gate was closed. Therefore, the young boy had to spend the night alone underneath his cart.

The wood-cutter's son, though young, was always mindful and was in the habit of contemplating the unique qualities of the Buddha. That night two ogres came to frighten him and to harm him. When one of the ogres pulled at the leg of the boy, he cried out, "I pay homage to the Buddha" (Namo Buddhassa). Hearing those words from the boy, the ogres got frightened and also felt that they must look after the boy. So, one of them remained near the boy, guarding him from all danger; the other went to the king's palace and brought the food-tray of King Bimbisāra. The two ogres then fed the boy as if he were their own son. At the palace, the ogre left a written message concerning the royal food--tray; and this message was visible only to the king.

In the morning, the king's men discovered that the royal food-tray was missing and they were very upset and very much frightened. The king found the message left by the ogre and directed his men where to look for it. The king's men found the royal food-tray among the firewood in the cart. They also found the boy who was still sleeping underneath the cart. When questioned, the boy answered that his parents came to feed him in the night and that he went to sleep contentedly and without fear after taking his food. The boy knew only that much and nothing more. The king sent for the parents of the boy, and took the boy and his parents to the Buddha. The king, by that time, had heard that the boy was always mindful of the unique qualities of the Buddha and also that he had cried out "Namo Buddhassa", when the ogre pulled at his leg in the night.

The king asked the Buddha, "Is mindfulness of the unique qualities of the Buddha the only dhamma that gives one protection against evil and danger, or is mindfulness of the unique qualities of the Dhamma equally potent and powerful?" To him the Buddha replied, "O king, my disciple! There are six things, mindfulness of which is a good protection against evil and danger."

Then the Buddha spoke in verse as follows:

Verse 296. Fully alert and ever vigilant are Gotama Buddha's disciples, who by day and by night are always mindful of the qualities of the Buddha.

Verse 297. Fully alert and ever vigilant are Gotama Buddha's disciples, who by day and by night are always mindful of the qualities of the Dhamma.

Verse 298. Fully alert and ever vigilant are Gotama Buddha's disciples, who by day and by night are always mindful of the qualities of the Saṁgha.

Verse 299. Fully alert and ever vigilant are Gotama Buddha's disciples, who by day and by night are always mindful of the component parts of the body.

Verse 300. Fully alert and ever vigilant are Gotama Buddha's disciples, whose mind by day and by night always takes delight in being compassionate (lit., harmless).

Verse 301. Fully alert and ever vigilant are Gotama Buddha's disciples, whose mind by day and by night always takes delight in the cultivation (of good-will towards all).

At the end of the discourse the boy and his parents attained Sotāpatti Fruition. Later they joined the Order and eventually they became arahats.

Verse 302

XXI (6) The Story of the Bhikkhu from the Conutry of the Vajjīs

While residing at the Veḷuvana monastery, the Buddha uttered Verse (302) of this book, with reference to a bhikkhu from Vesālī, a city in the country of the Vajjīs.

On the night of the full moon day of Kattika, the people of Vesālī celebrated the festival of the constellations (Nakkhatta) on a grand scale. The whole city was lit up, and there was much merry-making with singing, dancing, etc. As he looked towards the city, standing alone in the monastery, the bhikkhu felt lonely and dissatisfied with his lot. Softly, he murmured to himself, "There can be no one whose lot is worse than mine". At that instant, the spirit guarding the woods appeared to him, and said, "Those beings in niraya envy the lot of the beings in the deva world; so also, people envy the lot of those who live alone in the woods." Hearing those words, the bhikkhu realized the truth of those words and he regretted that he had thought so little of the lot of a bhikkhu.

Early in the morning the next day, the bhikkhu went to the Buddha and reported the matter to him. In reply, the Buddha told him about the hardships in the life of all beings.

Then the Buddha spoke in verse as follows:

Verse 302. It is hard to become a bhikkhu; it is hard to be happy in the practice of a bhikkhu. The hard life of a householder is painful; to live with those of a different temperament is painful. A traveller in saṁsāra is continually subject to dukkha; therefore, do not be a traveller in saṁsāra; do not be the one to be subject to dukkha again and again.

At the end of the discourse the bhikkhu attained arahatship.

Verse 303

XXI (7) The Story of Citta the Householder

While residing at the Jetavana monastery, the Buddha uttered Verse (303) of this book, with reference to Citta, a householder of Macchikāsanda town.

Citta, after hearing the Dhamma expounded by the Venerable Sāriputta, attained Anāgāmi Magga and Phala. One day, Citta loaded five hundred carts with food and other offerings for the Buddha and his disciples, and left for Sāvatthi, accompanied by three thousand followers. They travelled at the rate of one yojana a day and reached Sāvatthi at the end of a month. Then Citta went ahead with five hundred of his companions to the Jetavana monastery. While he was paying obeisance to the Buddha, masses of flowers dropped miraculously from above like showers of rain. Citta stayed at the monastery for one whole month offering alms-food to the Buddha and the bhikkhus and also feeding his own party of three thousand. All this time, the devas were replenishing his stock of food and other offerings.

On the eve of his return journey, Citta put all the things he had brought with him in the rooms of the monastery as offerings to the Buddha. The devas then filled up the empty carts with various items of priceless things. The Venerable Ānanda, seeing how Citta's riches were being replenished, asked the Buddha, "Venerable Sir! Is it only when Citta approached you that he is blessed with all these riches? Is he similarly blessed when he goes somewhere else?" To him the Buddha replied, "Ānanda, this disciple is fully endowed with faith and generosity; he is also virtuous and his reputation spreads far and wide. Such a one is sure to be revered and showered with riches wherever he goes."

Then the Buddha spoke in verse as follows:

Verse 303. He who is full of faith and virtue, who also possesses fame and fortune, is held in reverence wherever he goes.

Verse 304

XXI (8) The Story of Cūḷasubhaddā

While residing at the Jetavana monastery, the Buddha uttered Verse (304) of this book, with reference to Cūḷasubhaddā the daughter of Anāthapiṇḍika.

Anāthapiṇḍika and Ugga, the rich man from Ugga, studied under the same teacher when they were both young. Ugga had a son while Anāthapiṇḍika had a daughter. When their children came of age, Ugga asked for the consent of Anāthapiṇḍika to the marriage of their two children. So the marriage took place, and Cūḷasubhaddā, the daughter of Anāthapiṇḍika, had to stay in the house of her parents-in-law. Ugga and his family were followers of non-Buddhist ascetics. Sometimes, they would invite those non-Buddhist ascetics to their house. On such occasions, her parents--in-law would ask Cūḷasubhaddā to pay respect to those naked ascetics, but she always refused to comply. Instead, she told her mother-in-law about the Buddha and his unique qualities.

The mother-in-law of Cūḷasubhaddā was very anxious to see the Buddha when she was told about him by her daughter-in-law. She even agreed to let Cūḷasubhaddhā invite the Buddha for alms-food to their house. So, Cūḷasubhaddā prepared food and collected other offerings for the Buddha and his disciples. She then went up to the upper part of the house and looking towards the Jetavana monastery, she made offerings of flowers and incense and contemplate the unique qualities and virtues of the Buddha. She then spoke out her wish, "Venerable Sir! May it please you to come, with your disciples, to our house tomorrow. I, your devoted lay-disciple, most respectfully invite you. May this invitation of mine be made known to you by this symbol and gesture." Then she took eight fistfuls of jasmin and threw them up into the sky. The flowers floated through the air all the way to the Jetavana monastery and lay hanging from the ceiling of the congregation hall where the Buddha was expounding the Dhamma.

At the end of the discourse, Anāthapiṇḍika, the father of Cūḷasubhaddā, approached the Buddha to invite him to have alms-food in his house the following day. But the Buddha replied that he had already accepted Cūḷasubhaddā's invitation for the next day. Anāthapiṇḍika was puzzled at the reply of the Buddha and said, "But, Venerable Sir! Cūḷasubhaddā does not live here in Sāvatthi; she lives in Ugga at a distance of one hundred and twenty yojanas from here." To him the Buddha said, "True, householder, but the good are clearly visible as if they are in one's very presence even though they may be living at a distance".

Then the Buddha spoke in verse as follows:

Verse 304. Like the Himalayas, the good are visible even from afar; like arrows shot in the night, the wicked are not seen even though they may be near.

The next day, the Buddha came to the house of Ugga, the father-in-law of Cūḷasubhaddā. The Buddha was accompanied by five hundred bhikkhus on this trip; they all came through the air in decorated floats created by the order of Sakka, king of the devas. Seeing the Buddha in his splendour and glory, the parents-in-law of Cūḷasubhaddā were very much impressed and they paid homage to the Buddha. Then, for the next seven days, Ugga, and his family gave alms-food and made other offerings to the Buddha and his disciples.

Verse 305

XXI (9) The Story of the Thera Who Stayed Alone

While residing at the Jetavana monastery, the Buddha uttered Verse (305) of this book, with reference to a bhikkhu who stayed by himself. Because he usually stayed alone, he was known as Thera Ekavihāri.

Thera Ekavihāri did not mix much with other bhikkhus, but usually stayed by himself. All alone, he would sleep or lie down, or stand, or walk. Other bhikkhus thought ill of Ekavihāri and told the Buddha about him. But the Buddha did not blame him; instead, he said, "Yes, indeed, my son has done well; for, a bhikkhu should stay in solitude and seclusion".

Then the Buddha spoke in verse as follows:

Verse 305. He who sits alone, lies down alone, walks alone, in diligent practice, and alone tames himself should find delight in living in the forest.

End of Chapter Twenty-One: Miscellaneous.

Chapter XXII

The Chapter on Niraya (Nirayavagga)

Verse 306

XXII (1) The Story of Sundarī the Wandering Female Ascetic

While residing at the Jetavana monastery, the Buddha uttered Verse (306) of this book, with reference to Sundarī, a wandering female ascetic.

As the number of people revering the Buddha increased, the non-Buddhist ascetics found that the number of their following was dwindling. Therefore, they became very jealous of the Buddha; they were also afraid that things would get worse if they did not do something to damage the reputation of the Buddha. So, they sent for Sundarī and said to her, "Sundarī, you are a very beautiful and clever young lady. We want you to put Samaṇa Gotama to shame, by making it appear to others that you are having sexual dealings with him. By so doing, his image will be impaired, his following will decrease and many would come to us. Make the best use of your looks and be crafty."

Sundarī understood what was expected of her. Thus, late in the evening, she went in the direction of the Jetavana monastery. When she was asked where she was going, she answered, "I am going to visit Samaṇa Gotama; I live with him in the Perfumed Chamber of the Jetavana monastery." After saying this, she proceeded to the place of the non-Buddhist ascetics. Early in the morning the next day, she returned home. If anyone asked her from where she had come she would reply, "I have come from the Perfumed Chamber after staying the night with Samaṇa Gotama." She carried on like this for two more days. At the end of three days, those ascetics hired some drunkards to kill Sundarī and put her body in a rubbish heap near the Jetavana monastery.

The next day, the ascetics spread the news about the disappearance of Paribbājikā Sundarī. They went to the king to report the matter and their suspicion. The king gave them permission to search where they wished. Finding the body near the Jetavana monastery, they carried it to the palace. Then they said to the king, "O king, the followers of Gotama have killed this Paribbājikā and have thrown away her body in the rubbish heap near the Jetavana monastery to cover up the misdeed of their teacher." To them the king replied, "In that case, you may go 'round the town and proclaim the fact." So they went round the town carrying the dead body of Sundarī, shouting, "Look! What the followers of Gotama have done; see how they have tried to cover up the misdeed of Gotama!" The procession then returned to the palace. The bhikkhus living in the Jetavana monastery told the Buddha what those ascetics were doing to damage his reputation and impair his image. But the Buddha only said, "My sons, you just tell them this," and then spoke in verse as follows:

Verse 306. One who tells lies (about others) goes to niraya; one who has done evil and says "I did not do it", also goes to niraya. Both of them being evil-doers, suffer alike (in niraya) in their next existence.

The king next ordered his men to further investigate the murder of Sundarī. On investigation, they found out that Sundarī had died at the hands of some drunkards. So they were brought to the king. When questioned, the drunkards disclosed that they were hired by the ascetics to kill Sundarī and put her body near the Jetavana monastery. The king then sent for the non-Buddhist ascetics, and they finally confessed their role in the murder of Sundarī. The king then ordered them to go round the town and confess their guilt to the people. So they went round the town saying, "We are the ones who killed Sundarī. We have falsely accused the disciples of Gotama just to bring disgrace on Gotama. The disciples of Gotama are innocent, only we are guilty of the crime." As a result of this episode, the power, the glory and the fortune of the Buddha were very much enhanced.

Verse 307

XXII (2) The Story of Those Who Suffered for Their Evil Deeds

While residing at the Veḷuvana monastery, the Buddha uttered Verse (307) of this book, with reference to some petas.

Once, the Venerable Mahā Moggallāna was coming down the Gijjhakūṭa hill with Thera Lakkhaṇa when he saw some petas. When they were back at the monastery, Thera Mahā Moggallāna told Thera Lakkhaṇa, in the presence of the Buddha, that he had seen a peta who was just a skeleton. Then he added that he had also seen five bhikkhus with their body burning in flames. On hearing the statement about those bhikkhus, the Buddha said, "During the time of Kassapa Buddha, those bhikkhus had done much evil. For those evil deeds they had suffered in niraya and now they are serving out the remaining term of suffering as petas."

Then the Buddha spoke in verse as follows:

Verse 307. Many men wearing the yellow robe up to their necks who have an evil disposition and are unrestrained in thought, word and deed are reborn in niraya on account of their evil deeds.

Verse 308

XXII (3) The Bhikkhus Who Lived on the Bank of the Vaggumudā River

While residing at the Mahāvana forest near Vesālī, the Buddha uttered Verse (308) of this book, with reference to the bhikkhus who spent the vassa on the bank of the Vaggumudā River.

At that time, there was a famine in the country of the Vajjīs. So, to enable them to have enough food, those bhikkhus made it appear to the people that they had attained Magga and Phala although they had not done so. The people from the village, believing them and respecting them, offered much food to them leaving very little for themselves.

At the end of the vassa, as was customary, bhikkhus from all parts of the country came to pay homage to the Buddha. The bhikkhus from the bank of the river Vaggumudā also came. They looked hale and hearty while the other bhikkhus looked pale and worn out. The Buddha talked to all the bhikkhus and enquired how they fared during the vassa. To the bhikkhus from Vaggumudā River the Buddha specifically asked whether they had any difficulty in getting alms-food on account of the famine. They answered that they had no difficulty at all in getting alms-food.

The Buddha knew how those bhikkhus had managed to get enough alms-food. But he wanted to teach them on this point, so he asked, "How did you manage so well in getting alms-food throughout the vassa?" Then the bhikkhus told him how they discussed among themselves and decided that they should address one another in such a way that the villagers would think that they had really attained jhāna, Magga and Phala. Then the Buddha asked them whether they had really attained jhāna, Magga and Phala. When they answered in the negative, the Buddha reprimanded them.

Then the Buddha spoke in verse as follows:

Verse 308. It is better for one to eat a red-hot lump of iron burning like a flame than to eat alms-food offered by the people, if one is without morality (sīla) and unrestrained in thought, word and deed.

Verses 309 and 310

XXII (4) The Story of Khemaka, the Son of a Rich Man

While residing at the Jetavana monastery, the Buddha uttered Verses (309) and (310) of this book, with reference to Khemaka, the son of a rich man. Khemaka was also the nephew of the renowned Anāthapiṇḍika.

Khemaka, in addition to being rich, was also very good-looking and women were very much attracted to him. They could hardly resist him and naturally fell a prey to him. Khemaka committed adultery without compunction. The king's men caught him three times for sexual misconduct and brought him to the presence of the king. But King Pasenadi of Kosala did not take action because Khemaka was the nephew of Anāthapiṇḍika. So Anāthapiṇḍika himself took his nephew to the Buddha. The Buddha talked to Khemaka about the depravity of sexual misconduct and the seriousness of the consequences.

Then the Buddha spoke in verse as follows:

Verse 309. Four misfortunes befall a man who is unmindful of right conduct and commit sexual misconduct with another man's wife: acquisition of demerit, disturbed sleep, reproach, and suffering in niraya.

Verse 310. Thus, there is the acquisition of demerit, and there is rebirth in the evil apāya realms. The enjoyment of a scared man with a scared woman is short-lived, and the king also metes out severe punishment. Therefore, a man should not commit misconduct with another man's wife.

At the end of the discourse Khemaka attained Sotāpatti Fruition.

Verses 311, 312 and 313

XXII (5) The Story of the Obstinate Bhikkhu

While residing at the Jetavana monastery, the Buddha uttered Verses (311), (312) and (313) of this book, with reference to an obstinate bhikkhu.

Once, there was a bhikkhu who was feeling remorse for having unwittingly cut some grass. He confided about this to another bhikkhu. The latter was reckless and stubborn by nature, and he did not think much about committing small misdeeds. So he replied to the first bhikkhu, "Cutting grass is a very minor offence; if you just confide and confess to another bhikkhu you are automatically exonerated. There is nothing to worry about." So saying, he proceeded to uproot some grass with both hands to show that he thought very little of such trivial offences. When the Buddha was told about this he reprimanded the reckless, stubborn bhikkhu.

Then the Buddha spoke in verse as follows:

Verse 311. Just as kusa grass if badly held cuts that very hand, so also, the ill-led life of a bhikkhu drags that bhikkhu down to niraya.

Verse 312. An act perfunctorily performed, or a practice that is depraved, or a questionable conduct of a bhikkhu is not of much benefit.

Verse 313. If there is anything to be done, do it well; do it firmly and energetically; for the slack life of a bhikkhu scatters much dust (of moral defilements).

At the end of the discourse the reckless, obstinate bhikkhu realized the importance of restraint in the life of a bhikkhu and strictly obeyed the Fundamental Precepts for the bhikkhus. Later, through practice of Insight Meditation, that bhikkhu attained arahatship.

Verse 314

XXII (6) The Story of a Woman of Jealous Disposition

While residing at the Jetavana monastery, the Buddha uttered Verse (314) of this book, with reference to a woman who was by nature very jealous.

Once, a woman with a very strong sense of jealousy lived with her husband in Sāvatthi. She found that her husband was having an affair with her maid. So one day, she tied up the girl with strong ropes, cut off her ears and nose, and shut her up in a room. After doing that, she asked her husband to accompany her to the Jetavana monastery. Soon after they left, some relatives of the maid arrived at their house and found the maid tied up and locked up in a room. They broke into the room, untied her and took her to the monastery. They arrived at the monastery while the Buddha was expounding the Dhamma. The girl related to the Buddha what her mistress had done to her, how she had been beaten, and how her nose and ears had been cut off. She stood in the midst of the crowd for all to see how she had been mistreated. So the Buddha said, "Do no evil, thinking that people will not know about it. An evil deed done in secret, when discovered, will bring much pain and sorrow; but a good deed may be done secretly, for it can only bring happiness and not sorrow."

Then the Buddha spoke in verse as follows:

Verse 314. It is better not to do an evil deed; an evil deed torments one later on. It is better to do a good deed as one does not have to repent for having done it.

At the end of the discourse the couple attained **Sotāpatti Fruition.**

Verse 315

XXII (7) The Story of Many Bhikkhus

While residing at the Jetavana monastery, the Buddha uttered Verse (315) of this book, with reference to a group of bhikkhus who spent the vassa in a border town.

In the first month of their stay in that border town, the bhikkhus were well provided and well looked after by the townsfolk. During the next month the town was plundered by some robbers and some people were taken away as hostages. The people of the town, therefore, had to rehabilitate their town and reinforce fortifications. Thus, they were unable to look to the needs of the bhikkhus as much as they would like to and the bhikkhus had to fend for themselves. At the end of the vassa, those bhikkhus came to pay homage to the Buddha at the Jetavana monastery in Sāvatthi. On learning about the hardships they had undergone during the vassa, the Buddha said to them, "Bhikkhus, do not keep thinking about this or anything else; it is always difficult to have a carefree, effortless living. Just as the townsfolk guard their town, so also, a bhikkhu should be on guard and keep his mind steadfastly on his body."

Then the Buddha spoke in verse as follows:

Verse 315. As a border town is guarded both inside and outside, so guard yourself. Let not the right moment go by for those who miss this moment come to grief when they fall into niraya.

At the end of the discourse those bhikkhus attained arahatship.

Verses 316 and 317

XXII (8) The Story of the Nigaṇṭha Ascetics

While residing at the Jetavana monastery, the Buddha uttered Verses (316) and (317) of this book, with reference to Nigaṇtha ascetics, who covered only the front part of their bodies.

One day, some Niganthas went on an alms-round with their bowls covered with a piece of cloth. Some bhikkhus seeing them commented, "These Nigaṇṭha ascetics who cover the front part of the body are more respectable compared to those Acelaka ascetics who go about without wearing anything." Hearing this comment, those ascetics retorted, "Yes, indeed, we do cover up our front part (by covering our bowls); but we cover it up not out of shame in going naked. We only cover up our bowls to keep away dust from our food, for even dust contains life in it."

When the bhikkhus reported what the Nigaṇṭha ascetics said, the Buddha replied, "Bhikkhus, those ascetics who go about covering only the front part of their bodies are not ashamed of what they should be ashamed of, but they are ashamed of what they should not be ashamed of; because of their wrong view they would only go to bad destinations."

Then the Buddha spoke in verse as follows:

Verse 316. Those beings who are ashamed of what should not be ashamed of, who are not ashamed of what should be ashamed of, and who hold wrong views go to a lower plane of existence (duggati).

Verse 317. Those beings who see danger in what is not dangerous, who do not see danger in what is dangerous, and who hold wrong views go to a lower plane of existence (duggati).

At the end of the discourse many Nigaṇṭha ascetic became frightened and joined the Buddhist Order.

Verses 318 and 319

XXII (9) The Story of the Disciples of Non-Buddhist Ascetics

While residing at the Nigrodārāma monastery, the Buddha uttered Verses (318) and (319) of this book, with reference to some disciples of the Titthis (non--Buddhist ascetics).

The disciples of the Titthis did not want their children to mix with the children of the followers of the Buddha. They often told their children, "Do not go to the Jetavana monastery, do not pay obeisance to the bhikkhus of the Sakyan clan." On one occasion, while the Titthi boys were playing with a Buddhist boy near the entrance to the Jetavana monastery, they felt very thirsty. As the children of the disciples of the Titthis had been told by their parents not to enter a Buddhist monastery, they asked the Buddhist boy to go to the monastery and bring some water for them. The young Buddhist boy went to pay obeisance to the Buddha after he had had a drink of water, and told the Buddha about his friends who were forbidden by their parents to enter a Buddhist monastery. The Buddha then told the boy to tell the non-Buddhist boys to come and have water at the monastery. When those boys came, the Buddha gave them a discourse to suit their various dispositions. As a result, those boys became established in faith in the Three Gems i.e., the Buddha, the Dhamma and the Saṁgha.

When the boys went home, they talked about their visit to the Jetavana monastery and about the Buddha teaching them the Three Gems. The parents of the boys, being ignorant, cried, "Our sons have been disloyal to our faith, they have been ruined," etc. Some intelligent neighbours advised the wailing parents to stop weeping and to send their sons to the Buddha. Somehow, they agreed and the boys as well as their parents went to the Buddha.

The Buddha knowing why they had come spoke to them in verse as follows:

Verse 318. Beings who imagine wrong in what is not wrong, who do not see wrong in what is wrong, and who hold wrong views go to a lower plane of existence (duggati).

Verse 319. Beings who know what is wrong as wrong, who know what is right as right, and who hold right views go to a happy plane of existence (suggati).

At the end of the discourse all those people came to be established in faith in the Three Gems, and after listening to the Buddha's further discourses, they subsequently attained Sotāpatti Fruition.

End of Chapter Twenty-Two: Niraya.

Chapter XXIII

The Elephant (Nāgavagga)

Verses 320, 321 and 322

XXIII (1) On Subduing Oneself

While residing at the Ghositārāma monastery, the Buddha uttered Verses (320), (321) and (322) of this book, with reference to the patience and endurance manifested by himself when abused by the hirelings of Māgaṇḍiyā, one of the three queens of King Udena.

Once, the father of Māgaṇḍiyā, being very much impressed by the personality and looks of the Buddha, had offered his very beautiful daughter in marriage to Gotama Buddha. But the Buddha refused his offer and said that he did not like to touch such a thing which was full of filth and excreta, even with his feet. On hearing this remark both Māgaṇḍiyā's father and mother discerning the truth of the remark attained Anāgāmi Fruition. Māgaṇḍiyā, however, regarded the Buddha as her arch enemy and was bent on having her revenge on him.

Later, she became one of the three queens of King Udena. When Māgaṇḍiyā heard that the Buddha had come to Kosambī, she hired some citizens and their servants to abuse the Buddha when he entered the city on an alms-round. Those hirelings followed the Buddha and abused him using such abusive words as 'thief, fool, camel, donkey, one bound for niraya'. Hearing those abusive words, the Venerable Ānanda pleaded with the Buddha to leave the town and go to another place. But the Buddha refused and said, "In another town also we might be abused and it is not feasible to move out every time one is abused. It is better to solve a problem in the place where it arises. I am like an elephant in a battlefield; like an elephant who withstands the arrows that come from all quarters, I also will bear patiently the abuses that come from people without morality."

Then the Buddha spoke in verse as follows:

Verse 320. As an elephant in battlefield withstands the arrow shot from a bow, so shall I endure abuse. Indeed, many people are without morality.

Verse 321. Only the trained (horses and elephants) are led to gatherings of people; the King mounts only the trained (horses and elephants). Noblest among men are the tamed, who endure abuse.

Verse 322. Mules, thoroughbred horses, horses from Sindh, and great elephants are noble only when they are trained; but one who has tamed himself (through Magga Insight) is far nobler.

At the end of the discourse, those who had abused the Buddha realized their mistake and came to respect him; some of them attained Sotāpatti Fruition.

Verse 323

XXIII (2) The Story of the Bhikkhu Who Had Been a Trainer of Elephants

While residing at the Jetavana monastery, the Buddha uttered Verse (323) of this book, with reference to a bhikkhu who had previously been an elephant trainer.

On one occasion, some bhikkhus saw an elephant trainer and his elephant on the bank of the river Aciravatī. As the trainer was finding it difficult to control the elephant, one of the bhikkhus, who was an ex-elephant trainer, told the other bhikkhus how it could be easily handled. The elephant trainer hearing him did as told by the bhikkhu, and the elephant was quickly subdued. Back at the monastery, the bhikkhus related the incident to the Buddha. The Buddha called the ex-elephant trainer bhikkhu to him and said, "O vain bhikkhu, who is yet far away from Magga and Phala! You do not gain anything by taming elephants. There is no one who can get to a place where one has never been before (i.e., Nibbāna) by taming elephants; only one who has tamed himself can get there."

Then the Buddha spoke in verse as follows:

Verse 323. Indeed, not by any means of transport (such as elephants and horses) can one go to the place one has never been before (i.e., Nibbāna); but by thoroughly taming oneself, the tamed one can get to that place (i.e., Nibbāna).

Verse 324

XXIII. (3) The Story of an Old Brahmin

While residing at the Veḷuvana monastery, the Buddha uttered Verse (324) of this book, with reference to an old brahmin.

Once, there lived in Sāvatthi an old brahmin who had eight lakhs in cash. He had four sons; when each one of the sons got married, he gave one lakh to him. Thus, he gave away four lakhs. Later, his wife died. His sons came to him and looked after him very well; in fact, they were very loving and affectionate to him. In course of time, somehow they coaxed him to give them the remaining four lakhs. Thus, he was left practically penniless.

First, he went to stay with his eldest son. After a few days, the daughter-in-law said to him, "Did you give any extra hundred or thousand to your eldest son? Don't you know the way to the houses of your other sons?" Hearing this, the old brahmin got very angry and he left the eldest son's house for the house of his second son. The same remarks were made by the wife of his second son and the old man went to the house of his third son and finally to the house of his fourth and youngest son. The same thing happened in the houses of all his sons. Thus, the old man became helpless; then, taking a staff and a bowl he went to the Buddha for protection and advice.

At the monastery, the brahmin told the Buddha how his sons had treated him and asked for his help. Then the Buddha gave him some verses to memorize and instructed him to recite them wherever there was a large gathering of people. The gist of the verses is this: "My four foolish sons are like ogres. They call me 'father, father', but the words come only out of their mouths and not from their hearts. They are deceitful and scheming. Taking the advice of their wives they have driven me out of their houses. So, now I have got to be begging. Those sons of mine are of less service to me than this staff of mine." When the old brahmin recited these verses, many people in the crowd, hearing him, went wild with rage at his sons and some even threatened to kill them.

At this, the sons became frightened and knelt down at the feet of their father and asked for pardon. They also promised that starting from that day they would look after their father properly and would respect, love and honour him. Then, they took their father to their houses; they also warned their wives to look after their father well or else they would be beaten to death. Each of the sons gave a length of cloth and sent every day a food-tray. The brahmin became healthier than before and soon put on some weight. He realized that he had been showered with these benefits on account of the Buddha. So, he went to the Buddha and humbly requested him to accept two food-trays out of the four he was receiving every day from his sons. Then he instructed his sons to send two food-trays to the Buddha.

One day, the eldest son invited the Buddha to his house for alms-food. After the meal, the Buddha gave a discourse on the benefits to be gained by looking after one's parents. Then he related to them the story of the elephant called Dhanapāla, who looked after his parents. Dhanapāla when captured pined for the parents who were left in the forest.

Then the Buddha spoke in verse as follows:

Verse 324. The elephant called Dhanapāla, in severe must and uncontrollable, being in captivity, eats not a morsel, yearning for his native forest (i. e., longing to look after his parents).

At the end of the discourse, the old brahmin as well as his four sons and their wives attained Sotāpatti Fruition.

Verse 325

XXIII (4) The Story of King Pasenadi of Kosala

While residing at the Jetavana monastery, the Buddha uttered Verse (325) of this book, with reference to King Pasenadi of Kosala.

One day, King Pasenadi of Kosala went to the monastery to pay homage to the Buddha soon after having a heavy meal. The king was in the habit of taking one-quarter basketful (half a bushel of) cooked rice and meat curry. While he was in the presence of the Buddha, the king felt so drowsy that he kept on nodding and could hardly keep himself awake. Then he said to the Buddha, "Venerable Sir! I have been in great discomfort since I have taken my meal." To him the Buddha replied, "Yes, O king! Gluttons do suffer in this manner."

Then the Buddha spoke in verse as follows:

Verse 325. The stupid one who is lazy, gluttonous, and drowsy, who just wallows like a well-fed pig, is subject to repeated rebirths.

After hearing the discourse the king, having understood the message, gradually lessened the amount of food he took. As a result, he became much more active and alert and therefore also happy.

Vers 326

XXIII (5) The Story of Sāmaṇera Sānu

While residing at the Jetavana monastery, the Buddha uttered Verse (326) of this book, with reference to a young sāmaṇera named Sānu.

One day, Sāmaṇera Sānu was urged by older bhikkhus to go up on the dais and recite parts of the Pāḷi texts. When he had finished his recitation he solemnly called out, "May the merits gained by me today for reciting these sacred texts be shared by my mother and my father". At that time, the devas and the ogress who had been the mother of the young sāmaṇera in a previous existence were listening to his recitation. When they heard his words, the ogress was elated and promptly cried out, "My dear son, how happy I am to share your merit; you have done well, my son. Well done! Well done! (Sādhu! Sādhu!)." On account of Sāmaṇera Sānu, the mother ogress came to be very much respected and was given precedence in their assemblies by the devas and other ogres.

As the sāmaṇera grew older, he wanted to return to the life of a lay man; he went home and asked for his clothes from his mother. His mother did not want him to leave the Order and tried to dissuade him from leaving it, but he was quite firm in his decision. So, his mother promised to give him the clothes after his meal. As his mother was busy cooking his meal, the ogress, who was his mother of a past existence, thought, "If my son Sānu leaves the Order, I shall be put to shame and become a laughing stock among other ogres and devas; I must try and stop him leaving the Order." So, the young sāmaṇera was possessed by her; the boy rolled on the floor, muttering incoherently with saliva streaming out of his mouth. The mother got alarmed; neighbours came and tried to appease the spirits. Then, the ogress spoke out, "This sāmaṇera wants to leave the religious Order and return to the life of a lay man; if he does so he will not be able to escape from dukkha." After saying those words, the ogress left the body of the boy and the boy became normal again.

Finding his mother in tears and the neighbours crowding around him, he asked what had happened. His mother told him everything that had happened to him and also explained to him that to return to lay life after leaving it was very foolish; in fact, even though living he would be like a dead person. The sāmaṇera then came to realize his mistake. Taking the three robes from his mother, he went back to the monastery and was soon admitted as a bhikkhu.

When told about Sāmaṇera Sānu, the Buddha wishing to teach him about the restraint of mind said, "My son, one who does not restrain the mind which wanders about cannot find happiness. So, control your mind as a mahout controls an elephant."

Then the Buddha spoke in verse as follows:

Verse 326. In the past, this mind has wandered as it liked, wherever it liked, at its own pleasure. Now I will controt my mind wisely, as a mahout with his goad controls an elephant in must.

At the end of the discourse Thera Sānu comprehended the Four Noble Truths and later attained arahatship.

Verse 327

XXIII (6) The Story of the Elephant Called Pāveyyaka

While residing at the Jetavana monastery, the Buddha uttered Verse (327) of this book, with reference to the elephant, called Pāveyyaka.

Pāveyyaka when young was very strong; in due course, he became old and decrepit. One day, as old Pāveyyaka went into a pond he was stuck in the mire and could not get on to the shore. When King Pasenadi of Kosala was told about it, he sent an elephant trainer to help the elephant get out of the mire. The elephant trainer went to the site where the elephant was. There, he made the musicians strike up a martial tune. Hearing the military airs, the elephant felt as if he were in a battlefield; his spirits rose, he pulled himself with all his might, and was soon out of the mire.

When the bhikkhus told the Buddha about this he said, "Bhikkhus! Just as that elephant pulled itself out of the mire, so also, must you all pull yourselves out of the mire of moral defilements."

Then the Buddha spoke in verse as follows:

Verse 327. Take delight in mindfulness, guard your mind well. As an elephant stuck in mire pulls itself out, so also, pull yourself out of the mire of moral defilements.

At the end of the discourse the bhikkhus attained arahatship.

Verses 328, 329 and 330

XXIII (7) The Story of a Number of Bhikkhus

While residing in the Pālileyya forest where the elephant Pālileyyaka waited on him, the Buddha uttered Verses (328), (329) and (330) of this book, with reference to the bhikkhus from Kosambī.

Once, the bhikkhus of Kosambī split into two groups; one group followed the master of Vinaya and the other followed the teacher of the Dhamma. They did not listen even to the Buddha who exhorted them to make peace. So, the Buddha left them and spent the vassa all alone in the forest, where the elephant Pālileyyaka waited on him.

At the end of the vassa, the Venerable Ānanda went into the forest, accompanied by five hundred bhikkhus. Leaving the bhikkhus at some distance, the Venerable Ānanda approached the Buddha alone Then the Buddha told Ānanda to call the other bhikkhus. All of them came, paid obeisance to the

Buddha and said, "Venerable Sir! You must have had a hard time spending the vassa all alone in this forest." To this, the Buddha replied, "Bhikkhus, do not say so; the elephant Pālileyyaka had been looking after me all this time. He was, indeed, a very good friend, a true friend. If one has such a good friend one should stick to him; but if one cannot find a good friend it is better to stay alone."

Then the Buddha spoke in verse as follows:

Verse 328. If one finds a sagacious friend, who is a virtuous and steadfast companion, one should live with him joyfully and mindfully, overcoming all dangers.

Verse 329. If one cannot find a sagacious friend, who is a virtuous and steadfast companion, one should live alone like the king who gave up and left the country he had won, and like the elephant Mātaṅga roaming alone in the forest.

Verse 330. It is better to live alone; there is no fellowship with a fool. So one should live alone, do no evil, and be carefree like the elephant Mātaṅga roaming alone in the forest.

Verses 331, 332 333

XXIII (8) The Story of Māra

While residing in a monastery near the Himalayas, the Buddha uttered Verses (331), (332) and (333) of this book, with reference to Māra, who tried to entice him to rule as a king.

Once, while the Buddha was residing near the Himalayas, he found that many people were being ill-treated by some wicked kings. It then occurred to him whether it would be possible to prevent them from ill-treating those who should not be ill-treated and make the kings rule justly and wisely. Māra knew what the Buddha was thinking and planned to entice the Buddha to rule as a king. To him the Buddha replied, "O wicked Māra! Your teaching and my teaching are quite different. You and I cannot have any discussion. This is my teaching".

Then the Buddha spoke in verse as follows:

Verse 331. It is good to have friends when the need arises; it is good to be content with anything that is available; it is good to have merit when life is about to end; it is good to be rid of all dukkha.

Verse 332. In this world it is good to be dutiful to one's mother; also it is good to be dutiful to one's father. In this world it is good to minister unto samaṇas; also it is good to minister unto brāhmaṇas.

Verse 333. It is good to have virtue till old age, it is good to have unshakeable faith, it is good to gain wisdom, it is good to do no evil.

End of Chapter Twenty-three: The Elephant.

Chapter XXIV

Craving (Taṇhāvagga)

Verses 334, 335, 336 and 337

XXIV (1) The Story of Kapila the Fish

While residing at the Jetavana monastery, the Buddha uttered Verses (334), (335), (336) and (337) of this book, with reference to a fish with a lovely, golden colour and a stinking mouth.

During the time of Kassapa Buddha, there was a bhikkhu named Kapila, who was very learned in the Piṭakas. Because of his great learning he gained much fame and fortune; he also became very conceited and was full of contempt for other bhikkhus. When other bhikkhus pointed out to him, what was proper or not proper he invariably retorted, "How much do you know?" implying that he knew much more than those bhikkhus. In course of time, all good bhikkhus shunned him and only the bad ones gathered round him. On one sabbath day, while the bhikkhus were reciting the Fundamental Precepts for the bhikkhus (i.e., the Pātimokkha) Kapila said, "There is no such thing as Sutta, Abhidhamma, or Vinaya. It makes no difference whether you have a chance to listen to the Pātimokkha or not," etc., and left the congregation of the bhikkhus. Thus, Kapila was a hindrance to the development and growth of the Teaching (Sāsanā).

For this evil deed, Kapila had to suffer in niraya between the time of Kassapa Buddha and Gotama Buddha. Later, he was reborn as a fish in the Aciravatī River. That fish, as mentioned above, had a very beautiful golden body, but his mouth had a very horrid, offensive smell. One day, that fish was caught by some fishermen, and because it was so beautiful, they took it in a boat to the king. The king, in his turn, took the fish to the Buddha. When the fish opened its mouth, the horrid and offensive smell spread all around. The king then asked the Buddha why such a beautiful fish should have such a horrid and offensive smell. To the king and the audience, the Buddha explained, "O king! During the time of Kassapa Buddha there was a very learned bhikkhu who taught the Dhamma to others. Because of that good deed, when he was reborn in another existence, even as a fish, he was endowed with a golden body. But that bhikkhu was very greedy, proud and very contemptuous of others; he also disregarded the Disciplines and abused other bhikkhus. For these evil deeds, he was reborn in niraya, and now, he has become a beautiful fish with a mouth that stinks." The Buddha then turned to the fish and asked whether it knew where it would be going in its next existence. The fish answered that it would have to go again to niraya and it was filled with great despair, As predicted, on its death the fish was reborn in niraya, to undergo another term of continuous torment.

All those present hearing about the fish got alarmed. To them, the Buddha gave a discourse on the benefits of combining learning with practice.

Then the Buddha spoke in verse as follows:

Verse 334. In a man who is unmindful craving grows like a creeper. He runs from birth to birth, like a monkey seeking fruits in the forest.

Verse 335. In this world, sorrow grows in one who is overwhelmed by this vile craving that clings to the senses, just as well-watered bīraṇa grass grows luxuriantly.

Verse 336. In this world, sorrow falls away from one who overcomes this vile craving that is difficult to get rid of, just as water drops fall away from a lotus leaf.

Verse 337. Therefore, I will deliver this worthy discourse to all of you who have assembled here. Dig up the root of craving just as one who wishes to have the fragrant root digs up the bīraṇa grass. Do not let Māra destroy you again and again, as the flood destroys the reed.

Verses 338 to 343

XXIV (2) The Story of a Young Sow

While residing at the Veḷuvana monastery, the Buddha uttered Verses (338) to (343) of this book, with reference to a young sow.

On one occasion, while the Buddha was on an alms-round at Rājagaha, he saw a young dirty sow and smiled. When asked by the Venerable Ānanda, the Buddha replied, "Ānanda, this young sow was a hen during the time of Kakusandha Buddha. As she was then staying near a refectory in a monastery she used to hear the recitation of the sacred text and the discourses on the Dhamma. When she died she was reborn as a princess. On one occasion, while going to the latrine, the princess noticed the maggots and she became mindful of the loathsomeness of the body, etc. When she died she was reborn in the Brāhma realm as a puthujjana brahmā; but later due to some evil kamma, she was reborn as a sow. Ānanda! Look, on account of good and evil kamma there is no end of the round of existences.

Then the Buddha spoke in verse as follows:

Verse 338. Just as a tree with roots undamaged and firm grows again even though cut down, so also, if latent craving is not rooted out, this dukkha (of birth, ageing and death) arises again and again.

Verse 339. That man of wrong views, in whom the thirty-six streams (of craving) that flow towards pleasurable objects are strong, is carried away by his many thoughts connected with passion.

Verse 340. The stream of craving flows towards all sense objects; the creeper of craving arises (at the six sense-doors) and fixes itself (on the six sense objects). Seeing that creeper of craving growing, cut off its roots with Magga Insight.

Verse 341. In beings, there flows happiness that is smeared with craving; those beings attached to pleasure and seeking pleasure are, indeed, subject to birth and ageing.

Verse 342. People beset with craving are terrified like a hare caught in a snare; held fast by fetters and bonds they undergo dukkha (round of rebirths) again and again, for a long time.

Verse 343. People beset with craving are terrified like a hare caught in a snare. Therefore, one who wishes to free himself from craving should eradicate craving.

Verse 344

XXIV (3) The Story of an Ex-bhikkhu

While residing at the Veḷuvana monastery, the Buddha uttered Verse (344) of this book, with reference to a bhikkhu who was a pupil of the Venerable Mahākassapa.

As a pupil of the Venerable Mahākassapa, this bhikkhu had achieved the four mental absorptions (jhānas). But one day, as he went for alms-food to his uncle's house, he saw a woman and felt a great desire to have her. Then he left the Order of the bhikkhus. As a layman, he was a failure as he did not work hard. So, his uncle drove him out of the house, and subsequently he became mixed up with some thieves. All of them were caught by the authorities and were taken to the cemetery to be executed. The Venerable Mahākassapa saw his pupil as he was being let out and said to him, "My pupil, keep your mind steadfastly on a subject of meditation." As instructed, he concentrated and let himself be established in deep mental absorption. At the cemetery, while the executioners were making preparations to kill him, the ex-bhikkhu was very much composed and showed no signs of fear or anxiety. The executioners and the onlookers were awe-struck and very much impressed by the man's courage and composure and they reported about him to the king and also to the Buddha. The king gave orders to release the man. The Buddha on hearing about the matter sent his radiance and appeared to the thief as if in person.

Then the Buddha spoke to him in verse as follows:

Verse 344. Having left the forest of desire (i.e., the life of a householder), he takes to the forest of the practice (i.e., the life of a bhikkhu); but when he is free from the forest of desire he rushes back to that very forest. Come, look at that man who having become free rushes back into that very bondage.

At the end of the discourse, the thief who was steadfastly keeping his mind on the arising and perishing of the aggregates discerned the impermanent, unsatisfactory and non-self nature of all conditioned things and soon attained Sotāpatti Fruition. Later, he went to the Buddha at the Jetavana monastery where he was again admitted to the Order by the Buddha and he instantly attained arahatship.

Verses 345 and 346

XXIV (4) The Story on Imprisonment

While residing at the Jetavana monastery, the Buddha uttered Verses (345) and (346) of this book, with reference to some thieves who were kept in chains.

One day, thirty bhikkhus came into Sāvatthi for alms-food. While they were on their alms-round, they saw some prisoners being brought out with their hands and legs in chains. Back at the monastery, after relating what they had seen in the morning, they asked the Buddha whether there were any other bonds stronger than these. To them the Buddha answered, "Bhikkhus! These bonds are nothing compared to those of craving for food and clothing, for riches and for family. Craving is a thousand times, a hundred thousand times stronger than those chains, hand-cuffs and cages. That is the reason why the wise cut off craving and renounce the world and enter the Order of the bhikkhus.

Then the Buddha spoke in verse as follows:

Verses 345, 346. The wise do not say that bonds made of iron, of wood, and of hemp are strong bonds; they say that only passionate attachment to and care for gems and jewellery, children and wives are strong bonds. These drag one down (to lower planes of existence) and although they seem yielding are difficult to unfasten. The wise, cutting off this bond (of craving) and resolutely giving up sensual pleasures, renounce the world.

Verse 347

XXIV (5) The Story of Theri Khemā

While residing at the Veḷuvana monastery, the Buddha uttered Verse (347) of this book, with reference to Queen Khema.

Queen Khemā was the chief queen of King Bimbisara. She was very beautiful and also very proud.

The king wanted her to go to the Veḷuvana monastery and pay homage to the Buddha. But she had heard that the Buddha always talked disparagingly about beauty and she therefore tried to avoid seeing the Buddha. The king understood her attitude towards the Buddha; he also knew how proud she was of her beauty. So the king ordered his minstrels to sing in praise of the Veḷuvana monastery, about its pleasant and peaceful atmosphere, etc. Hearing them, Queen Khemā became interested and decided to set out for the Veḷuvana monastery.

When Queen Khemā arrived at the monastery, the Buddha was expounding the Dhamma to an audience. By his supernormal power, the Buddha made a very beautiful young lady appear, sitting not far from him, and fanning him. When Queen Khemā came to the audience hall, she alone saw the beautiful young lady. Comparing the exquisite beauty of the young lady to that of her own, Khemā realized that her beauty was much inferior to that of the young lady. As she looked again intently at the young lady her beauty began to fade gradually. In the end, she saw before her eyes an old decrepit being, which again changed into a corpse, her stinking body being attacked by maggots. At that instant, Queen Khemā realized the impermanence and worthlessness of beauty.

The Buddha knowing the state of her mind remarked, "O Khemā! Look carefully at this decaying body which is built around a skeleton of bones and is subject to disease and decay. Look carefully at the body which is thought of so highly by the foolish. Look at the worthlessness of the beauty of this young girl." After hearing this, Queen Khemā attained Sotāpatti Fruition.

Then the Buddha spoke in verse as follows:

Verse 347. Beings who are infatuated with lust fall back into the Stream of Craving they have generated, just as a spider does in the web it has spun. The wise, cutting off the bond of craving, walk on resolutely, leaving, all ills (dukkha) behind.

At the end of the discourse Queen khemā attained arahatship and was admitted to the Order and became the Chief Female Disciple of the Buddha.

Verse 348

XXIV (6) The Story of Uggasena

While residing at the Jetavana monastery, the Buddha uttered Verse (348) of this book, with reference to Uggasena, a rich man's son who fell in love with a dancer.

Once, a wandering theatrical troupe consisting of five hundred dancers and some acrobats came to Rājagaha and performed on the grounds of the palace of King Bimbisāra for seven days. There, a young dancer who was the daughter of an acrobat sang and danced on top of a long bamboo pole. Uggasena, the young son of a rich man, fell desperately in love with this dancer and his parents could not stop him from marrying her. He married the young dancer and followed the troupe. As he was not a dancer nor an acrobat, he was not of much use to the party. So, as the party moved from place to place, he had to help carry boxes, to drive the carts, etc.

In course of time, a son was born to Uggasena and his wife, the dancer. To this child, the dancer would often sing a song which ran thus: "O you, son of the man who keeps watch over the carts; the man who carries boxes and bundles! O you, son of the ignorant one who can do nothing!" Uggasena heard the song; he knew that his wife was referring to him and he was very much hurt and depressed. So he went to his father-in-law, the acrobat, and requested him to teach him acrobatics. After a year's training, Uggasena became a skilful acrobat.

Then, Uggasena went back to Rājagaha, and it was proclaimed that Uggasena would publicly demonstrate his skill in seven days' time. On the seventh day, a long pole was put up and Uggasena stood on top of it. At a signal given from below he somersaulted seven times on the pole. At about this time, the Buddha saw Uggasena in his vision and knew that time was ripe for Uggasena to attain arahatship. So, he entered Rājagaha and willed that the audience should turn their attention to him instead of applauding Uggasena for his acrobatic feats. When Uggasena saw that he was being neglected and ignored, he just sat on top of the pole, feeling very discontented and depressed. The Buddha then addressed Uggasena, "Uggasena, a wise man should abandon all attachment to the khandha aggregates and strive to gain liberation from the round of rebirths."

Then the Buddha spoke in verse as follows:

Verse 348. Give up the past, give up the future, give up the present. Having reached the end of existences, with a mind freed from all (conditioned things), you will not again undergo birth and decay.

At the end of the discourse Uggasena, who was still on top of the pole, attained arahatship. He came down and was soon admitted to the Order by the Buddha.

Verses 349 and 350

XXIV (7) The Story of Cūḷadhanuggaha, the Skilful Archer

While residing at the Jetavana monastery, the Buddha uttered Verses (349) and (350) of this book, with reference to a young bhikkhu, who was a skilful archer in one of his previous existences.

Once a young bhikkhu took his alms-food in one of the shelters specially built for bhikkhus in town. After his meal he felt like drinking water. So he went to a house and asked for some drinking water, and a young woman came out to give him some water. As soon as this young woman saw the young bhikkhu she fell in love with him. Wishing to entice him, she invited the young bhikkhu to come to her house whenever he felt thirsty. After some time, she invited him to her house for alms-food. On that day, she told him that they had everything they could wish for in the house, but that there was no male to look after their affairs, etc. Hearing those words, the young bhikkhu took the hint and he soon found himself to be more and more attached to the young, attractive woman. He became very much dissatisfied with his life as a bhikkhu and was getting thin. Other bhikkhus reported about him to the Buddha.

The Buddha called the young bhikkhu to his presence and said to him, "My son, listen to me. This young woman will be your undoing just as she had been to you in a previous existence. In one of your previous existences you were a very skilful archer and she was your wife. On one occasion, while the two of you were travelling, you came upon a gang of highwaymen. She fell in love with the gang leader. So, while you and the gang leader were engaged in fighting and you called out to her to give you the sword, she gave the sword to the robber who promptly killed you. Thus, she was the cause of your death. Now, too, she will be the cause of your ruin if you go after her and leave my Order for her sake."

Then the Buddha spoke in verse as follows:

Verse 349. In a man who is disturbed by (sensual) thoughts, whose passions are strong, and who keeps seeing objects as being pleasant, craving grows more and more. Indeed, he makes his bondage strong.

Verse 350. A man who takes delight in calming (sensual) thoughts, who is ever mindful, and meditates on the impurity (of the body, etc.) will certainly get rid (of craving); this man will cut the bond of Māra.

At the end of the discourse, the young bhikkhu attained Sotāpatti Fruition.

Verses 351 and 352

XXIV (8) The Story of Māra

While residing at the Jetavana monastery, the Buddha uttered Verses (351) and (352) of this book, with reference to Māra who had come to frighten Sāmaṇera Rāhula, son of Gotama Buddha.

On one occasion, a large number of bhikkhus arrived at the Jetavana monastery. To put up the guest bhikkhus, Sāmaṇera Rāhula had to go and sleep near the door, just outside the chamber of the Buddha. Māra, wanting to annoy the Buddha through his son, took the form of an elephant and encircling the head of the sāmaṇera with his trunk made an alarming noise hoping to frighten him. But Rāhula was unmoved. The Buddha, from his chamber, knew what was happening, and said, "O wicked Māra! Even a thousand such as you would not be able to frighten my son. My son has no fear, he is free from craving, he is vigilant, he is wise."

Then the Buddha spoke in verse as follows:

Verse 351. He who has attained arahatship is free from fear, free from craving, and free from moral defilements. He has cut off the thorns of existence (such as lust). This is the last existence (for him).

Verse 352. He who is free from craving and from attachment, who is skilled in the knowledge of the significance of terms, who knows the grouping of letters and their sequence is indeed called "one who has lived his last, a man of great wisdom, a great man."

Hearing the above words, Māra realized that the Buddha knew about his tricks and instantly disappeared.

Verse 353

XXIV (9) The Story of Upaka

The Buddha uttered Verse (353) of this book, in answer to the question put up by Upaka, a non--Buddhist ascetic, while the Buddha was on his way to the Deer Park (Migadāya) where the Group of Five Bhikkhus (Pañca Vaggīs) were staying. The Buddha was going there to expound the Dhammacakkappavattana Sutta to the Pañca Vaggīs, his old associates, viz., Kondañña, Bhaddiya, Vappa, Assaji, and Mahānāma. When Upaka saw Gotama Buddha, he was very much impressed by the radiant countenance of the Buddha and so said to him, "Friend, you look so serene and pure; may I know who your teacher is?" To him, the Buddha replied that he had no teacher.

Then the Buddha spoke in verse as follows:

Verse 353. I have overcome all, I know all, I am detached from all, I have given up all; I am liberated from moral defilements having eradicated craving, (i. e., I have attained arahatship). Having comprehended the Four Noble Truths by myself, whom should I point out as my teacher?

At the end of the discourse Upaka expressed neither approval nor disapproval but just nodded a few times and went on his way.

Verse 354

XXIV (10) The Story of the Questions Raised by Sakka

While residing at the Jetavana monastery, the Buddha uttered Verse (354) of this book, with reference to four questions raised by Sakka, king of the devas.

On one occasion, at a meeting of the devas in the Tāvatiṁsa realm, four questions were raised, but the devas failed to get the correct answers. Eventually, Sakka took these devas to the Buddha at the Jetavana monastery. After explaining their difficulty, Sakka presented the following four questions:

(a) Among gifts, which is the best?

(b) Among tastes, which is the best?

(c) Among delights, which is the best?

(d) Why is the eradication of craving said to be the most excellent?

To these questions, the Buddha replied, "Oh Sakka, the Dhamma is the noblest of all gifts, the best of all tastes and the best of all delights. Eradication of Craving leads to the attainment of arahatship and is, therefore, the greatest of all conquests."

Then the Buddha spoke in verse as follows:

Verse 354. The gift of the Dhamma excels all gifts; the taste of the Dhamma excels all tastes; delight in the Dhamma excels all delights. The eradication of Craving (i.e., attainment of arahatship) overcomes all ills (saṁsāra dukkha).

At the end of the discourse, Sakka said to the Buddha, "Venerable Sir, if the gift of the Dhamma excels all gifts why are we not invited to share the merit whenever gifts of the Dhamma are made? Venerable Sir! I pray that, from now on, we may be given a share in the merit of good deeds". Then the

Buddha asked all the bhikkhus to assemble and exhorted them to share the merit of all their good deeds with all beings.

Since then, it has become a custom to invite all beings from the thirty-one realms (bhūmis) to come and share merit whenever a good deed is done.

Verse 355

XXIV (11) The Story of a Childless Rich Man

While residing at the Jetavana monastery, the Buddha uttered Verse (355) of this book, with reference to a childless rich man.

On one occasion, King Pasenadi of Kosala came to pay homage to the Buddha. He explained to the Buddha that he was late because earlier that day a rich man had died in Sāvatthi without leaving any heirs, and so he had to confiscate all that man's property. Then, he proceeded to relate about the man, who, although very rich, was very stingy. While he lived, he did not give away anything in charity. He was reluctant to spend his money even on himself, and therefore, ate very sparingly and wore cheap, coarse clothes only. On hearing this the Buddha told the king and the audience about the man in a past existence. In that existence also he was a rich man.

One day, when a paccekabuddha came and stood for alms at his house, he told his wife to offer something to the paccekabuddha. His wife thought it was very rarely that her husband gave her permission to give anything to anybody. So, she filled up the alms-bowl with some choice food. The rich man again met the paccekabuddha on his way home and he had a look at the alms-bowl. Seeing that his wife had offered a substantial amount of good food, he thought, "Oh, this bhikkhu would only have a good sleep after a good meal. It would have been better if my servants were given such good food; at least, they would have given me better service." In other words, he regretted that he had asked his wife to offer food to the paccekabuddha. This same man had a brother who also was a rich man. His brother had an only son. Coveting his brother's wealth, he had killed his young nephew and had thus wrongfully inherited his brother's wealth on the latter's death.

Because the man had offered alms-food to the paccekabuddha he became a rich man in his present life; because he regretted having offered food to the paccekabuddha he had no wish to spend anything even on himself. Because he had killed his own nephew for the sake of his brother's wealth he had to suffer in niraya for seven existences. His bad kamma having come to an end he was born into the human world but here also he had not gained any good kamma. The king then remarked, "Venerable Sir! Even though he had lived here in the lifetime of the Buddha himself, he had not made any offering of anything to the Buddha or to his disciples. Indeed, he had missed a very good opportunity; he had been very foolish."

Then the Buddha spoke in verse as follows:

Verse 355. Wealth destroys the foolish; but it cannot destroy those who seek the other shore (i. e., Nibbāna). By his craving for wealth the fool destroys himself, as he would destroy others.

Verse 356 to 359

XXIV (12) The Story of Deva Aṅkura

While on a visit to the Tāvatiṁsa deva realm, the Buddha uttered Verses (356) to (359) of this book, with reference to a deva named Aṅkura.

The Buddha visited the Tāvatiṁsa deva realm to expound the Abhidhamma to Deva Santusita, who had been his mother. During that time, there was a deva named Indaka in Tāvatiṁsa. Indaka, in his last existence as a man, had offered a little alms-food to Thera Anuruddha. As this good deed was made to a thera within the period of the Buddha's Teaching he was amply rewarded for it. Thus, on his death he was reborn in the Tāvatiṁsa realm and was lavishly bestowed with the luxuries of the deva world. At that time, there was also another deva by the name of Aṅkura in Tāvatiṁsa who had given much in charity; in fact, many times more than what Indaka had given. But his charity was made outside the period of the Teaching of any of the Buddhas. So, in spite of his lavish and grand charities, he was enjoying the benefits of the life of a deva on a much smaller scale than Indaka, who had offered very little. As the Buddha was then at Tāvatiṁsa, Aṅkura asked him the reason for the discrepancy in gaining the benefits. To him the Buddha answered, "O deva! When giving charities and donations you should choose whom you give, for acts of charities are just like seeds. Seeds put into fertile soil will grow into strong, vigorous plants or trees and will bear much fruit; but you had sown your seed in poor soil, so you reap poorly."

Then the Buddha spoke in verse as follows:

Verse 356. Weeds damage fields; lust spoils all beings. Therefore, giving to those free from lust yields great benefit.

Verse 357. Weeds damage fields; ill will spoils all beings. Therefore, giving to those free from ill will yields great benefit.

Verse 358. Weeds damage fields; ignorance spoils all beings. Therefore, giving to those free from ignorance yields great benefit.

Verse 359. Weeds damage fields; covetousness spoils all beings. Therefore, giving to those free from covetousness yields great benefit.

End of Chapter Twenty-four: Craving

Chapter XXV

The Bhikkhu (Bhikkhuvagga)

Verses 360 and 361

XXV(1) The Story of Five Bhikkhus

While residing at the Jetavana monastery, the Buddha uttered Verses (360) and (361) of this book, with reference to five bhikkhus.

Once there were five bhikkhus in Sāvatthi. Each of them practised restraint of just one out of the five senses and each of them claimed that what he was practising was the most difficult. There were some heated arguments over this and they could not come to an agreement. Finally, they went to the Buddha to ask for his decision. The Buddha said to them, "Each of the senses is just as difficult to control as the other; but all bhikkhus must control all the five senses and not just one. Only those who control all the senses would escape from the round of rebirths."

Then the Buddha spoke in verse as follows:

Verse 360. Restraint in the eye is good, good is restraint in the ear; restraint in the nose is good, good is restraint in the tongue.

Verse 361. Restraint in body is good, good is restraint in speech; restraint in mind is good, good is restraint in all the senses. A bhikkhu restrained in all the senses is freed from all ills (saṁsāra dukkha).

Verse 362

XXV (2) The Story of a Bhikkhu Who Killed a Swan (Haṁsa)

While residing at the Jetavana monastery, the Buddha uttered Verse (362) of this book, with reference to a bhikkhu who killed a swan.

Once, there was a bhikkhu who was very skilful in throwing stones; he could even hit fast-moving objects without fail. One day, while sitting with another bhikkhu after having their bath in the Aciravatī River, he saw two swans flying at some distance. He told his friend that he would get one of the swans by throwing a stone at it. At that instant, the swan, hearing voices, turned its neck and the bhikkhu threw a pebble at the bird. The pebble went through one eye and came out of the other eye of the bird. The bird cried out in pain and agony and dropped dead at the feet of the young bhikkhu.

Other bhikkhus seeing the incident took the young bhikkhu to the Buddha. The Buddha reprimanded him and said, "My son, why have you killed this bird? Why especially you, a member of my Order, who should be practising loving-kindness to all beings and who should be striving ardently for liberation from the round of rebirths? Even during the period outside the Teaching, the wise practised morality and observed the precepts. A bhikkhu must have control over his hands, his feet and his tongue."

Then the Buddha spoke in verse as follows:

Verse 362. He who controls his hand, controls his foot, controls his speech, and has complete control of himself; who finds delight in Insight Development Practice and is calm; who stays alone and is contented;— him they call a bhikkhu.

Verse 363

XXV (3) The Story of Bhikkhu Kokālika

While residing at the Jetavana monastery, the Buddha uttered Verse (363) of this book, with reference to Bhikkhu Kokālika.

Bhikkhu Kokālika had abused the two Chief Disciples, the Venerable Sāriputta and the Venerable Mahā Moggallāna. For this evil deed Kokālika was swallowed up by the earth and had to suffer in Paduma Niraya. Learning about his fate, the bhikkhus remarked that Kokālika had to suffer grievously because he did not control his tongue. To those bhikkhus, the Buddha said, "Bhikkhus! A bhikkhu must have control over his tongue; his conduct must be good; his mind must be calm, subdued and not flitting about as it pleases."

Then the Buddha spoke in verse as follows:

Verse 363. The bhikkhu who controls his mouth (speech) who speaks wisely with his mind composed, who explains the meaning and the text of the Dhamma,— sweet are the words of that bhikkhu.

Verse 364

XXV (4) The Story of Thera Dhammarama

While residing at the Jetavana monastery, the Buddha uttered Verse (364) of this book, with reference to Thera Dhammārāma.

When it was made known to the disciples that the Buddha would realize parinibbāna in four months' time, most of the puthujjana bhikkhus (i.e., those who had not attained any of the Maggas) felt extremely depressed and were at a loss and did not know what to do. They just stayed close to the Buddha, hardly ever leaving his presence. However, there was a bhikkhu by the name of Dhammārāma who kept to himself and did not go near the Buddha. His intention was to strive most ardently to attain arahatship before the passing away of the Buddha. So he strove hard in Insight Meditation Practice. Other bhikkhus, not understanding his attitude and his noble ambition, misunderstood his behaviour.

Those bhikkhus took Dhammārāma to the Buddha and said to the Enlightened One, "Venerable Sir! This bhikkhu does not seem to have any affection or regard or reverence for you; he has been staying by himself while all the time other bhikkhus are staying close to Your Venerable presence." When other bhikkhus had said everything they wanted to say, Dhammārāma respectfully explained to the Buddha why he had not come to see the Buddha and also reported that he had been striving his utmost in Insight Meditation Practice.

The Buddha was satisfied and was very pleased with the explanation and conduct of Dhammārāma and he said, "My son Dammārāma, you have done very well. A bhikkhu who loves and respects me should act like you. Those who made offerings of flowers, scents and incense to me are not really paying me homage. Only those who practise the Dhamma are the ones who truly pay homage to me."

Then the Buddha spoke in verse as follows:

Verse 364. The bhikkhu who abides in the Dhamma, who delights in the Dhamma, who meditates on the Dhamma, and is ever mindful of the Dhamma, does not fall away from the Dhamma of the virtuous.

At the end of the discourse Thera Dhammārāma attained arahatship.

Verses 365 and 366

XXV (5) The Story of a Bhikkhu Who Associated With a Follower of Devadatta

While residing at the Jetavana monastery, the Buddha uttered Verses (365) and (366) of this book, with reference to a bhikkhu who was on friendly terms with a follower of Devadatta.

Once, a bhikkhu disciple of the Buddha, being very friendly with a follower of Devadatta, paid a visit to the monastery of Devadatta and stayed there for a few days. Other bhikkhus reported to the Buddha that he had been mixing with the followers of Devadatta and that he had even gone to the monastery of Devadatta, spent there a few days, eating, sleeping and apparently enjoying the choice food and the comforts of that monastery. The Buddha sent for that bhikkhu and asked him whether what he had heard about his behaviour was true. The bhikkhu admitted that he had gone to the monastery of Devadatta for a few days, but he told the Buddha that he had not embraced the teaching of Devadatta.

The Buddha then reprimanded him and pointed out that his behaviour made him appear like a follower of Devadatta. To him the Buddha said, "My son, even though you have not embraced the doctrine of Devadatta, you are going about as if you were one of his followers. A bhikkhu should be contented with what he gets and should not covet other people's gains. A bhikkhu who is filled with envy at the good fortune of others will not attain concentration (samādhi), or Insight, or the Path that leads to Nibbāna (Magga).

Only the bhikkhu who is contented with whatever he gets will be able to attain concentration, Insight and the Path."

Then the Buddha spoke in verse as follows:

Verse 365. One should not despise what one has received (by proper means), nor should one envy others their gains. The bhikkhu who envies others cannot attain Concentration (Samādhi).

Verse 366. Though he receives only a little, if a bhikkhu does not despise what he has received (by proper means), the devas will surely praise him who leads a pure life and is not slothful.

Verse 367

XXV (6) The Story of the Giver of the First-Fruits of His Labour

While residing at the Jetavana monastery, the Buddha uttered Verse (367) of this book, with reference to a brahmin who was in the habit of making five offerings of first-fruits in charity. The first-fruits here refer to the first-fruits of the field. The first-fruits of the field are given in charity at the time of harvesting, at the time of threshing, at the time of storing, at the time of cooking and at the time of filling the plate.

One day, the Buddha saw the brahmin and his wife in his vision and knew that time was ripe for the couple to attain Anāgāmi Fruition. Accordingly, the Buddha set out for their house and stood at the door for alms food. The brahmin who was then having his meal, facing the interior part of the house, did not see the Buddha. His wife who was near him saw the Buddha, but she was afraid that if her husband saw the Buddha standing at the door for alms-food, he would offer all his rice in the plate and, in that case, she would have to cook again. With this thought in her mind, she stood behind her husband so that he would not see the Buddha; then she quietly stepped backwards and slowly came to where the Buddha was standing, and whispered to him, "Venerable Sir! We do not have any alms-food for you today." But the Buddha had decided not to leave the house; he just shook his head. Seeing this gesture, the brahmin's wife could not control herself and she burst out laughing.

At that instant, the brahmin turned round and saw the Buddha. At once he knew what his wife had done, and he cried out, "O you, my wretched wife! You have ruined me." Then, taking up his plate of rice, he approached the Buddha and apologetically requested, "Venerable Sir! Please accept this rice which I have partly consumed." To him the Buddha replied, "O brahmin! Any rice is suitable for me, whether it is not yet consumed, or is partly consumed, or even if it is the last remaining spoonful." The brahmin was very much surprised by the Buddha's reply; at the same time, it made him happy because his offer of rice was accepted by the Buddha. The brahmin next asked the Buddha by what standard a bhikkhu was judged and how a bhikkhu was defined. The Buddha knew that both the brahmin and his wife had already learned something about mind and body (nāma-rūpa); so he answered, "O brahmin! One who is not attached to mind and body is called a bhikkhu."

Then the Buddha spoke in verse as follows:

Verse 367. He who does not take the mind-and-body aggregate (nāma-rūpa) as "I and mine", and who does not grieve over the dissolution (of mind-and-body) is, indeed, called a bhikkhu.

At the end of the dicourse both the brahmin and his wife attained Anāgāmi Fruition.

Verses 368 to 376

XXV (7) The Story of a Great Many Bhikkhus

While residing at the Jetavana monastery, the Buddha uttered Verses (368) to (376) of this book, with reference to nine hundred bhikkhus.

Once there was a very rich lady in the town of Kuraraghara, about one hundred and twenty yojanas from Sāvatthi. She had a son who had become a bhikkhu; his name was Soṇa. On one occasion, Bhikkhu Soṇa passed through his home town. On his return from the Jetavana monastery his mother met him and organized a grand charity in his honour. Having heard that Bhikkhu Soṇa could expound the Dhamma very well she also requested him to expound the Dhamma to her and other people of the home town. Bhikkhu Soṇa complied with her request. So a pavilion was built and a meeting was organized for Bhikkhu Soṇa to give a discourse. There was a large gathering at the pavilion; the mother of the bhikkhu also went to listen to the Dhamma expounded by her son. She took all the members of her household with her leaving only a maid to look after the house.

While the lady was away, some thieves broke into the house. Their leader, however, went to the pavilion where the mistress of the house was, sat down near her and kept an eye on her. His intention was to get rid of her should she return home early on learning about the theft at her house. The maid seeing the thieves breaking into the house went to report the matter to her mistress, but the lady only said, "Let the thieves take all my money, I don't care; but do not come and disturb me while I am listening to the Dhamma. You'd better go back." So the maid went home.

There the girl saw the thieves breaking into the room where her mistress kept all her silverware. Again she went to the pavilion where her mistress was and reported to her that thieves were taking away her silverware, but she was given the same answer as before. So she had to go back to the house. There she saw the thieves breaking into the room where her mistress kept her gold and she reported the matter to her mistress. This time, her mistress shouted at her, "O dear! Let the thieves take whatever they wish to take; why do you have to come and worry me again when I am listening to a discourse on the Dhamma? Why did you not go back when I told you to? Don't you dare come near me again and say things about the theft or the thieves."

The leader of the gang of thieves who was close at hand heard everything the lady had said and he was extremely surprised. Her words also kept him thinking, "If we take away the property of this wise and noble person, we will surely be punished; we might even be struck by lightning and our heads broken into many pieces." The leader got alarmed over this possibility and he hurried back to the house of the lady and made his followers return all the things they had taken. He then took all his followers to where the mistress of the house was; she was still at the pavilion, listening attentively to the Dhamma.

Thera Soṇa finished his exposition on the Dhamma with the crack of dawn and came down from the dais from where he had expounded the Dhamma. The leader of the thieves approached the rich, noble lady, paid respect to her and revealed his identity to her. He also related to her how they had plundered her house and also that they had returned all her property on hearing her words to her maid, who reported the theft to her during the night. Then, the leader and all the thieves asked the lady to forgive them for having wronged her. Then, they asked Thera Soṇa to admit them to the Order of bhikkhus. After the admission, each one of the nine hundred bhikkhus took a subject of meditation from Thera Soṇa and went to the nearby forest to practise meditation in seclusion.

From a distance of one hundred and twenty yojanas, the Buddha saw those bhikkhus and sent forth his radiance to them so that he seemed to be sitting in their midst.

Then noticing their individual dispositions, the Buddha spoke in verse as follows:

Verse 368. The bhikkhu who lives exercising loving--kindness and is devoted to the Teaching of the Buddha will realize Nibbāna—the Tranquil, the Unconditioned, the Blissful.

Verse 369. O bhikkhu, bale out the water (of wrong thoughts) from this boat (your body); when empty it will sail swiftly; having cut off passion and ill will you will realize Nibbāna.

Verse 370. Cut off the five (the lower five fetters); give up the five (the upper five fetters); and develop the five (controlling faculties). The bhikkhu who has freed himself of the five bonds (passion, ill will, ignorance, pride and wrong view) is called "One who has crossed the flood (of saṁsāra)."

Verse 371. O Bhikkhu, meditate, and do not be unmindful; do not let your mind rejoice in sensual pleasures. Do not be unmindful and swallow the (hot) lump of iron; as you burn (in niraya) do not cry, "This, indeed, is suffering."

Verse 372. There can be no concentration in one who lacks wisdom; there can be no wisdom in one who lacks concentration. He who has concentration as well as wisdom is, indeed, close to Nibbāna.

Verse 373. The bhikkhu who goes into seclusion (to meditate), whose mind is tranquil, who clearly perceives the Dhamma, experiences the joy which transcends that of (ordinary) men.

Verse 374. Every time he clearly comprehends the arising and the perishing of the khandhas, he finds joy and rapture. That, to the wise, is the way to Nibbāna (the Deathless).

Verse 375. For a wise bhikkhu in this Teaching, this is the beginning (of the practice leading to Nibbāna): control of the senses, contentment, and restraint according to the Fundamental Precepts.

Verse 376. Associate with good friends, who are energetic and whose livelihood is pure; let him be amiable and be correct in his conduct. Then, (frequently) feeling much joy he will make an end of dukkha (of the round of rebirths).

At the end of each verse, one hundred out of the nine hundred bhikkhus attained arahatship.

Verse 377

XXV (8) The Story of Five Hundred Bhikkhus

While residing at the Jetavana monastery, the Buddha uttered Verse (377) of this book, with reference to five hundred bhikkhus.

Five hundred bhikkhus from Sāvatthi, after taking a subject of meditation from the Buddha, set out for the forest to practise meditation. There, they noticed that the jasmin flowers which bloomed in the early morning dropped off from the plants onto the ground in the evening. Then the bhikkhus resolved that they would strive hard to free themselves from all moral defilements even before the flowers were shed from the plants. The Buddha, through his supernormal power, saw them from his Perfumed Chamber. He therefore sent forth his radiance to them and made them feel his presence. To them the Buddha said, "Bhikkhus! As the withered flower is shed from the plant, so also, should a bhikkhu strive to free himself from the round of rebirths."

Then the Buddha spoke in verse as follows:

Verse 377. O bhikkhus! As the jasmin (vassikā) plant sheds its withered flowers, so also, should you shed passion and ill will.

At the end of the discourse the five hundred bhikkhus attained arahatship.

Verse 378

XXV (9) The Story of Thera Santakāya

While residing at the Jetavana monastery, the Buddha uttered Verse (378) of this book, with reference to Thera Santakāya.

There was once a thera named Santakāya, who had been a lion in his past existence. It is said that lions usually go out in search of food one day and then rest in a cave for the next seven days without moving. Thera Santakāya, having been a lion in his last existence, behaved very much like a lion. He moved about very little; his movements were slow and steady; and he was usually calm and composed. Other bhikkhus took his behaviour to be very queer and they reported about him to the Buddha. After hearing the account given by the bhikkhus, the Buddha said to all of them, "Bhikkhus! A bhikkhu should be calm and composed; he should behave like Santakāya."

Then the Buddha spoke in verse as follows:

Verse 378. The bhikkhu who is calm in body, calm in speech, and calm in mind, who is well-composed and has given up (lit., vomited) worldly pleasures, is called a "Tranquil One"

At the end of the discourse Thera Santakāya attained arahatship.

Verses 279 and 380

XXV (10) The Story of Thera Naṅgalakula

While residing at the Jetavana monastery, the Buddha uttered Verses (379) and (380) of this book, with reference to Thera Naṅgala.

Naṅgala was a poor field labourer in the service of a farmer. One day, a bhikkhu, seeing him ploughing a field in his old clothes, asked him if he would like to become a bhikkhu. When he replied in the affirmative, the bhikkhu took him along to the monastery and made him a bhikkhu. After the admission to the Order, as instructed by his teacher, he left his plough and his old clothes in a tree not far away from the monastery. Because the poor man had left his plough to join the Order, he was known as Thera Naṅgala (naṅgala=plough). Due to better living conditions at the monastery Thera Naṅgala became healthier and soon put on weight. However, after some time, he grew tired of the life of a bhikkhu and often felt like returning to home-life. Whenever this feeling arose in him, he would go to the tree near the monastery, the tree where he had left his plough and his old clothes. There he would reproach himself saying, "O you shameless man! Do you still want to put on these old rags and return to the hard, lowly life of a hired labourer?" After this, his dissatisfaction with the life of a bhikkhu would disappear and he would go back to the monastery. Thus, he went to the tree at an interval of every three or four days, to remind himself of the wretchedness of his old life.

When other bhikkhus asked him about his frequent visits to the tree, he replied, "I have to go to my teacher." In course of time, he attained arahatship and he stopped going to the tree. Other bhikkhus, noticing this, asked him teasingly, "Why don't you go to your teacher now?" To those bhikkhus, he replied, "I used to go to my teacher because I had need of him; but now, I have no need to go to him." The bhikkhus understood what he meant by his answer and they went to the Buddha and reported, "Venerable Sir! Thera Naṅgala claims to have attained arahatship. It cannot be true; he must be boasting, he must be telling lies." To them the Buddha said, "Bhikkhus! Do not say so; for Naṅgala is not telling lies. My son Naṅgala. by reproaching himself and correcting himself, has indeed attained arahatship."

Then the Buddha spoke in verse as follows:

Verse 379. O bhikkhu, by yourself exhort yourself, and examine yourself; thus guarding yourself and being mindful, you will live in peace.

Verse 380. One indeed is one's own refuge, (how could anyone else be one's refuge?) One indeed is one's own haven; therefore, look after yourself as a horse dealer looks after a thoroughbred.

Verse 381

XXV (11) The Story of Therā Vakkali

While residing at the Veḷuvana monastery, the Buddha uttered Verse (381) of this book, with reference to Thera Vakkali.

Vakkali was a brahmin who lived in Sāvatthi. One day when he saw the Buddha going on an alms--round in the city, he was very much impressed by the noble appearance of the Buddha. At the same time, he felt much affection and great reverence for the Buddha and asked permission to join the Order just to be near him. As a bhikkhu, Vakkali always kept close to the Buddha; he did not care much about other duties of a bhikkhu and did not at all practise concentration meditation. So, the Buddha said to him, "Vakkali, it will be of no use to you by always keeping close to me, looking at my face. You should practise concentration meditation; for, indeed, only the one who sees the Dhamma sees me. One who does not see the Dhamma does not see me. So, you must leave my presence." When he heard those words Vakkali felt very depressed. He left the Buddha as ordered, and climbed the Gijjhakūṭa hill with the intention of committing suicide by jumping down from the peak.

The Buddha, knowing full well the extent of Vakkali's grief and despondency, reflected that because of his great sorrow and despondency Vakkali might miss the chance of attaining the Maggas. Accordingly, he sent forth his radiance to Vakkali, made him feel his presence and appeared as if in person to Vakkali. With the Buddha near him, Vakkali soon forgot all his sorrow; he became cheerful and very much heartened.

To him the Buddha spoke in verse as follows:

Verse 381. The bhikkhu who frequently feels joy and is devoted to the Teaching of the Buddha will realize Nibbāna— the Tranquil, the Unconditioned, the Blissful.

At the end of the discourse Vakkali attained arahatship.

Verse 382

XXV (12) The Story of Sāmaṇera Sumana

While residing at the Pubbārāma monastery, the Buddha uttered Verse (382) of this book, with reference to Sāmaṇera Sumana.

Sāmaṇera Sumana was a pupil of Thera Anuruddha. Although he was only seven years old he was an arahat, endowed with supernormal powers. Once, when his teacher Anuruddha was ill at a monastery in a forest of the Himalayas, he fetched water from the Anotatta lake which was five hundred yojanas away from the monastery. The journey was made not by land but by air through his supernormal power. Later, Thera Anuruddha took Sāmanera Sumana to the Buddha, who was then sojourning at Pubbārāma, the monastery donated by Visākhā.

There, other young bhikkhus and samaṇeras teased him by patting his head, or pulling his ears, nose and arms, and jokingly asked him if he was not feeling bored. The Buddha saw them and thought that he would make those young bhikkhus see the rare qualities of young Sāmaṇera Sumana. So it was made known by the Buddha that he wanted some samaṇera to get a jar of water from the Anotatta lake. The Venerable Ānanda searched among the bhikkhus and sāmaṇeras of the Pubbārāma monastery, but there was none who was able to undertake the job. Finally, the Venerable Ānanda asked Sāmaṇera Sumana who readily agreed to fetch water from the Anotatta lake. He took a big golden jar from the monastery and soon brought the water from the Anotatta lake for the Buddha. As before, he went to the Anotatta lake and came back by air through his supernormal power.

At the congregation of the bhikkhus in the evening, the bhikkhus told the Buddha about the wonderful trip made by Sāmaṇera Sumana. To them the Buddha said, "Bhikkhus, one who practises the Dhamma vigilantly and zealously is capable of attaining supernormal powers, even though he is young."

Then the Buddha spoke in verse as follows:

Verse 382. A bhikkhu who, though young, devotes himself to the Teaching of the Buddha lights up the world, as does the moon freed from a cloud.

End of Chapter Twenty-five: **The Bhikkku.**

Chapter XXVI

The Brāhmaṇa (Brāhmaṇavagga)

Verse 383

XXVI (1) The Story of a Brahmin Who Had Great Faith

While residing at the Jetavana monastery, the Buddha uttered Verse (383) of this book, with reference to a brahmin, who showed extreme devotion to some buikkhus.

Once, in Sāvatthi, there lived a brahmin who became extremely devoted to the Buddha and his Teaching, after hearing a discourse given by the Buddha. Every day, he invited the bhikkhus to his house for alms-food. When the bhikkhus arrived at his house, he addressed them as "arahats" and respectfully requested them to enter his house. When thus addressed, the puthujjana bhikkhus and the arahats felt embarassed and they decided not to go to the brahmin's house the next day.

When the brahmin found that the bhikkhus did not come to his house again he felt unhappy. He went to the Buddha and told him about the bhikkhus not coming to his house. The Buddha sent for those bhikkhus and asked for explanation. The bhikkhus told the Buddha about the brahmin addressing all of them as arahats. The Buddha then asked them whether they felt any false pride and undue elation when they were thus addressed. The bhikkhus answered in the negative. To them the Buddha said, "Bhikkhus, if you don't feel any false pride and undue elation when addressed as arahats, you are not guilty of breaking any of the rules of discipline of the bhikkhus. The fact is that the brahmin addressed you so because he was extremely devoted to the arahats. So, my sons, you should strive hard to get rid of craving and attain arahatship."

Then the Buddha spoke in verse as follows:

Verse 383. O brāhmaṇa, cut off the stream of craving with diligence, and abandon sense desires. O brāhmaṇa, perceiving the cessation of the conditioned, be an arahat who realizes Nibbāna, the Unconditioned.

Verse 384

XXVI (2) The Story of Thirty Bhikkhus

While residing at the Jetavana monastery, the Buddha uttered Verse (384) of this book, with reference to thirty bhikkhus.

On one occasion, thirty bhikkhus came to pay homage to the Buddha. The Venerable Sāriputta, seeing that time was ripe and proper for those bhikkhus to attain arahatship, approached the Buddha and asked a question, solely for the benefit of those bhikkhus. The question was this: "What are the two dhammas?" To this the Buddha replied, "Sāriputta! Tranquillity and Insight Meditation are the two dhammas."

Then the Buddha spoke in verse as follows:

Verse 384. When the brāhmaṇa is well-established in the two dhammas (i.e., the practice of Tranquillity and Insight Meditation), then, in that knowing one, all fetters are destroyed.

At the end of the discourse all the thirty bhikkhus attained arahatship.

Verse 385

XXVI (3) The Story of Mara

While residing at the Jetavana monastery, the Buddha uttered Verse (385) of this book, with reference to Mara.

On one occasion, Māra came to the Buddha disguised as a man and asked him, "Venerable Sir! You often say the word 'pāraṁ'; what is the meaning of that word?" The Buddha, knowing that it was Māra who was asking that question, chided him, "O wicked Māra! The words 'pāraṁ' and 'apāraṁ' have nothing to do with you. 'Pāraṁ' which means 'the other shore' can be reached only by the arahats who are free from moral defilements."

Then the Buddha spoke in verse as follows:

Verse 385. Him I call a brāhmana who has for him neither this shore (i.e., the sense bases) nor the other shore (i.e., the sense objects), and who is undistressed and free from moral defilements.

Verse 386

XXVI (4) The Story of a Certain Brahmin

While residing at the Jetavana monastery, the Buddha uttered Verse (386) of this book, with reference to a brahmin.

One day, a brahmin thought to himself, "Gotama Buddha calls his disciples 'brāhmaṇa'. I also am a brahmin by caste. Shouldn't I also be called a brāhmaṇa?" So thinking, he went to the Buddha and posed this question. To him the Buddha replied, "I do not call one a brāhmaṇa simply because of his caste; I only call him a brāhmaṇa, who has attained arahatship."

Then the Buddha spoke in verse as follows:

Verse 386. Him I call a brāhmaṇa, who dwells in seclusion practising Tranquillity and Insight Meditation and is free from taints (of moral defilements); who has performed his duties, and is free from moral intoxicants (āsavas) and has reached the highest goal (arahatship).

At the end of the discourse the brahmin attained Sotāpatti Fruition.

Verse 387

XXVI (5) The Story of Thera Ananda

While residing at the Pubbārāma monastery, the Buddha uttered Verse (387) of this book, with reference to the Venerable Ānanda.

It was the full moon day of the seventh month (Assayuja) when King Pasenadi of Kosala came to visit the Buddha. The king was then resplendent in his full royal regalia. At that time, Thera Kāludāyī was also present in the same room sitting at the edge of the congregation. He was in deep mental absorption (jhāna), his body bright and golden. In the sky, the Venerable Ānanda noticed that the sun was setting and the moon was just coming out, both the sun and the moon radiating rays of light.

The Venerable Ānanda looked at the shining splendour of the king, of the thera, and of the sun and the moon, Finally. the Venerable Ananda looked at the

The verse runs thus:

Ye dhammā hetuppa bhavā
tesaṁ hetuṁ tathāgato āha
tesañca yo nirodho
evaṁ vādī mahā samaṇo.

It means:

The Tathāgata has declared the cause and also the cessation of all phenomena which arise from a cause. This is the doctrine held by the Great Samaṇa.

When the verse was only half-way through, Upatissa attained Sotāpatti Fruition.

As promised, Upatissa went to his friend Kolita to inform him that he had found the true dhamma. Then the two friends, accompanied by two hundred and fifty followers, went to the Buddha who was then at Rājagaha. When they arrived at the Veḷuvana monastery, they asked permission to enter the Buddhist Order, and both Upatissa and Kolita, together with their two hundred and fifty followers, were admitted as bhikkhus. Upatissa, son of Sārī, and Kolita, son of Moggali, then came to be known as Sāriputta and Moggallāna. Soon after their admission to the Order, the Buddha expounded to them a dhamma and the two hundred and fifty bhikkhus attained arahatship; but Moggallāna and Sāriputta attained arahatship only at the end of seven days and fifteen days respectively. The reason for the delay in their attainment of arahatship was that they had made a wish for Chief Discipleship, which required much more striving to achieve perfection.

The Venerable Sāriputta always remembered that he had been able to. meet the Buddha and attain the Deathless through the Venerable Assaji. So, he always paid obeisance in the direction where his teacher was and he always went to bed with his head lying in the same direction. Other bhikkhus who were staying with him at the Jetavana monastery misinterpreted his actions and said to the Buddha, "Venerable Sir! The Venerable Sāriputta still worships the various directions, viz., the East, the South, the West, the North, the Nadir and the Zenith, as he has done before as a brahmin youth; it seems as if he has not yet given up his old beliefs." The Buddha sent for the Venerable

Sāriputta and Sāriputta explained to the Buddha that he was only paying obeisance to his teacher, the Venerable Assaji, and that he was not worshipping the various directions. The Buddha was satisfied with the explanation given by the Venerable Sāriputta and said to the other bhikkhus, "Bhikkhus! The Venerable Sāriputta was not worshipping the various directions; he was only paying obeisance to his teacher and benefactor, through whom he had attained the Deathless. It is quite right and proper for him to pay homage to such a teacher."

Then the Buddha spoke in verse as follows:

Verse 392. If from somebody one should learn the Teaching of the Buddha, he should respectfully pay homage to that teacher, as a brahmin worships the sacrificial fire.

Verse 393

XXVI (10) The Story of Jaṭila the Brahmin

While residing at the Jetavana monastery, the Buddha uttered Verse (393) of this book, with reference to Jaṭila, a brahmin ascetic who wore matted hair.

Once, a brahmin ascetic thought to himself that the Buddha called his disciples 'brāhmaṇas' and that he being a brahmin by birth should also be called a 'brāhmaṇa'. Thinking thus, he went to see the Buddha and put forward his view. But the Buddha rejected his view and said. "O brahmin, I do not call one a brahmaṇa because he keeps his hair matted or simply because of his birth; I call one a brāhmaṇa only if he fully comprehends the Four Noble Truths."

Then the Buddha spoke in verse as follows:

Verse 393. Not by wearing matted hair, nor by lineage, nor by caste, does one become a brāhmaṇa; only he who realizes the Truth and the Dhamma is pure; he is a brāhmaṇa.

Verse 394

XXVI (11) The Story of a Deceitful Brahmin

While residing at the Kūṭāgāra monastery in Vesālī, the Buddha uttered Verse (394) of this book, with reference to a deceitful brahmin.

Once, a deceitful brahmin climbed up a tree near the city-gate of Vesālī and kept himself hanging upside down like a bat from one of the branches of the tree. From this very awkward position, he kept on muttering, "O people! Bring me a hundred heads of cattle, many pieces of silver and a number of slaves. If you do not bring these to me, and if I were to fall down from this tree and die, this city of yours will surely come to ruin." The people of the town, fearing that their city might be destroyed if the brahmin were to fall down and die, brought all the things he demanded and pleaded with him to come down.

The bhikkhus hearing about this incident reported to the Buddha and the Buddha replied that the deceitful one could only cheat the ignorant people but not the wise ones.

Then the Buddha spoke in verse as follows:

Verse 394. O foolish one! What is the use of your wearing matted hair? What is the use of your wearing a garment made of antilope skin? In you, there is a forest (of moral defilements); you clean yourself only externally.

Verse 395

XXVI (12) The Story of Kisāgotamī

While residing at the Gijjhakūṭa hill, the Buddha uttered Verse (395) of this book, with reference to Kisāgotamī.

On one occasion, Sakka, king of the devas, came with his followers to pay homage to the Buddha. At the same time, Therī Kisāgotamī, by her supernormal power came through the sky to pay homage to the Buddha. But when she saw Sakka and his entourage paying homage to the Buddha, she retreated. Sakka, seeing her, asked the Buddha who the lady was, and the Buddha replied, "O Sakka! She is my daughter Kisāgotamī. Once, she came to me in sorrow and distress through the loss of her son and I made her see the impermanent, the unsatisfactory and the non-self nature of all conditioned things. As a consequence of that she attained Sotāpatti Fruition, joined the Order, and became an arahat. She is one of my eminent female disciples and is matchless in the ascetic practice of wearing robes made from rags collected from a dust heap."

Then the Buddha spoke in verse as follows:

Verse 395. Him I call a brāhmaṇa who wears robes made from rags (picked up from a dust heap), who is lean with veins standing out, who meditates alone in the forest.

Verse 396

XXVI (13) The Story of a Brahmin

While residing at the Jetavana monastery, the Buddha uttered Verse (396) of this book, with reference to a brahmin.

Once, a brahmin from Sāvatthi thought that since the Buddha called his disciples 'brāhmaṇas', he should also be called a 'brāhmaṇa' because he was born of brahmin parents. When he told the Buddha about this, the Buddha replied to him, "O brahmin! I do not call him a brāhmaṇa just because he is born of brahmin parents. I call him a brāhmaṇa only if he is free from moral defilements and has cut off all clinging to existence."

Then the Buddha spoke in verse as follows:

Verse 396. I do not call him a brāhmaṇa just because he is born from the womb of a brāhmaṇa mother. He is just a bhovādi brahmin if he is not free from moral defilements. Him I call a brāhmaṇa, who is free from moral defilements and from attachment.

At the end of the discourse that brahmin attained Sotāpatti Fruition.

Verse 397

XXVI (14) The Story of Uggasena, the Son of a Rich Man[1]

While residing at the Jetavana monastery, the Buddha uttered Verse (397) of this book, with reference to Uggasena, son of a rich man.

---

1. This story is the continuation of the story mentioned in Chapter XXIV, story number (6).

After marrying a dancer from a theatrical troupe, Uggasena was trained by his father-in-law who was an acrobat, and became very skilful in acrobatics. One day while he was demonstrating his skill, the Buddha came on the scene. After hearing the Buddha's teaching Uggasena attained arahatship while he was still performing his feats on top of a long bamboo pole. After that, he climbed down from the pole and pleaded with the Buddha to accept him as a bhikkhu and was accordingly admitted into the Order.

One day, when other bhikkhus asked him whether he did not have any feeling of fear while climbing down from such a great height (i.e., about ninety feet), he answered in the negative. The bhikkhus took that to mean that Uggasena was claiming to have attained arahatship even then. So, they went to the Buddha and said, "Venerable Sir! Uggasena claims himself to be an arahat; he must be telling lies." To them the Buddha replied, "Bhikkhus, one who has cut off all fetters, like my son Uggasena, has no fear."

Then the Buddha spoke in verse as follows:

Verse 397. Him I call a brāhmaṇa, who has cut off all fetters and is fearless, who is beyond attachment and is free from moral defilements.

Verse 398

XXVI (15) The Story of Two Brahmins

While residing at the Jetavana monastery, the Buddha uttered Verse (398) of this book, with reference to two brahmins.

Once there lived in Sāvatthi two brahmins, each of whom owned a bullock. Each claimed that his bullock was better and stronger. At last, they agreed to put their animals to a test. So they went to the bank of the Aciravatī River and there they filled up a cart with sand. One after the other, the bullocks pulled the cart, but they only pulled in vain, because the cart did not move and only the ropes broke off. The bhikkhus seeing this reported to the Buddha and the Buddha said to them, "Bhikkhus! It is easy to break off the straps which you can see with your eyes; anyone can break them or cut them. But my sons, a bhikkhu should cut the strap of ill will and the thong of craving which are within you and which bind you."

Then the Buddha spoke in verse as follows:

Verse 398. Him I call a brāhmaṇa, who has cut the strap (of ill will), the thong (of craving) and the cord (of wrong views together with latent defilements), who has lifted the bar that fastens the door (of ignorance), and who knows the Truth.

At the end of the discourse five hundred bhikkhus attained arahatship.

Verse 399

XXVI (16) The Story of the Abusive Brahmin Brothers

While residing at the Veḷuvana monastery, the Buddha uttered Verse (399) of this book, with reference to the abusive Bhāradvāja brothers.

Once there was a brahmin, whose wife was in the habit of blurting out a string of words whenever she sneezed or when something or someone touched her unawares. One day, the brahmin invited some of his friends to a meal and suddenly she blurted out some words. Since she was a Sotāpanna, the words "Namo tassa bhagavato arahato sammāsambhuddassa" automatically came out of her mouth. These words of veneration to the Buddha were very much disliked by her husband, the brahmin. So, in anger, he went to the Buddha hoping to put some challenging questions to the Buddha. His first question was, "What do we have to kill to be able to live happily and peacefully?" and his second question was, "Killing of what dhamma do you approve of?" To these questions, the Buddha replied, "O brahmin, to be able to live happily and peacefully, one will have to kill ill will (dosa). Killing one's ill will is liked and praised by the Buddhas and the arahats." After hearing the Buddha, the brahmin was so impressed and satisfied with the answer that he asked to be permitted to enter the Order. Accordingly, he entered the Order and later became an arahat.

This brahmin had a brother who was very notorious for his abusive words and was known as Akkosaka Bhāradvāja, the abusive Bhāradvāja. When Akkosaka Bhāradvāja heard that his brother had joined the Order of the bhikkhus, he was furious. He went straightaway to the monastery and abused the Buddha. The Buddha in his turn asked, "O brahmin, let us suppose you offered some food to some guests and they left the house without taking the food. Since the guests did not accept your food, to whom would that food belong?" To this question the brahmin answered that the food would be his. On receiving that answer, the Buddha said, "In the same way, O brahmin, since I do not accept your abuse, the abuse would only go back to you." Akkosaka Bhāradvāja instantly realized the sagacity of those words and he felt a great respect for the Buddha. He also entered the Order and in due course became an arahat.

After Akkosaka Bhāradvāja had entered the Order, his two younger brothers also came to see the Buddha with the same intention of abusing the Buddha. They too were made to see the light by the Buddha and they also, in their turn, entered the Order. Eventually, both of them became arahats.

One evening, at the congregation of the bhikkhus, the bhikkhus said to the Buddha, "O how wonderful and how great are the virtues of the Buddha! The four brahmin brothers came here to abuse the Buddha; instead of arguing with them, he made them see the light, and as a result, the Buddha has become a refuge to them." To them, the Buddha replied, "Bhikkhus! Because I am patient and forbearing, and do no wrong to those who do me wrong, I have become a refuge to many."

Then the Buddha spoke in verse as follows:

Verse 399. Him I call a brāhmaṇa, who, without anger endures abuse, beating and being bound, and to whom the strength of patience is like the strength of an army.

Verse 400

XXVI (17) The Story of Thera Sāriputta

While residing at the Veḷuvana monastery, the Buddha uttered Verse (400) of this book, with reference to the Venerable Sāriputta.

While the Buddha was in residence at the Veḷuvana monastery, the Venerable Sāriputta, accompanied by five hundred bhikkhus, entered Nālaka Village and stood at the door of the house of his own mother for alms-food. His mother invited them into the house. But while she was offering food to her son she said, "O you consumer of left-overs, you who have abandoned eighty crores to become a bhikkhu, you have ruined us." Then, she offered alms-food to the other bhikkhus and said to them rudely, "You all have used my son as your attendant; now eat your food." The Venerable Sāriputta said nothing in reply but he just meekly took his bowl and came back to the monastery. Back at the monastery, the bhikkhus told the Buddha how the Venerable Sāriputta had patiently borne the scolding and abuses of his mother. To them, the Buddha said that arahats never get angry, they never lose their temper.

Then the Buddha spoke in verse as follows:

Verse 400. Him I call a brāhmaṇa, who is free from anger, who practises austerity, who is virtuous and free from craving, who is controlled in his senses and for whom this body (i.e., existence) is the very last.

Verse 401

XXVI (18) The Story of Theri Uppalavaṇṇā[1]

While residing at the Jetavana monastery, the Buddha uttered Verse (401) of this book, with reference to Therī Uppalavaṇṇā.

Once, some bhikkhus were talking about the arahat Therī Uppalavaṇṇā being molested by the young Nanda who was then swallowed up by the earth. In this connection, they asked the Buddha whether arahats do not enjoy sensual pleasures as they have the same physical make-up like any other people. To them the Buddha replied, "Bhikkhus! Arahats do not enjoy sensual pleasures; they do not indulge in sensual pleasures, for they do not cling to objects of sense and to sensual pleasures, just as water does not cling to the lotus leaf or the mustard seed to the tip of an awl."

---

1. This story is the continuation of the story given in Chapter V (Story number 10), Verse 69.

Then the Buddha spoke in verse as follows:

Verse 401. Him I call a brāhmaṇa, who does not cling to sensual pleasures, just as water does not cling to a lotus leaf, or the mustard seed to the tip of an awl.

Verse 402

XXVI (19) The Story of a Certain Brahmin

While residing at the Jetavana monastery, the Buddha uttered Verse (402) of this book, with reference to a certain brahmin, whose slave became an arahat.

Once, there was a young slave of a brahmin. One day, fleeing from the house of his master he joined the Order of the bhikkhus, and in due course, he attained arahatship. On one occasion, while he went on an alms-round with the Buddha, his former master, the brahmin, saw him and grabbed him firmly by the robe. When the Buddha asked what the matter was, the brahmin explained that the young bhikkhu was his slave at one time. To him the Buddha said, "This bhikkhu has laid down the burden (of the khandhas)." The brahmin took that to mean that his slave had become an arahat. So to make sure, he asked the Buddha whether it was true that the young bhikkhu had become an arahat, and the Buddha confirmed his statement.

Then the Buddha spoke in verse as follows:

Verse 402. Him I call a brāhmaṇa, who even in this existence realizes the end of dukkha (i.e., Nibbāna), who has laid down the burden (of the khandhas) and who is free from moral defilements.

At the end of the discourse the brahmin attained Sotāpatti Fruition.

Verse 403

XXVI (20) The Story of Therī Khemā[1]

While residing at the Gijjhakūṭa hill, the Buddha uttered Verse (403) of this book, with reference to Therī Khemā.

1. See also Verse 347, Chapter XXIV, Story No. (5).

One night, Sakka, king of the devas, came with his followers to pay homage to the Buddha. While they were with the Buddha, Therī Khemā, by her supernormal power, also came through the sky to pay homage to the Buddha. But because Sakka and his company were there with the Buddha, she just paid obeisance to the Buddha, and soon left him. Sakka asked the Buddha who that bhikkhunī was and the Buddha replied, "She is one of my pre-eminent disciples; she is known as Therī Khemā. She is matchless amongst the bhikkhunīs in wisdom and she knows how to differentiate the right way from the wrong way.

Then the Buddha spoke in verse as follows:

Verse 403. Him I call a brāhmaṇa, who is wise and is profound in his knowledge, who knows the right way from the wrong way, and who has attained the highest goal (i.e., arahatship).

Verse 404.

XXVI (21) The Story of Thera Tissa

While residing at the Jetavana monastery, the Buddha uttered Verse (404) of this book, with reference to Thera Tissa.

Thera Tissa, after taking a subject of meditation from the Buddha, went to a mountain side. There, he found a cave which suited him and he decided to spend the three months of the rainy season (vassa) in that cave. So he stayed in the cave and went to the village for alms-food every morning. In the village, there was a certain elderly woman who regularly offered him alms-food. In the cave, there also lived the guardian spirit of the cave. As the thera was one whose practice of morality was pure, the cave-spirit dared not live in the same cave with the noble thera; at the same time, he did not have the courage to ask the thera to leave the place. So he thought of a plan that would enable him to find fault with the thera and thus cause him to leave the cave.

The cave-spirit possessed the son of the elderly woman from the house where the thera usually went for his alms-food. He caused the boy to behave in a very peculiar way, turning his head backwards, and rolling his wide open eyes. His mother got alarmed and was in tears. The cave-spirit, who possessed the boy, then said, "Let your teacher, the thera, wash his feet with water and pour that water on the head of your son." The next day, when the thera came to her house for alms-food, she did as she was advised by the cave-spirit and the boy was left in peace. The cave-spirit went back to the cave and waited at the entrance for the return of the thera. When the thera returned from his alms-round, the cave-spirit revealed himself and said, "I am the spirit guarding this cave. O you physician, do not enter this cave." The thera knew that he had lived a clean life from the day he had become a thera, so he replied that he did not remember practising medicine. Then the cave-spirit accused him that in that very morning he had cured a young boy possessed by an ogre at the house of the elderly woman. But the thera reflected that it was not, in fact, practising medicine and he realized that even the cave-spirit could find no other fault with him. That gave him a delightful satisfaction (pīti) with himself, and abandoning pīti and concentrating hard on Insight Meditation he attained arahatship then and there, while still standing at the entrance to the cave.

As the thera had now become an arahat, he advised the cave-spirit to leave the cave. The thera continued to stay there till the end of the vassa, and then he returned to the Buddha. When he told the other bhikkhus about his encounter with the cave-spirit, they asked him whether he did not get angry with the cave-spirit when he was forbidden to enter the cave. The thera answered in the negative but they did not believe him. So they went to the Buddha and said, "Thera Tissa claims himself to be an arahat; he is not speaking the truth." To them the Buddha replied, "Bhikkhus, my son Tissa was speaking the truth when he said he did not get angry. He has indeed become an arahat; he is no longer attached to anyone; he has no occasion to get angry with anyone nor any need to associate with others."

Then the Buddha spoke in verse as follows:

Verse 404. Him I call a brāhmaṇa, who associates not with the householder or with the homeless one, or with both, who is free from sensual desire, and has few wants.

Verse 405

XXVI (22) The Story of a Certain Bhikkhu

While residing at the Jetavana monastery, the Buddha uttered Verse (405) of this book, with reference to a certain bhikkhu.

Once, a bhikkhu after taking a subject of meditation from the Buddha went to a forest to practise meditation. After he had attained arahatship he came back to the Buddha to offer his deep and profound gratitude to the Buddha. On his way, he passed through a village. Just as he was going through the village, a woman having quarrelled with her husband came out of her house and followed the bhikkhu. The husband coming after his wife, seeing her behind the bhikkhu, thought that the bhikkhu was taking his wife away. So he shouted at the bhikkhu and threatened to beat him. His wife entreated him not to beat the bhikkhu, but that made him more furious. As a result, the thera was beaten black and blue by the husband. After beating the bhikkhu to his heart's content, he took away his wife along with him and the bhikkhu continued on his way.

On arrival at the Jetavana monastery, other bhikkhus saw the bruises over the whole body of the bhikkhu and they attended to his bruises. When they asked him if he did not get angry with the man who had beaten him so sorely, he answered in the negative. So the other bhikkhus went to the Buddha and reported that the bhikkhu had falsely claimed to have attained arahatship. To them the Buddha replied, "Bhikkhus! Arahats have laid aside the stick and the sword. They do not get angry even if they are beaten." Thus, the Buddha confirmed that the bhikkhu had, indeed, become an arahat.

Then the Buddha spoke in verse as follows:

Verse 405. Him I call a brāhmaṇa, who has laid aside the use of force towards all beings, the perturbed as well as the unperturbed (i.e., arahats), and who does not kill or cause others to kill.

Verse 406

XXVI (23) The Story of Four Sāmaṇeras

While residing at the Jetavana monastery, the Buddha uttered Verse (406) of this book, with reference to four sāmaṇeras who were arahats.

Once, the wife of a brahmin sent her husband the brahmin to the Jetavana monastery to invite four bhikkhus to an alms-meal at their house. She told him to specifically request for senior bhikkhus who were also true brāhmaṇas. But four seven year old arahat sāmaṇeras, viz., Saṁkicca, Paṇḍita, Sopāka and Revata were sent along with him. When his wife saw the young sāmaṇeras she was very much dissatisfied and blamed the brahmin for bringing such young sāmaṇeras who were even younger than her grandson. She was, in fact, furious with her husband, and so she sent him back to the monastery to get older bhikkhus. In the meantime she refused to give the young sāmaṇeras the higher seats reserved for the bhikkhus; they were given lower seats and she did not offer them alms-food.

When the brahmin arrived at the monastery, he met the Venerable Sāriputta and invited him to his house. When the Venerable Sāriputta arrived at the house of the brahmin, he saw the four young arahat sāmaṇeras and asked them if they had been offered alms-food yet. On learning that the arahat sāmaṇeras had not been given alms-food yet and also that food had been prepared only for four persons the Venerable Sāriputta returned to the monastery without accepting alms-food from the house of the brahmin. So his wife sent the brahmin back again to the monastery to get another senior bhikkhu. This time, the Venerable Mahā Moggallāna came along with the brahmin, but he also returned to the monastery without accepting alms-food when he learned that the young sāmaṇeras had not been offered alms-food and also that food had been prepared only for four persons.

By this time, the sāmaṇeras were feeling hungry. Sakka, king of the devas, seeing the state of things took the form of an old brahmin and came to the house. The brahmin and his wife paid respect to the old brahmin and offered him a seat of honour, but Sakka just sat on the ground and paid respect to the four sāmaṇeras. Then he revealed that he was Sakka. Seeing that Sakka himself was paying respect to the young sāmaṇeras, the brahmin couple offered alms-food to all the five. After the meal, Sakka and the sāmaṇeras manifested their supernormal power by going right up into the sky through the roof. Sakka went back to his celestial abode, the sāmaṇeras returned to the monastery.

When other bhikkhus asked the sāmaṇeras whether they did not get angry when the brahmin couple refused to offer alms-food to them, they answered in the negative. The bhikkhus not believing them reported to the Buddha that the four young sāmaṇeras were falsely claiming to be arahats. To them the Buddha said, "Bhikkhus, arahats bear no ill will towards those who are hostile to them."

Then the Buddha spoke in verse as follows:

Verse 406. Him I call a brāhmaṇa, who is not hostile to those who are hostile, who is peaceful (i.e., has laid aside the use of force) to those with weapons, and who is without attachment to objects of attachment.

Verse 407

XXVI (24) The Story of Thera Mahāpanthaka

While residing at the Veḷuvana monastery, the Buddha uttered Verse (407) of this book, with reference to Thera Mahāpanthaka, elder brother of Cūḷapanthaka[1].

Thera Mahāpanthaka was already an arahat when his younger brother Cūḷapanthaka joined the Order. Cūḷapanthaka was born a dullard because he had made fun of a very dull bhikkhu in one of his past existences. Cūḷapanthaka could not even memorize one verse in four months' time. Mahāpanthaka was disappointed with his younger brother and asked him to leave the monastery as he was not worthy of the Order.

It was in this connection that, on one occasion, the bhikkhus asked the Buddha why Mahāpanthaka, even though he was an arahat, turned his younger brother Cūḷapanthaka out of the monastery They also added

1. See also Verse 25, Chapter II, story number (3).

"Do the arahats still lose their temper? Do they still have moral defilements like ill will in them?" To them the Buddha replied, "Bhikkhus! Arahats have no moral defilements like passion and ill will in them. My son Mahāpanthaka acted as he did with a view to benefiting his brother and not out of ill will."

Then the Buddha spoke in verse as follows:

Verse 407. Him I call a brāhmaṇa, from whom passion ill will, pride and detraction have fallen off, like a mustard seed from the tip of an awl.

Verse 408

XXVI (25) The Story of Thera Pilindavaccha

While residing at the Veḷuvana monastery, the Buddha uttered Verse (408) of this book, with reference to Thera Vaccha, who was also known as Thera Pilindavaccha, due to his offensive ways.

Thera Pilindavaccha had a very offensive way of addressing people; he would often say, "Come here, you wretch", or "Go there, you wretch" and such other things. Other bhikkhus reported about him to the Buddha. The Buddha sent for him, and spoke to him on the matter. Then, on reflection the Buddha found that for the past five hundred existences, the thera had been born only in the families of the brahmins, who regarded themselves as being superior to other people. So the Buddha said to the bhikkhus, "Bhikkhus! Thera Vaccha addresses others as 'wretch' only by force of habit acquired in the course of his five hundred existences as a brahmin, and not out of malice. He has no intention of hurting others, for an arahat does not harm others."

Then the Buddha spoke in verse as follows:

Verse 408. Him I call a brāhmaṇa, who speaks gentle, instructive and true words, and who does not offend anyone by speech.

Verse 409

XXVI (27) The Story of a Certain Thera

While residing at the Jetavana monastery, the Buddha uttered Verse (409) of this book, with reference to a certain thera.

One day, a brahmin from Sāvatthi put his upper garment outside his house to air it. A thera found that garment as he was going back to the monastery. Thinking that it was a piece of cloth thrown away by someone and therefore ownerless, the thera picked it up. The brahmin looking out of his window saw the thera picking up the piece of clothing and came after the thera, abusing and accusing him. "You shaven head! You are stealing my clothing", he said; the thera promptly returned the piece of clothing to the brahmin.

Back at the monastery, the thera related the above incident to other bhikkhus, and they made fun of him and jokingly asked him whether the cloth was long or short, coarse or fine. To this question the thera answered, "Whether the clothing is long or short, coarse or fine matters not to me; I am not at all attached to it.", Other bhikkhus then reported to the Buddha that the thera was falsely claiming himself to be an arahat. To them the Buddha replied, "Bhikkhus! The thera speaks the truth; an arahat does not take anything that is not given him."

Then the Buddha spoke in verse as follows:

Verse 409. Him I call a brāhmaṇa, who, in this world, takes nothing that is not given him, be it long or short, big or small, good or bad.

Verse 410

XXVI (27) The Story of Thera Sāriputta

While residing at the Jetavana monastery, the Buddha uttered Verse (410) of this book, with reference to Thera Sāriputta.

On one occasion, Thera Sāriputta accompanied by five hundred bhikkhus went to a monastery near a small village to spend the vassa. At the end of the vassa, Thera Sāriputta wanted robes for young bhikkhus and sāmaṇeras. So he said to the bhikkhus, "If people come to offer robes, send them to me or inform me"; and then he left for the Jetavana monastery to pay homage to the Buddha. Other bhikkhus misunderstood Thera Sāriputta's instructions, and said to the Buddha, "Venerable Sir! Thera Sāriputta is still attached to material things like robes and other requisites of a bhikkhu." To them the Buddha replied, "Bhikkhus! My

festivities were going on in Sāvatthi, the parents of Sundarasamudda missed him very much; they also felt sorry for their son who was missing all the enjoyment and they wept. As they were weeping, a courtesan came to them and asked what the matter was. On hearing about their son, the courtesan said, "If I could make your son leave the Order and return to the life of a lay man how would you reward me?" The parents answered that they would make her rich. The courtesan then asked for a large sum of money and left for Rājagaha with a number of followers.

At Rājagaha, she rented a house with seven-tiered pinnacles on the route where Thera Sundarasamudda would come on his alms-round. She prepared good food and waited for him. On the first few days, she offered alms-food to the thera at the door of her house. Later, she invited him to come inside. Meanwhile, she paid money to some children to come and play just outside the house about the time the thera usually came on his alms-round. This gave her the excuse that it was very dusty and noisy on the ground floor; with this excuse she invited the thera to the top floor to have his alms--food. The thera consented and went up and as soon as he had entered the room, the courtesan closed the door. Then she started seducing the thera. She said to the thera, "Venerable Sir! Please be my youthful and energetic husband, and I will be your dearly beloved wife. After our long and happy wedded life we can both leave it to enter the Order and strive our very best to attain Nibbāna." When he heard these words the thera suddenly realized his mistake and got alarmed. Then he said to himself, "Indeed, by being negligent and unmindful I have made a great mistake."

At that instant, the Buddha saw from his Perfumed Chamber what was happening to Thera Sundarasamudda at Rājagaha. He called the Venerable Ānanda and said to him, "Ānanda! On an upper storey of a pinnacled building in Rājagaha, there now goes on a struggle between Sundarasamudda and a courtesan; but in the end the thera will be the winner." After saying this to Ānanda, the Buddha sent forth his radance to the thera, made him feel his presence, and said, "My son! Be resolute and get rid of love of wealth and sensual pleasures."

Then the Buddha spoke in verse as follows:

Verse 415. Him I call a brāhmaṇa, who, in this world, has given up sensual pleasures, and leaving the home-life has become a bhikkhu; who has eradicated sensual desires and has come to the end of existence.

At the end of the discourse the thera attained arahatship, and by supernormal power passed through the roof into the sky and went to the Buddha.

Verse 416

XXVI (33) The Story of Thera Jaṭila

While residing at the Veḷuvana monastery, the Buddha uttered Verse (416) of this book, with reference to Thera Jaṭila.

Soon after the passing away (parinibbāna) of Kassapa Buddha, an arahat thera went round for donations to build a gold stupa where the relics of Kassapa Buddha were to be enshrined. The thera came to the house of a goldsmith while he and his wife were engaged in a heated quarrel. The goldsmith shouted at the thera and said, "You had better throw your stupa into the water and go away." His wife then said to the goldsmith, "If you are angry with me you should abuse me only; you can even beat me if you like; but why do you have to abuse the Buddha and the thera? Surely, you have done a grievous wrong!" Hearing her words, the goldsmith realized the enormity of the wrong he had done and wanted to make atonement for it. So, he made some gold flowers, put them into three gold pots and offered them to be put into the relic chamber of the stupa of Kassapa Buddha.

In his present existence he was conceived in the womb of a rich man's daughter who had had an illicit love affair. When the child was born, she put it into a pot and floated it down the stream. A young woman who was bathing in the stream saw the child in the pot and took it with her. She adopted him and named him Jaṭila. Later, on the advice of a thera the woman sent Jaṭila to Taxila where he had his education. While at Taxila the thera arranged for him to stay at the house of a merchant who was a disciple of his. In due course, Jatila married the daughter of the merchant. Soon after the marriage, a large mound of gold appeared in the backyard of the house which was newly built for the couple. Three sons were born out of this marriage. After that, Jaṭila joined the Order and attained arahatship within a few days.

On one occasion, as the Buddha went on an alms-round with five hundred bhikkhus including Jaṭila, they came to the house of the sons of Jaṭila. His sons offered alms-food to the Buddha and his disciples for fifteen days. Some time afterwards, the bhikkhus asked Jaṭila whether he was still attached to his mound of gold and his sons, and he answered that he had no more attachment to them. The bhikkhus then said to the Buddha that Jaṭila was falsely claiming to have attained arahatship. To them the Buddha said, "Bhikkhus! Jaṭila has got rid of craving and pride; he has indeed attained arahatship."

Then the Buddha spoke in verse as follows:

Verse 416. Him I call a brāhmaṇa, who, in this world, has given up craving, and leaving the home-life has become a bhikkhu; who has eradicated craving and has come to the end of existence.

Verse 416*

XXVI (34) The Story of Thera Jotika

While residing at the Veḷuvana monastery, the Buddha uttered Verse (416) of this book, with reference to Thera Jotika.

Jotika was a famous rich man from Rājagaha. He lived in a stately mansion with seven tiered pinnacles. There were seven walls around his mansion, each of which had an entrance guarded by celestial demons. The fame of his wealth spread far and wide, and many people came to see his mansion. On one occasion, King Bimbisāra came to visit Jotika; he also brought his son Ajātasattu with him. Ajātasattu seeing the grandeur of Jotika's mansion vowed that he would not allow Jotika to live in such a magnificent mansion when he became king. On the king's departure from his house Jotika presented the king with a large

---

*Story No. (33) and (34) of this chapter have the same verse.

priceless ruby. It was the custom of Jotika to give presents to all visitors who came to see him.

When Ajātasattu ascended the throne, after killing his father, he came with his soldiers to take the mansion of Jotika by force. But as all the gates were well guarded by celestial demons, Ajātasattu and his soldiers had to retreat. Ajātasattu fled to the Veḷuvana monastery and he found Jotika listening to a discourse given by the Buddha. Seeing Jotika at the feet of the Buddha, Ajātasattu exclaimed, "After making your guards fight me, you are now pretending to be listening to a discourse!" Jotika realized that the king had gone to take his place by force and that he had been compelled to retreat.

In a past existence, Jotika had made a solemn wish that his property might not be taken away from him against his wish, and this wish had been fulfilled. So Jotika said to King Ajātasattu, "O king! My property cannot be taken away against my wish." Saying this, he stretched out his ten fingers and asked the king to take off the twenty rings he was wearing on his fingers. The king tried hard to take them off but did not succeed. Jotika then asked the king to spread out a piece of cloth and as Jotika put his fingers on to the cloth, all his rings easily slipped off. After he had given all his rings to King Ajātasattu, Jotika asked the Buddha that he might be permitted into the Order. Soon after entering the Order, Jotika attained arahatship.

One day, when other bhikkhus asked him whether he had any more craving left in him for his mansion, his wealth and his wife, he answered that he did not have any more craving for them. The bhikkhus then went to the Buddha and said, "Venerable Sir! Thera Jotika claims to have attained arahatship; he is telling lies." To them the Buddha said, "Bhikkhus! Jotika speaks the truth; he does not have any more craving in him. He is now an arahat."

Then the Buddha spoke in verse as follows:

Verse 416. Him I call a brāhmaṇa, who, in this world, has given up craving, and leaving the home-life has become a bhikkhu; who has eradicated craving and has come to the end of existence.

Verse 417

XXVI (35) The Story of Thera Naṭaputtaka

While residing at the Jetavana monastery, the Buddha uttered Verse (417) of this book, with reference to Thera Naṭaputtaka, who was the son of a dancer.

Once, the son of a dancer was going round the streets singing and dancing when he had a chance to listen to a discourse given by the Buddha. After listening to the discourse, he entered the Order and attained arahatship soon afterwards. One day, while the Buddha and the bhikkhus including Naṭaputtaka were going on an alms-round, they came across the son of another dancer dancing in the street. Seeing the young man dancing, the other bhikkhus asked Naṭaputtaka whether he still liked dancing. And Naṭaputtaka answered, "No, I do not." The bhikkhus then went to the Buddha and told him that Thera Naṭaputtaka was falsely claiming to have attained arahatship. Thereby, the Buddha said, "Bhikkhus! Naṭaputtaka has gone beyond all bonds of attachment; he has become an arahat."

Then the Buddha spoke in verse as follows:

Verse 417. Him I call a brāhmaṇa, who has given up attachment to (sensual pleasures of) human life, has transcended attachment to (sensual pleasures of) deva life and is completely free from all attachment.

Verse 418

XXVI (36) The Story of Thera Naṭaputtaka

While residing at the Veḷuvana monastery, the Buddha uttered Verse (418) of this book, with reference to another Thera Naṭaputtaka, son of another dancer.

As in the previous story, the son of a dancer had entered the Order and had attained arahatship. Other bhikkhus went to the Buddha and told him about Thera Naṭaputtaka claiming to have attained arahatship. To them the Buddha said, "Bhikkhus! Naṭaputtaka has given up taking delight in all things."

Then the Buddha spoke in verse as follows:

Verse 418. Him I call a brāhmaṇa, who has given up taking delight (in sensual pleasures) and not taking delight (in solitude); who has attained perfect peace and is free from moral defilements; who has overcome all the five khandhas (lit., the world) and is diligent.

Verses 419 and 420

XXVI (37) The Story of Thera Vaṅgīsa

While residing at the Jetavana monastery, the Buddha uttered Verses (419) and (420) of this book, with reference to Thera Vaṅgīsa.

Once, in Rājagaha, there was a brahmin by the name of Vaṅgīsa who by simply tapping on the skull of a dead person could tell whether that person was reborn in the world of the devas, or of the human beings, or in one of the four lower worlds (apāyas). The brahmins took Vaṅgīsa to many villages and people flocked to him and paid him ten, twenty or a hundred to find out from him where their various dead relatives were reborn.

On one occasion, Vaṅgīsa and his party came to a place not far from the Jetavana monastery. Seeing those people who were going to the Buddha, the brahmins invited them to come to Vaṅgīsa who could tell where their relatives had been reborn. But the Buddha's disciples said to them, "Our teacher is one without a rival, he only is the Enlightened One." The brahmins took that statement as a challenge and took Vaṅgīsa along with them to the Jetavana monastery to compete with the Buddha. The Buddha, knowing their intention, instructed the bhikkhus to bring the skulls of a person reborn in niraya, of a person reborn in the animal world, of a person reborn in the human world, of a person reborn in the deva world and also of an arahat. The five were then placed in a row. When Vaṅgīsa was shown those skulls he could tell where the owners of the first four skulls were reborn; but when he came to the skull of the arahat he was at a loss. Then the Buddha said, "Vaṅgīsa, don't you know? I do know where the owner of that skull is." Vaṅgīsa then asked the Buddha to let him have the magical incantation (mantra) by which he could thus know; but the Buddha told him that the mantra could be given only to a bhikkhu. Vaṅgīsa then told the brahmins to wait outside the monastery while he was being taught the mantra. Thus Vaṅgīsa became a bhikkhu and, as a bhikkhu, he was instructed by the Buddha to contemplate the thirty-two constituents of the body. Vaṅgīsa diligently practised meditation as instructed by the Buddha and attained arahatship within a short time.

When the brahmins who were waiting outside the monastery came to ask Vaṅgīsa whether he had acquired the mantra, Vaṅgīsa said, "You all had better go now; as for me, I should no longer go along with you." Other bhikkhus hearing him thought he was tellling lies, so they went to the Buddha and said, "Venerable Sir! Vaṅgīsa is falsely claiming to have attained arahatship." To them the Buddha said, "Bhikkhus! Vaṅgīsa really knows the death and rebirth of beings."

Then the Buddha spoke in verse as follows:

Verse 419. Him I call a brāhmaṇa, who knows the death and rebirth of beings in every detail, who is detached, who follows the good practice and knows the Four Noble Truths.

Verse 420. Him I call a brāhmaṇa, whose destination the devas or gandhabbas or men do not know, who has eradicated moral intoxicants and is an arahat.

Verse 421

XXVI (38) The Story of Therī Dhammadinnā

While residing at the Veḷuvana monastery, the Buddha uttered Verse (421) of this book, with reference to Therī Dhammadinnā.

Once, there was a lay-disciple of the Buddha named Visākha in Rājagaha. After hearing the Buddha's discourses again and again Visākha attained Anāgāmi Fruition and he said to his wife, "Please accept all my property; from today, I'm not going to take part in any of the affairs of the house." His wife Dhammadinnā retorted, "Who would swallow the spittle you have thrown up?" Then she asked permission from him to enter the Order and became a bhikkhunī. After becoming a bhikkhunī she went to a monastery in a small village in the company of other bhikkhunīs to practise meditation. Within a short time, she attained arahatship and returned to Rājagaha.

Visākha, hearing that Dhammadinnā had returned, went to see her and asked her some questions. When he asked her about the first three maggas she answered him; but when he asked her questions on the arahatta magga and phala she said, "O lay-disciple! This matter is out of your depth; if you want, you may go and ask the Buddha." When Visākha asked the Buddha, the Buddha said, "Dhammadinnā has already answered your question. If you ask me I shall have to give the same answer." Saying this the Buddha confirmed the fact that Dhammadinnā had attained arahatship.

Then the Buddha spoke in verse as follows:

Verse 421. Him I call a brāhmaṇa, who does not cling to the past, future and present khandha aggregates and who is free from moral defilements and attachment.

Verse 422

XXVI (39) The Story of Aṅgulimāla

While residing at the Jetavana monastery, the Buddha uttered Verse (422) of this book, with reference to Thera Aṅgulimāla.

On one occasion, King Pasenadi and Queen Mallikā made an alms-offering to the Buddha and his bhikkhus numbering five hundred in all, on a scale which could not be surpassed by anyone else. At that ceremony, each bhikkhu was to have an elephant holding a white umbrella over his head as a sunshade. However, they could get only four hundred and ninety-nine trained elephants and so they had to put in an untrained elephant and it was allotted to hold the umbrella over Thera Aṅgulimāla. Every one was afraid that the untrained elephant might give trouble, but when brought near Thera Aṅgulimāla it was quite docile.

It was with reference to this incident that the bhikkhus later asked Aṅgulimāla whether he did not get frightened or not. To this question Aṅgulimāla answered that he was not frightened. The bhikkhus then went to the Buddha and said that Thera Aṅgulimāla claimed to have attained arahatship. To them the Buddha said, "Bhikkhus! It is quite true that Aṅgulimāla was not afraid; those who are like him are also not afraid."

Then the Buddha spoke in verse as follows:

Verse 422. Him I call a brāhmaṇa, who is fearless like a bull, who is noble and diligent, who is a seeker of high moral virtues and a conqueror (of three Māras), who is free from craving, who has been cleansed of moral defilements and knows the Four Noble Truths.

Verse 423

XXVI (40) The Story of Devahita the Brahmin

While residing at the Jetavana monastery, the Buddha uttered Verse (423) of this book, with reference to Devahita, a brahmin.

On one occasion, the Buddha suffered from a gastric ailment and he sent Thera Upavāṇa to get some hot water from Devahita the brahmin. The brahmin was very pleased to have this rare opportunity to offer something to the Buddha. So, in addition to hot water he also gave the thera some molasses for the Buddha. At the monastery Thera Upavāṇa gave a warm bath to the Buddha; after the bath he offered the Buddha a mixture of molasses and hot water. After drinking the mixture there was instant relief. The brahmin then came and asked the Buddha, "Venerable Sir! An offering made to whom gives one the greatest benefit?" To him the Buddha said, "Brahmin! An offering made to one who has given up all evil is the most beneficial."

Then the Buddha spoke in verse as follows:

Verse 423. Him I call a brāhmaṇa, who knows past existences, who sees the celestial as well as the lower worlds, who has reached the end of rebirths, who, with Magga Insight, has become an arahat and has accomplished all that is to be accomplished for the eradication of moral defilements.

At the end of the discourse the brahmin became established in the faith in the Three Gems (the Buddha, the Dhamma and the Saṁgha) and became a lay-disciple of the Buddha.

End of Chapter Twenty-sixt The Brāhmaṇa.

END OF THE DHAMMAPADA

GLOSSARY

(A)

Ābhassara brahmā: The radiant brahmās of the abode of the second Rūpāvacara Jhāna Brahmā realm.
Abhidhamma: Philosophical exposition of the Dhamma.
Accantaṁ: Excessive, veritable, truly, really.
Accutaṁ: Deathless, i.e., Nibbāna.
Addhagū: A traveller.
Āgāraṁ: A house, building, hall.
Aggasāvaka: Chief Disciple.
Ahethayaṁ: Without damaging, without harming.
Amata: Deathless, synonym for Nibbāna.
Anāgāmī: One who has attained Anāgāmi or the third Magga.
Anakkhato: Too great to be described; ineffable; an epithet of Nibbāna.
Anāsavā: Free from āsavas (moral intoxicants).
Anatta: No soul; non-self; no substance.
Andhakārena: Darkness.
Anicca: Impermanence.
Anīgho: Free from harm.
Animitta: The Signless, i.e., no sign of craving, ill will and wrong view. It is an epithet of Nibbāna.
Anudhammacārī: One who acts in conformity with the dhamma.
Anuloma: The order of arising.
Anumodanā: Expression of appreciation or approval.
Anuttaraṁ: Supreme, incomparable, highest.
Āpatti: Violation of disciplinary rules for bhikkhus; an offence.
Āpatti, Saṁghādisesa: Offences which require penance and suspension from the Order.
Apāya: Miserable existences, the four Lower Worlds.
Appamāda: Mindfulness, heedfulness, vigilance.
Appicchatā: Contentment, frugality.
Arahat: One who has attained the fourth and final Magga, and for whom existences have come to an end.

(A)

Ariya : The noble one; one who has entered the Path, i.e., one who has realized at least one of the four Maggas.

Āsavā : Āsavas; moral intoxicants.

Asadisadāna : Incomparable or unrivalled alms-giving.

Atidhonacārinaṁ : One who transgresses or indulges too much in the use of the four requisites of a bhikkhu.

Attadantassa : One who is self-controlled.

Attakilamathānuyoga: Self-mortification.

Aṭṭhaṅgikomaggo : The Path of Eight Constituents; the Path pointed out by the Buddha for liberation from the round of existences. The eight constituents are: right view, right thinking, right speech, right action, right living, right effort, right mindfulness and right concentration.

Ātura : Ailing, diseased.

Āyatanā : Ayatanas; sense-bases and sense-objects.

(B)

Bāla : The foolish, the ignorant, the dull.

Bhaddo / Bhadro : Good, excellent, worthy.

Bhante : Venerable Sir.

Bhikkhu : A member of the Buddhist Order (the Saṁgha).

Bhikkhunī : A female member of the Buddhist Order.

Bhūtagāma sikkha: The disciplinary rule forbidding bhikkhus to cut vegetation.

Bodhi ñāṇa or sabbaññuta ñāṇa : Supreme Enlightenment; the all comprehending wisdom.

Brahmadaṇḍa : Brahma punishment, i.e., to be ignored.

Brāhmaṇa : In Buddhism, one in whom craving is extinguished. The term also applies to the Buddhas and the Paccekabuddhas.

Byāpāda/Vyāpāda : Ill will, anger, hatred.

(C)

Caturo padā	: Cattāri ariyasaccāni or the Four Noble Truths.
Cetiya	: Stupa, shrine.
Citta	: Mind, thought, consciousness.

(D)

Dāna	: Charity, alms-giving.
Dhammadhāra	: One who is versed in the Dhamma.
Daṇḍa	: Stick, weapon, punishment, penalty.
Dhamma	: The doctrine of the Buddha.
Dhammā	: Dhammas; all conditioned and unconditioned phenomena.
Dhammajīvino	: One who earns his living according to the dhamma (c.f. samājiva).
Dhammaṭṭha	: Just, righteous.
Dhammaṭṭho	: One who abides by the law.
Dhammamuttamaṁ	: The Noble Dhamma or the Highest Dhamma (the Nine Transcendentals). The Nine Transcendentals are: four Maggas, four Phalas and Nibbāna.
Diso	: Enemy.
Dosa	: Hatred, anger, ill will, trouble, stain, blemish, defect, taint.
Dhīro	: The wise; one endowed with wisdom, fortitude, energy, and courage.
Dhutaṅga	: Austerity or purification practice.
Dibbacakkhu ñāṇa	: The divine power of sight.
Duggati	: Unhappy destinations or existences; the four Lower Worlds.
Dukkha	: Dukkha as a Noble Truth cannot be translated and is therefore left untranslated. In the context of feeling it is translated as suffering or pain.
Dussīlo	: Immoral, wicked.

(E)

Etadaggaṁ	: The chief; the best; pre-eminence.

(G)

Gacche	: To go, to proceed, to reach.
Gahapati	: Householder.
Gantha	: Bond or tie.

(G)

Gāthā : A verse, a stanza.
Gati : Course, going, movement, destination.

(J)

Jano : Man, person, people, the world.
Jarā : Ageing, old age, decay.
Jāti : Birth.
Jhāna : Concentration, tranquillity, mental absorption.

(K)

Kahāpaṇa : A certain weight or a coin which may be of copper or silver or gold.
Kalyāṇa puthujjana: Virtuous worldling.
Kāmasukhallikānuyoga : Excessive sensual indulgence.
Katapuñño : Doer of good deeds.
Khandhā : Khandhas, aggregates (of existence).
Kilesā : Moral defilements.
Kodha : Anger.
Kukkucca : Worry.
Kusala : Good, merit, skill.
Kusito : An idle person.

(L)

Lokuttarā Dhammā: The nine Transcendentals, viz., the four Maggas, the four Phalas and Nibbāna.

(M)

Maccudheyyaṁ : The realm of the king of Death.
Maccurājassa : The king of Death.
Magga : The Path, ariya aṭṭhaṅgika magga, the Path of eight constituents; the Path leading to Nibbāna.
Magga : Road, path, course.
Majjhimapaṭipadā: The Middle Path; the Noble Path of Eight Constituents.
Malaṁ : Impurity, dirt, stain, taint, rust, cause of destruction.
Mallikā : Arabian jasmin.
Mando : A stupid or dull person.

(M)

Māna : Pride, conceit.
Mettā : Loving-kindness, good will.
Moghajiṇṇo : One grown old in vain.
Moha : Ignorance, bewilderment.
Muddha : Head, top, summit.
Modati : To rejoice.

(N)

Nakkhattarājā : The moon.
Nagaraṁ : A town or city.
Naro : Man.
Nātho : Refuge, protector.
Niccaṁ : Lasting, always.
Nikkha : A weight of gold or a gold ornament or a gold coin.
Niraya or Naraka : A region of continuous and extreme mental and physical pain. It is a plane of existence from which one can be liberated depending on the working of one's good kamma. It is often translated as hell.

(O)

Ogho : Flood, torrent.

(P)

Pabbajita : One who leaves the household life for the homeless life of a recluse; one who has given up the impurity of the household life to become a bhikkhu.
Paccekabuddha : One who is Self-Enlightened like the Buddha but cannot teach others.
Padaṁ : Path, way, footprint, words of the Doctrine, Nibbāna.
Padipaṁ : Light, lamp.
Pakiṇṇaka : Miscellaneous.
Pamatto : Careless; negligent.
Paṇḍita : The wise, the learned.
Pāpa : Evil, bad.
Pāpakārī : Evil doer.
Paribbājaka : A wandering ascetic.
Paribbājikā : A female wandering ascetic.
Parinibbāna : Passing away of a Buddha or an arahat.

(P)

Parittas : Religious stanzas that are usually recited for protection against harmful influences.

Peta : A miserable, always hungry being in a lower world.

Pīti : Delight; delightful satisfaction: joy.

Paṭiccasamuppāda: Doctrine of Dependent Origination.

Paṭiloma : The order of cessation.

Pharuso : Harsh, unkind, savage.

Piya : Affection.

Pubbenivāsānussati-ñāṇa: The power of recollection of past existences.

Pupphaṁ : A flower.

Purisājañño : The noblest of men; a Buddha.

Puthujjana : Worldling; a common man; one who has not attained any of the Maggas.

(R)

Rāga : Passion, lust, desire.

Rakkhato : One who keeps watch.

Rati : Delight, pleasure, attachment.

(S)

Sacca : Truth, the four Noble Truths.

Saddhā : Faith, belief, confidence.

Sādhurūpo : A good hearted man.

Sahassa : Thousand.

Sahitaṁ / **Saṁhitaṁ** } : The Buddhist text.

Sakka : King of the devas.

Saḷāyatana : The six sense bases, the six fields of sense perception.

Samādhi : Concentration attained through meditation.

Samāpatti : Sustained deep mental absorption; sustained absorption in concentration.

Samatha : Tranquillity, concentration.

Saṁsāra : Round of rebirths, round of existences.

Saṁgha : The Buddhist Order.

Saṁyojanaṁ : A fetter. There are ten fetters of human passion which bind man to the round of rebirths.

Santimaggaṁ : The Path that leads to Nibbāna; i,e., the Path of Eight Constituents.

(S)

Sappurisa	: Good and pious people; virtuous persons.
Sārambhakathā	: Malicious talk, overbearing talk.
Sassataditthi	: Eternity-belief.
Sati	: Mindfulness. heedfulness, awareness.
Sāvaka	: A disciple of the Buddha.
Sekha	: One who practises the Dhamma and has entered the Path, but has not yet become an arahat.
Sīla	: Morality, moral practice or conduct, moral concept.
Socati	: To grieve, to mourn.
Sotāpatti Magga and Phala	: Sotāpatti Magga is the first Magga attained by one who has entered the current of emancipation. This is followed immediately by Sotāpatti Phala, the 'fruit' or 'fruition' of Stream-Entering.
Sugati or Suggati	: Happy plane of existence or destination.
Sukha	: Happiness, satisfactoriness, well-being, bliss.
Suññata	: The Void, i.e., Void of craving, ill will and wrong view. It is also an epithet of Nibbāna.

(T)

Tādino	: One who is calm or tranquil, or unperturbed.
Tagara	: Rhododendron.
Taṇhā	: 'Thirst', desire, craving.
Taṇhakkhaya	: The extinction of craving, synonym for Nibbāna.
Tapacariya / **Tapacaraṇaṁ**	: The practice of religious austerities.
Tappati	: To burn, to suffer, to be tormented.
Tathāgata	: One who has found the Truth; synonym for the Buddhas.
Thera	: A senior member of the Buddhist Order, but often applied to bhikkhus in general.
Thina-middha	: Sloth and torpor.
Tisaraṇa	: The Three Gems, the Three Refuges viz., the Buddha, the Dhamma and the Saṁgha.

(U)

Ucchedadiṭṭhi : Annihilation-belief.
Udāna : Verse or stanza of exultation.
Udayabbayaṁ : The arising and the dissolving of the five aggregates (khandhas).
Udayabbayañāṇa : Knowledge of the arising and the dissolving of the five aggregates(khandhas).
Uddhaṁsoto : One who is going upstream, i.e., one who is bound for the "pure abodes" (Suddhāvāsa Brahmā realms).
Upādāna : Clinging, grasping attachment.
Uposatha sīla : The eight moral precepts; the observance of Sabbath.
Uppādo : Springing up, appearance, birth.
Upāsaka : A lay-disciple of the Buddha.
Upasanto : The Peaceful; one who has extinguished the fire of moral defilments.

(V)

Vācā : Word, speech.
Vassa : Rainy season; rainy season retreat; resident period of the rains.
Vassikā : Spanish jasmin.
Vedanā : Feeling, sensation.
Vicikicchā : Doubt.
Vilomāni : Faults, failings.
Vimokkha : Liberation from existence; Nibbāna.
Vinaya : Disciplinary rules of the Buddhist Order.
Vissāsa : Trust; intimacy.
Viveka : Solitude, detachment, Nibbāna.

(Y)

Yamaka : Pair, double, twin.
Yāmaṁ : Watches of the night; also used metaphorically for the three stages in a man's life.
Yathābūta : In reality, as things are.
Yoga : Bond or attachment. The four attachments are: attachment to sensual pleasure, to existence, to wrong views, and to ignorance.
Yogakkhemaṁ : Secure from the four yogas, an epithet of Nibbāna.

INDEX TO FIRST LINES OF PĀḶI VERSES

[Figures indicate verse numbers]

K

M

N

N

O

P

P

R

S

U

V

Y

Y

Y